D0132139

Microsoft®

Excel® 2010 Plain & Simple

Curtis D. Frye

PUBLISHED WITH THE AUTHORIZATION OF MICROSOFT CORPORATION BY:
O'Reilly Media, Inc.
1005 Gravenstein Highway North
Sebastopol, California 95472

Copyright © 2010 Curtis D. Frye.

Complying with all applicable copyright laws is the responsibility of the user. All rights reserved. Without limiting the rights under copyright, no part of this document may be reproduced, stored in or introduced into a retrieval system, or transmitted in any form or by any means (electronic, mechanical, photocopying, recording, or otherwise), or for any purpose, without express written permission of O'Reilly Media, Inc.

Printed and bound in the United States of America.

2 3 4 5 6 7 8 9 10 11 QGT 6 5 4 3 2 1

Microsoft Press books are available through booksellers and distributors worldwide. For further information about international editions, contact your local Microsoft Corporation office or contact Microsoft Press International directly at fax (425) 936-7329. Visit our Web site at *www.microsoft.com/mspress*. Send comments to *mspinput@microsoft.com*.

Microsoft, Microsoft Press, ActiveX, Excel, FrontPage, Internet Explorer, PowerPoint, SharePoint, Webdings, Windows, and Windows 7 are either registered trademarks or trademarks of the Microsoft group of companies. Other product and company names mentioned herein may be the trademarks of their respective owners.

The example companies, organizations, products, domain names, e-mail addresses, logos, people, places, and events depicted herein are fictitious. No association with any real company, organization, product, domain name, e-mail address, logo, person, place, or event is intended or should be inferred.

This book expresses the author's views and opinions. The information contained in this book is provided without any express, statutory, or implied warranties. Neither the authors, Microsoft Corporation, nor its resellers, or distributors will be held liable for any damages caused or alleged to be caused either directly or indirectly by this book.

Acquisitions and Developmental Editor: Kenyon Brown
Production Editor: Kristen Borg
Editorial Production: Online Training Solutions, Inc.
Proofreader: Nancy Sixsmith
Technical Reviewer: Mark Reddin
Compositor: Nellie McKesson
Illustrator: Robert Romano
Indexer: Ginny Munroe

ISBN: 978-0-7356-2727-7 [2011-06-03]

To Virginia

Contents

Acknowledgments xiii

1 Introduction: About This Book 1

No Computerese! 1
Useful Tasks... 2
...And the Easiest Way to Do Them 2
A Quick Overview 2
A Few Assumptions 4
A Final Word (or Two) 4

2 What's New and Improved in Excel 2010 5

Managing Excel Files and Settings in Backstage View 6
Previewing Data Using Paste Preview 6
Customizing the Excel 2010 User Interface 6
Summarizing Data Using More Accurate Functions 6
Summarizing Data Using Sparklines 7
Visualizing Data Using Improved Conditional Formats 7
Creating and Displaying Math Equations 8
Editing Pictures Within Excel 2010 8

3 Getting Started with Excel 2010 9

Surveying the Excel Program Window 10
Starting Excel 12
Finding and Opening Existing Workbooks 14
Using File Properties 17
Creating a New Workbook 19

Working with Multiple Workbooks 20
Sizing and Viewing Windows 21
Zooming In or Out on a Worksheet 22
Viewing a Worksheet in Full-Screen Mode 23
Saving and Closing an Excel Workbook 24
Using the Excel Help System 26

4 **Building a Workbook** **29**

Understanding How Excel Interprets Data Entry 30
Navigating the Worksheet 31
Selecting Cells 32
Entering Text in Cells 34
Entering Numbers in Cells 36
Entering Dates and Times in Cells 37
Entering Data Using Fills 39
Entering Data with Other Shortcuts 40
Creating an Excel Table 41
Editing Cell Contents 44
Inserting a Symbol in a Cell 45
Creating Hyperlinks 46
Cutting, Copying, and Pasting Cell Values 50
Clearing Cell Contents 53
Using the Office Clipboard 54
Undoing or Redoing an Action 56
Finding and Replacing Text 57
Checking the Spelling of Your Worksheet 59

5 Managing and Viewing Worksheets 61

Viewing and Selecting Worksheets . . . 62
Renaming Worksheets . . . 63
Moving Worksheets . . . 64
Copying Worksheets . . . 66
Inserting and Deleting Worksheets . . . 67
Hiding or Showing a Worksheet . . . 68
Changing Worksheet Tab Colors . . . 69
Inserting, Moving, and Deleting Cells . . . 70
Inserting, Moving, and Deleting Columns and Rows . . . 72
Hiding and Unhiding Columns and Rows . . . 75
Entering Data and Formatting Many Worksheets at the Same Time . . . 76
Changing How You Look at Excel Workbooks . . . 78
Naming and Using Worksheet Views . . . 80

6 Using Formulas and Functions 83

Creating Simple Cell Formulas . . . 85
Assigning Names to Groups of Cells . . . 86
Using Names in Formulas . . . 88
Creating a Formula That References Values in an Excel Table . . . 89
Creating Formulas That Reference Cells in Other Workbooks . . . 90
Summing a Group of Cells Without Using a Formula . . . 93
Creating a Summary Formula . . . 94
Summing with Subtotals and Grand Totals . . . 95
Exploring the Excel Function Library . . . 97

Using the IF Function 99
Checking Formula References 100
Debugging Your Formulas 102

7 Formatting the Cell 105

Formatting Cell Contents 106
Formatting Cells Containing Numbers 108
Formatting Cells Containing Dates 110
Adding Cell Backgrounds and Shading 111
Formatting Cell Borders 113
Defining Cell Styles 115
Aligning and Orienting Cell Contents 119
Formatting a Cell Based on Conditions 121
Changing How Conditional Formatting Rules Are Applied 126
Stop When a Condition Is Met 126
Displaying Data Bars, Icon Sets, or Color Scales Based on Cell Values 128
Deleting Conditional Formats 130
Copying Formats with Format Painter 131
Merging or Splitting Cells or Data 132

8 Formatting the Worksheet 135

Applying Workbook Themes 136
Coloring Sheet Tabs 139
Changing a Worksheet's Gridlines 140
Changing Row Heights and Column Widths 142
Inserting Rows or Columns 144

Moving Rows and Columns 146
Deleting Rows and Columns 147
Outlining to Hide and Show Rows and Columns 148
Hiding Rows and Columns 150
Protecting Worksheets from Changes 152
Locking Cells to Prevent Changes 153

9 Printing Worksheets 155

Previewing Worksheets Before Printing 156
Printing Worksheets with Current Options 158
Choosing Whether to Print Gridlines and Headings 159
Choosing Printers and Paper Options 160
Printing Part of a Worksheet 162
Printing Row and Column Headings on Each Page 163
Setting and Changing Print Margins 164
Setting Page Orientation and Scale 166
Creating Headers and Footers 168
Adding Graphics to a Header or a Footer 171
Setting and Viewing Page Breaks 173

10 Customizing Excel to the Way You Work 175

Opening Ready-to-Use Workbook Templates 176
Adding Commands to the Quick Access Toolbar 179
Modifying the Ribbon User Interface 181
Controlling Which Error Messages Appear 189
Defining AutoCorrect and AutoFormat Entries 192

11 Sorting and Filtering Worksheet Data 197

Sorting Worksheet Data 198
Creating a Custom Sort List 200
Filtering Data Quickly with AutoFilter 202
Creating an Advanced Filter 205
Validating Data for Correctness During Entry 207

12 Summarizing Data Visually Using Charts 211

Creating a Chart Quickly 213
Changing a Chart's Appearance 215
Formatting Chart Legends and Titles 217
Changing the Body of a Chart 219
Customizing Chart Data 222
Working with Common Charts 225
Working with Uncommon Charts 227
Adding a Trendline to a Chart 228
Summarizing Data Using Sparklines 229

13 Enhancing Your Worksheets with Graphics 233

Adding Graphics to Worksheets 235
Adding Drawing Objects to a Worksheet 236
Adding Fills to Drawing Objects 238
Adding Effects to Drawing Objects 241
Customizing Pictures and Objects 243
Aligning and Grouping Drawing Objects 246
Using WordArt to Create Text Effects in Excel 249
Inserting Clip Art into a Worksheet 251

Inserting and Changing a Diagram 252
Creating an Organization Chart 254
Adding an Equation to a Shape 258

14 Sharing Excel Data with Other Programs 261

Linking and Embedding Other Files 263
Exchanging Table Data Between Excel and Word 265
Copying Excel Charts and Data into PowerPoint 267
Exchanging Data Between Access and Excel 269
Importing a Text File 271

15 Using Excel in a Group Environment 273

Sharing Workbooks in Excel 274
Commenting in Cells 275
Tracking Changes in Workbooks 277
Accepting or Rejecting Changes 278
Saving Worksheets to the Web 280
Dynamically Update Worksheets Published to the Web 281
Retrieving Web Data Using Excel 282
Modifying Web Queries 284
Interacting over the Web Using XML 286

Index 289

What do you think of this book? We want to hear from you!

Microsoft is interested in hearing your feedback so we can continually improve our books and learning resources for you. To participate in a brief online survey, please visit:

www.microsoft.com/learning/booksurvey/

Acknowledgments

A book is a team effort. I'd like to extend my sincere thanks to Kristen Borg, who shepherded this book through the production process;, Mark Reddin, who provided a rigorous technical edit; John Pierce, who copyedited the text; Robert Romano, who served as our graphic artist; Nellie McKesson, who laid out the pages; and Ginny Munroe, who prepared the index.

1 Introduction: About This Book

In this section:

- No Computerese!
- A Quick Overview
- A Few Assumptions
- A Final Word (or Two)

If you want to get the most from your computer and your software with the least amount of time and effort—and who doesn't?—this book is for you. You'll find *Microsoft Excel 2010 Plain & Simple* to be a straightforward, easy-to-read reference tool. With the premise that your computer should work for you, not you for it, this book's purpose is to help you get your work done quickly and efficiently so that you can get away from the computer and live your life.

No Computerese!

Let's face it—when there's a task you don't know how to do but you need to get it done in a hurry, or when you're stuck in the middle of a task and can't figure out what to do next, there's nothing more frustrating than having to read page after page of technical background material. You want the information you need—nothing more, nothing less—and you want it now! It should be easy to find and understand.

That's what this book is all about. It's written in plain English—no jargon. There's no single task in the book that takes more than a couple pages. Just look up the task in the index or the table of contents, turn to the page, and there's the information you need, laid out in an illustrated, step-by-step format. You don't get bogged down by the whys and wherefores: Just follow the steps, and get your work done.

Occasionally, you might have to turn to another page if the procedure you're working on is accompanied by a See Also. That's because a lot of tasks overlap, and I didn't want to keep repeating myself. I've scattered some useful tips here and there, and thrown in a Try This or a Caution once in a while, but by and large I've tried to remain true to the heart and soul of a Plain & Simple book, which is that the information you need should be available to you at a glance.

Useful Tasks...

Whether you use Microsoft Excel 2010 at home or on the road, I've tried to pack this book with procedures for everything I could think of that you might want to do, from the simplest tasks to some of the more esoteric ones.

...And the Easiest Way to Do Them

Another thing I've tried to do in this book is find and document the easiest way to accomplish a task. Excel 2010 often provides a multitude of methods to accomplish a single end result—which can be daunting or delightful, depending on the way you like to work. If you tend to stick with one favorite and familiar approach, I think the methods described in this book are the way to go. If you like trying out alternative techniques, go ahead! The intuitiveness of Excel 2010 invites exploration, and you're likely to discover ways of doing things that you think are easier or that you like better than mine. If you do, great! It's exactly what the developers of Excel 2010 had in mind when they provided so many alternatives.

A Quick Overview

Your computer probably came with Excel 2010 preinstalled, but if you do have to install it yourself, Setup makes installation so simple that you won't need my help anyway. So, unlike many computer books, this one doesn't start with installation instructions and a list of system requirements.

Next, you don't have to read the sections of this book in any particular order. You can jump in, get the information you need, and then close the book and keep it near your computer until the next time you need to know how to get something done. But that doesn't mean I scattered the information about with wild abandon. I've organized the book so that the tasks you want to accomplish are arranged in two levels—you find the general type of task you're looking for under a main section title such as "Formatting the Worksheet," "Summarizing Data Visually Using Charts," "Using Excel in a Group Environment," and so on. Then, in each of those sections, the smaller tasks within the main task are arranged in a loose progression from the simplest to the more complex.

Section 1 introduces the book, while Section 2 fills you in on the most important new features of Excel 2010. The biggest difference between Excel 2010 and previous versions is that all the file management tasks, such as saving and printing, are now gathered into a single place called Microsoft Office Backstage view. This section also describes new and improved capabilities for previewing how copied data will appear when you paste it into a worksheet, how you can customize the Excel 2010 program window, how new functions improve the accuracy of your calculations, how to summarize data visually using compact charts called sparklines, how to visualize data using improved conditional formats, how to edit images in Excel 2010, and how to add math equations to your worksheets.

Sections 3 and 4 cover the basics: starting Excel 2010 and shutting it down, sizing and arranging program windows, navigating in a workbook, using the user interface ribbon to have Excel do what you want it to do, and working with multiple Excel documents at the same time. Section 3 also introduces galleries, which are collections of preset formats you can apply to worksheets, charts, and other Excel objects, and shows you how to get help from within Excel and on the Web. Section 4 contains a lot of useful information about entering text and data, including shortcuts you can use to enter an entire series of numbers or dates by typing values in just one or two cells. You'll also learn about using the Office Clipboard to manage items you cut and paste, running the spelling checker to ensure you haven't made any errors in your workbook, and finding and replacing text to update changes in information such as customer addresses or product names.

Section 5 is all about managing and viewing worksheets—the "pages" of a workbook. In this section, you'll find out about selecting, renaming, moving, copying, inserting, and deleting worksheets, rows, columns, and cells. In Section 6, you'll get to know formulas and functions. You use formulas to calculate values, such as finding the sum of the values in a group of cells. Once you're up to speed on creating basic formulas, you'll learn how to save time by copying a formula from one cell and pasting it into as many other cells as you like. Finally, you'll extend your knowledge of formulas by creating powerful statements using the function library in Excel 2010.

Section 7 focuses on making your workbooks' cells look great. Here's where you'll learn techniques to make your data more readable, such as by changing font sizes and font colors, and adding colors and shading to cells. Section 8 describes similar techniques you can apply to your worksheets, such as moving, inserting, and deleting rows and columns, applying worksheet themes, and coloring sheet tabs to call attention to important information.

Section 9 is all about printing your Excel documents, whether that means printing all or just a portion of your results. Your productivity should increase after reading Section 10, where you'll learn how to customize Excel 2010 for the way you work. I'll show you how to add commands to the Quick Access Toolbar, customize the tabs on the ribbon user interface, control which error messages appear, define rules Excel uses to replace oft-misspelled words, create workbooks from built-in templates, and create custom workbook templates you can use to create new workbooks based on those formats.

Section 11 is about sorting and filtering your data, techniques you can use to limit the data displayed in a worksheet and determine the order in which it is presented. Do you need to see all of the sales for a specific product but don't want to bother with the rest of the data for the moment? No problem.

A picture is worth ten thousand words (according to Confucius; the modern version of the saying shorts you by nine thousand words), and in Section 12 I'll show you how to use the new Excel 2010 charting engine to create and use charts—including the new sparkline charts—to summarize your data visually. In Section 13, you'll learn how to enhance your worksheets by adding graphics and pictures. You'll be surprised to learn just how easy it is to insert clip art, add a special text effect, or resize a photo you added to a worksheet.

Sections 14 and 15 are all about sharing the data in your Excel worksheets—whether it's with your colleagues, on the Internet, or with other programs. Section 14 shows you how to make Excel 2010 interact with other Microsoft Office 2010 programs, such as by embedding documents from other programs in your Excel workbooks, exchanging data between Excel and Word, or importing a text file into an Excel worksheet. In Section 15, you'll learn how to use Excel in a group environment, to add comments to your worksheets, and to accept or reject the comments made by others. You'll also learn how to publish a worksheet to the Web, as well as how to pull information from the Internet directly into your worksheets. This section also introduces XML (an abbreviation for Extensible Markup Language), a handy technology that enables you to exchange data between spreadsheet applications.

A Few Assumptions

I had to make a few educated guesses about you, my audience, when I started writing this book. Perhaps you just use Excel for personal reasons, tracking your household budget, doing some financial planning, or recording your times for weekend bike races. Maybe you run a small, home-based business, or you're an employee of a corporation where you use Excel to analyze and present sales or production data. Taking all these possibilities into account, I assumed you need to know how to create and work with Excel workbooks and worksheets, summarize your data in a variety of ways, format your documents so that they're easy to read, and then print the results or share them over the Web or distribute your data both ways.

Another assumption I made is that—initially, anyway—you use Excel 2010 just as it came, meaning that you'd be working with the standard user interface. I like the new user interface, so that's what I've described in the procedures and graphics throughout this book.

A Final Word (or Two)

I had three goals in writing this book:

- Whatever you want to do, I want the book to help you get it done.
- I want the book to help you discover how to do things you didn't know you wanted to do.
- And, finally, if I've achieved my first two goals, I'll be well on the way to the third, which is for my book to help you enjoy using Excel 2010. I think that's the best gift I could give you to thank you for buying my book.

I hope you'll have as much fun using *Microsoft Excel 2010 Plain & Simple* as I've had writing it. The best way to learn is by doing, and that's how I hope you'll use this book.

Jump right in!

2 What's New and Improved in Excel 2010

In this section:

- Managing Excel Settings and Files in Backstage View
- Previewing Data Using Paste Preview
- Customizing the Excel 2010 User Interface
- Summarizing Data Using More Accurate Functions
- Summarizing Data Using Sparklines
- Visualizing Data Using Improved Conditional Formats
- Creating and Displaying Math Equations
- Editing Pictures Within Excel 2010

One of the first things you'll notice about Microsoft Excel 2010 is that the program incorporates the Microsoft Fluent interface, also known as the ribbon, which was introduced in Excel 2007. If you've been using Excel 2003 or an earlier version of Excel, you'll need to spend only a little bit of time working with the new user interface to bring yourself back up to your usual proficiency. If you used Excel 2007, you'll immediately notice one significant change: the Microsoft Office Button, located at the top-left corner of the program window in Excel 2007, has been replaced by the File tab.

This section of the book introduces many of the new and improved features in Excel 2010: managing settings and files in Backstage view, controlling paste options using Paste Preview, customizing the Excel 2010 program window, summarizing data using improved functions, summarizing data using compact charts called sparklines, visualizing data using improved conditional formats, editing pictures in Excel 2010, and creating and displaying math equations.

Managing Excel Files and Settings in Backstage View

After releasing the 2007 Microsoft Office System, the Microsoft Office User Experience team re-examined the programs' user interfaces to determine how they could be improved. During this process, the team discovered that it was possible to divide user tasks into two categories: "in" tasks, such as formatting and formula creation, which affect the contents of the workbook directly, and "out" tasks, such as saving and printing, which can be considered workbook management tasks.

When the User Experience and Excel teams focused on the Excel 2007 user interface, they discovered that several workbook-management tasks were sprinkled among the ribbon tabs that contained content-related tasks. The Excel team moved all the workbook-management tasks under the File tab, which users can click to display these commands in the new Backstage view.

Previewing Data Using Paste Preview

One of the most common tasks undertaken by Excel users involves cutting or copying a worksheet's contents, such as text or numbers, and pasting that data into either the same workbook or a separate Microsoft Office document. You have always been able to paste data from the Clipboard and control which formatting elements are pasted into the destination; however, in versions prior to Excel 2010, you had to select a paste option, observe the results, and (often) undo the paste and try another option until you found the option that produced the results you needed.

In Excel 2010, you can take advantage of the new Paste Preview capability to see how your data will appear in the worksheet before you commit to pasting it. By hovering the mouse pointer over any of the icons in the Paste Options palette, you can see a preview; switch between options to discover the one that makes your pasted data appear the way you want it to.

Customizing the Excel 2010 User Interface

When the Microsoft Office User Experience team designed the ribbon interface for Excel 2007, they allowed users to modify the program window by adding, moving, and deleting commands on the Quick Access Toolbar. In Excel 2010, users can still modify the Quick Access Toolbar, but they also have much more ability to change the ribbon interface. Users can hide or display built-in ribbon tabs, change the order of built-in ribbon tabs, add custom control groups to a ribbon tab, and create custom ribbon tabs that, in turn, can contain custom groups. These custom groups provide easy access to existing ribbon controls as well as custom controls that run macros stored in the workbook.

Summarizing Data Using More Accurate Functions

In previous versions of Excel, the program contained statistical, scientific, engineering, and financial functions that could return inaccurate results in some relatively rare circumstances. For Excel 2010, the Excel programming team identified the functions that returned inaccurate results and collaborated with academic and industry analysts to improve the functions' accuracy.

The Excel team also changed the naming conventions used to identify the program's functions. This change is most noticeable with regard to the program's statistical functions. Excel 2010 also contains more accurate statistical summary and test functions. The Excel programming team chose to retain the older functions to ensure that workbooks created in Excel 2010 would be compatible with workbooks created in previous versions of the program.

It is possible in Excel 2010 to create formulas using the older functions. The Excel team assigned these functions to a new group called Compatibility functions. These older functions appear at the bottom of the Formula AutoComplete list, but they are marked with an icon that's different from the icon for newer functions. Additionally, the ScreenTip that appears when you hover the mouse pointer over an older function's name indicates the function is included for backward compatibility only.

Summarizing Data Using Sparklines

In his book *Beautiful Evidence*, Edward Tufte describes sparklines as "intense, simple, word-sized graphics." In Excel 2010, sparklines take the form of small charts that summarize data in a compact space. These small but powerful additions to Excel 2010 enhance the program's reporting and summary capabilities.

Adding a sparkline to a summary worksheet provides context for the single value, such as an average or total, displayed in the worksheet. Excel 2010 includes three types of sparklines: line, column, and win/loss. A line sparkline is a line chart that displays a data trend over time. A column sparkline summarizes data by category, such as sales by product line or by month. Finally, win/loss sparklines indicate whether the points in a data series are positive, zero, or negative.

Visualizing Data Using Improved Conditional Formats

In Excel 2007, the Excel programming team greatly improved your ability to change a cell's format based on the cell's contents. One new conditional format, data bars, indicated a cell's relative value by the length of the bar within the cell that contained the value. The cell in the range that contained the smallest value displayed a zero-length bar, and the cell that contained the largest value displayed a bar that spanned the entire cell width.

Excel 2010 data bars' default behavior has been changed so that bar length is calculated in comparison to a baseline value such as zero. If you prefer, you can display values based on the Excel 2007 method or change the comparison value to something other than zero. Excel 2010 data bars also differ from those in Excel 2007 in that they display negative values and positive values in different colors. In addition, data bars representing negative values extend to the left of the baseline, not to the right. In Excel 2007, the conditional formatting engine placed the zero-length data bar in the cell that contained the smallest value, regardless of whether that value was positive or negative.

You have much more control over your data bars' formatting in Excel 2010 than in Excel 2007. When you create a data bar in Excel 2010, it has a solid color fill, not a gradient fill like the bars in Excel 2007. The gradient fill meant that the color of the Excel 2007 data bars faded as the bar extended to the right, making the cells' relative values harder to discern. In Excel 2010 you can select a solid or gradient fill style, apply borders to data bars, and change the fill and border colors for both positive and negative values.

Creating and Displaying Math Equations

Scientists and engineers who use Microsoft Excel to support their work often want to include equations in their workbooks to help explain how they arrived at their results. Excel 2010 includes an updated equation designer that enables you to create any equation you require. The new editor has several common equations, such as the quadratic formula and the Pythagorean Theorem, built in, but it also contains numerous templates you can use to create custom equations quickly.

Editing Pictures Within Excel 2010

When you present data in an Excel workbook, you can insert images into your worksheets to illustrate aspects of your data. For example, a shipping company could display a scanned image of a tracking label or a properly prepared package. Rather than having to edit your images in a separate program and then insert them into your Excel 2010 workbook, you can insert the image and then modify it by using the editing tools built in to Excel 2010.

One very helpful capability that is new in Excel 2010 is the ability to remove the background elements of an image. Removing an image's background enables you to create a composite image in which the foreground elements are placed in front of another background. For example, you could focus on a flower's bloom and remove most of the leaves and stem from the photo. After you isolate the foreground image, you can place the bloom in front of another background.

3 Getting Started with Excel 2010

In this section:

- Surveying the Excel Program Window
- Starting Excel
- Finding and Opening Existing Workbooks
- Using File Properties
- Creating a New Workbook
- Working with Multiple Workbooks
- Sizing and Viewing Windows
- Zooming In or Out on a Worksheet
- Viewing a Worksheet in Full-Screen Mode
- Saving and Closing an Excel Workbook
- Using the Excel Help System

Microsoft Excel 2010 is designed to help you store, summarize, and present data relevant to your business or home life. You can create spreadsheets to track products and sales or—just as easily—build spreadsheets to keep track of your personal investments or your kids' soccer scores. Regardless of the specific use you have in mind, Excel is a versatile program you can use to store and retrieve data quickly.

Working with Excel is pretty straightforward. The program has a number of preconstructed workbooks you can use for tasks such as tracking work hours for you and your colleagues or computing loan payments, but you also have the freedom to create and format workbooks from scratch, giving you the flexibility to build any workbook you need.

This section of the book covers the basics: how to start Excel and shut it down, how to open Excel documents, how to change the Excel window's size and appearance, and how to get help from within the program. There's also an illustrated overview of the Excel window, with labels for the most important parts of the program, and a close-up look at the new user interface. You can use the images in this section as touchstones for learning more about Excel.

Surveying the Excel Program Window

In many ways, an Excel worksheet is like the ledger in your checkbook. The page is divided into rows and columns, and you can organize your data using these natural divisions as a guide. The box formed by the intersection of a row and a column is called a cell. You can identify an individual cell by its column letter and row number. This combination, which identifies the first cell in the first column as cell A1, is called a cell reference. The following graphic shows you the important features of the Excel 2010 screen.

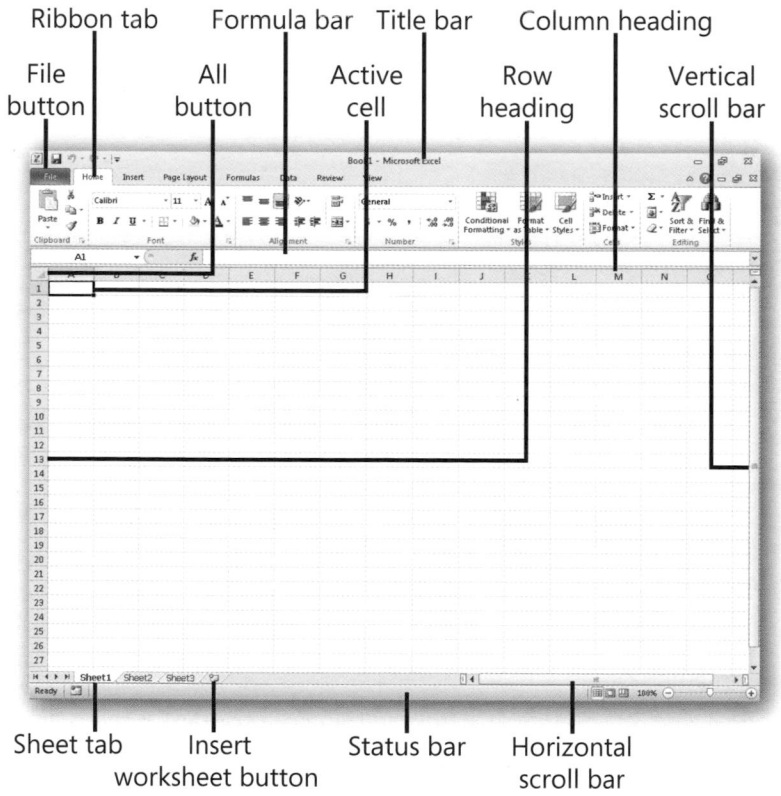

Work with the User Interface

Excel 2010 incorporates the Microsoft Office Fluent interface introduced in the 2007 Microsoft Office system. In versions of Office prior to Office 2007, you had to look through dozens of toolbars and menus to find specific commands. In Excel 2010, you can find what you need in one place: the ribbon at the top of the screen.

Work with Galleries

After you enter your data in a worksheet, you can change the appearance of data and objects within the worksheet by using galleries that appear on the user interface. The ribbon has three types of galleries: galleries that appear in a dialog box, galleries that appear as a drop-down menu when you click a user interface item, and galleries that appear within the user interface itself. The graphic on the right shows a styles gallery.

Excel 2010 lets you see how formatting will appear before you apply a formatting change. Rather than make you apply the change and then remove it if you don't like how it turned out, when you hover your mouse pointer over a style in a gallery, Excel 2010 generates a live preview of how your data or object will appear if you apply that style. All you need to do is move your mouse to see what your objects will look like when you're finished.

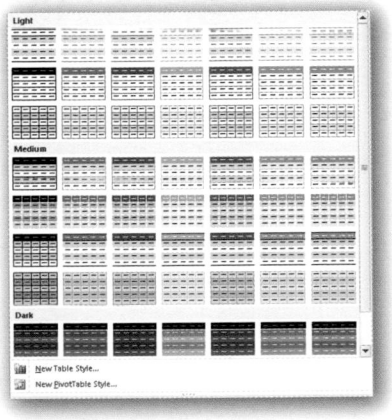

Tip

If positioning your mouse pointer over an icon in a gallery doesn't result in a live preview, that option might be turned off in your copy of Excel 2010. To turn Live Preview on, click the File tab, and click Options to display the Excel Options dialog box. Click General, select the Enable Live Preview check box, and click OK.

Starting Excel

After you install Excel on your computer, you can start it from the Start menu, which opens the program with a new, blank workbook, or by double-clicking an Excel file already on your computer.

Start Excel with a Blank Workbook

1. Click the Start button on the taskbar.
2. Point to All Programs.
3. Click Microsoft Office.
4. Click Microsoft Excel 2010.

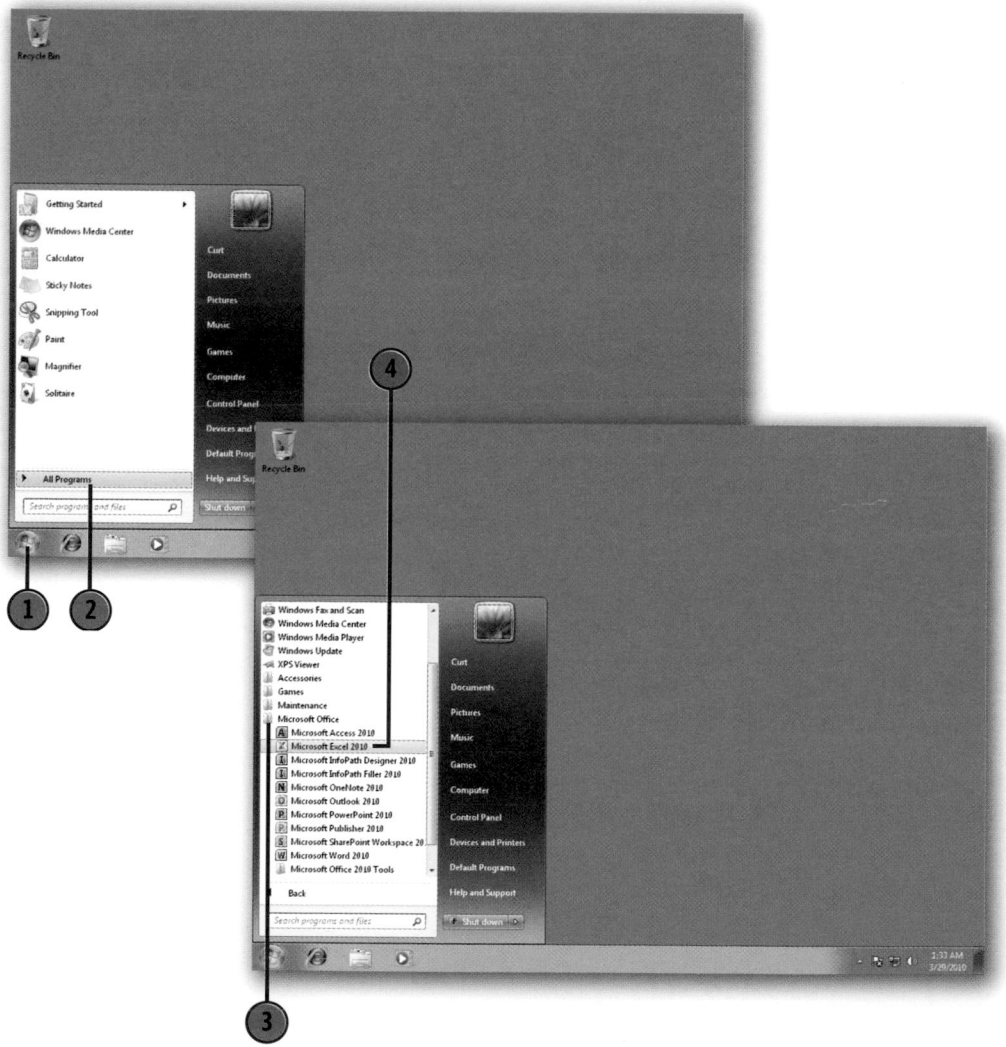

Tip

Pressing Ctrl+Esc also opens the Start menu.

Open an Existing Workbook

1. Click the Start button on the taskbar.
2. Click Computer.
3. Navigate to the folder that contains the file you want to open.
4. Double-click the file you want to open.

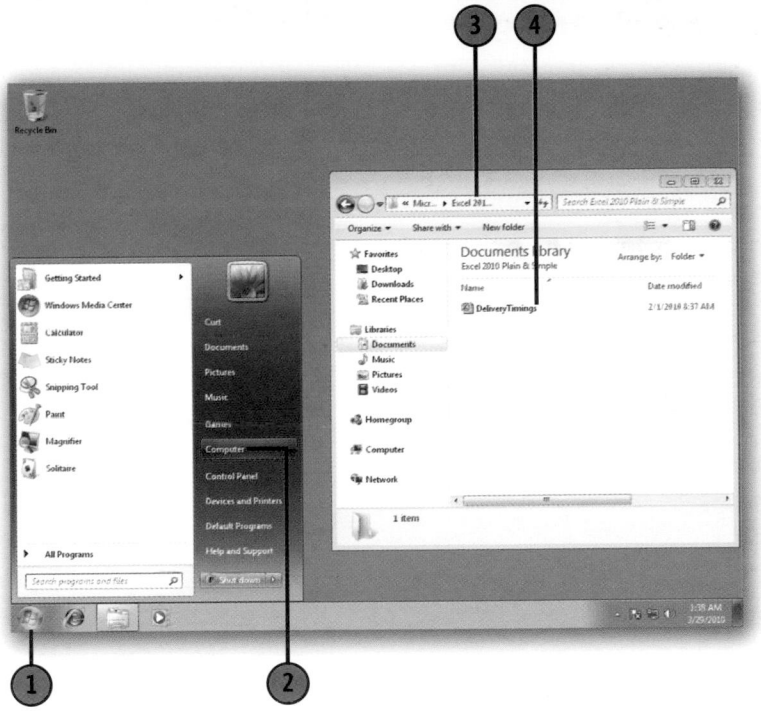

Tip

In Windows 7, if Microsoft Excel 2010 appears as an item on the Start menu, hovering the mouse pointer over Microsoft Excel 2010 displays a list of the most recently opened Excel workbooks. You can click any of these workbooks to open it in Excel 2010.

Finding and Opening Existing Workbooks

After you create an Excel workbook, you will probably want to open it again, whether to verify the contents, add or update data, or copy data from one workbook to another. If you don't know the exact name of the file you want to open, but you do know some of the data it contains, you can search for the file and open it after you locate it.

Open a Workbook

1. Click the File tab.
2. Click Open.
3. Navigate to the folder that contains the workbook you want to open.
4. Click the workbook.
5. Click Open.

Tip

You can also display the Open dialog box by pressing Ctrl+O.

Open a Recently Used Workbook

1. Click the File tab.
2. Click Recent.
3. Click the workbook you want to open.

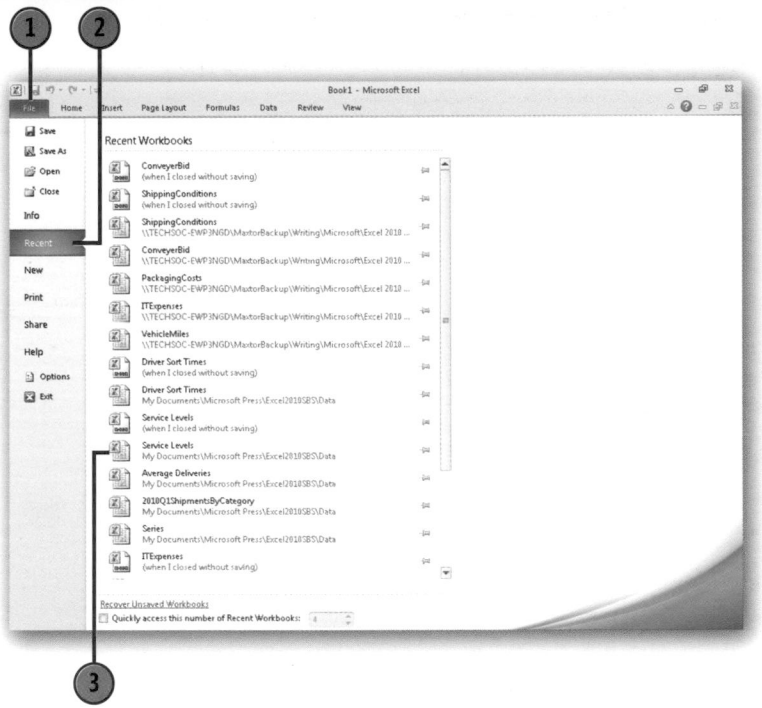

Search for a Workbook by Name and Open It

1. Click the Start button on the taskbar.
2. Type the first few characters of the name of the file you want to find or the word you want to find in a document.
3. Click the file you want to open, or continue to step 4 for more options.
4. Click See More Results.
5. Click Custom.
6. Select the locations you want to search.
7. Click OK.
8. Click a file name in the Search Results list to open the file.

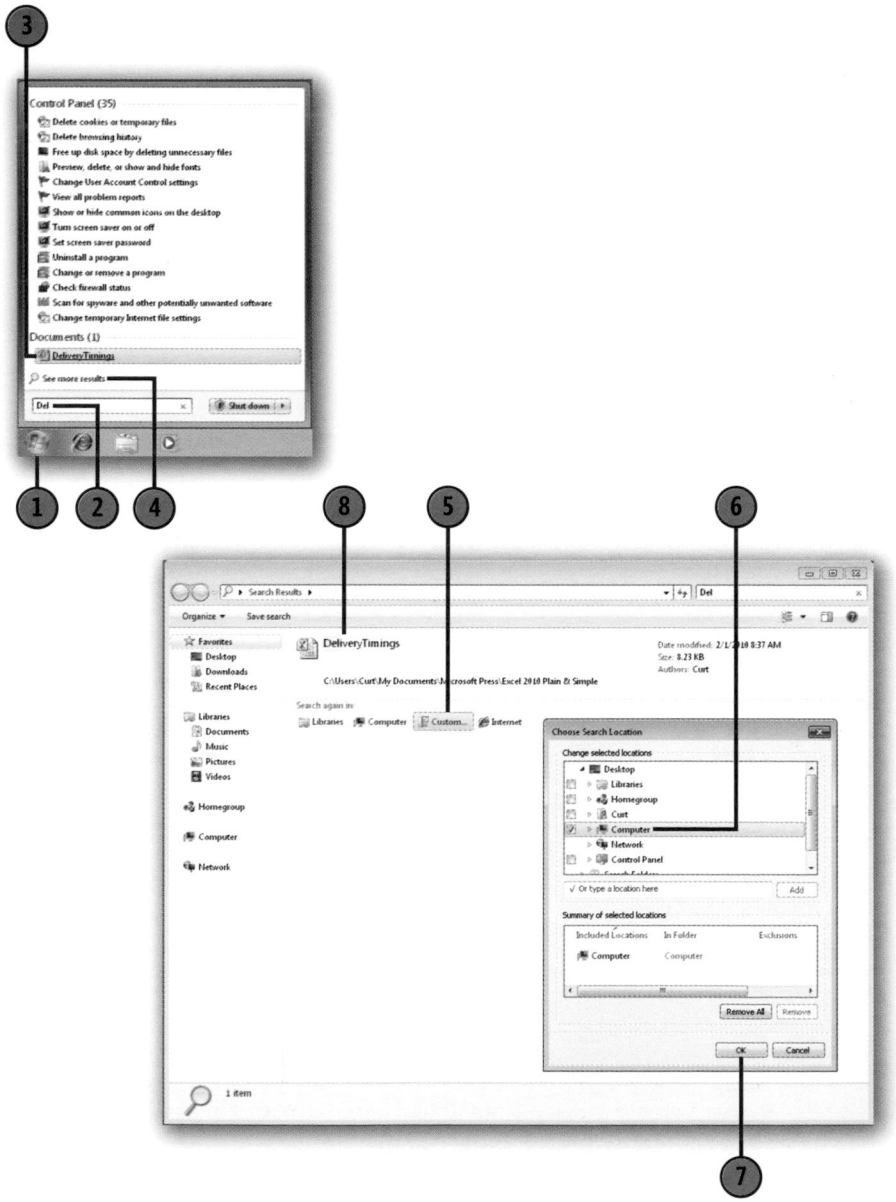

Using File Properties

Finding files can be difficult on computers you share with your colleagues or if you've been using the same computer for a long time and have created a lot of workbooks. You can make it easier to find your files by adding descriptive terms to their Properties fields. If you enter a term in a Properties field, you can search using that term, even if it doesn't occur within the body of the workbook.

Set File Properties

1. Open the file to which you want to assign property values.
2. Click the File tab.
3. Click Properties.
4. Click Show Document Panel.
5. Add information describing your file.

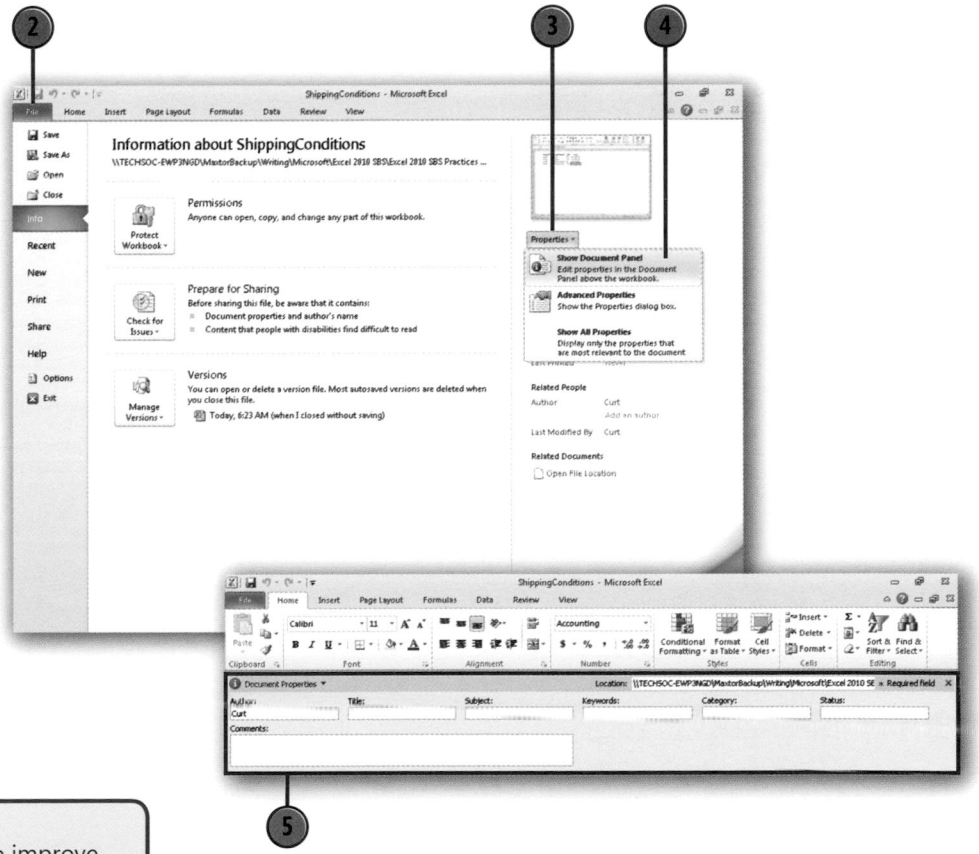

Tip

Adding words to the Keywords field is a great way to improve search results. Just type a word, press the Spacebar, and then type the next word. There's no need to use commas.

Define Custom Properties

1. Open the file to which you want to assign property values.
2. Click the File tab.
3. Click Properties.
4. Click Advanced Properties.
5. Click the Custom tab.
6. Type the name of the custom property.
7. Select the type of data contained in the property.
8. Type a value for the property.
9. Click Add.
10. Click OK.

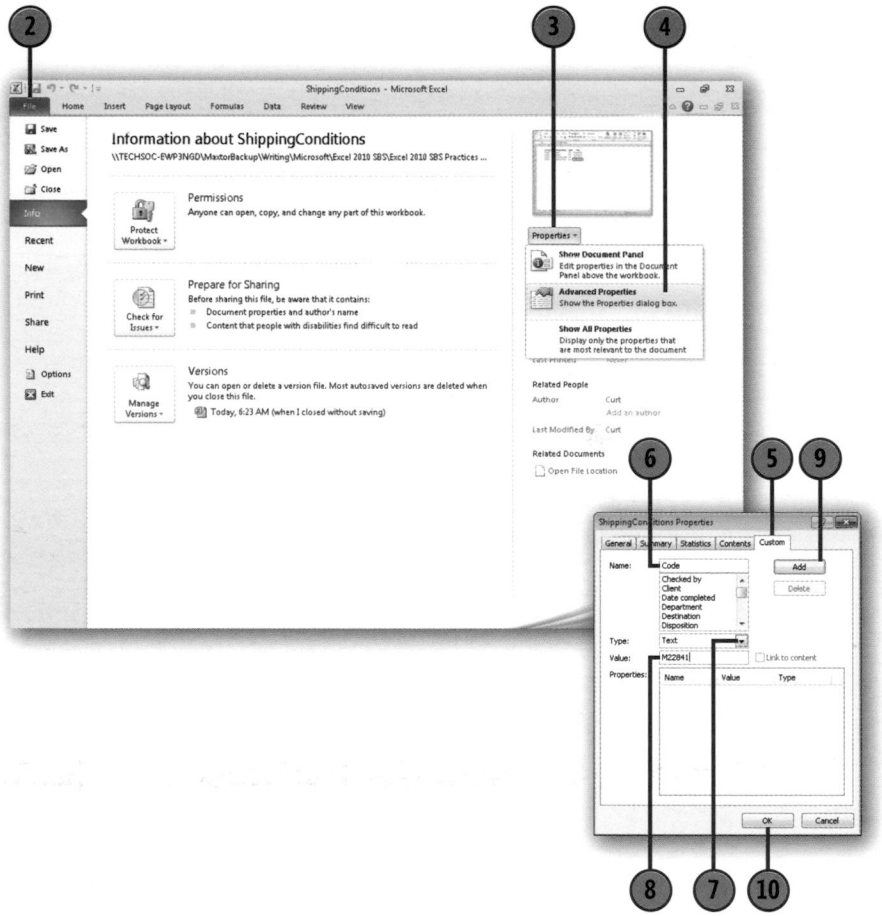

Try This!

Excel comes with a set of predefined custom properties, such as Checked By and Date Completed. To use an existing custom property, display the Custom tab of the Properties dialog box, click the name of the custom property, type a value for the property in the Value box, and click OK.

Creating a New Workbook

As a general rule, you should create a new workbook any time you need a place to store data on a new subject. For example, you might track your company's sales in one workbook, the products your company offers in another, and your employees' personal information and salaries in another.

Create a New Workbook

1. Click the File tab.
2. Click New.
3. Click Blank Workbook.
4. Click Create.

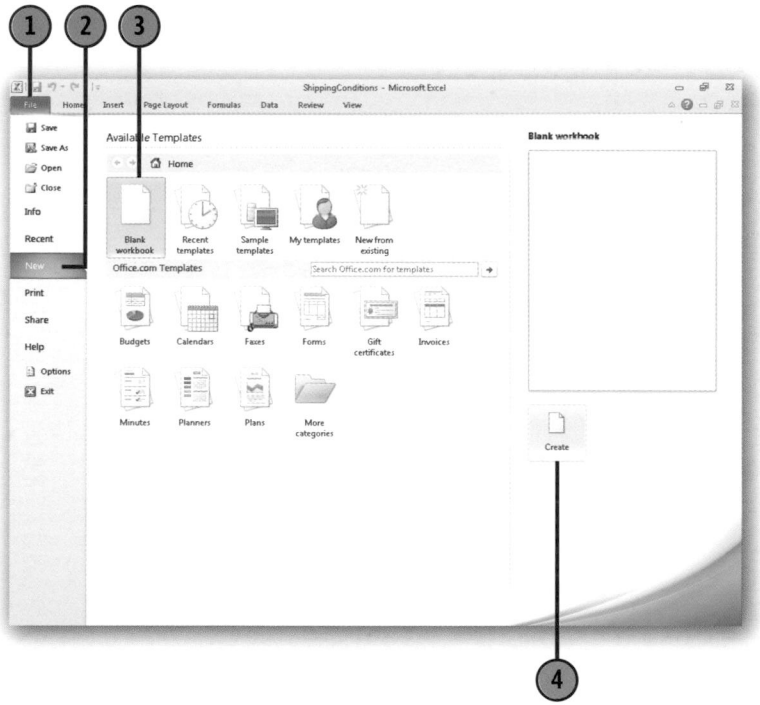

Tip

You can create a new, blank workbook by pressing Ctrl+N at any time you are not in Backstage view (which appears when you click the File tab). To exit Backstage view, click any tab on the ribbon.

Working with Multiple Workbooks

When you create an Excel workbook for each subject of your business, you sometimes need to look at data from more than one workbook to make your decisions. In cases like this, you can switch between workbooks by choosing the workbook's name from the list displayed when you click the Switch Windows button on the View tab. You can also choose one of several arrangements so that you can work with your workbooks effectively.

Switch Between Open Workbooks

1. Click the View tab.
2. Click Switch Windows.
3. Click the name of the workbook you want to display.

Show More Than One Workbook

1. Click the View tab.
2. Click Arrange All.
3. Select the arrangement you want.
4. Click OK.

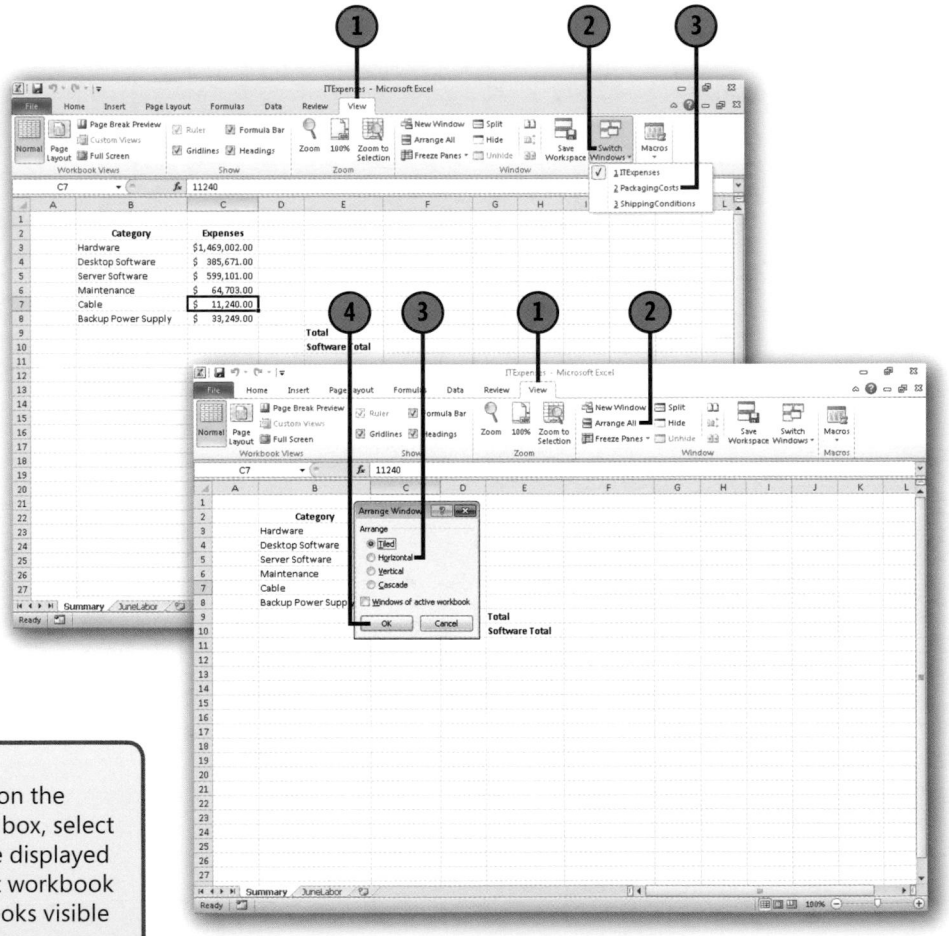

Try This!

Open three workbooks; then, in the Window group on the View tab, click Arrange All. In the Arrange All dialog box, select the Cascade option, and click OK. The workbooks are displayed with a slight overlap, with the full contents of the first workbook displayed and the title bars of the other two workbooks visible behind the first workbook.

Sizing and Viewing Windows

You work with windows in the Excel program the same way you work with windows on your desktop. You can make a workbook's window as large as the screen itself. If you have more than one workbook open at a time, you can choose from several display arrangements to order the windows most effectively.

Resize a Window

- Click the Maximize button to make the window take up the entire screen.
- Click the Minimize button to represent the window as a button on the taskbar.
- Click the Restore button to return the window to its previous size.
- Drag the left or right border of the window to resize it horizontally.
- Drag the top or bottom border of the window to resize it vertically.
- Drag a corner to resize the window both horizontally and vertically.
- Drag the window's title bar to change its position.

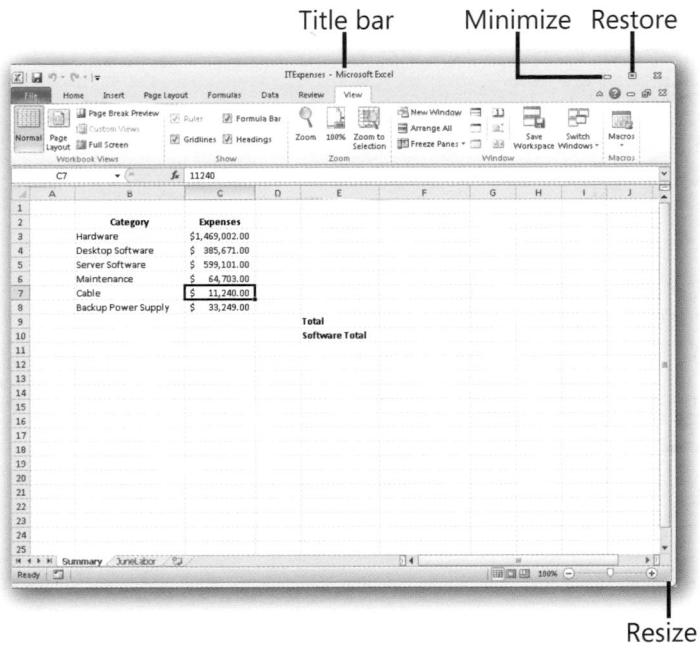

Tip

The Maximize and Restore buttons are actually two states of the same "window size" button, so you never see them on a window at the same time.

Zooming In or Out on a Worksheet

If you are not satisfied with how much of your worksheet you can see, you can make the worksheet larger or smaller without changing the window size. When you zoom out on a worksheet, you can see the overall layout, but it might be difficult to read the data in individual cells. To get a better look at the data in your cells, you can zoom in on your worksheet.

Zoom In or Out

- Click the Zoom In control to make your window's contents 10 percent larger per click.
- Click the Zoom Out control to make your window's contents 10 percent smaller per click.
- Drag the Zoom slider control, shown in the figure, to the left to zoom out or to the right to zoom in.

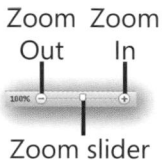

Zoom In or Out to a Custom Zoom Level

1. Click the View tab.
2. Click Zoom.
3. Select the Custom option.
4. Type a new zoom level in the Custom field.
5. Click OK.

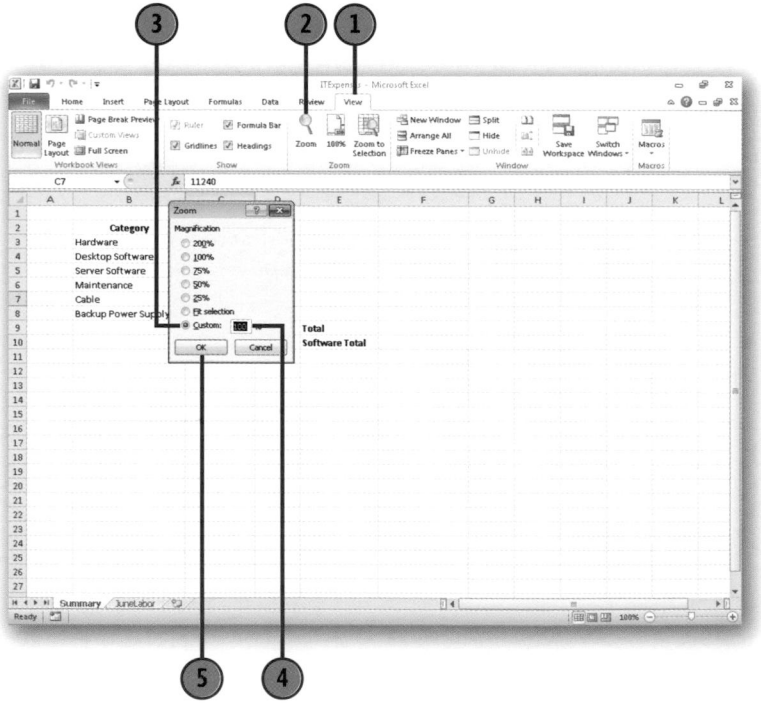

Tip

The maximum zoom level is 400 percent; the minimum zoom level is 10 percent.

Viewing a Worksheet in Full-Screen Mode

Occasionally, you'll want to see as much of a worksheet as possible. An easy way to temporarily hide the user interface ribbon at the top of the Excel window and the status bar at the bottom is to display the workbook in full-screen mode. Unlike with the Maximize command, which affects only one worksheet, in full-screen mode you can view multiple worksheets simultaneously. If you want to format or otherwise manipulate the contents of your worksheet, you can right-click a cell or an object to display a shortcut menu.

You can find the Close Full Screen command at the bottom of the shortcut menu that appears when you click a cell.

Turn Full-Screen Mode On

1. Click the View tab.
2. Click Full Screen.

Turn Full-Screen Mode Off

1. Right-click a worksheet cell.
2. Choose Close Full Screen.

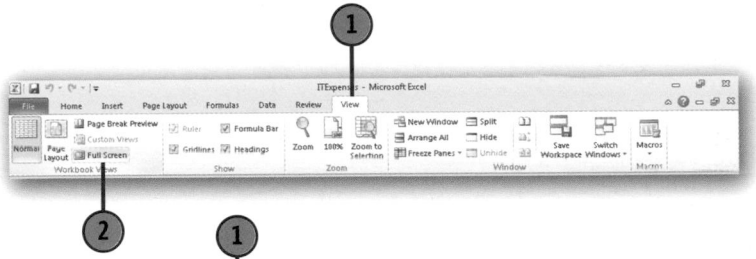

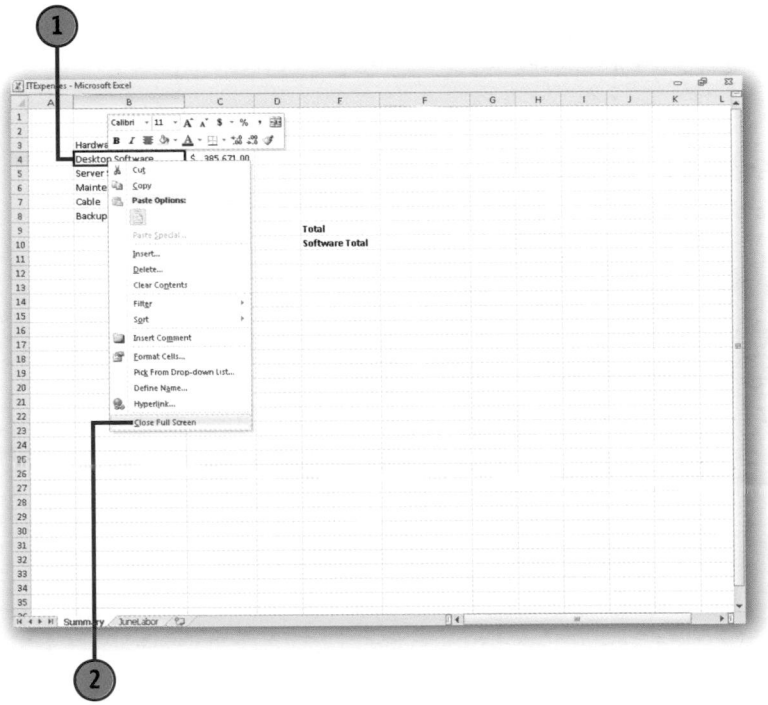

Saving and Closing an Excel Workbook

There's nothing more frustrating than losing a few minutes or even hours of work because you forget to save your file. When you close your workbook, Excel checks to see whether it has changed since the last time you saved it. If it has been changed, you're asked whether you want to save your workbook before you close it. If you want to save multiple versions of the same workbook, you can create a copy of your file by saving it with a different name. Also, if you usually open workbooks that are saved in folders other than Documents, you can change the folder that Excel displays by default in the Open and Save As dialog boxes.

Save a Workbook

1. Click the Save button on the Quick Access Toolbar.

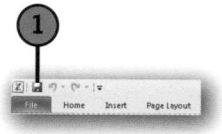

Save a Workbook with a New Name

1. Click the File tab.
2. Click Save As.
3. Navigate to the directory where you want to save your file.
4. Type a new file name.
5. Click Save.

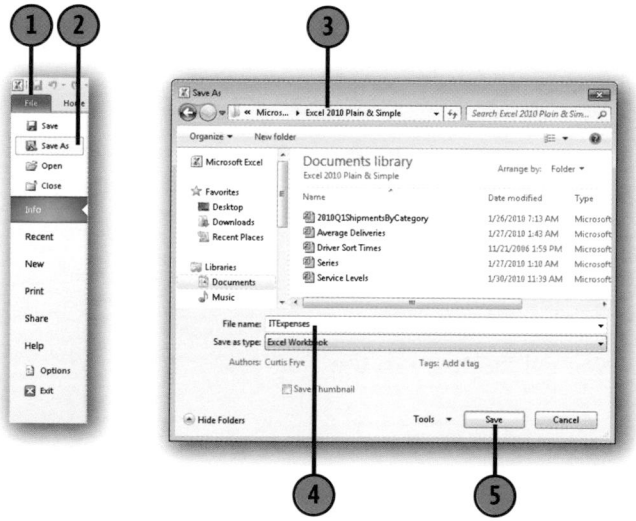

Tip

You can also save a workbook by pressing Ctrl+S. A good rule of thumb is to save your workbook every time you make a change you would hate to have to make again.

Change the Default File Folder

1. Click the File tab.
2. Click Options.
3. Click Save.
4. In the Default File Location box, type the path for the folder you want to appear by default.
5. Click OK.

Close a Workbook

1. Click the File tab.
2. Click Close.
3. If a dialog box appears asking whether you want to save any unsaved changes, you can do any of the following:
   - Click Save to save the workbook using the same name and location.
   - Click Don't Save to discard all the changes made since the workbook was last saved.
   - Click Cancel to return to the workbook.

Exit Excel

1. Click the File tab.
2. Click Exit.

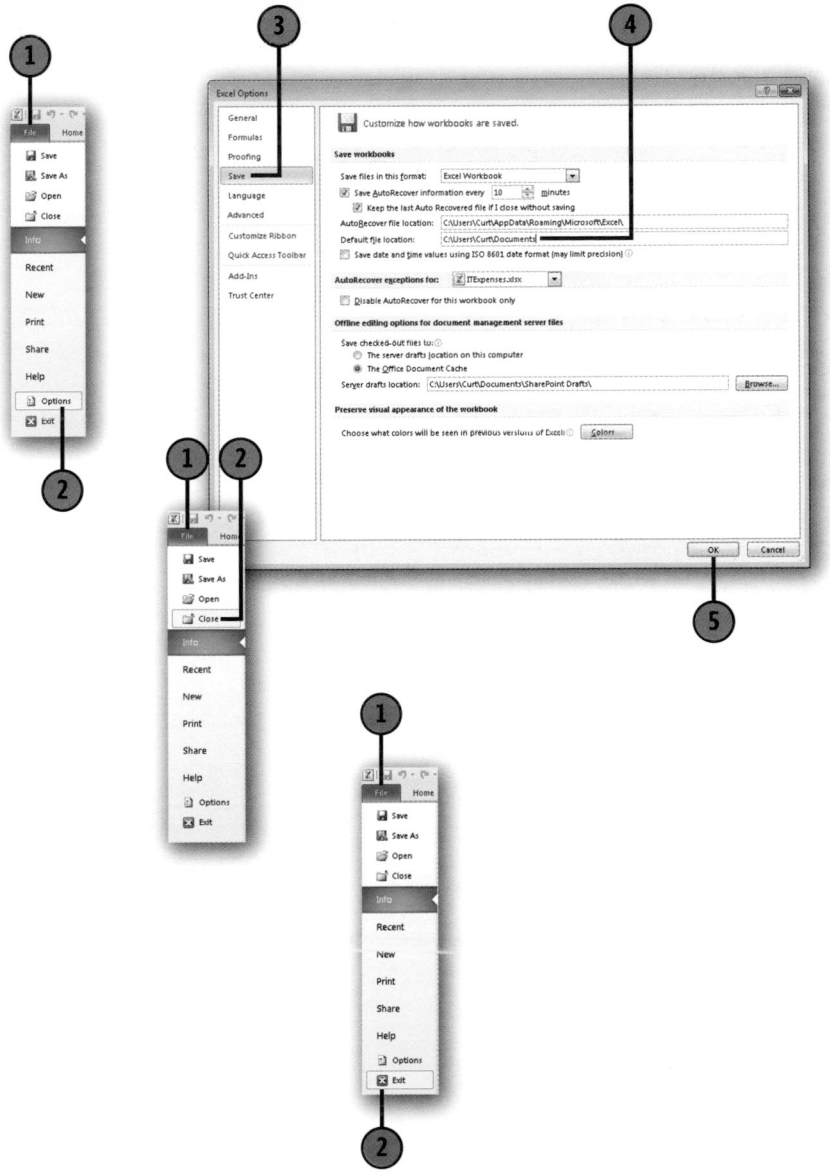

Using the Excel Help System

If you need to get help for using Excel, you can look in a number of places. One option is to right-click an object (such as a worksheet or a graphic) to see a list of things you can do with the object. You can also open the Excel Help files and browse through them to find the answer to a specific question or just to explore.

Get Microsoft Excel Help

1. Click the Microsoft Excel Help button.

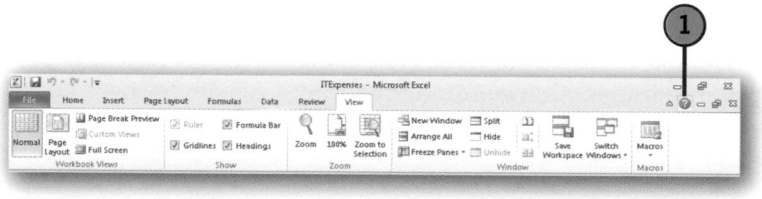

Get Suggested Commands from Shortcut Menus

1. Right-click any Excel object to see the shortcut menu of commands.
2. Click a command.

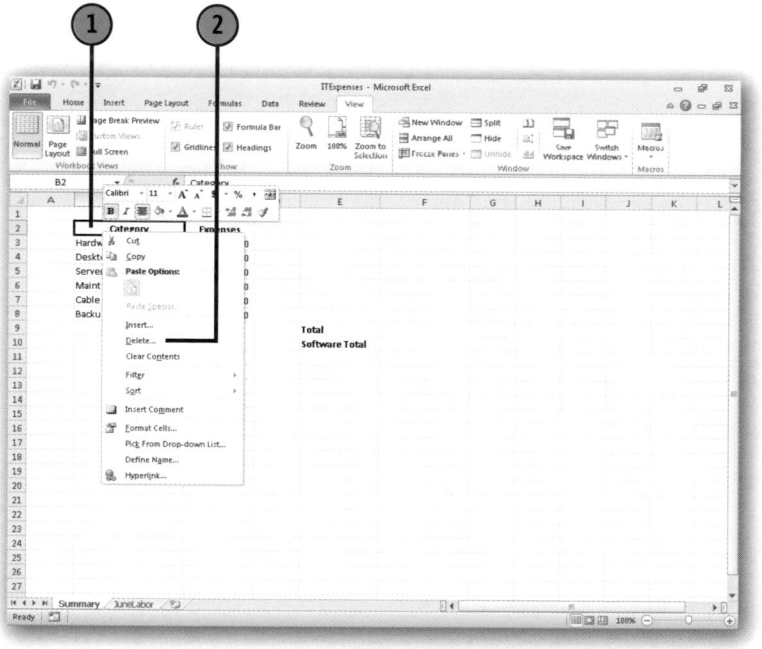

Get Help on the Web

1. Click the Microsoft Office Excel Help button.
2. Type your search terms.
3. Click the Search button.
4. Browse the topics displayed for help and resources.

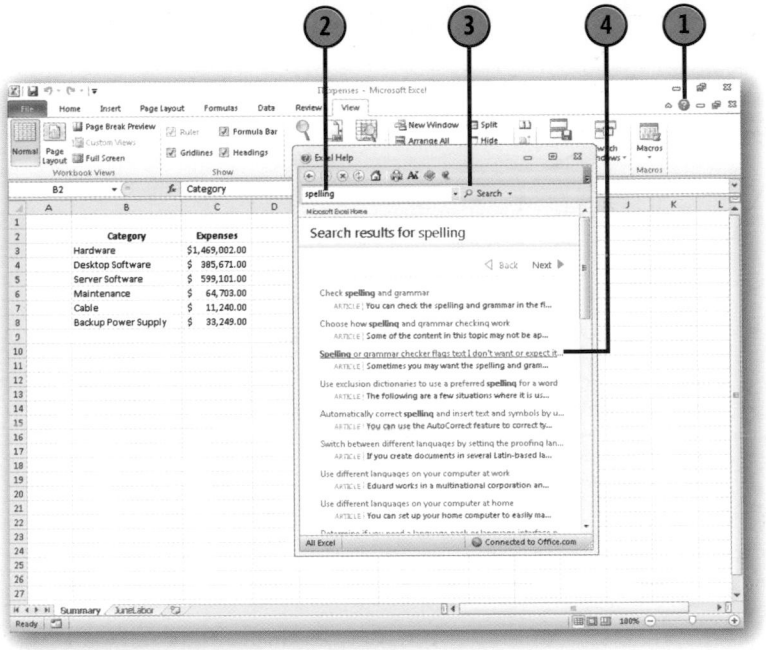

Tip

You can visit the Microsoft Office Online site directly by opening your Web browser and typing *http://office.microsoft.com/* in the Address box. You can find numerous links to help and how-to files on that page.

4 Building a Workbook

In this section:

- Navigating the Worksheet and Selecting Cells
- Entering Data in Cells
- Entering Data Using Fills
- Entering Data with Other Shortcuts
- Creating an Excel Table
- Editing Cell Contents
- Inserting a Symbol in a Cell
- Creating Hyperlinks
- Cutting, Copying, and Pasting Cell Values
- Undoing or Redoing an Action
- Finding and Replacing Text
- Checking the Spelling of Your Worksheet

One of the real strengths of Microsoft Excel 2010 is that the program makes it easy for you to enter large quantities of data. When you type text, Excel remembers what you entered in previous cells in the same column and offers to complete the current entry for you. The good news is that you need to type Arkadelphia only once. After the first time, typing the first few letters gives Excel enough information to guess the city's name. Entering a series of numbers, dates, or days also goes quickly and smoothly. If you want to enter a long series of numbers, dates, or even weekdays, you can type one or two values and have Excel fill in the remaining values in the series! These techniques, combined with formatting and other skills you'll learn elsewhere in this book, make data entry nearly painless.

Understanding How Excel Interprets Data Entry

Excel makes it easy for you to enter data in a worksheet by guessing the type of data you're entering and applying the appropriate formatting to that data. It's important to remember that because Excel is a computer program, it has some limitations. For example, Excel performs calculations using decimal values, such as .5, rather than fractions, such as ½; however, if you do want to express some of your data as fractions and not as decimal values, you can do so by changing the cell's format to Fraction. In either case, you can save the data in your preferred format.

Another aspect of this bias toward decimal values is that entering dates and times is much easier than it would be if you had to type out a full date, such as February 3, 2010. For example, if you type 2/3 in a cell and press Enter, Excel recognizes the text as an abbreviation for the third day of the month of February and displays the data as 3-Feb.

You can choose the format you want for dates and times by selecting the cells that will hold dates or times, clicking the Home tab on the ribbon, and then clicking the Font dialog box launcher to display the Format Cells dialog box. Inside the dialog box, click the Number tab, and then click Date in the list of categories. The available date formats appear on the right. From there, just click the format you want, and click OK. If you want the data in a cell to appear as a fraction, click the Number tab, click the Fraction category, specify the type of fraction on the right, and click OK. The following figure shows the Number tab with the Fraction category selected.

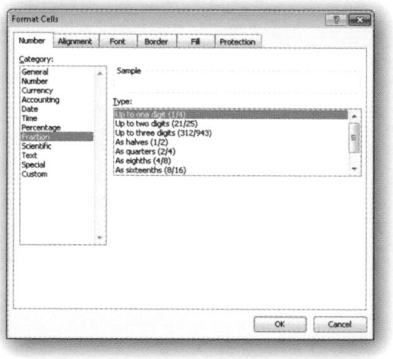

Navigating the Worksheet

Using the mouse and keyboard, you can move from cell to cell in a worksheet, move up or down a page at a time, or move to the first or last cell in a row. The following table lists the keyboard shortcuts you can use in addition to the scroll bars and sheet tabs you use with your mouse.

Navigate Your Workbook Using the Keyboard

Key	Action
Left arrow	Move one cell left.
Right arrow	Move one cell right.
Up arrow	Move one cell up.
Down arrow	Move one cell down.
Enter	Move one cell down.
Tab	Move one cell to the right.
Ctrl + Home	Move to cell A1.
Ctrl + End	Move to the last used cell in the worksheet.
Page Up	Move up one page.
Page Down	Move down one page.
Ctrl + arrow key	Move to the next cell with data in the direction of the arrow key. If there is not another cell with data in that direction, you move to the last cell in the worksheet in that direction.

Selecting Cells

Whenever you make changes to cells in a worksheet, you can save time by applying the changes to similar cells at the same time. You used to be limited to selecting cells that were contiguous, but in Excel 2010 you can select groups of cells that aren't even next to each other! If your worksheet stores dates in cells with other information in cells in between, you can select all the date cells and apply a format to them at the same time.

Select a Contiguous Group of Cells

- Drag from the upper-left cell you want to select to the lower-right cell.

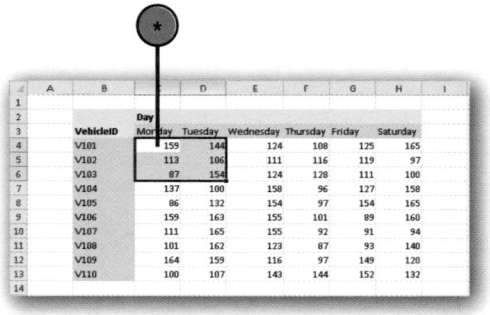

	VehicleID	Day Monday	Tuesday	Wednesday	Thursday	Friday	Saturday
4	V101	159	144	124	108	125	165
5	V102	113	106	111	116	119	97
6	V103	87	154	124	128	111	100
7	V104	137	100	158	96	127	158
8	V105	86	132	154	97	154	165
9	V106	159	163	155	101	89	160
10	V107	111	165	155	92	91	94
11	V108	101	162	123	87	93	140
12	V109	164	159	116	97	149	120
13	V110	100	107	143	144	152	132

Select a Noncontiguous Group of Cells

1. Drag from the upper-left cell you want to select to the lower-right cell to select the first set of cells.
2. Hold down the Ctrl key, and drag to select another set of cells.

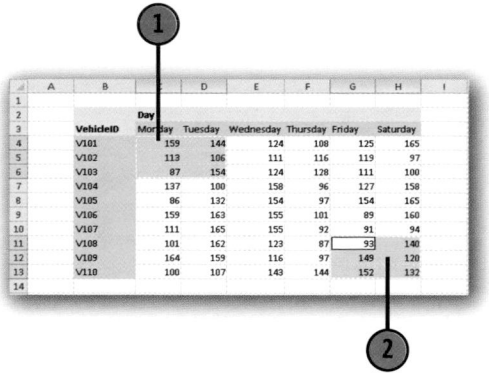

	VehicleID	Day Monday	Tuesday	Wednesday	Thursday	Friday	Saturday
4	V101	159	144	124	108	125	165
5	V102	113	106	111	116	119	97
6	V103	87	154	124	128	111	100
7	V104	137	100	158	96	127	158
8	V105	86	132	154	97	154	165
9	V106	159	163	155	101	89	160
10	V107	111	165	155	92	91	94
11	V108	101	162	123	87	93	140
12	V109	164	159	116	97	149	120
13	V110	100	107	143	144	152	132

Select Rows or Columns

1. Click the header for the first row or column you want to select.
2. Hold down the Shift key, and click the header for the last row or column you want to select.

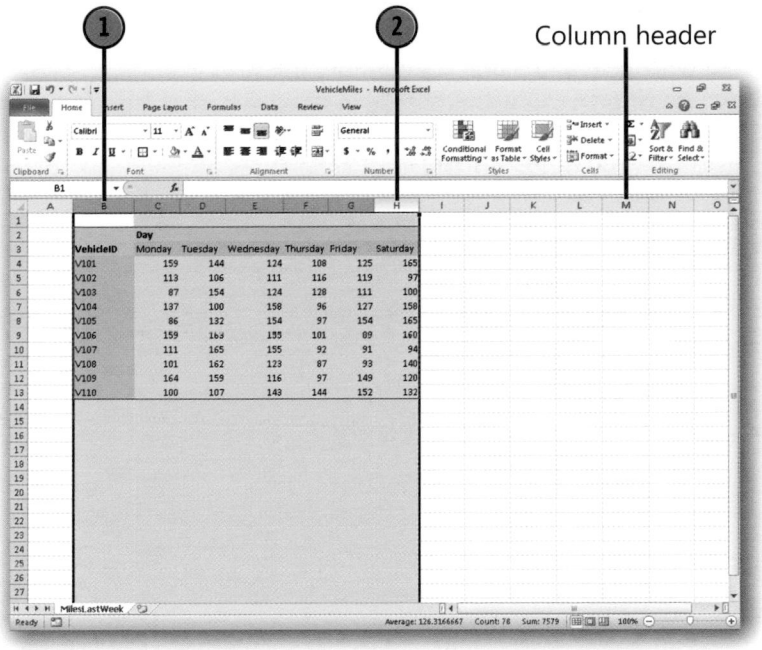

Select Noncontiguous Rows or Columns

- Hold down the Ctrl key, and then click the headers of the rows or columns you want to select.

Tip

To cancel the selection of a group of cells, rows, or columns, click any cell in the worksheet.

Entering Text in Cells

No workbook worthy of the name stays empty for long. You can type any sort of text you want directly in a cell, whether the text is a label identifying the data in a row or column or an explanation reminding you and your colleagues of any limitations on the data to be entered in a cell. Most text entered in Excel workbooks is short enough to fit on one line, but if you want to have the text in a cell appear on two or more lines and break at a specific location, you can easily insert a line break.

Enter Text as One Line

1. Click the cell in which you want to enter text.
2. Type the text you want to appear.
3. Press Enter.

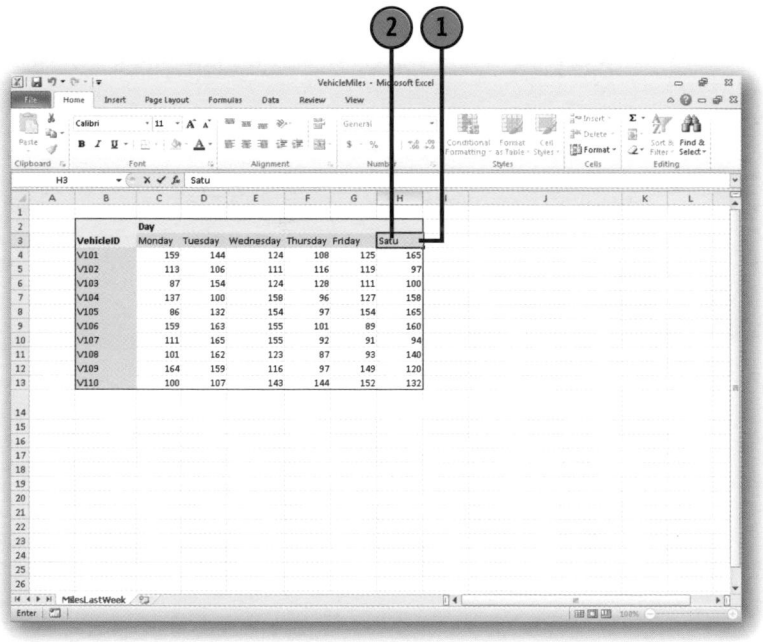

Tip

In Excel 2010, the formula bar doesn't expand to display all the information in a cell. To scroll through the contents of the formula bar one line at a time, use the scroll buttons at the right edge of the formula bar. To display the formula bar's entire contents, click the Expand Formula Bar control to the right of the formula bar. When you expand the formula bar, the Expand Formula Bar control changes to the Collapse Formula Bar control; clicking it returns the formula bar to its original one-line height.

See Also

For information about how to make your columns wider to allow more text to appear within a cell, see "Resize a Column" on page 143.

Enter Text with Forced Line Breaks

1. Click the cell in which you want to enter text.
2. Type the text you want to appear on the first line. Press Alt+Enter to insert a line break.
3. Type the text you want to appear on the second line, and then press Enter.

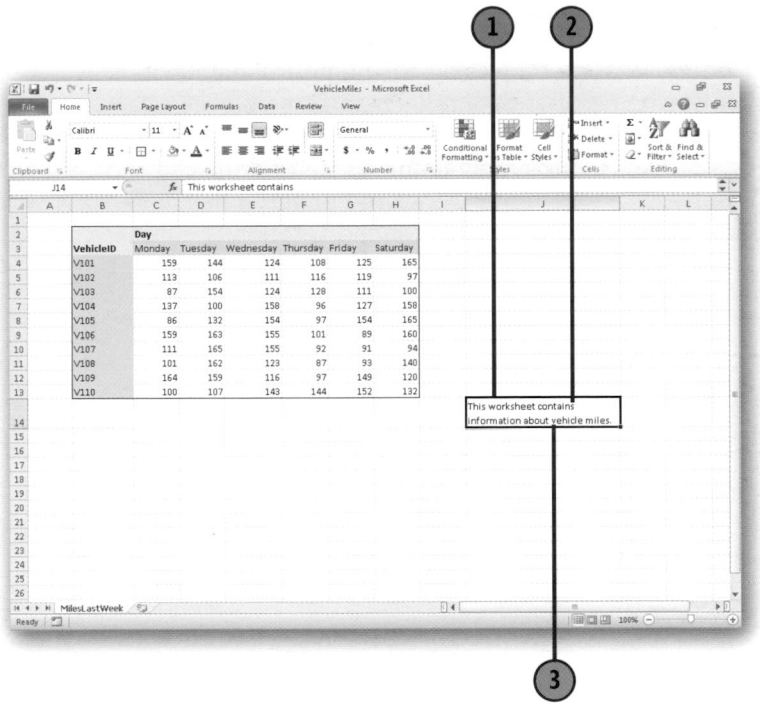

	Day					
VehicleID	Monday	Tuesday	Wednesday	Thursday	Friday	Saturday
V101	159	144	124	108	125	165
V102	113	106	111	116	119	97
V103	87	154	124	128	111	100
V104	137	100	158	96	127	158
V105	86	132	154	97	154	165
V106	159	163	155	101	89	160
V107	111	165	155	92	91	94
V108	101	162	123	87	93	140
V109	164	159	116	97	149	120
V110	100	107	143	144	152	132

Try This!

Type a long line of text in a cell that is in an empty row. The text in this cell will extend over the other columns. Click the cell to the right of the one you just entered text in, type some text in it, and press Enter. The overlapping text in the previous column is now hidden.

Entering Numbers in Cells

The backbone of any workbook is the numerical data in its worksheets, whether that data reflects sales, employee salaries, or the quantity of a given product you have in inventory. Entering numbers in Excel is as simple as clicking the cell and typing, but you can also enter very large or very small numbers using scientific notation. In scientific notation, a number with a positive exponent is written as 1.00E+06, which is read as "one times ten to the sixth power." Numbers that are less than one can be written with negative exponents. For example, the number .001 would be written as 1.00E-03 and read as "one times ten to the negative third power."

Enter Numbers

1. Click the cell in which you want to enter a number.
2. Type a numerical value.
3. Press Enter.

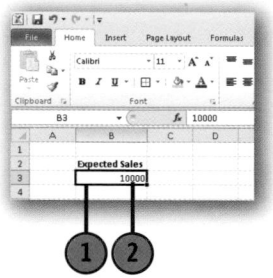

Enter Numbers Using Scientific Notation and Exponents

1. Click the cell in which you want to enter a number.
2. Type the base number you want.
3. Type E.
4. Type the exponent you want.
5. Press Enter.

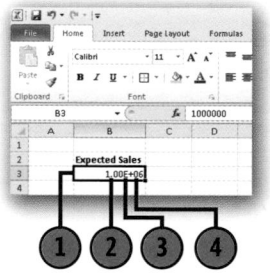

See Also

For information about applying number formatting such as dollar and percent signs instead of typing them, see "Formatting Cells Containing Numbers" on page 108.

Tip

You can type a number but have it interpreted as a text value by typing ' (an apostrophe) before the number value. The apostrophe will not appear in the cell, but a green icon will appear in the corner of the cell; clicking the cell exposes formatting options you can apply to the data.

Entering Dates and Times in Cells

Dates are extremely important in any business or personal situation, so Excel takes care to get them right. Excel understands dates no matter how you type them, so feel free to type them as needed. You can always change the formatting later.

Enter a Date

1. Click the cell in which you want to enter a date.
2. Type the month, day, and year, with each number separated by a slash (/) or a hyphen (-).
3. Press Enter.

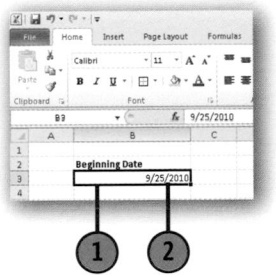

Enter a Time

1. Click the cell in which you want to enter a time.
2. Type the hour, a colon (:), and the minutes. Press the Spacebar, and type a or p for A.M. or P.M.
3. Press Enter.

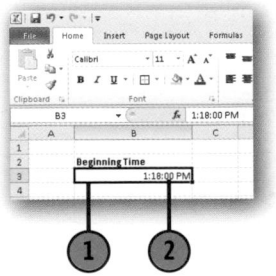

Enter a Date and Time

1. Click the cell in which you want to enter a date and time.
2. Type a date, press the Spacebar, and then type a time.
3. Press Enter.

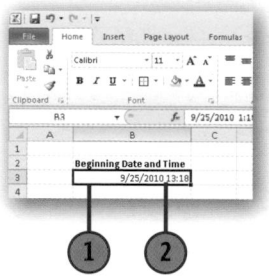

Enter the Current Date and Time

1. Click the cell in which you want to enter the current date and time.
2. Type =NOW().
3. Press Enter.

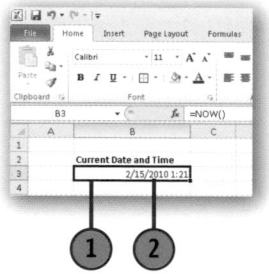

Caution

Different countries have different customs for writing dates. For example, 07/04/10 could mean July 4, 2010, or April 7, 2010, depending on where you live.

See Also

For more information about formatting cells with dates, see "Formatting Cells Containing Dates" on page 110.

Entering Data Using Fills

Entering a long series of data such as the days in the month, weekdays, or a series of numbers with a definite progression is tedious. As you type or paste the data, it's easy to forget which months have 31 days or on which day of the week the first of a month falls. Excel makes entering such series simple: Using AutoFill, you can type a label or value in one cell and assign it to many other cells; type labels or values in two or more cells and have Excel extend the series based on the relationship of the cell entries; or even extend dates by a day, a month, or a year.

Fill Data Using AutoFill

1. Type the label or value you want to appear in multiple cells.
2. Drag the Fill handle down or across the cells you want to fill.

Use AutoFill to Enter a Series of Values

1. Type the first label or value for your list.
2. Type the second label or value for your list.
3. Select the two cells.
4. Drag the Fill handle to the cell containing the last label or value in the series.

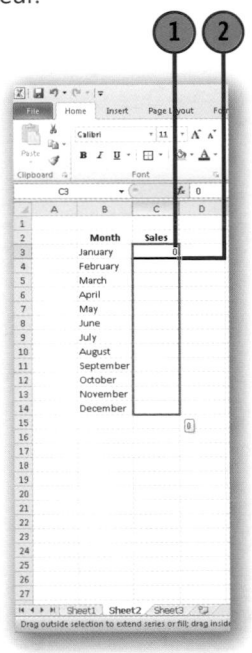

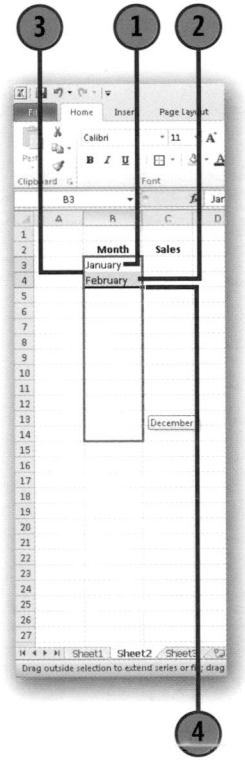

Tip

If you hold down the Ctrl key as you drag the Fill handle, Excel changes how it fills in your series. For example, if dragging the Fill handle would normally copy a single value into the cells you drag over, dragging while holding down the Ctrl key causes the value to increment (for example, dragging the Fill handle of a cell that contains the value "1" increments the value to 2, then 3, and so on).

Try This!

Type 1/1/2010 in cell A1, and then drag the Fill handle across the cells you want to fill. Excel fills your cells by increasing the day for every entry. Now click the AutoFill Options button that appears, and click Fill Years.

Entering Data with Other Shortcuts

Excel gives you lots of ways to enter data quickly. The less time you spend typing data, the more time you have to analyze and make decisions based on what the data tells you. One way Excel offers to help you enter data is to recognize whether the first few characters of the text you're typing matches text from another cell in the same column; if the text matches, Excel offers to complete the rest of that text. If it's the text you want, you can accept it and move on. If not, just keep typing.

A similar way Excel simplifies data entry is by letting you pick the value for the active cell from a list of existing values in a column. This technique is not that important for a small worksheet, but when you're working with page after page of data, seeing a sorted list of possible values is a real help.

Enter Data with AutoComplete

1. Type the beginning of an entry.
2. Press Tab to accept the AutoComplete value.

Pick Data from a List

1. Right-click a cell in a column with existing values, and then click Pick From Drop-Down List from the short-cut menu.
2. Click the item in the list you want to enter.

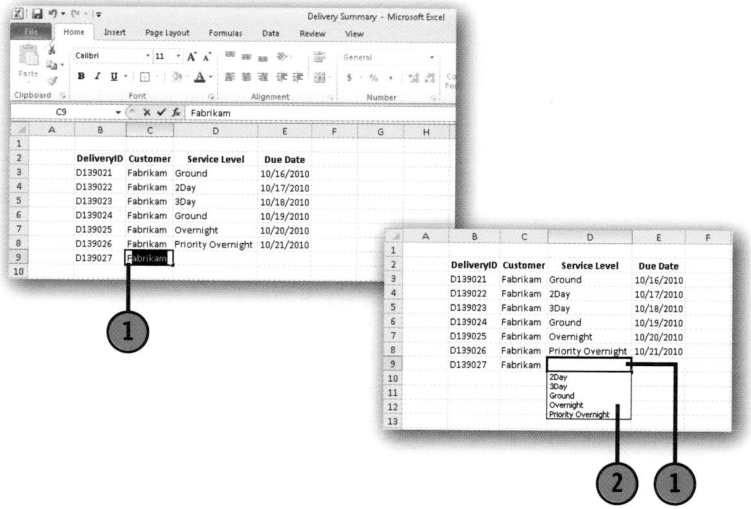

Caution

AutoComplete works only if the text or data you are entering is similar to text already in the same column.

Tip

You can also display the Pick From Drop-Down List items by selecting the cell in which you want to enter the value and pressing Alt+Down arrow.

Creating an Excel Table

One popular way to maintain data in Excel is by creating a data list. A list describes one type of object, such as orders, sales, or contact information. Structurally, a list consists of a header row, which contains labels describing the data in each column, and data rows, which contain data about a particular instance of the list's subject. For example, if you use a list to store your customer's contact information, you could have a separate column for the customer's first name, last name, street address, city, state, postal code, and telephone number. Each row in a list would contain a particular customer's information.

In Excel 2010, you can store your data lists in an Excel table. An Excel table is an object that you can refer to in your formulas and use to summarize your data.

Create an Excel Table

1. Type your table headers in a single row.
2. Type your first data row directly below the header row.
3. Click any cell in the range in which you want to create a table.
4. On the Home tab, click Format As Table.
5. Click the table style you want to use.
6. Verify that Excel identified the data range correctly.
7. If your table has headers, select the My Table Has Headers check box.
8. Click OK.

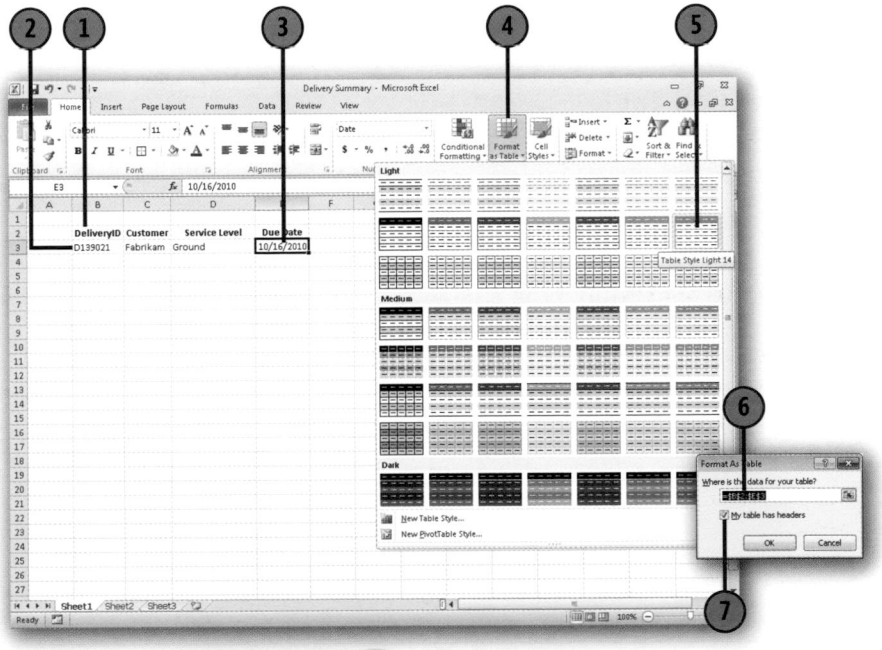

Tip

You can display the Create Table dialog box by clicking any cell in an existing cell range and pressing Ctrl+L. If you click OK, Excel 2010 creates an Excel table using the default Excel table style.

Add Data to an Excel Table

Follow either of these steps:

- Click the cell at the bottom-right corner of the Excel table, and press Tab to create a new table row.
- Type data in the cell below the bottom-left corner of the Excel table, and press Tab. Excel makes the new row part of the Excel table.

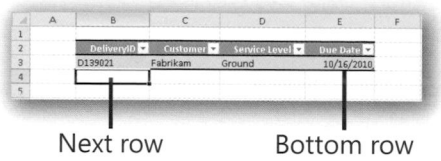

Rename an Excel Table

1. Click any cell in the Excel table.
2. On the ribbon, under Table Tools, click the Design tab.
3. In the Properties group, type a new name for your Excel table, and press Enter.

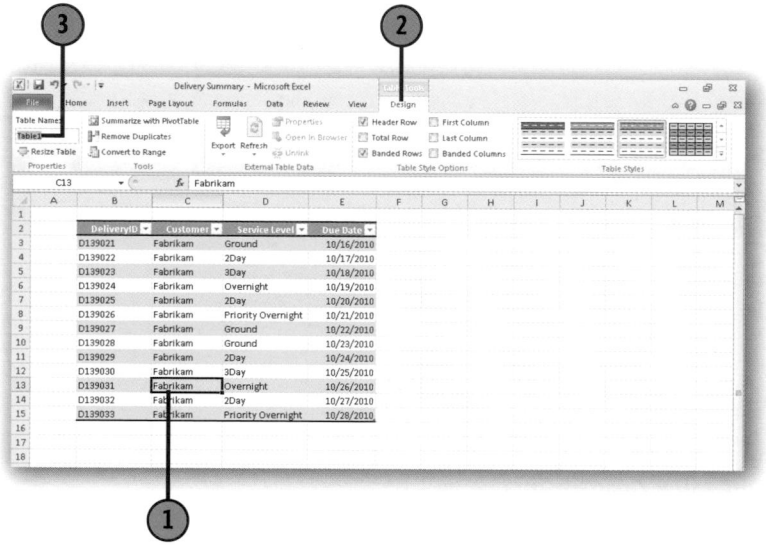

Try This!

Display an Excel table that takes up more than one screen vertically and scroll down the workbook page. When the table's header row reaches the top of the screen, it freezes in place, but the data rows continue scrolling. Now you don't have to remember which column is which; the labels are right there!

Resize an Excel Table

- Drag the resize handle at the bottom-right corner of the Excel table to add or remove table rows or columns.

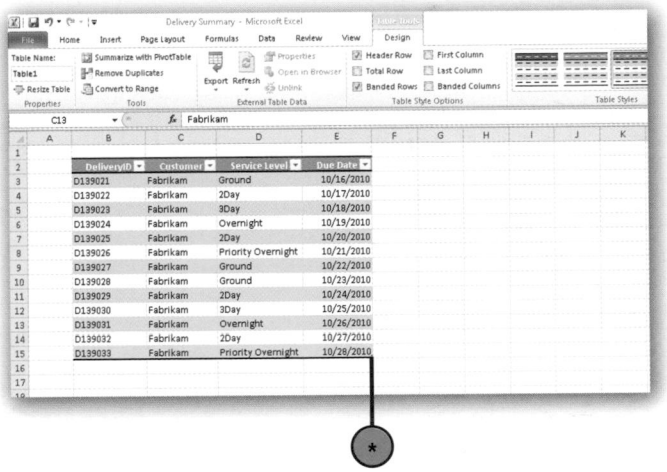

Select an Excel Table Column

- Click the header of the column you want to select.

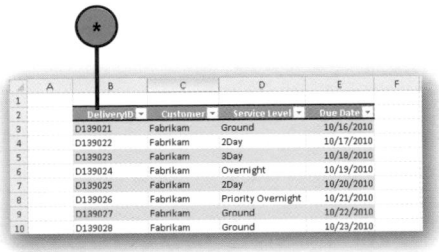

Caution

Be sure not to click the filter arrow at the right edge of an Excel table's column header; doing so displays the column's filter options, which, although useful, doesn't enable you to select the entire column.

Editing Cell Contents

You're not stuck with the first data you enter in a cell. In fact, you can change the value completely, delete it, or update it to reflect a supplier's new business name or a customer's new address. You also are not stuck with only one way to edit the data; you can edit the data either in the formula bar or directly in the cell.

Edit Cell Contents in the Formula Bar

1. Click the cell you want to edit.
2. Select the text you want to edit in the formula bar.
3. Type the new text, and press Enter.

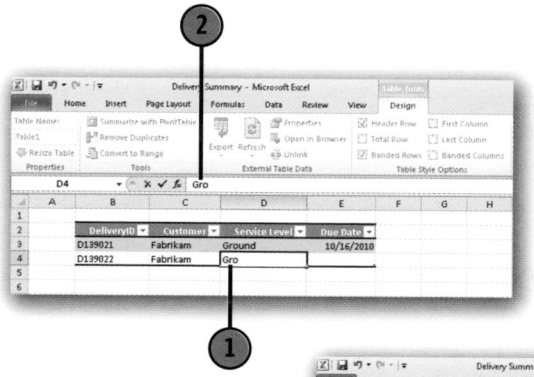

Edit Cell Contents Directly in the Cell

1. Double-click the cell you want to edit.
2. Select the text you want to edit.
3. Type the new text, and press Enter.

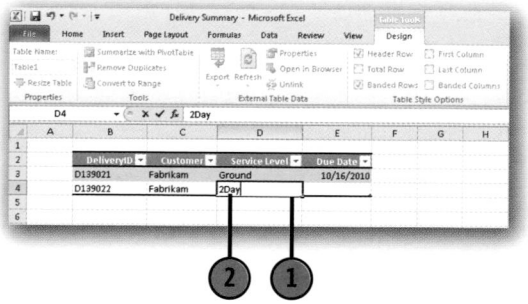

Tip

If you're editing a cell and decide you don't want to keep your edits, press the Esc key to return the cell to its previous state.

Tip

If you double-click a cell but aren't able to edit its contents, another user might have turned off this option. To turn on in-cell editing, click the File tab, and click Options. In the Excel Options dialog box, click Advanced to display the Advanced page of the dialog box. In the Editing Options group, select the Allow Editing Directly In Cells check box, and click OK.

Inserting a Symbol in a Cell

Not every bit of information can be communicated effectively using text. If your worksheet is meant for public consumption and you mention another company's products, you might want to include a trademark (™) or another symbol to recognize that company's intellectual property. Excel—and the other Office programs—have lots of symbols you can use. If you use a symbol in the course of your everyday business, you can probably find it in Excel.

Add a Symbol to a Cell

1. Click the Insert tab.
2. Click Symbol.
3. Click the Font down arrow.
4. Select the font from which you want to pick the symbol.
5. Click the symbol you want to insert.
6. Click Insert.
7. Click Close.

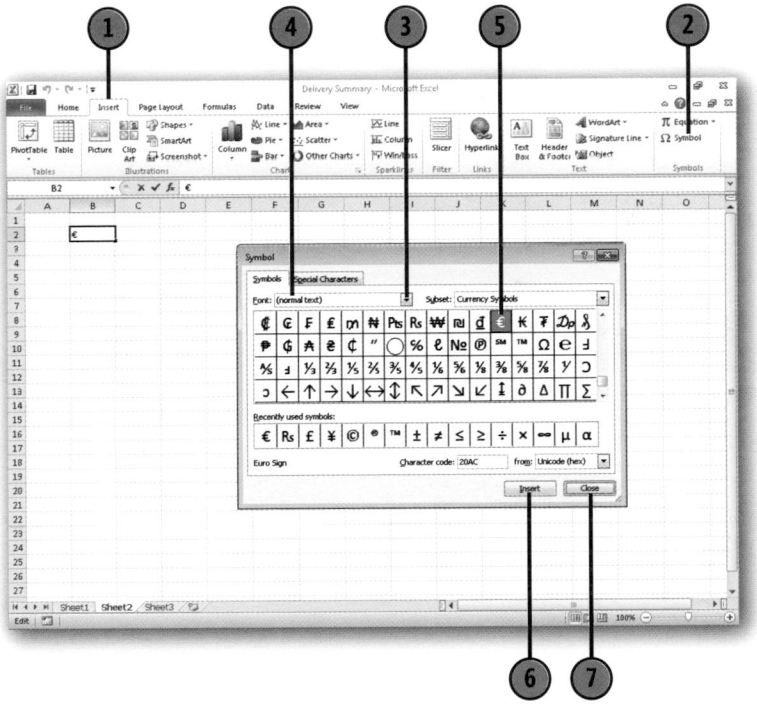

Tip

If you want to insert more than one symbol consecutively (in the same cell), click the first symbol, click the Insert button, click the next symbol, click the Insert button again, and so on. When you're done inserting symbols, click the Close button.

Creating Hyperlinks

One of the hallmarks of the World Wide Web is that documents published on the Web can have references, or hyperlinks, to points in the same document or to other Web documents. One great way to take advantage of this feature is to create a workbook in which you track sales by product and have a cell at the end of each product's row with a hyperlink to in-depth product information. That information could be on another worksheet in the same workbook, in another file on your computer, in a file on another computer, or on a Web page. Another type of hyperlink is the mailto hyperlink, which, when clicked, lets you send an e-mail message to the address referred to in the link.

Add a Hyperlink to a Place in the Same File

1. Click the cell where you want to place a hyperlink.
2. Click the Insert tab.
3. Click Hyperlink.
4. Click Place In This Document.
5. Click the sheet to which you want to link.
6. Type the cell reference of the cell to which you want to link.
7. Type a short phrase to describe the hyperlink's target.
8. Click OK.

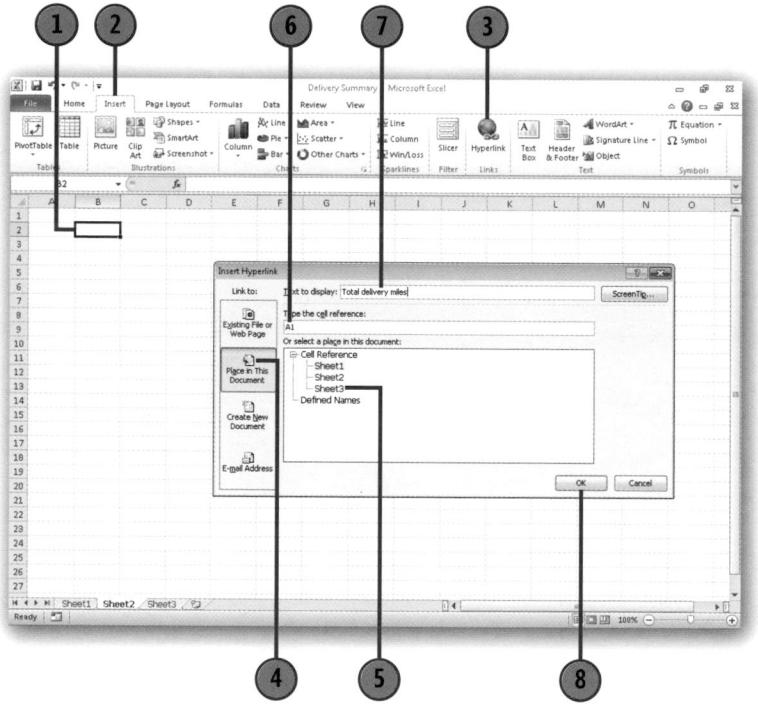

Tip

Excel 2010 also enables you to create links to any named ranges or Excel tables in your workbook.

Add a Hyperlink to Another File

1. Click the cell in which you want to place a hyperlink.
2. Click the Insert tab.
3. Click Hyperlink.
4. Click Existing File Or Web Page.
5. Click Current Folder.
6. Click the file to which you want to link.
7. Type a short phrase to describe the hyperlink's target.
8. Click OK.

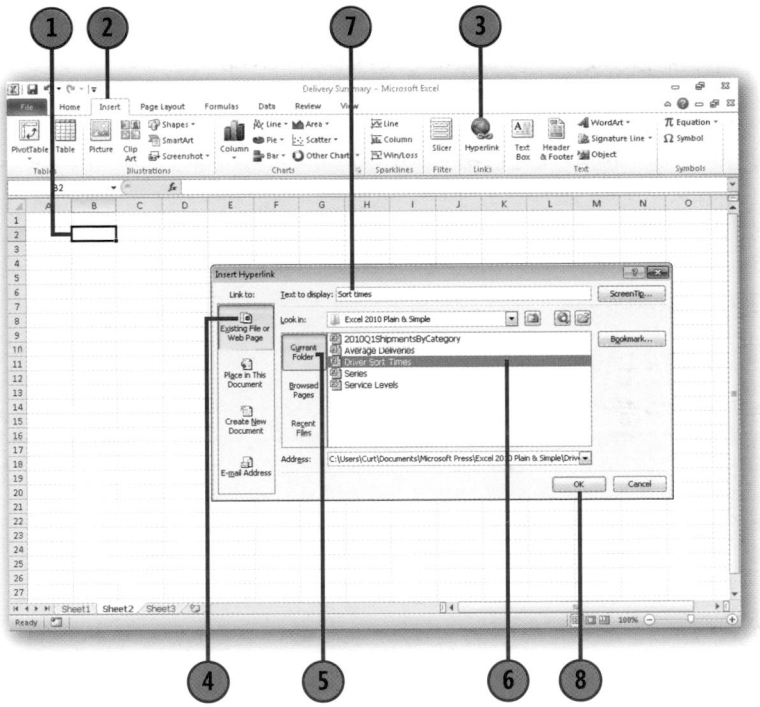

Tip

You can view recently used files by clicking Recent Files in the Look In pane.

Add a Hyperlink to a Web Page

1. Click the cell in which you want to place a hyperlink.
2. Click the Insert tab.
3. Click Hyperlink.
4. Click Existing File Or Web Page.
5. Click Browsed Pages.
6. Click the Web page to which you want to link.
7. Type a short phrase to describe the hyperlink's target.
8. Click OK.

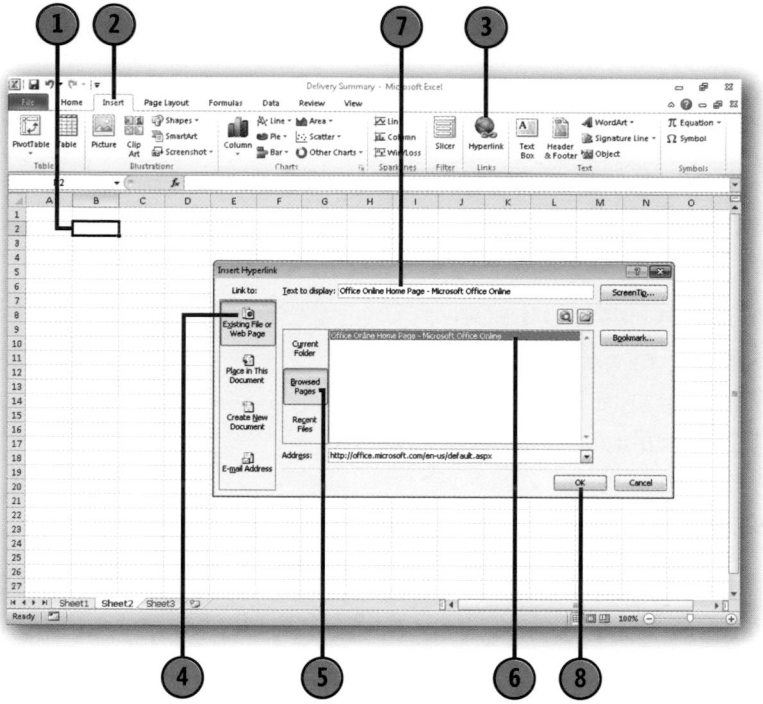

Caution

When you click Browsed Pages, the Insert Hyperlink dialog box displays all the Web pages you visited recently.

Add a Mailto Hyperlink

1. Click the cell in which you want to place a hyperlink.
2. Click the Insert tab.
3. Click Hyperlink.
4. Click E-Mail Address.
5. Type the e-mail address to which you want to link.
6. Type text describing the hyperlink.
7. Type a default subject for the e-mail message.
8. Click OK.

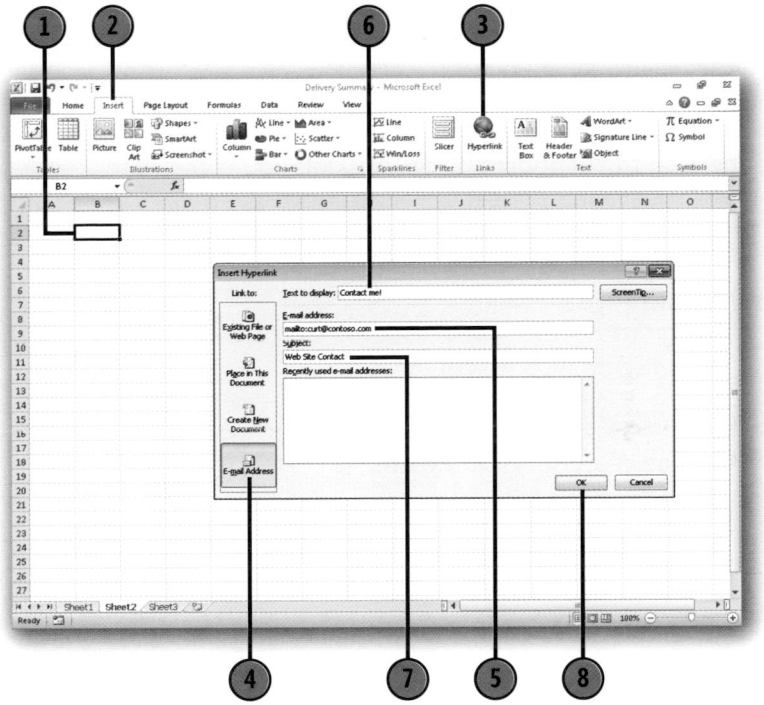

Tip

You can type just the target e-mail address in the E-Mail Address field. Excel adds the mailto: prefix for you.

Cutting, Copying, and Pasting Cell Values

After you enter values in one or more cells, you can copy the values and paste them into another cell, remove the values from the cells and paste them elsewhere, or just cut the values and leave them on the Clipboard. Excel 2010 lets you control how the pasted values appear in your worksheet. When you click the Paste button's down arrow, you can hover your mouse pointer over any of the icons to display a live preview of how the pasted data will appear if you select that paste formatting option. Pointing to another icon displays the result of selecting that paste option, and clicking an icon pastes your copied items using the icon's paste options.

Cut a Cell Value

1. Select the cells you want to cut.
2. Click the Home tab.
3. In the Clipboard group, click the Cut button.

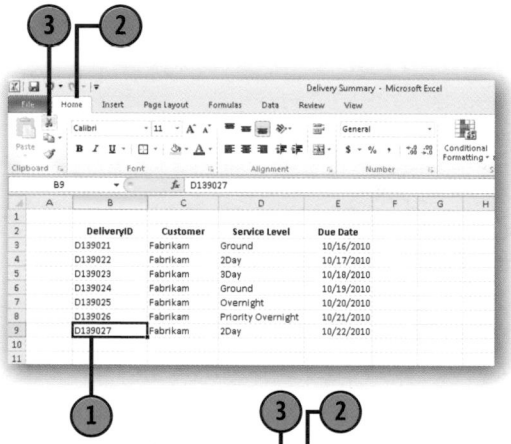

Copy a Cell Value

1. Select the cells you want to copy.
2. Click the Home tab.
3. In the Clipboard group, click the Copy button.

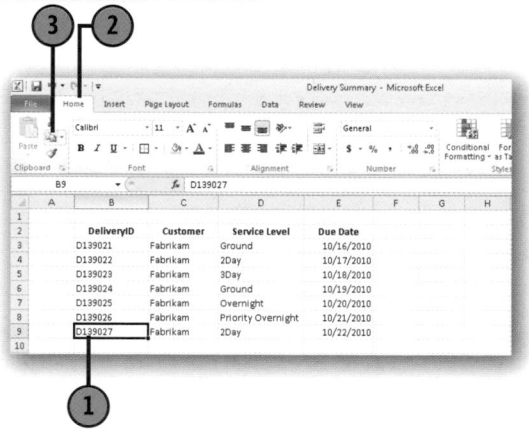

Pasting Values with More Control

When you cut or copy cells, you write a copy of the cells' contents and formatting to the Clipboard. When you paste the cells back into a worksheet, Excel pastes the values, formulas, and formatting associated with the cells. You're not limited to such simple pasting behavior, however; you can choose to paste just the cell's formula, just a formula's result, paste everything except the cells' borders, or even paste an image of the item that you can click to display the item you copied.

The following table lists the advanced paste options you can use.

Option	Action
Paste	Performs the standard paste operation.
Formulas	Pastes the formulas from the cells you copied.
Formulas & Number Formatting	Pastes the formulas and number formatting from the cells you copied.
Keep Source Formatting	Pastes the contents of the cells you copied and retains the copied cells' formatting.
Keep Source Column Widths	Pastes the contents of the cells you copied and makes the columns into which you paste the copied data the same width as the source columns.
Values	If the copied cell contains a formula, pastes the result of the formula into the target cell.
Values & Number Formatting	If the copied cell contains a formula, pastes the result of the formula and the cell's number formatting into the target cell.
Values & Source Formatting	If the copied cell contains a formula, pastes the result of the formula and the cell's formatting into the target cell.
Formatting	Pastes the copied cell's formatting into the target cell.
No Borders	Pastes the contents of the copied cells without including any borders drawn around the cells.
Transpose	Exchanges the rows and columns of the copied data.
Paste Link	Creates a link to the copied item; does not create a new copy of the item.
Paste Special	Displays the Paste Special dialog box.
Paste As Hyperlink	Pastes a text hyperlink to the copied item.
Linked Picture	Pastes an image that, when clicked, activates a hyperlink to the copied item.
Picture	Pastes an image of the copied item's appearance (for example, pasting a picture of a chart doesn't create a new chart).
Copy As Picture	Copies an image of the selected item's appearance to the Clipboard.

Paste Values with More Control

1. Cut or copy a value, and then click the cell into which you want to paste your values.
2. Click the Home tab.
3. In the Clipboard group, click the Paste button's down arrow.
4. Hover the mouse pointer over an option in the palette to generate a live preview.
5. Select the action you want to take.

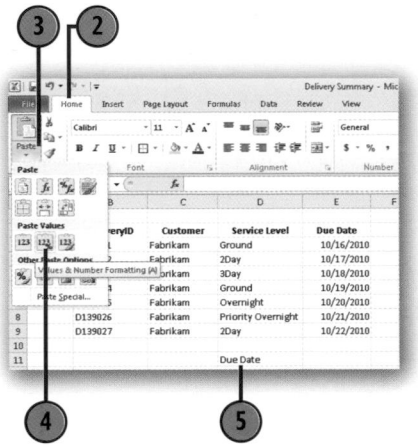

Tip

After you paste data you've cut or copied from a cell, Excel displays an option button asking how you want to format the data you're pasting. The options that appear depend on the formatting of the data you copied or cut.

Clearing Cell Contents

If you're lucky, you won't have to replace the data and formatting you've entered in a workbook; however, there might be times when you want to clear the data, formatting, or contents of a group of cells. Clearing is like cutting, but clearing differs because you have the option to leave the formatting in the cell from which you remove the data. When you cut a cell's contents, Excel removes the cell's contents and formatting.

Clear a Cell

1. Select the cell you want to clear.
2. Click the Home tab.
3. In the Editing group, click the Clear button.
4. Select the type of clearing you want.

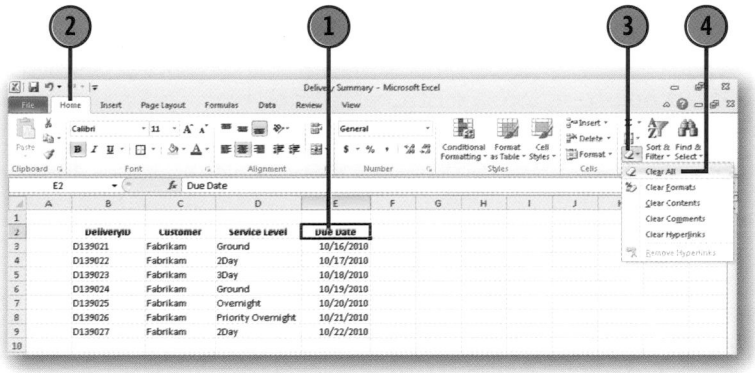

Tip

If all you want to do is clear the cell contents, click the cell you want to clear, and then press Delete.

Using the Office Clipboard

When you work in Excel, you can take advantage of the flexibility that comes with its place in the Office suite by using the Office Clipboard. The Office Clipboard keeps track of the last 24 items you've cut or copied from any Office document. You can open the Office Clipboard and then paste any of its contents into your workbook. If an item that you know you won't use again resides on the Office Clipboard, you can always remove it.

Display the Contents of the Office Clipboard

1. Click the Home tab.
2. Click the Clipboard dialog box launcher.

Paste an Item from the Office Clipboard

1. Click the cell into which you want to paste a Clipboard item.
2. Click the Clipboard item you want to paste.

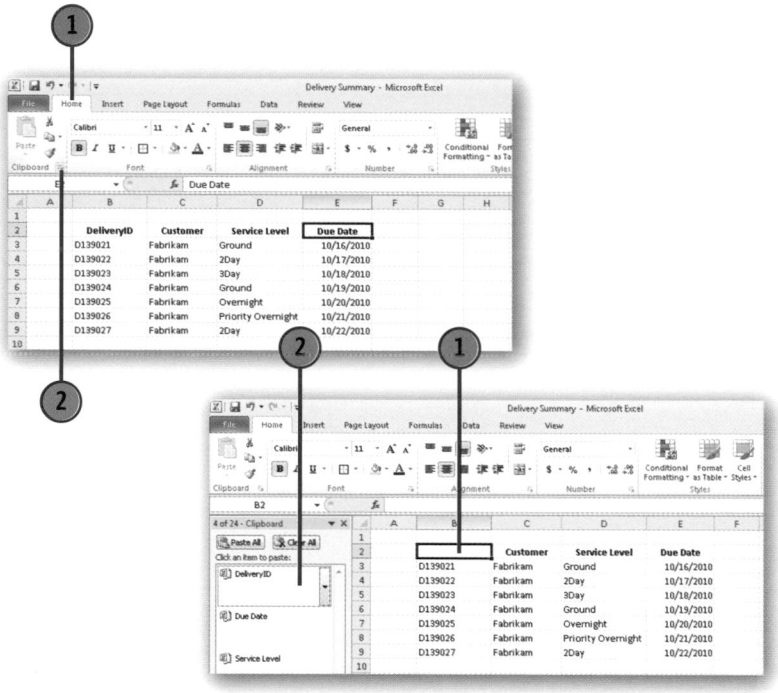

Tip

You can paste every item from the Clipboard into your application by clicking Paste All.

Clear an Item from the Office Clipboard

1. Point to the Clipboard item you want to delete.
2. Click the down arrow that appears next to the item.
3. Click Delete.

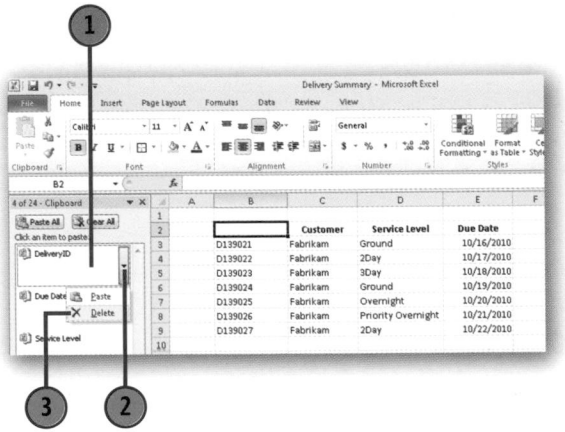

Tip

You can remove all entries from the Office Clipboard by clicking Clear All.

Undoing or Redoing an Action

One of the strengths of Excel is how easily it lets you change the formatting, layout, and structure of your workbooks. The problem, of course, is that you might not have made the exact change you wanted. If that's the case, and you haven't closed the workbook since you made the change you want to get rid of, you can easily undo your changes by clicking the Undo button on the Quick Access Toolbar. Excel keeps a record of your changes, which you can see by clicking the down arrow at the right edge of the Undo button. When you reverse a change by clicking the Undo button, Excel displays the Redo button. Clicking the Redo button, as you might expect, reapplies the last change you undid. If you have made a change but haven't clicked the Undo button, Excel displays the Repeat button, which you can click to apply the last change to a new selection.

Undo or Redo an Action

Follow either of these steps:

- Click the Undo button.
- Click the Redo button.

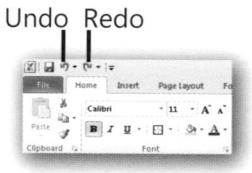

Finding and Replacing Text

After you enter data into a workbook, you might need to search the document for a particular word or, if one of your suppliers changes the name of a product, replace some or all instances of a word or phrase. You can do just that using Find and Replace in Excel.

Find a Word or Value

1. Click the Home tab.
2. In the Editing group, click Find & Select.
3. Click Find.
4. Type the text you want to find.
5. Click Find Next.
6. Click Close.

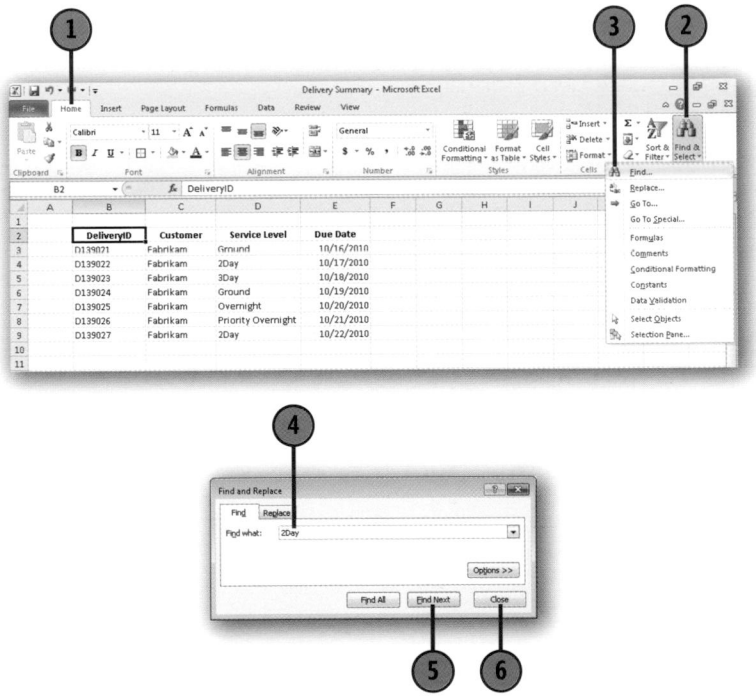

Replace a Word or Value

1. Click the Home tab.
2. In the Editing group, click Find & Select.
3. Click Replace.
4. Type the text you want to replace.
5. Type the text you want to take the place of the existing text.
6. Click Find Next, and follow any of these steps:
   - Click Replace to replace the text.
   - Click Find Next to skip this instance of the text and move to the next time it occurs.
   - Click Replace All to replace every instance of the text.
7. Click Close.

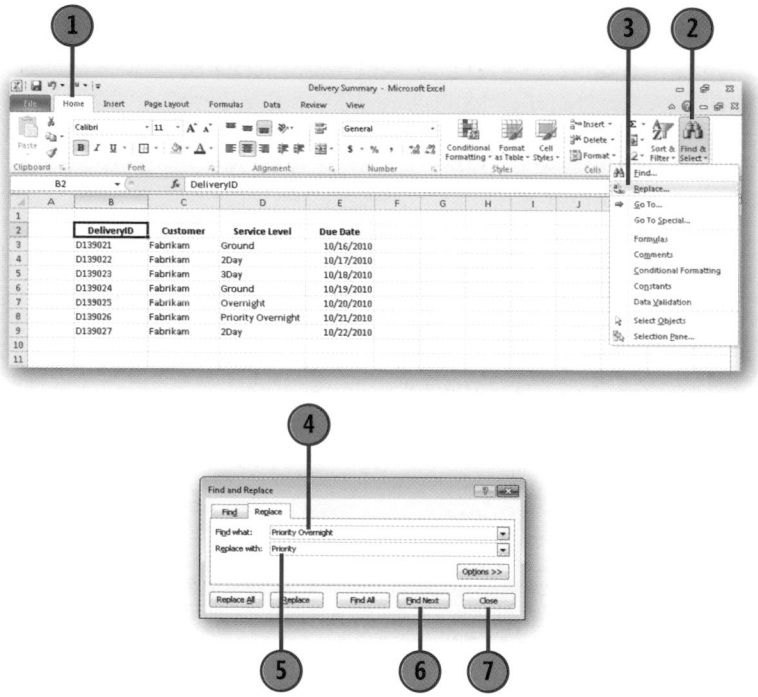

Caution

Clicking Replace All is a quick way to change every occurrence of one value to another value, but it can also have unintended consequences. For example, changing "ear" to "bear" would change "hearing" to "hbearing." It's much safer to use Find Next and verify each change.

Checking the Spelling of Your Worksheet

After you create a workbook and fill it with data, labels, and explanatory text, you should always use the Excel spelling checker to check your text for misspellings. If Excel finds a word it doesn't recognize, the spelling checker asks you whether it's correct and might suggest alternatives. You can have Excel ignore a word once or for the entire document, choose one of the program's suggestions, or even add new words to the dictionary. Products are often given unique names, so adding them to the dictionary Excel uses to check all documents will save you a lot of time.

Check Spelling

1. Click the Review tab.
2. In the Proofing group, click Spelling. If you are asked whether you want to save your work, do so.
3. Follow any of these steps:
   - Click Ignore Once to ignore the current misspelling.
   - Click Ignore All to ignore all instances of the misspelled word.
   - Click Add To Dictionary to add the current word to the dictionary.
   - Click AutoCorrect to create an AutoCorrect entry that replaces the misspelled word with the word highlighted in the Suggestions list.
   - Click the correct spelling, and then click Change to replace the current misspelling with the correct word.
   - Click the correct spelling, and then click Change All to replace all instances of the current misspelling with the correct word.
   - Click Cancel to stop checking spelling.
4. Click OK to clear the dialog box that appears after the spelling check is complete.

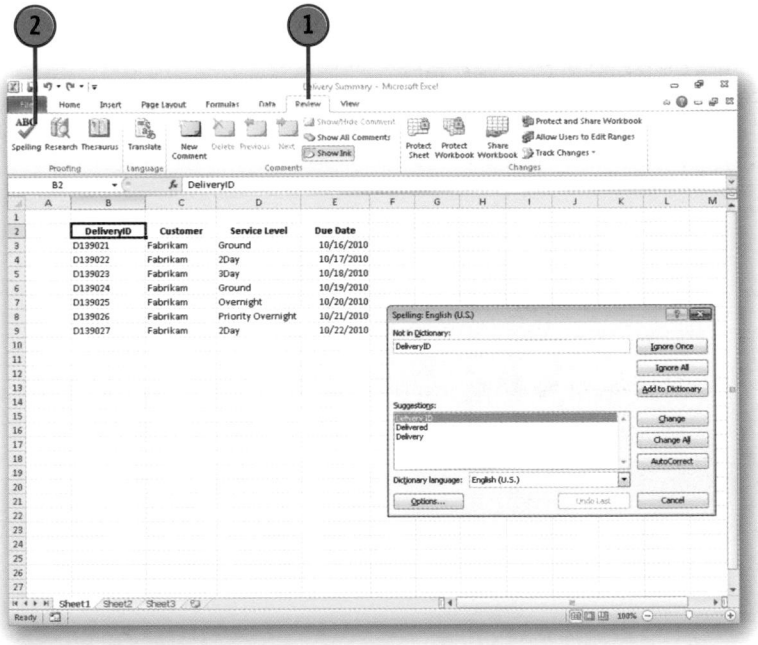

Tip

If you don't start checking spelling with cell A1 selected, Excel checks spelling to the end of the worksheet and then displays a dialog box asking if you want to continue checking from the beginning of the worksheet. Click Yes to continue.

5 Managing and Viewing Worksheets

In this section:

- Viewing and Selecting Worksheets
- Renaming Worksheets
- Moving and Copying Worksheets within a Workbook or between Workbooks
- Inserting and Deleting Worksheets
- Inserting and Deleting Columns, Rows, and Cells
- Hiding and Unhiding Columns and Rows
- Freezing Worksheet Rows and Columns
- Splitting a Worksheet into Independent Areas
- Saving Custom Worksheet Views

After you build your workbook, you can reorganize it as needed. If you use data in a specific worksheet often, you can move the worksheet to the front of the workbook. Similarly, if you often switch between two worksheets, you can put their sheet tabs next to each other so that you don't have to spend as much time moving from one worksheet to the other. Another way you can save time is to enter the same data or apply the same formatting to multiple cells in several worksheets at the same time.

Finally, you can change how Microsoft Excel 2010 displays your data in a workbook. If you have a series of headings in the first row of a worksheet, they don't have to disappear when you scroll down. Instead, you can have Excel freeze the rows at the top of the screen and scroll down as far as you want without losing your guides at the top.

Viewing and Selecting Worksheets

Every Excel workbook should hold data on a given subject, such as products you carry, your customers, or your sales. By the same token, every page, or worksheet, in a workbook should store part of the workbook's data. One way to divide your data is by time. For example, if you track your sales by the hour, you could easily fit a month's worth of data in a worksheet; at most you would need 31 rows to cover every day and, if your store were open around the clock, 24 columns to take care of the hours. You can view individual worksheets quickly, and it's simple to work with more than one worksheet at a time.

Select Multiple Worksheets

1. Click the sheet tab of the first worksheet you want to select.
2. Hold down the Ctrl key, and click the sheet tabs of additional worksheets you want to select.

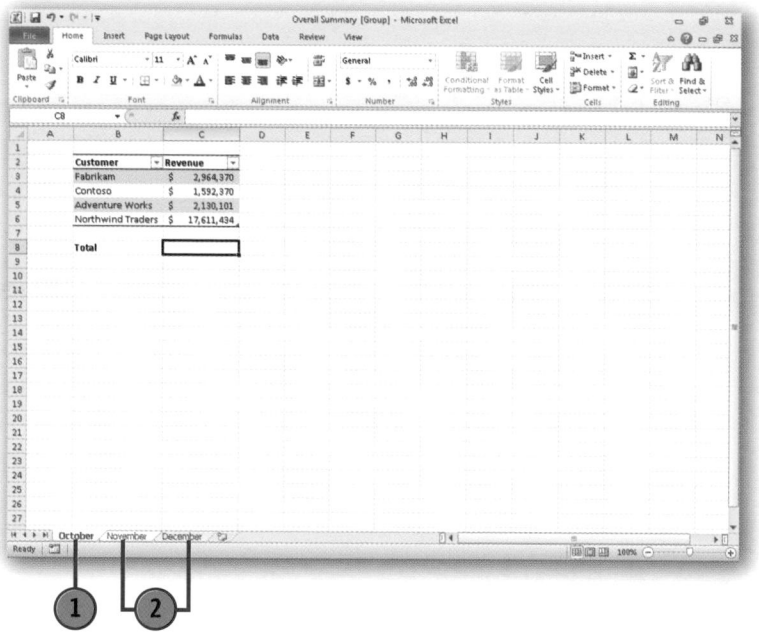

Tip

To select multiple adjacent worksheets, click the first worksheet, hold down the Shift key, and then click the last sheet tab you want to select.

See Also

For information about adding worksheets to a workbook, see "Inserting and Deleting Worksheets" on page 67.

Tip

You can select all worksheets in a workbook by right-clicking any sheet tab and choosing Select All Sheets from the shortcut menu.

Renaming Worksheets

When you create a workbook, Excel names your worksheets Sheet1, Sheet2, and Sheet3. Those names are fine when you first create a workbook, but after you add data to several worksheets, naming the sheet tabs helps you and your colleagues find the data you're looking for. As always, if you think of a better name for your worksheets, or even want to change the name of a worksheet temporarily to make it stand out, you can rename a worksheet any time you want.

Change the Name of a Worksheet

1. Double-click the sheet tab of the worksheet you want to rename.
2. Type the new name of the worksheet, and press Enter.

Moving Worksheets

Business needs change—the data that was so important yesterday might be of only passing significance today. In fact, if a new customer sends a big order your way, you might spend most of your time adding to and reading from a worksheet you haven't looked at more than twice in the previous month. If that worksheet is at the back of your workbook, you can move it to the front to make it easier to find in the workbook. Or, if you keep every other worksheet relating to that customer in a separate workbook, you can move the worksheet from its current spot to its rightful place in the other workbook.

Move Worksheets Within the Workbook

1. Drag the sheet tab of the worksheet you want to move.

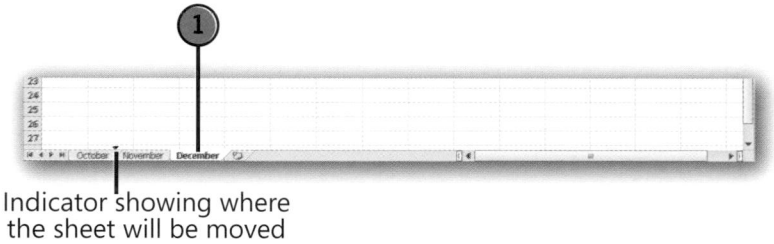

Move Worksheets to Another Workbook

1. Open the workbook that will receive the worksheets.
2. Switch to the workbook that contains the worksheets you want to move, hold down the Ctrl key, and click the sheet tabs of the worksheets you want to move.
3. Right-click the selection.
4. Choose Move Or Copy from the shortcut menu.
5. Click the To Book down arrow.
6. Click the workbook to which you want to move the worksheets.
7. Click OK.

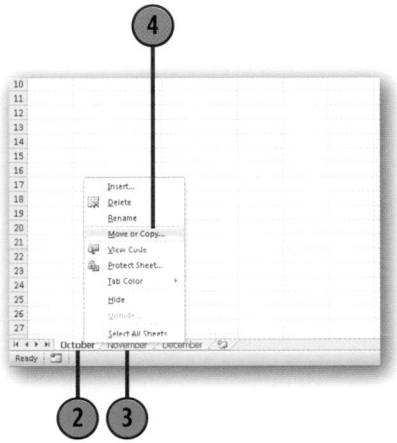

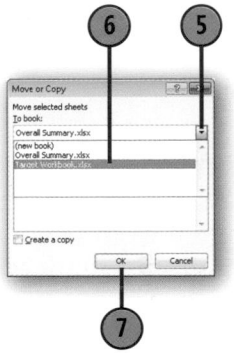

Tip

If you want to position a worksheet last in a workbook, right-click the worksheet you want to move, choose Move Or Copy from the shortcut menu, click Move To End, and click OK.

Tip

If the destination workbook has a different Office theme applied to it, selecting the Match Destination Theme check box causes the copied worksheet to take on the target workbook's formatting.

Copying Worksheets

After you finish adding data to a worksheet—such as at the end of a calendar month, when you create a new worksheet to store data for the next month—you might want to include the entire worksheet as part of a monthly overview presentation to your general manager. Rather than keep all the worksheets in their original workbooks and flip from document to document when you create your presentation, you can copy the worksheet from the current workbook (and any other worksheets with data you want to include) to a central document. Going from worksheet to worksheet is much easier than going from workbook to workbook!

Copy Worksheets Within the Workbook

1. Hold down the Ctrl key, and drag the worksheet you want to copy to the new location.

Copy Worksheets to Another Workbook

1. Open the workbook that will receive the new worksheets.
2. Switch to the workbook that contains the worksheets you want to copy, hold down the Ctrl key, and click the sheet tabs of the worksheets you want to copy.
3. Right-click the selection.
4. Choose Move Or Copy from the shortcut menu.
5. Select the Create A Copy check box.
6. Click the To Book down arrow.
7. Click the workbook to which you want to copy the worksheet(s).
8. Click OK.

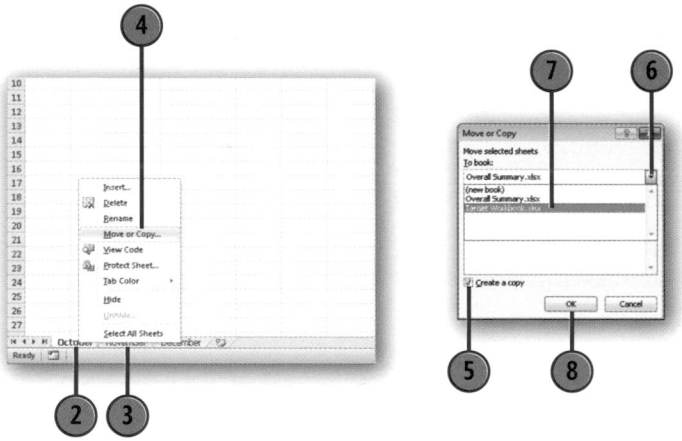

Caution

If you don't hold down the Ctrl key while you drag the sheet tab of the worksheet you want to copy, you just move the worksheet to a new location in the workbook.

Tip

Select the New Book option from the To Book list to copy the selected worksheet or worksheets to a new workbook.

Inserting and Deleting Worksheets

If you haven't changed Excel from the way it was installed, any workbooks you create will contain three worksheets. Three worksheets are plenty of room if you're working at home and are perhaps more than you need for small projects, but you'll run out of space quickly if you're tracking products or monthly sales. Adding or deleting a worksheet takes just a moment, but if you want to delete a worksheet, be sure you're getting rid of the right one!

Insert a Blank Worksheet

1. Right-click the sheet tab of the worksheet that follows the location where you want to insert a worksheet.
2. Choose Insert from the shortcut menu.
3. Double-click Worksheet.

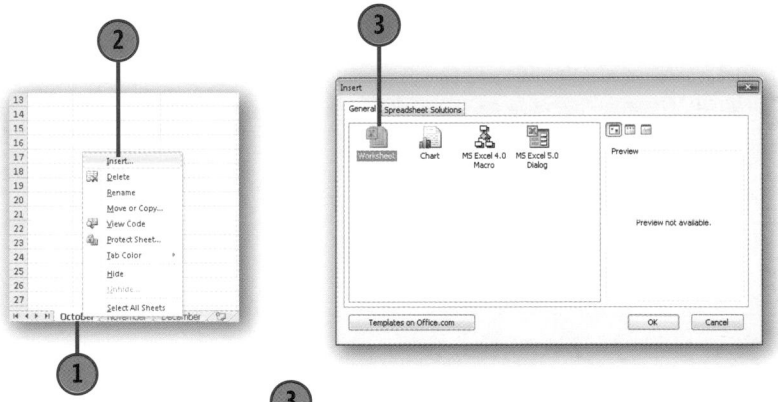

Delete One or More Worksheets

1. Hold down the Ctrl key, and click the sheet tabs of the worksheets you want to delete.
2. Right-click the selection.
3. Choose Delete from the shortcut menu.
4. Click Delete to confirm that you want to delete the worksheets.

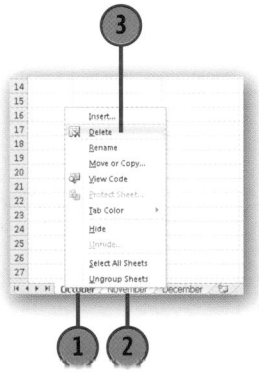

Tip

If you want to insert a worksheet at the end of the workbook, click the Insert Worksheet button at the right edge of the tab bar.

Caution

If you have data in the worksheet that you want to delete, deleting the worksheet erases all the data in that worksheet. This operation is not reversible.

Hiding or Showing a Worksheet

If you build a workbook that contains a lot of worksheets, you might find it easier to navigate the workbook if you can't see the sheet tabs of the worksheets you're not using. You can hide the sheet tabs of worksheets so that they don't appear in the Excel window, reducing clutter and letting you find the worksheets you are using with no trouble.

Hide or Unhide a Worksheet

1. Hold down the Ctrl key, and click the sheet tabs of the worksheets you want to hide.
2. Right-click any selected worksheet tab, and then choose Hide.

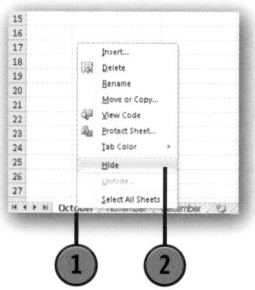

Unhide a Hidden Worksheet

1. Right-click any worksheet tab.
2. Click Unhide.
3. Click the worksheet you want to unhide.
4. Click OK.

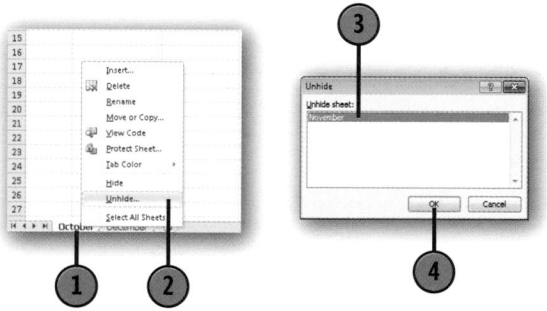

Tip

After you unhide a worksheet, Excel displays that worksheet immediately.

Changing Worksheet Tab Colors

A great way to make any worksheet element stand out is to change it to a color that contrasts with the other colors used in the worksheet. In Excel, you can change the color of sheet tabs. For example, you can change the color of a sheet tab in a workbook in which you track sales for a year with a worksheet for each month. Rather than move the current worksheet to the front of the list, which would put the worksheets out of order, you can change the color of the sheet tab to make it stand out. When the month ends, you can remove the color from that sheet tab and apply it to the new month's sheet tab.

Color a Sheet Tab

1. Hold down the Ctrl key, and click the sheet tabs you want to color.
2. Right-click the selection, and point to Tab Color on the shortcut menu.
3. Select the color you want.

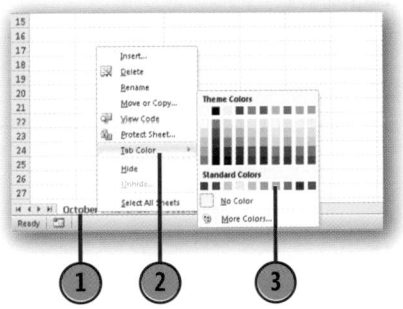

Tip

If you don't see the tab color you want in the Tab Color palette, click More Colors to display the Colors dialog box.

Inserting, Moving, and Deleting Cells

There's very little that's more frustrating than creating a large worksheet and discovering that you forgot to enter data in a few cells. If you're new to Excel, you might be tempted to cut the existing cells and paste them a few cells below their current location to make room for the new data. But that's too much like work; there's an easier way to insert a few cells to give you the room you need. Similarly, it's not that difficult to move a group of cells to a new location in your worksheet or to delete a group of cells that contains data you entered by accident. After you insert or delete cells, you can choose how to move existing cells to make room for the new cells or to fill in the space left by the deleted cells.

Insert Cells in a Worksheet

1. Select the cells in the spot where you want to insert new cells.
2. Click the Home tab.
3. In the Cells group, click the Insert button's down arrow.
4. Click Insert Cells.
5. Select the option button representing how you want to move the existing cells to make room for the inserted cells.
6. Click OK.

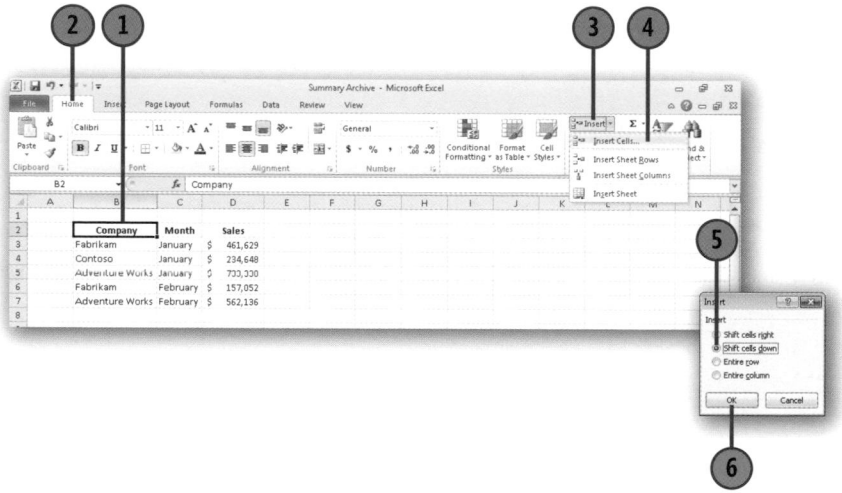

Move Cells in a Worksheet

1. Select the cells you want to move.
2. Move the mouse pointer over the outline of the selected cells.
3. Drag the cells to the new location.

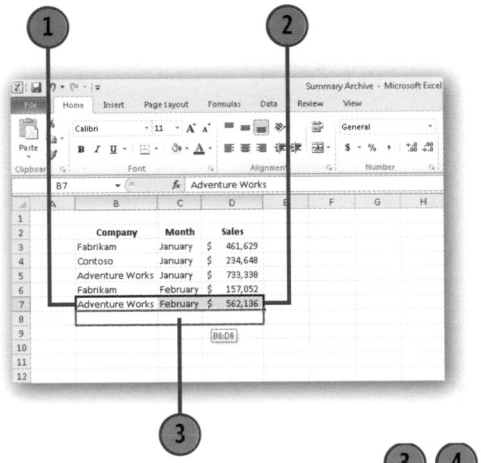

Delete Cells in a Worksheet

1. Select the cells you want to delete.
2. Click the Home tab.
3. In the Cells group, click the Delete button's down arrow.
4. Click Delete Cells.
5. Select the option button representing how you want the remaining cells to fill in the deleted space.
6. Click OK.

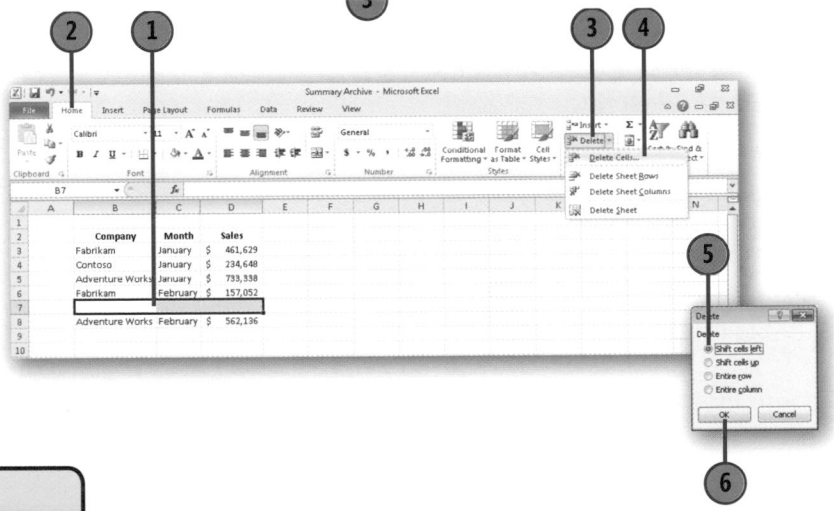

Caution

Because Excel doesn't highlight an entire row or column when you click a single cell, it is possible to be a bit inaccurate if you attempt to delete a row or column by clicking a cell and then clicking the Entire Row or Entire Column option in the Delete dialog box. It's better to follow the procedure listed in the following section, where you click the row or column header, so you can see the entire row or column to be deleted.

Tip

As you drag the cells in the worksheet, Excel displays an outline where the cells would go when you release the left mouse button.

Inserting, Moving, and Deleting Columns and Rows

After you create a worksheet and begin filling in your data, you might decide to insert a row or column to add data you didn't think to include when you started. For example, a customer might want to add a product to an order. To accommodate this new data, you can insert a blank row below the last row in their existing order and add the new item there. You can do the same with columns; you can even use the Insert Options button to format the new rows or columns.

On the other hand, there might be times when you no longer need to use a particular row or column. Whether you placed an extra column to add some white space between the main body of data and a summary calculation or a row holds the contact information of a customer who asked to be removed from your list, you can delete the row or column quickly and easily. Or, if you want to change a column or row's position, you can move a group of columns or rows to another location in the worksheet.

Insert a Row in a Worksheet

1. Right-click the row header below where you want the new row to appear.
2. Choose Insert from the shortcut menu.

Insert a Column in a Worksheet

1. Right-click the column header to the right of where you want the new column to appear.
2. Choose Insert from the shortcut menu.

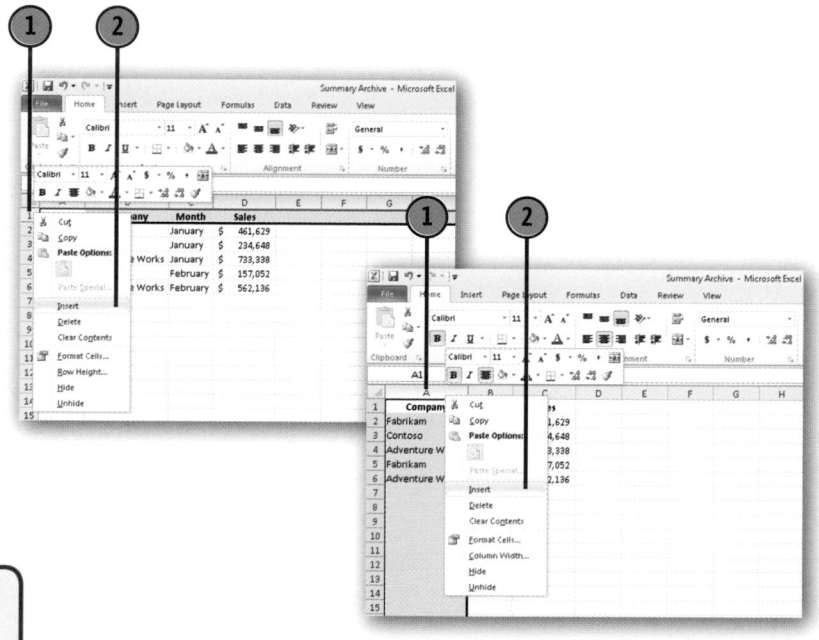

Tip

If you want to insert more than one row or column at a time, select the number of adjacent rows or columns equal to the number you want to insert, and then choose the appropriate command from the Insert menu.

Set Insert Options

1. After inserting rows or columns, click the Insert Options button.
2. Select the type of formatting you want the new cells to have.

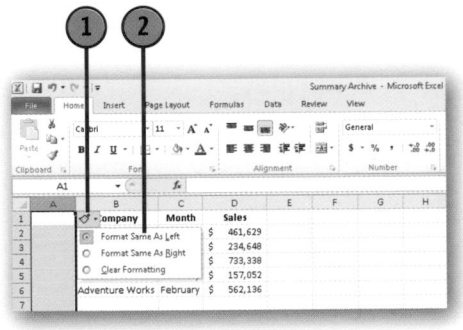

Delete Rows or Columns

1. Select the rows or columns you want to delete.
2. Right-click a header in the selection, and choose Delete from the shortcut menu.

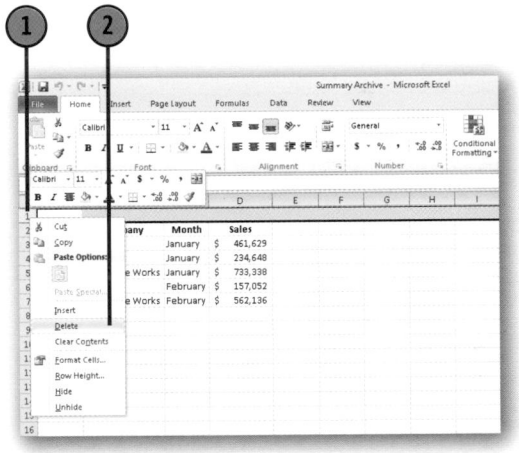

Tip

The Insert Options button appears only if the cells above or below the insertion point have special formatting.

Caution

Formulas that reference cells in the columns or rows you delete will no longer work. The Error action tells you there is an Invalid Cell Reference Error and gives you options to fix the problem. #REF! appears in the damaged cell.

Move One or More Rows

1. Select the rows you want to move.
2. Click the Home tab.
3. Click the Cut button.
4. Click the first cell in the row where you want the rows to be moved.
5. Click Paste.

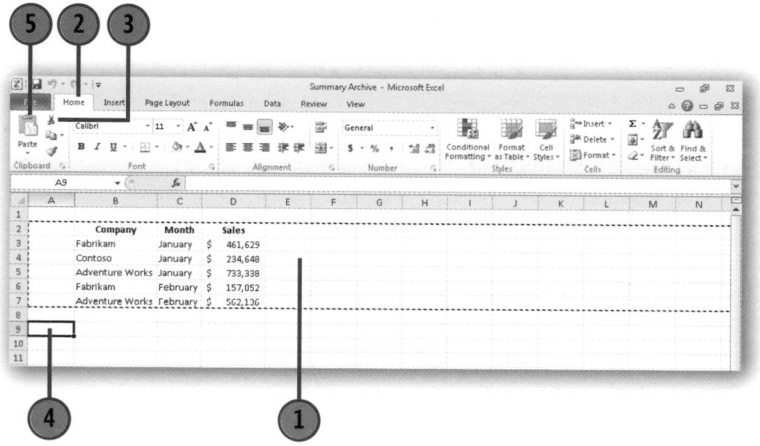

Move One or More Columns

1. Select the columns you want to move.
2. Click the Home tab.
3. Click the Cut button.
4. Click the first cell in the column where you want to move the columns.
5. Click Paste.

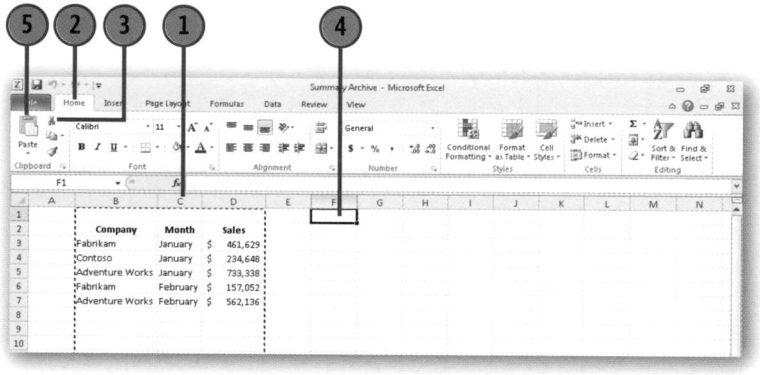

Hiding and Unhiding Columns and Rows

If you're working with a worksheet that contains lots of data, you might need to refer to the contents of rows or columns that aren't close enough on the worksheet to appear on the same screen. Rather than scroll back and forth to access the data you need, you can hide any intervening rows or columns so that everything you need to see is displayed on the screen at the same time. The rows or columns you hide are only gone temporarily. The data hasn't been deleted; it's just been moved out of your way while you don't need it.

Hide Rows or Columns

1. Select the rows or columns you want to hide.
2. Right-click a row or column header in the selection, and choose Hide from the shortcut menu.

Unhide Rows or Columns

1. Click the row or column header of the row above or the column to the left of the rows or columns you want to unhide.
2. Hold down the Shift key, and click the row or column header of the row below or the column to the right of the rows or columns you want to unhide.
3. Right-click the selection, and choose Unhide from the shortcut menu.

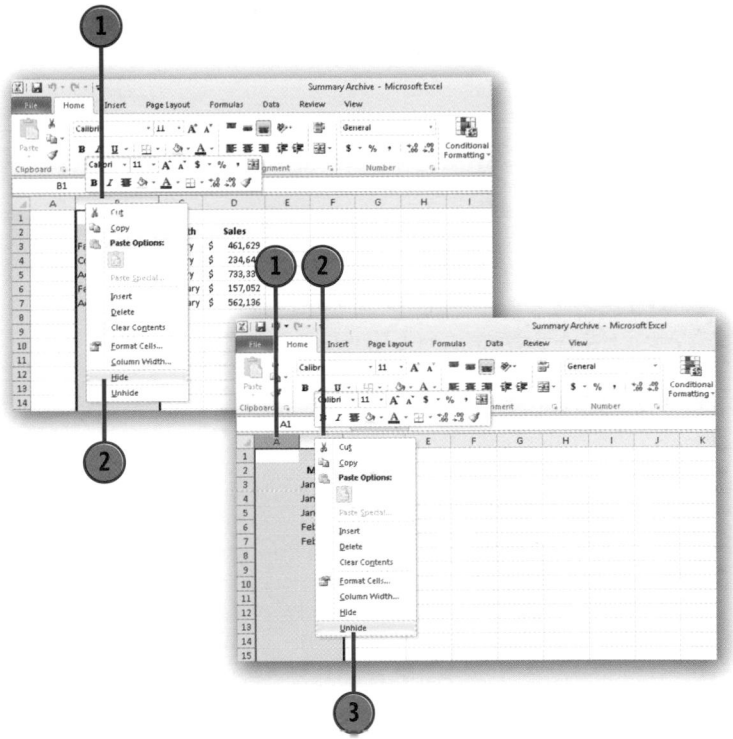

Tip

There are two ways you can tell that hidden rows or columns are in a worksheet. First, whenever rows or columns are hidden, row numbers or column letters are missing. For example, if rows 2, 3, and 4 are hidden, the first two visible rows of the worksheet are labeled row 1 and row 5.

The other way you can tell that a worksheet contains hidden rows or columns is that a thick line appears on the border of the row header or column header where the rows or columns would otherwise appear.

Entering Data and Formatting Many Worksheets at the Same Time

After you work with Excel for a while, you'll probably develop standard worksheets you use over and over. When working with worksheets that follow a common layout, you might want to enter a set of data across multiple worksheets. For example, you might have a set of column headers you want to appear on several worksheets, and you would like to avoid creating them from scratch for each individual worksheet. In Excel 2010, you can save lots of time by entering data and formatting in equivalent blocks of cells on multiple worksheets. If you have existing data you want to paste into several worksheets at the same time, you can do that as well.

Enter and Format Data on Several Worksheets at One Time

1. Hold down the Ctrl key, and click the sheet tabs of the worksheets you want to edit.
2. Select the cell or cells in which you want to enter the data.
3. Type the data you want to appear in the same cell or cells on the worksheets you selected.
4. Right-click the selected cells.
5. Using the Mini toolbar, specify the formatting options you want.
6. Press Enter.
7. Click the sheet tab of any unselected worksheet.

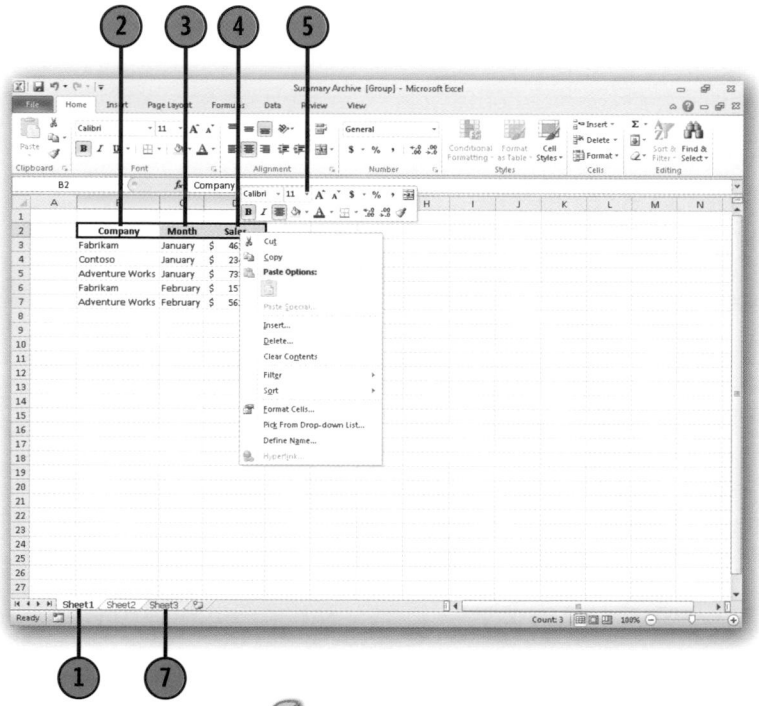

Tip

If you want to format your cells using controls that aren't available on the Mini toolbar, right-click the cell(s) and choose Format Cells to display the Format Cells dialog box.

Tip

If you select all of your workbook's worksheets, you can ungroup them by right-clicking any selected worksheet's sheet tab and then clicking Ungroup Sheets.

Copy Cells from One Worksheet to a Group of Worksheets

1. Click the Home tab.
2. Select the cells you want to copy.
3. Click the Copy button.
4. If you're copying the data to another worksheet, hold down the Ctrl key, and click the sheet tabs of the worksheets you want to receive the copied data.
5. Click the cell you want to receive the data.
6. Click Paste.

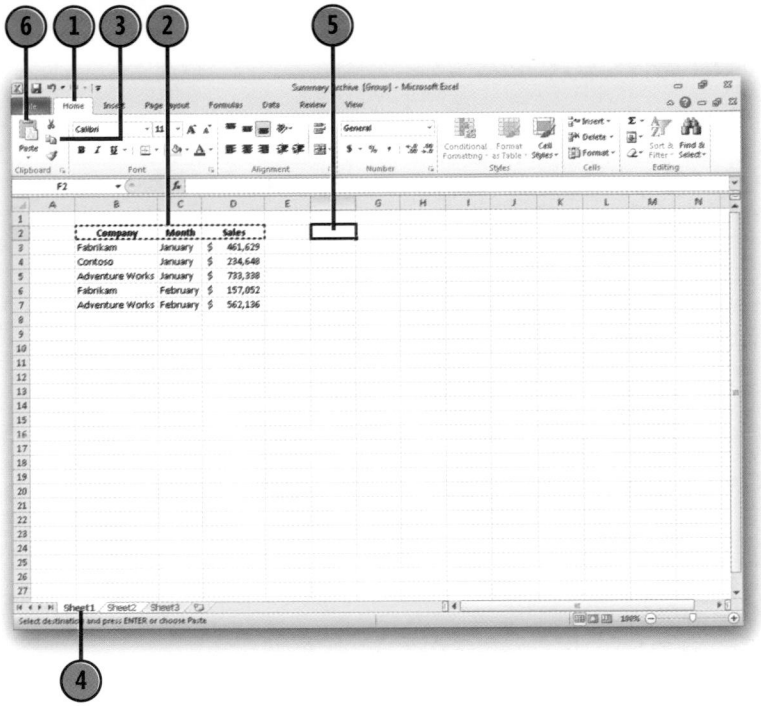

Changing How You Look at Excel Workbooks

When you're examining your Excel data to make a business decision, you might need to look at data from more than one worksheet, or even more than one workbook. Hourly sales totals can help determine when you need more staff on the floor, but if you keep track of the number of customers in the store as well, you might find that your great sales on Monday mornings come from landscape architects loading up for the week. In that case, you would be better off having your warehouse staff and not your counter clerks show up to handle the load.

You can open more than one workbook at a time and arrange them on the screen so that you can read data from both sources at the same time. You can do something similar if you have relevant data in two parts of the same worksheet. If you can't see everything you need to see, you can split the worksheet into two or four units, all with independent scroll bars.

View Different Parts of One Worksheet at the Same Time

1. Click the cell where you want to split the worksheet.
2. Click the View tab.
3. In the Window group, click Split.

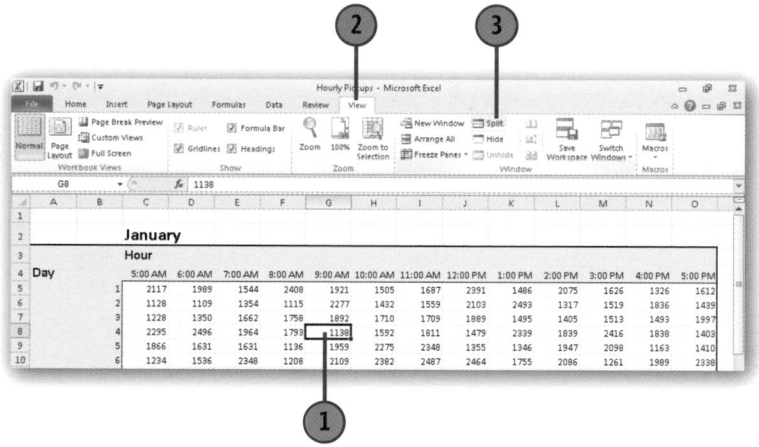

Tip

To remove a worksheet split, click the View tab and then, in the Window group, click Split.

Tip

To split a worksheet into two regions instead of four, click the first cell in the row or column where you want to create the split.

View Multiple Workbooks at the Same Time

1. Open all the workbooks you want to view.
2. Click the View tab.
3. Click Arrange All.
4. Select the option representing the target arrangement.
5. Click OK.

View Multiple Parts of a Worksheet by Freezing Panes

1. Click the cell below and to the right of where you want to freeze the worksheet.
2. Click the View tab.
3. In the Window group, click Freeze Panes.
4. Click one of the following items:
   - Freeze Panes, which keeps the cells above or to the left of the current selection visible at all times
   - Freeze Top Row, which keeps the top row visible at all times
   - Freeze First Column, which keeps the lettmost column visible at all times

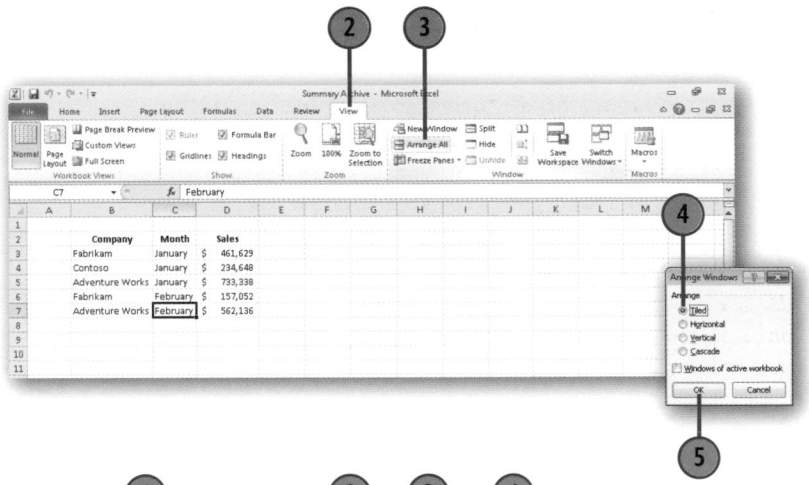

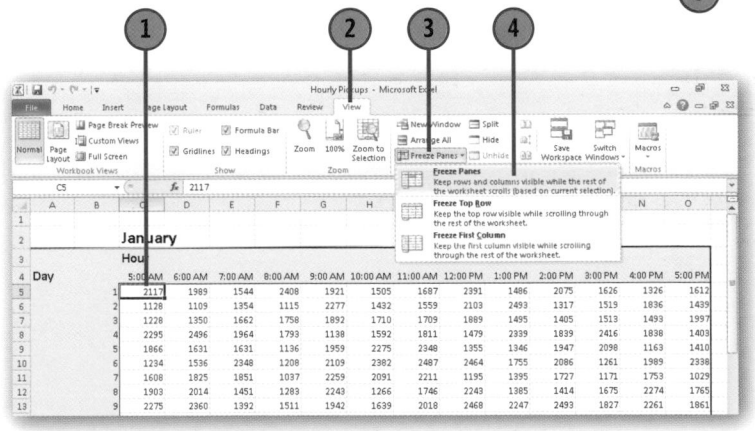

Caution

All the workbooks will be arranged like this unless you select the Windows Of Active Workbook check box, which applies the arrangement only to the active workbook.

Naming and Using Worksheet Views

After you set up your Excel worksheets so that you can read them effectively, you don't need to re-create the arrangement every time you run Excel. Instead, you can record the arrangement—which includes splits, frozen rows and columns, and hidden cells—in a view. Views are especially handy for worksheets that are used by different people, all of whom need different information. Different views can be created for each person, so if the data one person views spans many columns, you can set the print settings to Landscape mode for that view.

Name the Current View of the Worksheet

1. Arrange your Excel window as you would like it to appear.
2. Click the View tab.
3. Click Custom Views.
4. Click Add.
5. Type the name of the view.
6. Select what you want to include in the view.
7. Click OK.

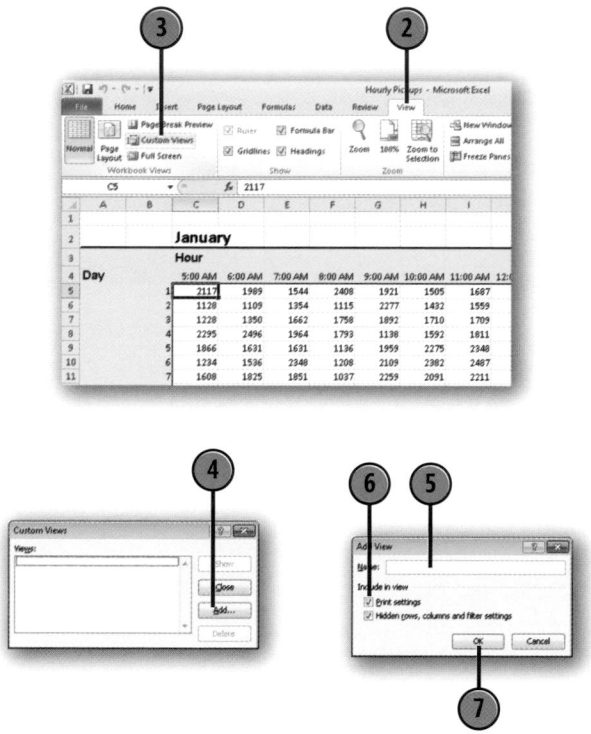

Caution

You can't create a custom view in a workbook that contains an Excel table.

Switch to Another View of the Worksheet

1. Click the View tab.
2. Click Custom Views.
3. Click the view you want.
4. Click Show.

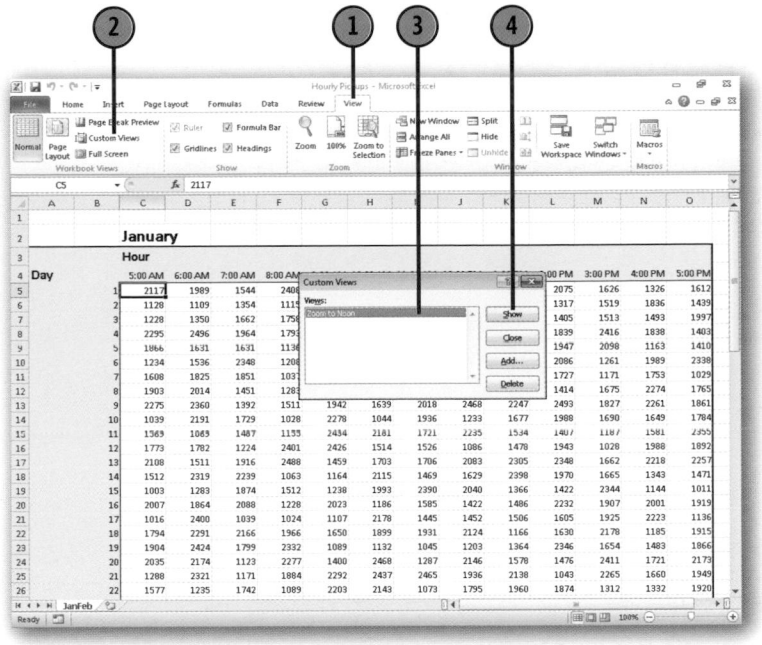

Tip

To delete a custom view, on the View tab, in the Workbook Views group, click Custom Views. Then, in the Custom Views dialog box, click the View you want to delete and click Delete. Click Yes to verify that you want to delete the custom view, and then click Close.

6 Using Formulas and Functions

In this section:

- Understanding Formulas and Cell References in Excel
- Creating and Editing Formulas
- Creating, Editing, and Deleting Named Ranges
- Using Named Ranges in Formulas
- Summarizing the Values in Groups of Cells
- Creating Formulas That Reference Cells in Other Workbooks
- Summing with Subtotals and Grand Totals
- Exploring the Excel Function Library
- Creating Conditional Functions
- Debugging Your Formulas

Microsoft Excel 2010 workbooks allow you to do much more than simply store and organize your data. One important task you can perform in Excel is to summarize the values in related cells. Whether those cells represent the sales for a day at your store, the returns from your personal investments, or your times in bicycle races, you can find the total or average of the values, identify the minimum or maximum value in a group, or perform dozens of other calculations on your data. Many times you can't access the information you want without referencing more than one cell; it's also often true that you'll use the data in the same group of cells in more than one calculation. Excel makes it easy to reference a number of cells at once, letting you build your calculations quickly.

Understanding Formulas and Cell References in Excel

After you add your data to a worksheet, you can summarize the data by creating formulas. A formula is an expression that performs calculations on your data. For example, in a worksheet that lists hourly sales for a day in a single row of cells, you can build a formula in the last cell in that row to find the total of all sales for the day. You can also build the formula to calculate the average or find the lowest or highest hourly value.

When you build a formula, you need to identify the worksheet cells that provide the values for the formula and the operations you want to perform on those values. To identify a cell, you give its cell reference. The first cell in the first column is cell A1, meaning column A, row 1. If you examine a formula, you sometimes see a cell reference written as $A$1, rather than just A1. The difference is that cell references written with the dollar signs are absolute references, meaning the reference doesn't change when the formula is copied to another cell. Cell references written without the dollar signs are relative references, which do change when the formula with the references is copied to another cell.

The benefit of relative references is that you can write a formula once, copy it to as many other cells as you like, and have Excel update the formulas to reflect the new cells. As an example, consider the worksheet in the following figure, which tracks the number of hourly package pickups for a month.

The cells in column P contain formulas that calculate the sum of the hourly pickup values in column C through column O. The formula in cell P5, =SUM(C5:O5), finds the sum of cells in row 5, corresponding to January 1. When you copy the formula from cell P5 to cell P6, the formula changes to =SUM(C6:O6). Excel notices that you copied the formula to a new row and assumes that you want the formula to work on that data. Had you written the formula as =SUM($C$5:$O$5), however, Excel would notice that the formula used absolute references and would copy the formula as =SUM($C$5:$O$5).

If you want to reference a value from a cell in another workbook, you can do that. Excel uses 3D references, which means that any cell in any workbook can be described by three pieces of information:

- The name of the workbook
- The name of the worksheet
- The cell reference

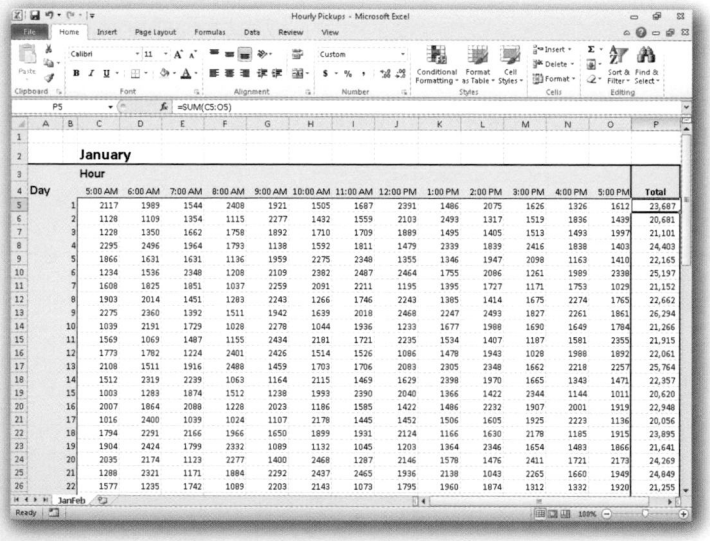

Here's the reference for cell Q38 on the January worksheet in the Y2010ByMonth workbook:

[Y2010ByMonth.xlsx]
January!$Q$38

The good news is that you don't need to remember how to create these references yourself. If you want to use a cell from another workbook in a formula, all you need to do is click the cell where you want to use the value, start the formula, and then click the cell in the other workbook. Excel fills in the reference for you.

Creating Simple Cell Formulas

Building calculations in Excel is pretty straightforward. If you want to find the sum of the values in two cells, you just type an equal sign (=), the reference of the first cell, a plus sign (+), and the reference of the second cell. The formula you enter appears on the formula bar, where you can examine and edit it.

Build a Formula

1. Click the cell in which you want to enter a formula.
2. Type =.
3. Type the expression representing the calculation you want to perform.
4. Press Enter.

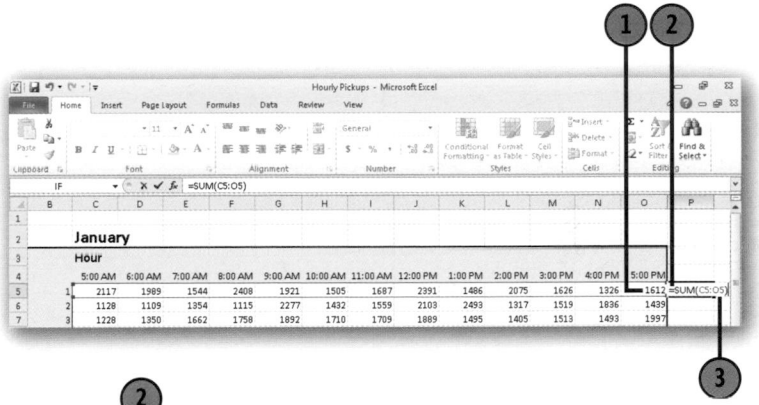

Edit a Formula

1. Click the cell you want to edit.
2. Select the part of the formula you want to edit in the formula bar.
3. Make any changes that you want.
4. Press Enter.

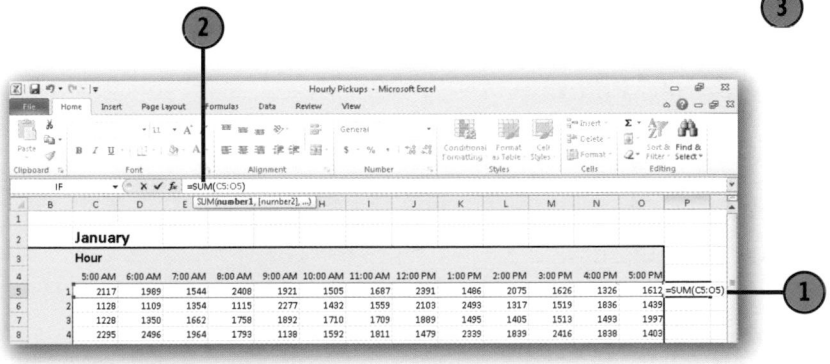

Try This!

Click the Excel Help button. Then, in the Excel Help dialog box, type common formulas in the Search box, press Enter, and click Examples Of Commonly Used Formulas in the list of available topics. The Help file that appears has quite a few examples of formulas you might want to create.

Caution

Be sure that there's no space before the equal sign in your formula. If there is, Excel interprets the cell's contents as text, not a formula.

Assigning Names to Groups of Cells

When you work with large amounts of data, it's easy to lose track of which cells contain which data. In addition, it can be difficult to locate data in workbooks you didn't create. Although you might always store product prices in one worksheet column, there's no guarantee that your colleagues will follow the same pattern! One way to prevent confusion is to define a named range for any cell group that holds specific information. For example, in a worksheet with customer order data, you can define the Totals named range to represent the cells in which the total for each order is stored. After you define the named range, you can display its contents, rename it, or delete it.

Create a Named Range

1. Select the cells you want to name.
2. Click the Name Box on the Formula Bar.
3. Type the name you want for the range.
4. Press Enter.

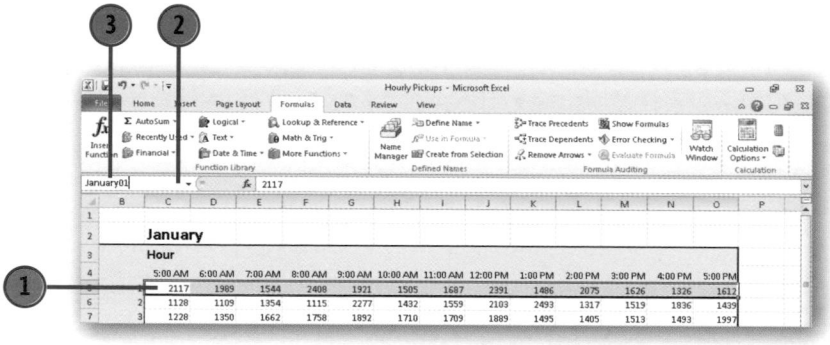

Go to a Named Range

1. Click the Name Box down arrow.
2. Click the range to which you want to go.

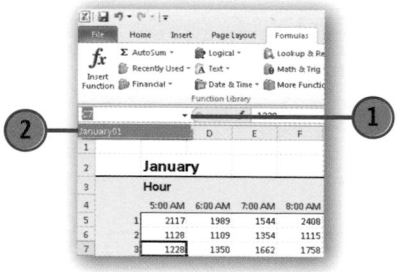

Caution

The name you give your named range shouldn't duplicate a potential cell address. For example, typing DAY1 in a formula would reference cell DAY1. To avoid this problem, either ensure that your ranges have names that begin with at least four letters (the last column is XFD) or use an underscore to separate the letters from the rest of the name. The name DAY1 isn't valid, but the name DAY_1 is.

See Also

For information about selecting cells from several parts of the same worksheet, see "Select a Noncontiguous Group of Cells" on page 32.

Delete a Named Range

1. Click the Formulas tab.
2. Click Name Manager.
3. Click the named range you want to delete.
4. Click Delete.
5. Click OK to clear the confirmation dialog box that appears.
6. Click Close.

Rename a Named Range

1. Click the Formulas tab.
2. Click Name Manager.
3. Click the named range you want to rename.
4. Click Edit.
5. Type a new name for the range.
6. Click OK.
7. Click Close.

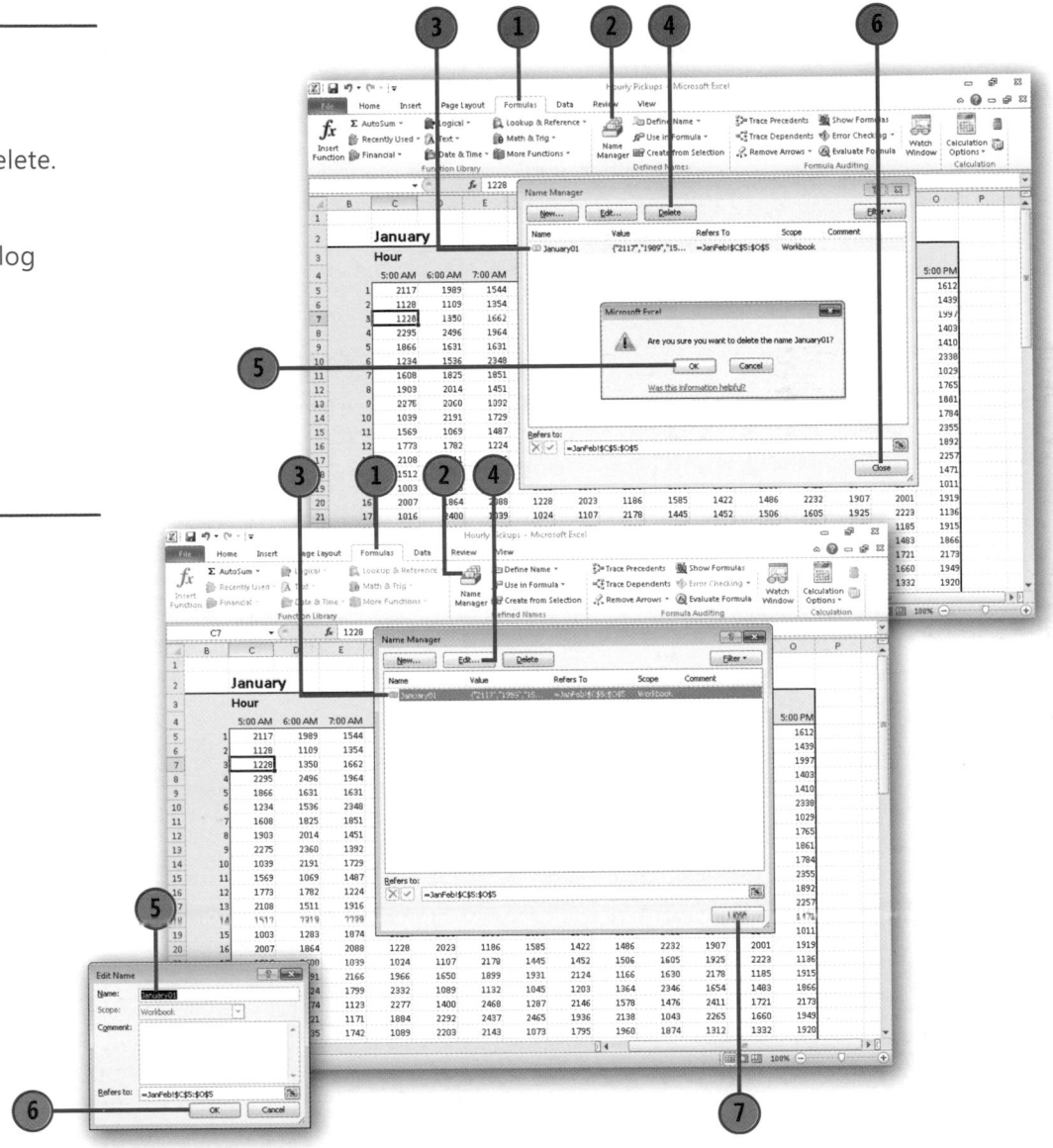

Using Names in Formulas

When you define a named range, you create a shortcut that you can use to refer to a group of cells. A great way to use named ranges is in formulas. Instead of entering the references of every cell you want to use in your calculation, you can type the name of the range. When you reference named ranges in formulas, your formulas are shorter and easier to understand. Rather than seeing a series of cell references you need to examine, you and your colleagues can rely on the named ranges to understand the goal of a calculation.

Create a Formula with a Named Range

1. Click the cell in which you want to enter a formula.
2. Type = followed by the formula you want. When you want to use a range that has a name, start typing the name instead of the cell address.
3. Click the named range in the Formula AutoComplete list that appears.
4. Press Enter.

Excel 2010 further streamlines formula creation with Formula AutoComplete. Remember that when you start typing a value into a cell, Excel examines the previous values in that column and offers to let you complete the entry by pressing Tab or Enter. Now, when you start typing a named range's name into a formula, Excel recognizes that you might be entering a named range and displays a list of named ranges (as well as built-in functions) available in the active workbook. All you have to do is click the named range you want, and it's included in the formula immediately.

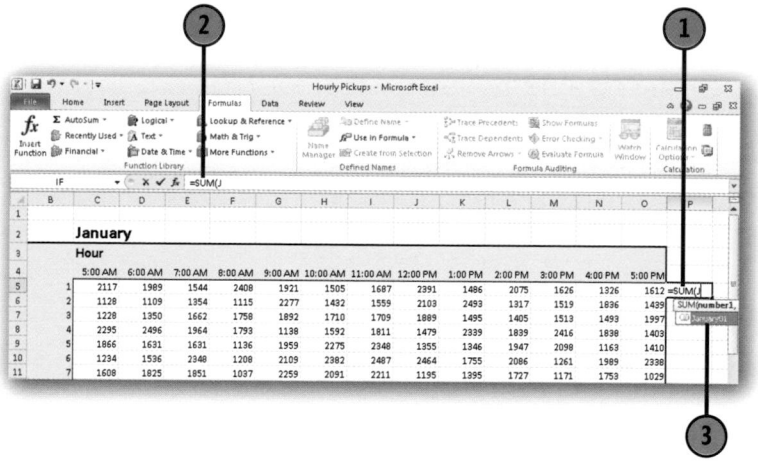

Tip

If you change the name of a range of cells, Excel automatically makes the name change in every one of your formulas.

Creating a Formula That References Values in an Excel Table

In previous versions of Excel, it was a challenge to create named ranges that included an entire column in a data list. Suppose that you created a named range that encompassed the existing cells in a data column, such as the cell range A3:A44; if you added data to cell A45, you would need to change the cells in the named range's definition. Yes, there is a complicated way to create a dynamic named range in Excel 2003 and earlier versions, but you don't have to worry about it in Excel 2010. All you need to do is create an Excel table (as shown in "Creating an Excel Table" on page 41) and select the headers of the columns that contain the data you want to summarize in your formulas.

Create a Formula with an Excel Table Reference

1. Click the cell in which you want to create the formula.
2. Type =, followed by the function to include in the formula and a left parenthesis; for example, =SUM(would be a valid way to start.
3. Type the name of the Excel table.
4. Type a left square bracket.
5. Click the name of the table column.
6. Type a right square bracket, a right parenthesis, and press Enter.

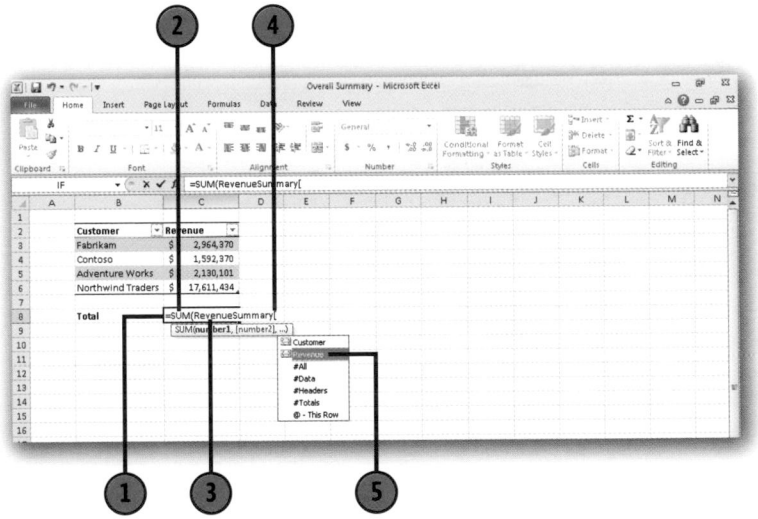

Tip

To include more than one table column in a formula, either hold down the Shift key, select the column header of the first column to use in the formula, and then click another column to select everything in the span between the two columns, or hold down the Ctrl key and click the other column headers you want to use. Excel includes the references in the formula.

Creating Formulas That Reference Cells in Other Workbooks

One of the strengths of Excel is that you aren't limited to using cells from the current workbook in your formulas. If you want, you can use data from any other workbook in your calculations. For example, you might have a workbook in which you track monthly advertising sales for your newsletter. If you want to create a new workbook to summarize all income and expenses for your publication, you can do so. By letting you create formulas that reference cells from more than one workbook, Excel makes it easy for you to organize your workbooks so that each workbook holds data about a specific subject. Not only can you find the data easily, you can reference it anywhere else.

After you create links between workbooks, you can have Excel update your calculation if the data in the linked cell changes. You can also change the cell to which you linked, or if the workbook with the cell to which you linked has been moved or deleted, you can delete the link and have Excel store the last value from the calculation.

Use Cells from Other Workbooks in a Formula

1. Open the workbook with the cell you want to reference in your formula.
2. In the workbook where you want to create the formula, click the View tab.
3. Click Arrange All.
4. Select the Tiled option.
5. Click OK.

(continued on next page)

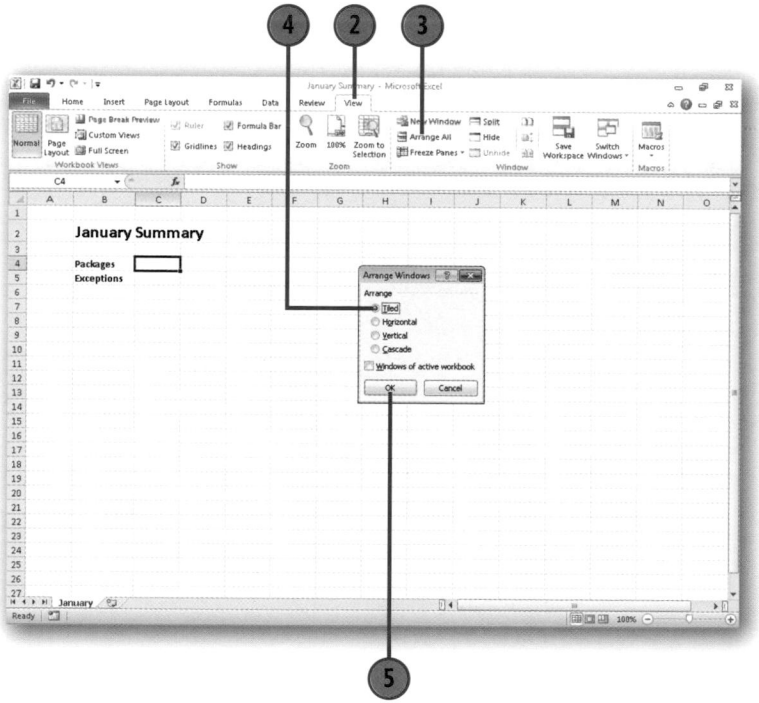

Use Cells from Other Workbooks in a Formula *(continued)*

6. Click the cell where you want to create the formula.
7. Type = followed by the first part of the formula.
8. Select the cells with the values you want to use in the formula.
9. Press Enter.

Break Links to Other Workbooks and Convert to Values

1. Click the cell that contains the formula you want to edit.
2. Select the part of the formula representing the link you want to break.
3. Press F9.
4. Press Enter.

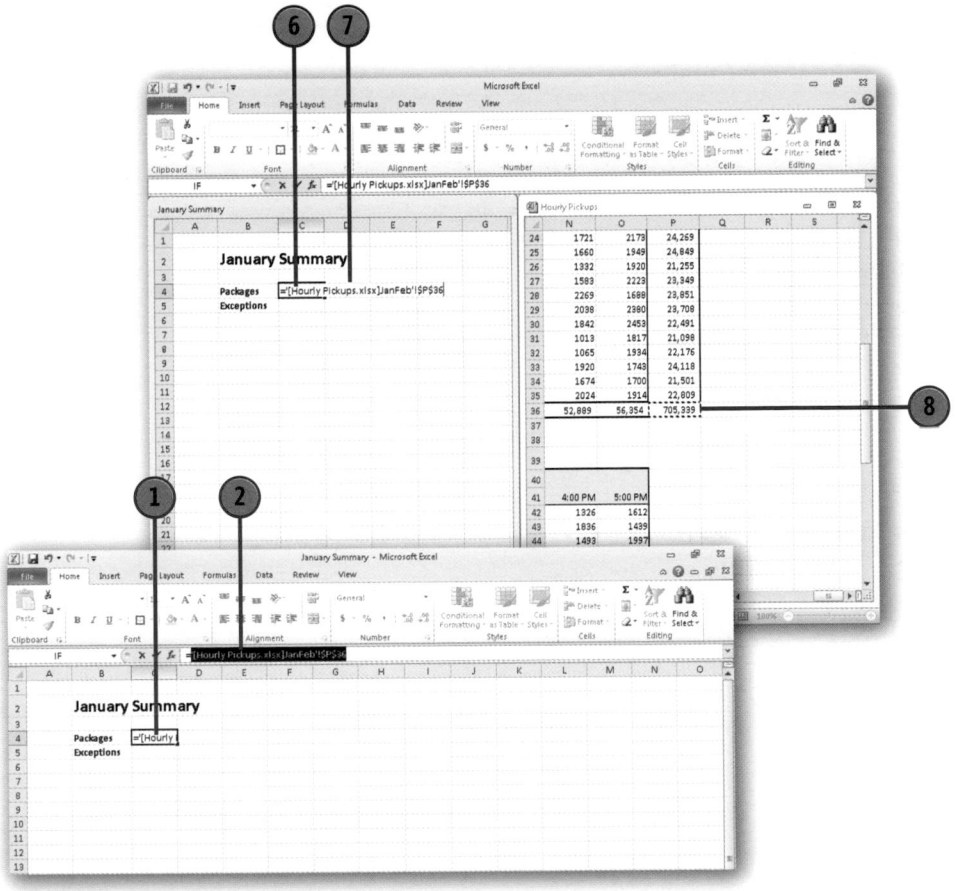

Tip

You can use the techniques here to link to a cell on a different worksheet in the same workbook. Just create the formula, and when you want to put in the cell reference, move to the target worksheet and click the appropriate cell.

Refresh Links

1. Click the Data tab.
2. In the Connections group, click Refresh All.

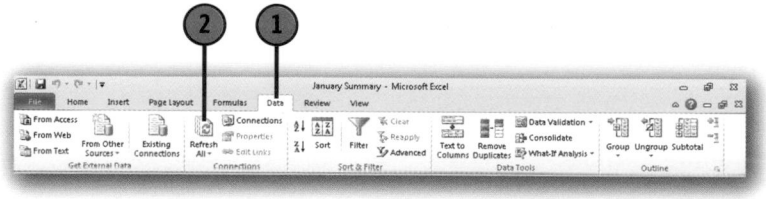

Change Links to Different Workbooks

1. Click the Data tab.
2. In the Connections group, click Edit Links.
3. Click the link you want to change.
4. Click Change Source.
5. Click the workbook with the new cell to which you want to link.
6. Click OK.
7. Select the sheet from which to update values.
8. Click OK.
9. Click Close.

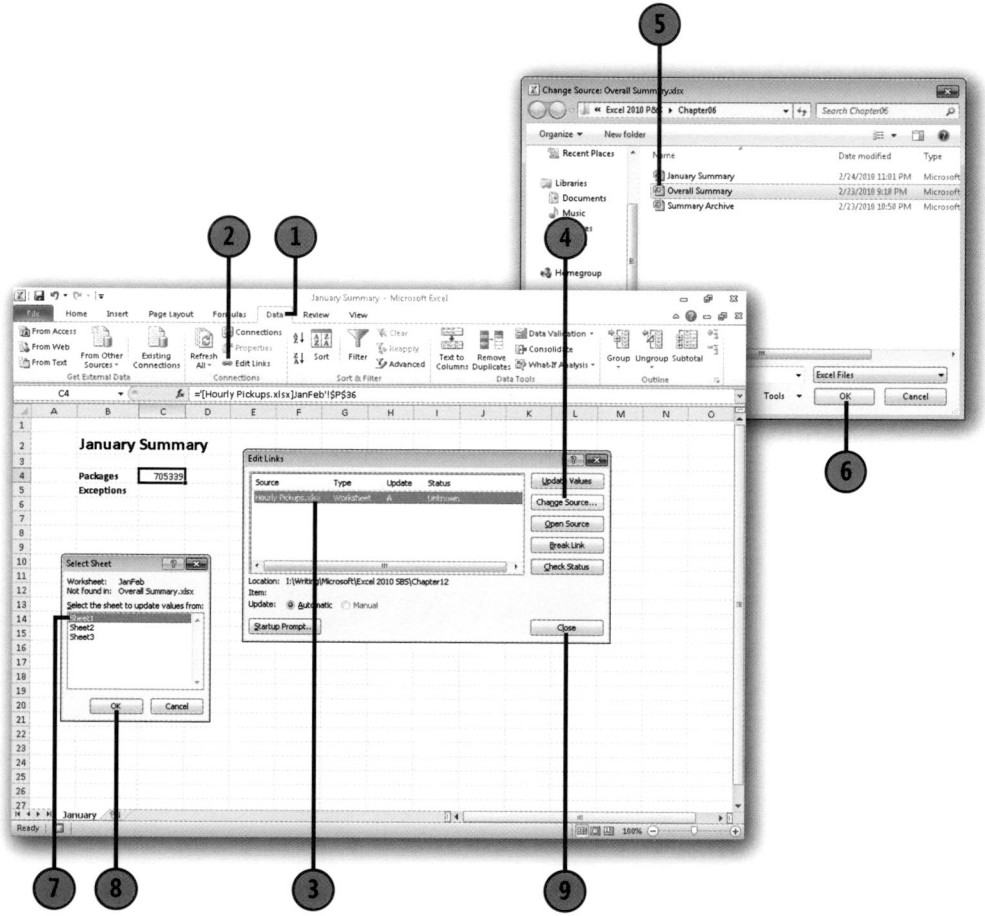

Summing a Group of Cells Without Using a Formula

Sometimes, such as when you're entering data into a worksheet or you're curious to find out the sum or average of the values in a few cells, it's too much work to find a blank cell and write a formula to calculate the sum or average for the cells. Rather than make you create a separate formula, Excel counts the number of cells selected, calculates a running total and average for the currently selected cells, and displays the results on the status bar. Finding the sum, average, and count of the values in the selected cells are the most commonly used operations, so Excel calculates those values by default. You can choose from several other operations, however, or even tell Excel not to calculate a running total for any selected cells.

Summarize Data in a Group of Cells

1. Select the cells you want to summarize.

Find the Total, Average, or Other Values of Cell Data

1. Right-click the status bar, and choose the summary operations you want from the shortcut menu.

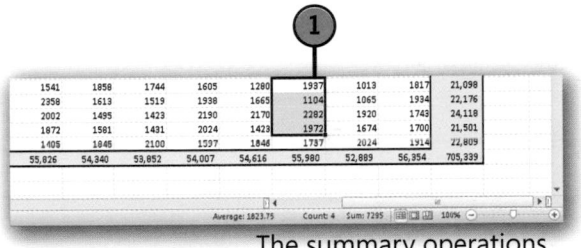

The summary operations and results of the summaries appear on the status bar

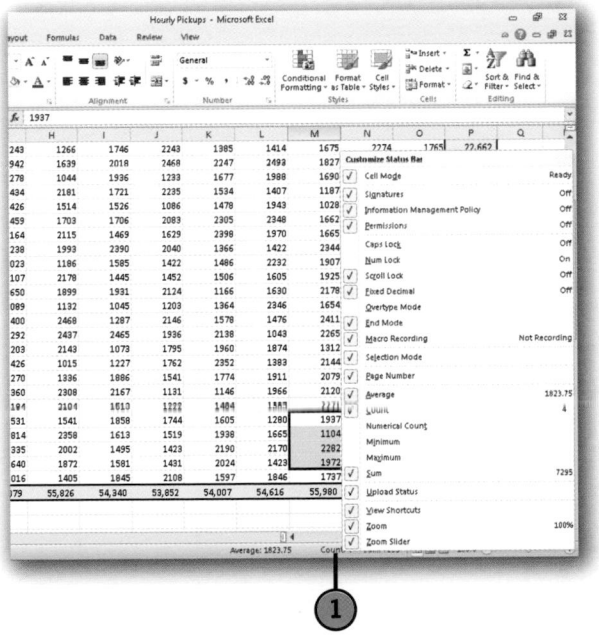

Tip

Active summary operations are checked on the shortcut menu. Clicking a checked summary operation turns off that operation.

Creating a Summary Formula

After you enter data into a worksheet, you can create formulas to summarize the values and display the result of the calculation. You can summarize the values in a group of cells in many ways: You can find the total or average of the cell values, identify the maximum or minimum value in the group, or simply count the number of cells containing values. You can create these formulas by clicking the cell below or to the right of the cells you want to summarize, displaying either the Home tab or the Formulas tab, and clicking the AutoSum button. (The button appears on both tabs.) Clicking the AutoSum button itself creates a SUM formula, which finds the arithmetic sum of the values, but you can choose other calculations by clicking the AutoSum button's down arrow. After you create the formula you want, you can use the result in other calculations.

Create an AutoSum Formula

1. Click the cell where you want the summary value to appear.
2. Click the Home tab.
3. Click the AutoSum down arrow.
4. Click the AutoSum function you want to use.
5. If necessary, select the cells with the data you want to summarize.
6. Press Enter.

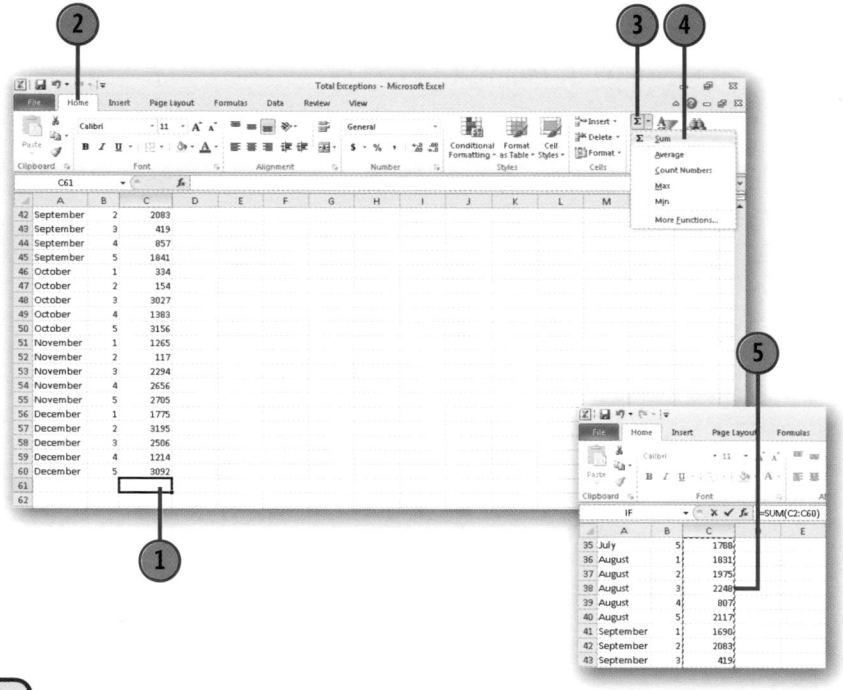

See Also

For information about finding a running total for a group of cells without creating a formula, see "Summing a Group of Cells Without Using a Formula" on page 93.

Summing with Subtotals and Grand Totals

You frequently need to organize the data in an Excel worksheet by one or more criteria. For example, you might have a worksheet in which you list yearly sales for each product you offer, with the products broken down by category. If your data is organized this way, you can have Excel calculate a subtotal for each category of products. When you create a subtotal, you identify the cells with the values to be calculated and the cells that identify the change from one category to the next; Excel updates the subtotal and grand total for you if the value of any cell changes.

Create a Subtotal

1. Click any cell in the range you want to subtotal.
2. Click the Data tab.
3. In the Outline group, click Subtotal.
4. Click the At Each Change In down arrow.
5. Click the value on which you want to base the subtotals.
6. Click the Use Function down arrow.
7. Click the subtotal function you want to use.
8. Select which columns should have subtotals calculated.
9. Click OK.

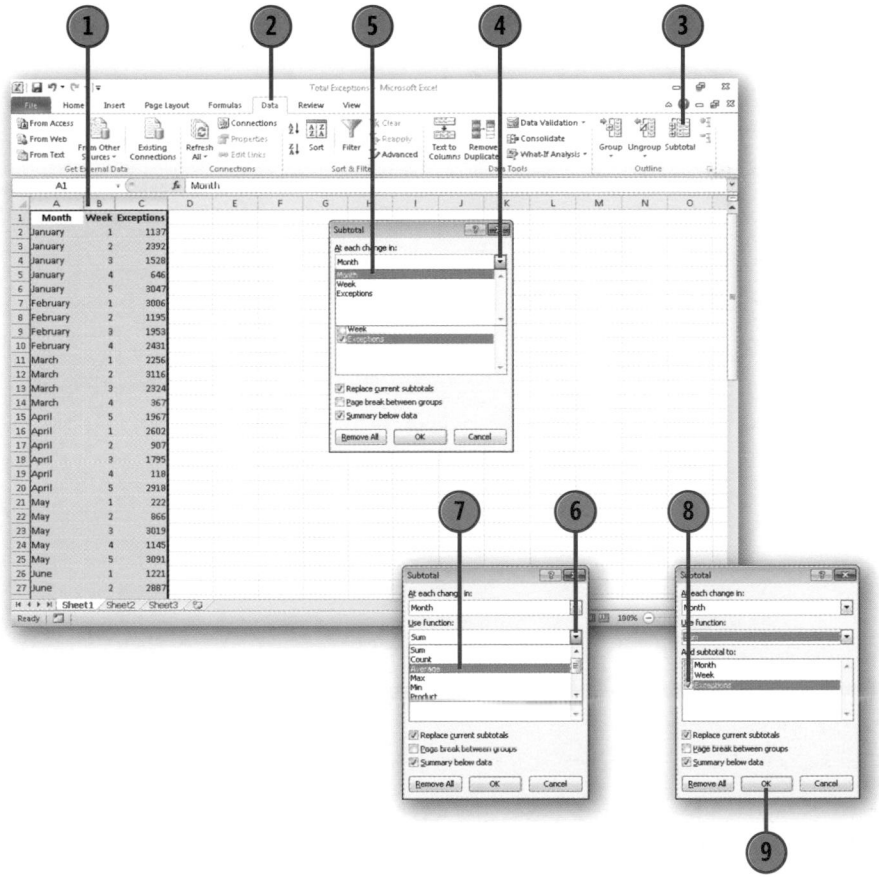

Remove a Subtotal

1. Click any cell in the subtotaled range.
2. Click the Data tab.
3. Click Subtotal.
4. Click Remove All.

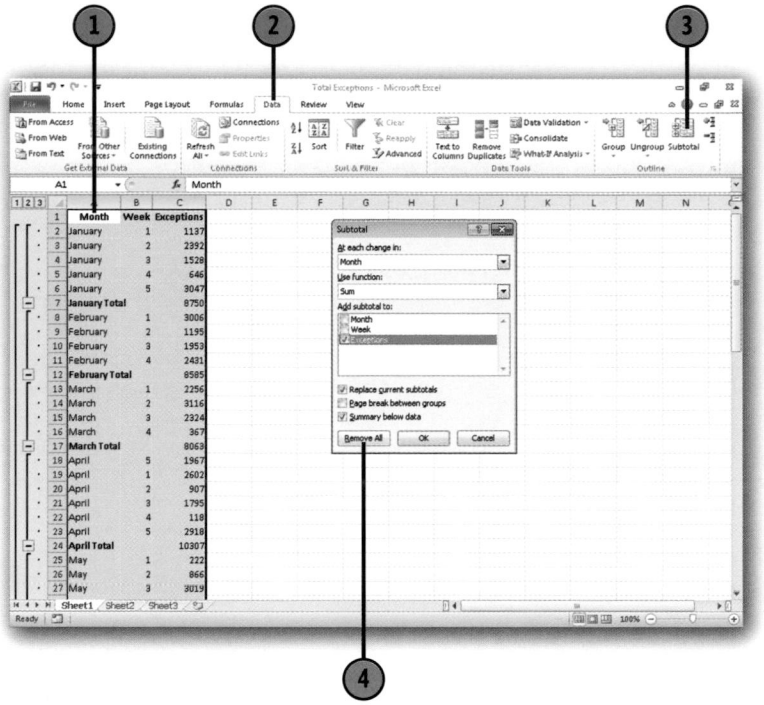

Exploring the Excel Function Library

You can create dozens of different functions in Excel. You can use Excel functions to determine mortgage payments, perform scientific calculations, or find the square root of a number. The best way to become familiar with the formulas available in Excel is to display the Insert Function dialog box and move through the listed functions, clicking the ones that look interesting. When you click a function, its description appears at the bottom of the dialog box.

Another way to get information about a function is to view the ScreenTip that appears next to the function. If you double-click a cell with a function, a ScreenTip with the function's structure and expected values appears below it. Clicking an element of the structure points to the cell or cells providing that value.

List Functions Available from the Excel Library

1. Click the Insert Function button.
2. Display the drop-down list, and click the function category you want to view.
3. Click the function you want to examine.
4. Click OK.
5. Click Cancel to close the Function Arguments dialog box.

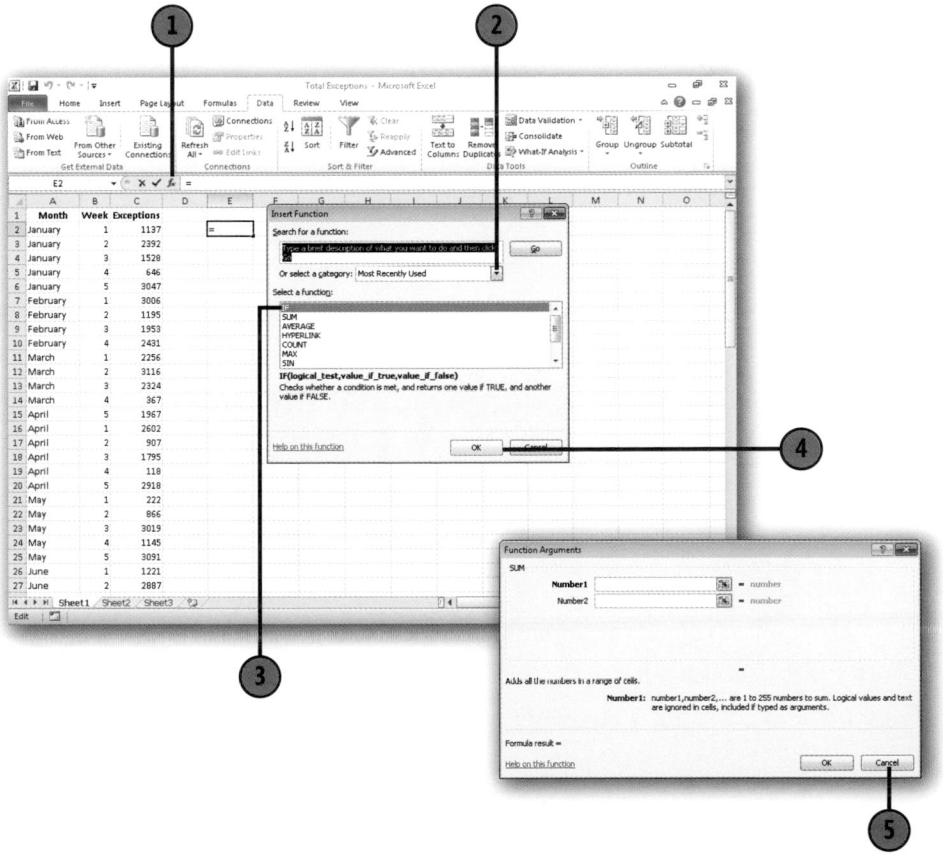

Use Function ScreenTips

1. Double-click a cell that contains a formula.
2. In the ScreenTip, click the function name to open the Help file entry for the function.
3. Click the Close button to close the Help window.
4. Click an argument to select the cells to which it refers.

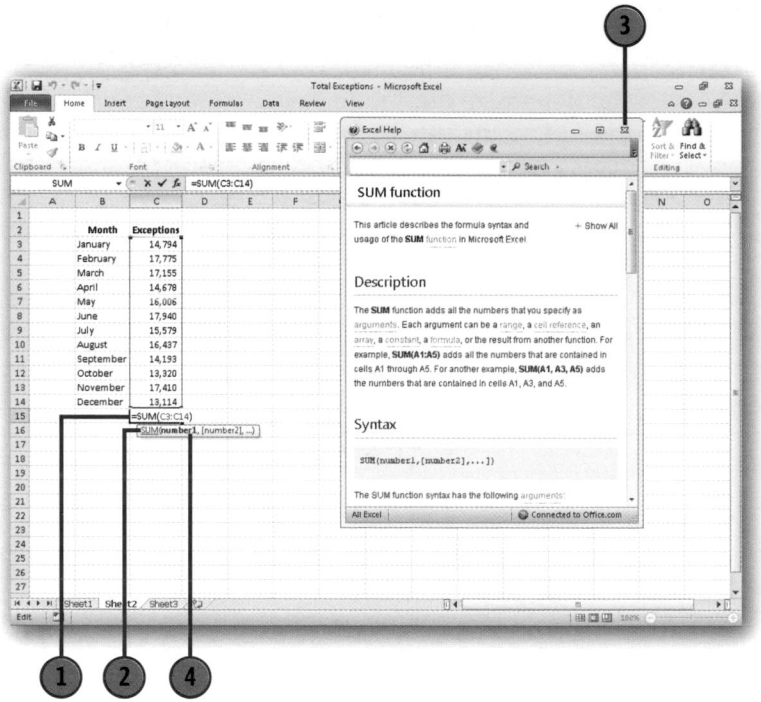

Using the IF Function

In addition to calculating values based on the contents of other cells, you can have Excel take different actions based on the contents of those other cells by using the IF function. For example, if you create a workbook to track the times of riders in a bicycle-racing club, you can create a formula to compare each rider's time to his previous time. When someone's most recent time is the lowest time in the group, you can have Excel display Personal Best in the cell with the formula, alerting you to congratulate the rider in your next club newsletter.

Create an IF Function

1. Click the cell in which you want to enter an IF function.
2. Click the Formulas tab.
3. Click Logical.
4. Click IF.
5. Type a conditional statement that evaluates to true or false.
6. Type the text you want to appear if the condition is true.
7. Type the text you want to appear if the condition is false.
8. Click OK.

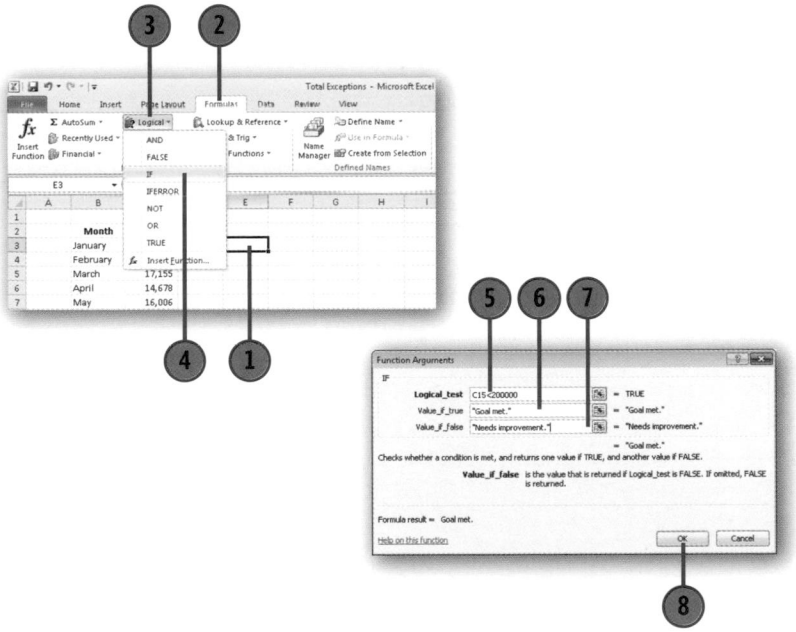

Caution

The text message must be enclosed in quotation marks.

Tip

You can also create an expression in the Value_If_True and Value_If_False boxes. Excel displays the result of the expression in the appropriate box.

Checking Formula References

When you create a formula that draws values from several different places in your workbook—or from other workbooks—it can be difficult to see what's going wrong if your formula isn't producing the expected results. Excel helps you locate a cell's precedents (the cells the formula uses in its calculation) and dependents (the cells that depend on the current cell to calculate their own values). To help you find what you need to check your formulas, Excel groups all the tools you need on the Formula Auditing group on the Formulas tab.

Find Cell Precedents and Dependents

1. Click the cell you want to examine.
2. Click the Formulas tab.
3. Using the controls in the Formula Auditing group, follow either of these steps:
   - Click Trace Precedents.
   - Click Trace Dependents.

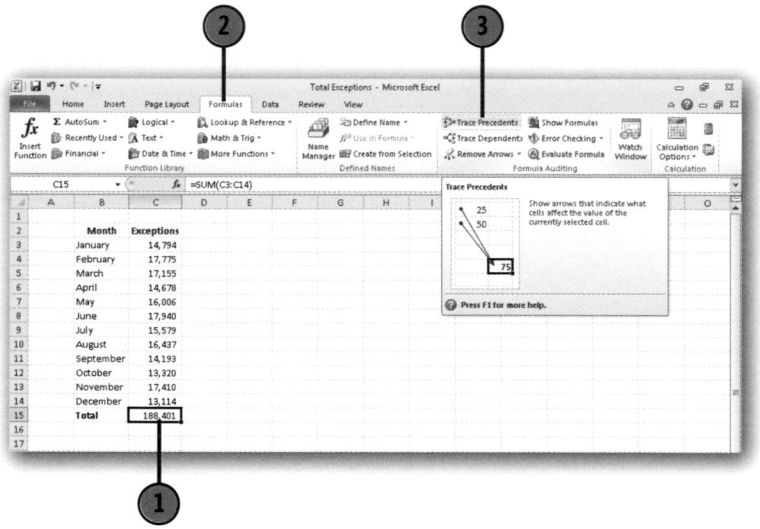

Remove Tracer Arrows

1. Click the Formulas tab.
2. Click the Remove Arrows down arrow, and follow any of these steps:
   - Click Remove Arrows to remove all arrows.
   - Click Remove Precedent Arrows to remove the precedent arrows.
   - Click Remove Dependent Arrows to remove the dependent arrows.

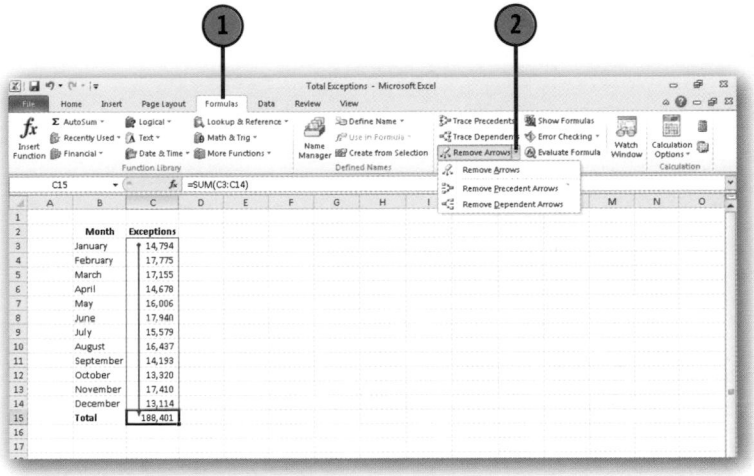

Tip

Tracer arrows are particularly effective when they're used to examine formulas that include named ranges. When you refer to a named range, you know what the indicated cells are supposed to represent.

Debugging Your Formulas

When you share a workbook with your colleagues, some of the values in that workbook might change rapidly as new data is entered. For example, workbook data probably will change quickly if you are evaluating stock prices. Stock market values change frequently, so your data will as well. You can monitor the value in a cell even while you're using another workbook by setting a watch. When you set a watch, the values of the cells you're monitoring appear in the Watch Window.

Another way you can monitor your data is to check the result of part of a calculation by using the Evaluate Formula dialog box. When you click the Evaluate Formula button, Excel displays the formula in the active cell and the subtotal for part of the calculation. You can move through the formula bit by bit, with Excel showing you the result of each piece of the formula.

Monitor a Formula for Changes

1. Click the Formulas tab.
2. Click Watch Window.
3. Click Add Watch.
4. Select the cells you want to watch.
5. Click Add.
6. Click Watch Window.

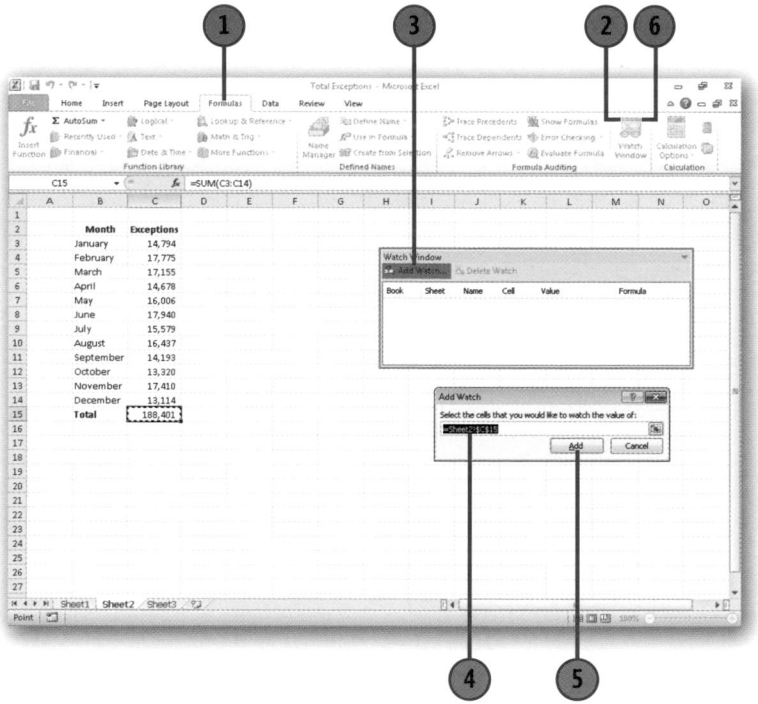

Delete a Watch

1. Click the Formulas tab.
2. Click Watch Window.
3. Click the watch you want to delete.
4. Click Delete Watch.
5. Click the Close button.

Evaluate Parts of a Formula

1. Click the cell with the formula you want to evaluate.
2. Click the Formulas tab.
3. Click Evaluate Formula.
4. Click Evaluate (one or more times) to move through the formula's elements.
5. Click Close.

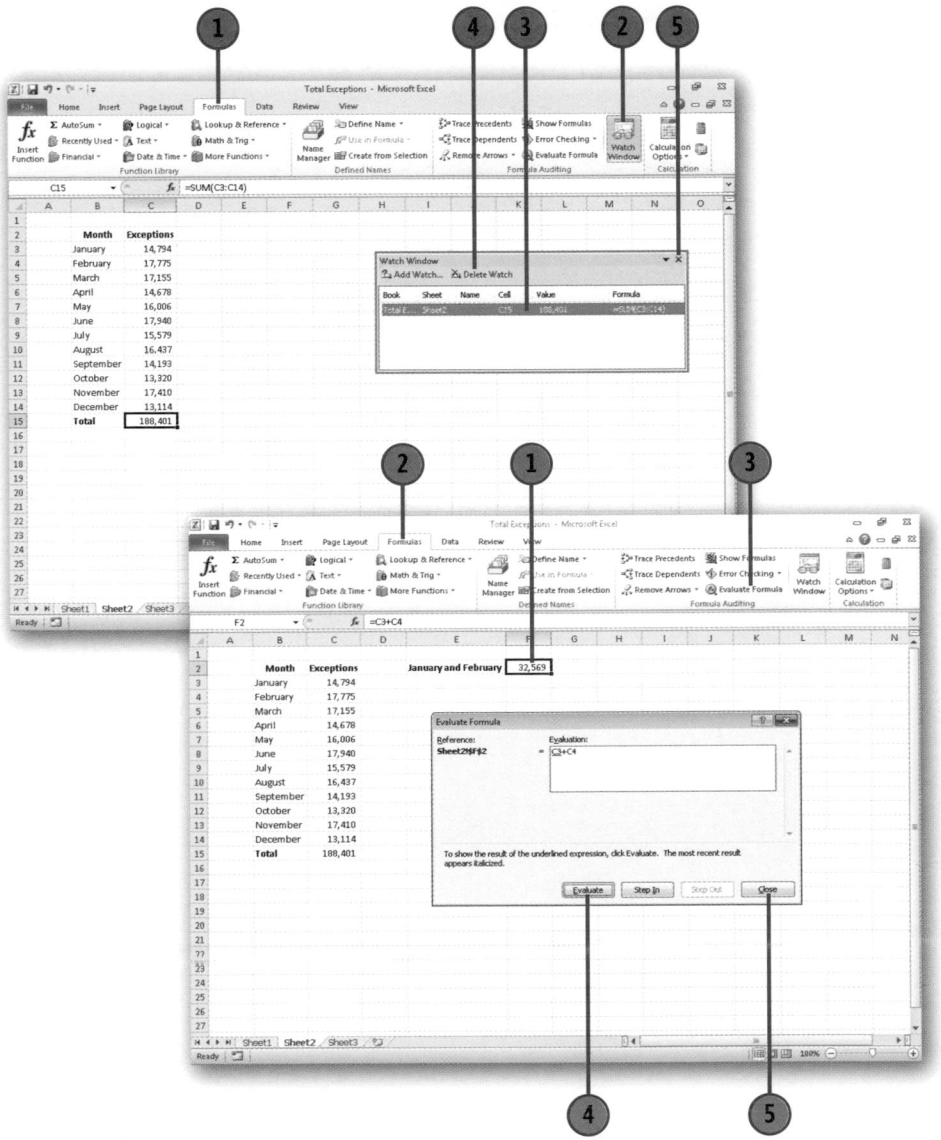

7 Formatting the Cell

In this section:

- Formatting Cells and Cell Contents
- Adding Cell Backgrounds and Formatting Cell Borders
- Defining Cell Styles and Aligning and Orienting Cell Contents
- Applying Conditional Formatting
- Displaying Data Bars, Icon Sets, or Color Scales Based on Cell Values
- Copying Formats with Format Painter
- Merging or Splitting Cells or Data

Microsoft Excel 2010 helps you manage large quantities of data with ease. One of the ways you can accomplish this is by changing how the program displays the data in your worksheet. For example, you can easily change the size of characters displayed in a cell, add color to emphasize important cells, or changecel the orientation of text within a cell. Excel 2010 also enables you to change a cell's formatting based on the contents of the cell by creating conditional formats. Although you had the ability to create these conditional formats in previous versions of Excel, Excel 2010 greatly expands the type and number of formats you can create.

Formatting Cell Contents

Some cells have values that need to stand out. Whether the value is a grand total for a year's sales or a label that lets your colleagues know that data they enter in the worksheet must be within certain limits, you can change the font used to display the data; make the text larger or smaller; or make the text appear bold, italicized, or underlined. You can apply these settings by using the controls on the Home tab of the ribbon or on the Mini toolbar, but formatting cell contents isn't an all-or-nothing proposition. You can choose to format a word or even a single character in a cell.

Change Font and Font Size

1. Select the cells you want to format.
2. Click the Home tab.
3. Click the Font down arrow.
4. Click the font you want.
5. Click the Font Size down arrow.
6. Click the font size you want.

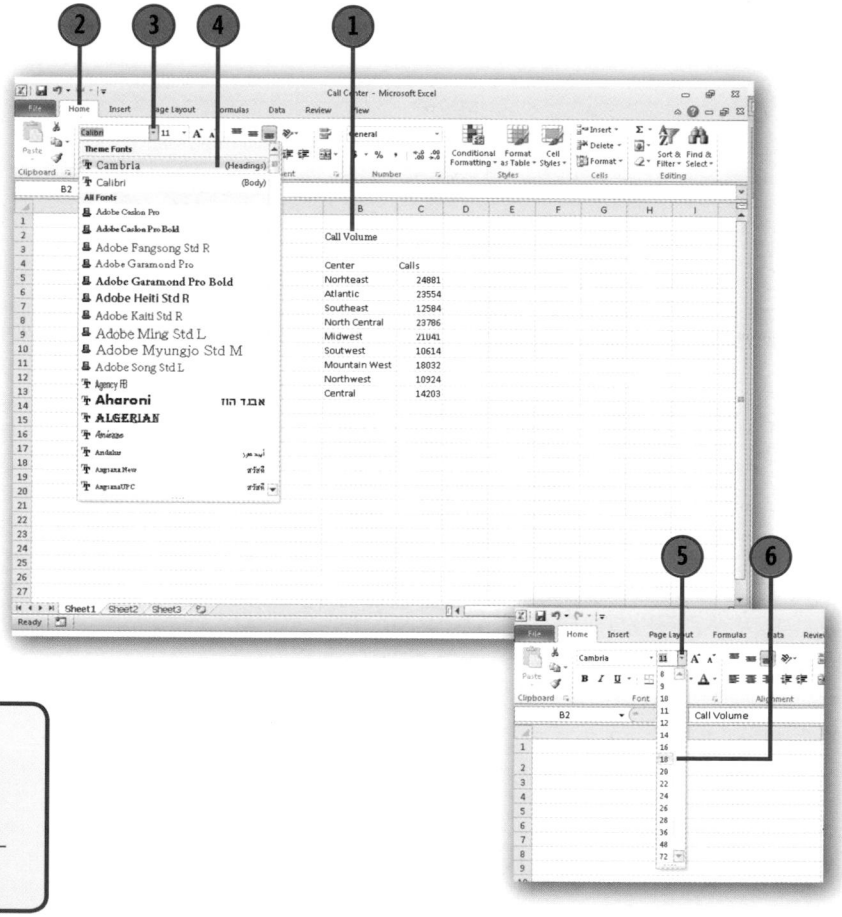

Tip

You can display the Format Cells dialog box, which contains a wider range of cell formatting controls, by selecting a group of cells, right-clicking any selected cell, and choosing Format Cells. You can also display the Format Cells dialog box by clicking the Font group's dialog box launcher.

Change Text Appearance

1. Select the cells you want to format.
2. Click the Home tab.
3. Use the tools in the Font, Alignment, and Number groups to change your text's appearance.

Format Part of a Cell's Contents

1. Click the cell with the data you want to format.
2. In the formula bar, select the contents of the cell you want to format.
3. If necessary, click the Home tab.
4. Use the controls in the Font group on the ribbon to apply the changes you want.

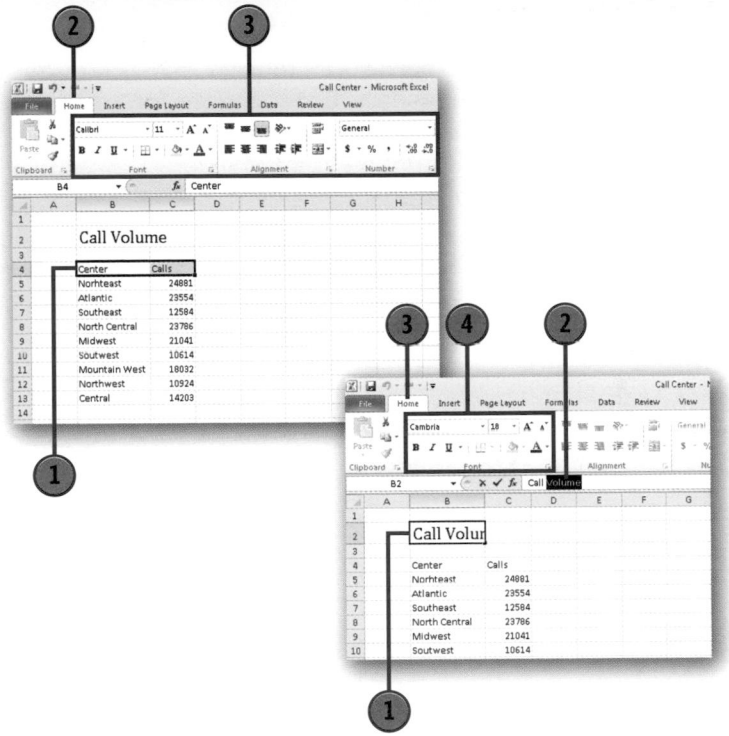

Caution

When you select multiple cells to change their appearance, the range you select might have a combination of cells that already have formatting applied to them and cells that have no formatting applied. If this is the case, you might have to click the buttons multiple times until all the cells are formatted how you want them.

Formatting Cells Containing Numbers

Numerical data plays a central role in Excel workbooks; therefore, it stands to reason that you have lots of options for choosing how you want your numbers to appear. Two frequently used formats are the Accounting number style, which displays a cell's contents as a monetary value, and Percent, which multiplies a value by 100 and adds a percent sign to the end. The two biggest benefits of formatting data as a percent are that you save a lot of time (and avoid mistakes) by not typing the decimal point or percent sign yourself and that you can tell the values are percentages at a glance.

Two other options for formatting your numbers are to display the values in a cell with commas every third digit and to increase or decrease the number of digits to the right of the decimal point. Although two decimal places are sufficient for most financial data, you may need to track currency exchange amounts to three or four decimal places.

Display Numerical Values As Currency and Percentages

1. Select the cells you want to format.
2. Click the Home tab.
3. Using the tools in the Number group, follow any of these steps:
   - Click the Accounting Number Format button to apply the currency style with two decimal places. You can choose a currency symbol other than your default (which is the $ sign in the United States) by clicking the down arrow at the right edge of the Accounting Number Format button.
   - Click the Percent Style button to add a percent sign with no decimal places.
   - Click the Comma Style button to add a comma format with two decimal places.

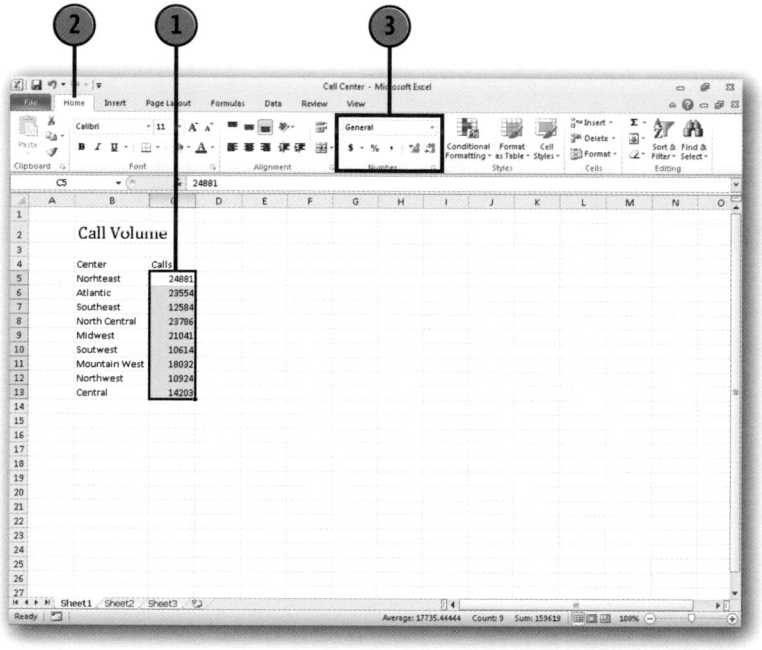

Set the Number of Decimal Places

1. Select the cells you want to format.
2. Click the Home tab.
3. Follow either of these steps:
   - Click the Increase Decimal button in the Number group on the ribbon.
   - Click the Decrease Decimal button in the Number group on the ribbon.

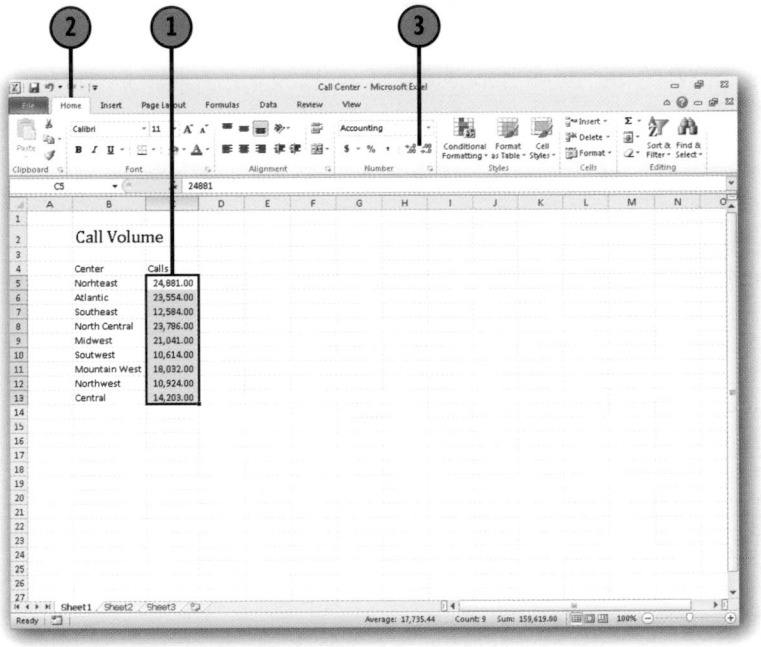

Tip

When you create a worksheet, you should apply the numerical formatting you want to all the cells in which you'll store numbers of a certain type. That way, when you type the data later (or copy it from another document), it will be formatted correctly.

Formatting Cells Containing Dates

In many cases, knowing when something happened is just as important as knowing what happened. If you run a garden supply store or nursery, for example, it's useful to know that you get most of your customers on the weekends but that you make most of your large sales (most likely to landscape architects and other stores) during the week. Excel recognizes when you enter a date in a cell and applies the program's default format to the date. There are many date formats to choose from, though—pick the one you like the best!

Set a Date Format

1. Select the cells you want to format as a date.
2. Click the Home tab.
3. In the Number group, click the dialog box launcher.
4. Click the Number tab.
5. Click Date.
6. Click the date format you want.
7. Click OK.

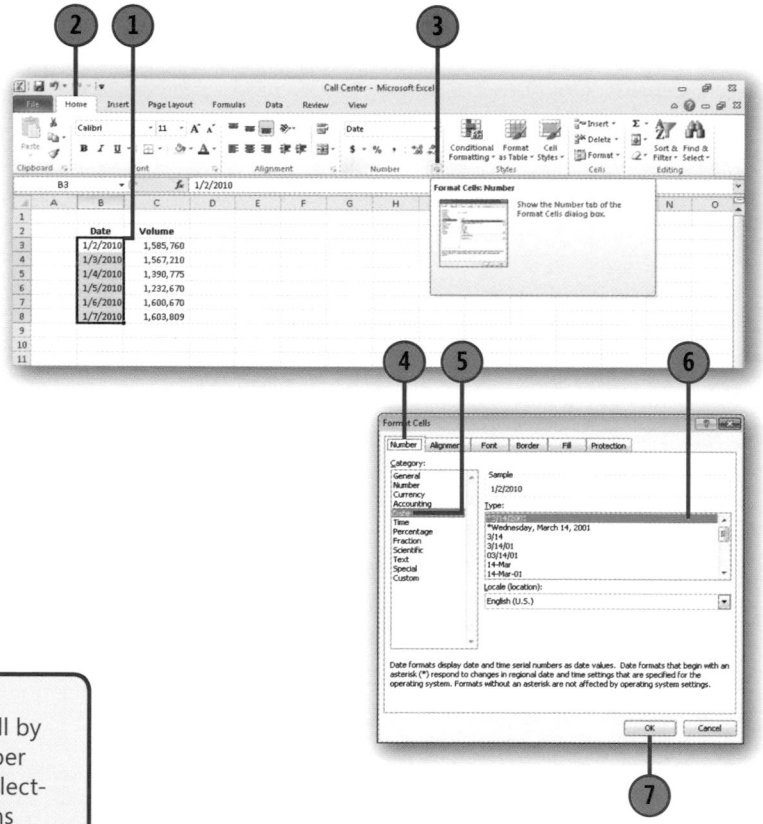

Tip

You can apply the Short Date or Long Date format to a cell by selecting the cell and then, on the Home tab, in the Number group, clicking the Number Format box's list arrow and selecting Short Date or Long Date. If the cell you format contains the date August 2, 2010, the Short Date format displays it as 8/2/2010 and the Long Date format displays it as Monday, August 2, 2010.

Adding Cell Backgrounds and Shading

Sometimes creating or applying a workbook theme is too much work. If all you want to do is highlight the value in a cell by changing the cell's background to red, you don't need to go to the trouble of finding the theme that includes red as one of its colors. Instead, you can simply change the background color of cells to make those cells stand out. Be sure there's enough contrast between the background and text colors, however. Very little is worse than having to squint at the monitor to read text that blends in with the background color.

Add Background Color

1. Select the cells you want to change.
2. Click the Home tab.
3. In the Font group, click the Fill Color down arrow.
4. Select the background color you want.

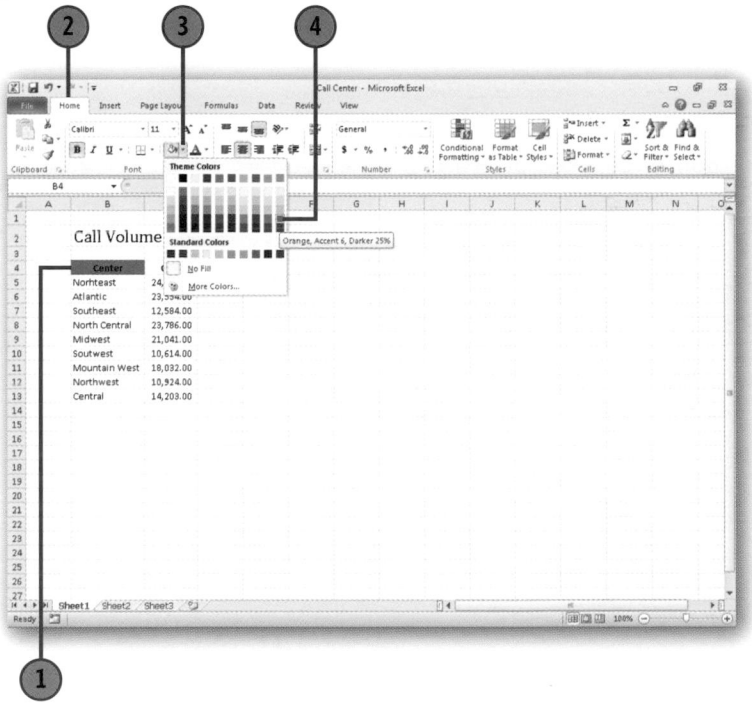

Tip

When you hover your mouse pointer over a color in the Fill Color palette, Excel 2010 displays a live preview of how your worksheet will appear if that color is applied.

Tip

After you apply a color, the Fill Color button changes to reflect your most recent choice. Clicking the button, rather than the down arrow at the right edge of the button, applies the previous choice to the active selection.

Change Background Shading

1. Select the cells you want to change.
2. Right-click the selection, and click Format Cells on the shortcut menu.
3. Click the Fill tab.
4. Click the Pattern Color down arrow, and then select the color you want.
5. Click the Pattern Style down arrow, and then select the pattern you want.
6. Click OK.

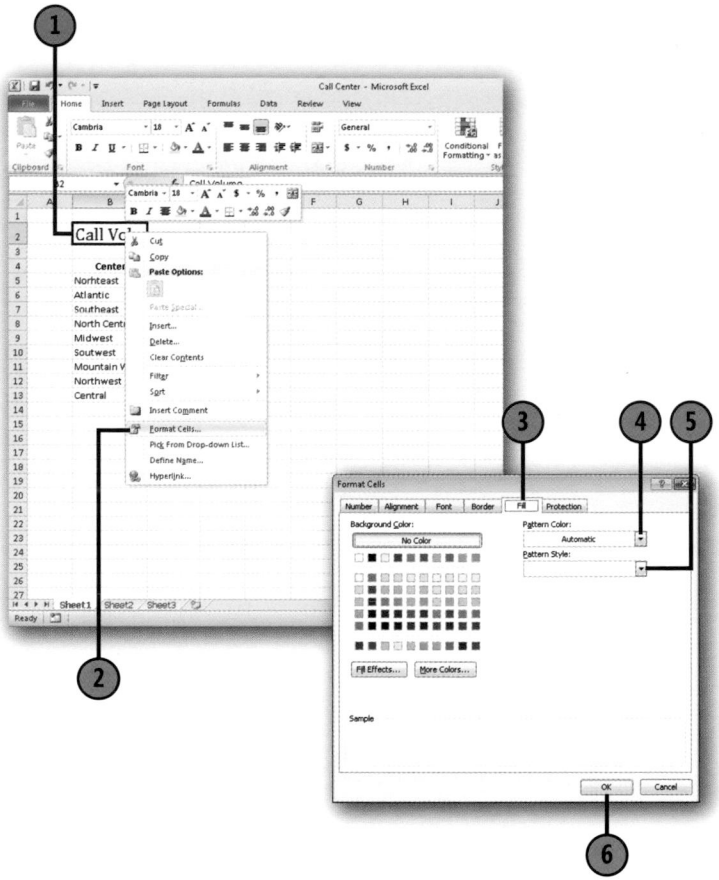

Formatting Cell Borders

The grid that appears on the standard worksheet uses light gray lines to mark cell boundaries, but those boundary lines don't distinguish one area of the worksheet from another.

One way you can make a group of cells stand out from other groups is to draw a border on the edge of the cells. You can also change the color of any border you add to your worksheet.

Draw Borders

1. Select the cells around which you want to draw a border.
2. Click the Home tab.
3. Click the Border button's down arrow.
4. Click the type of border you want to apply.

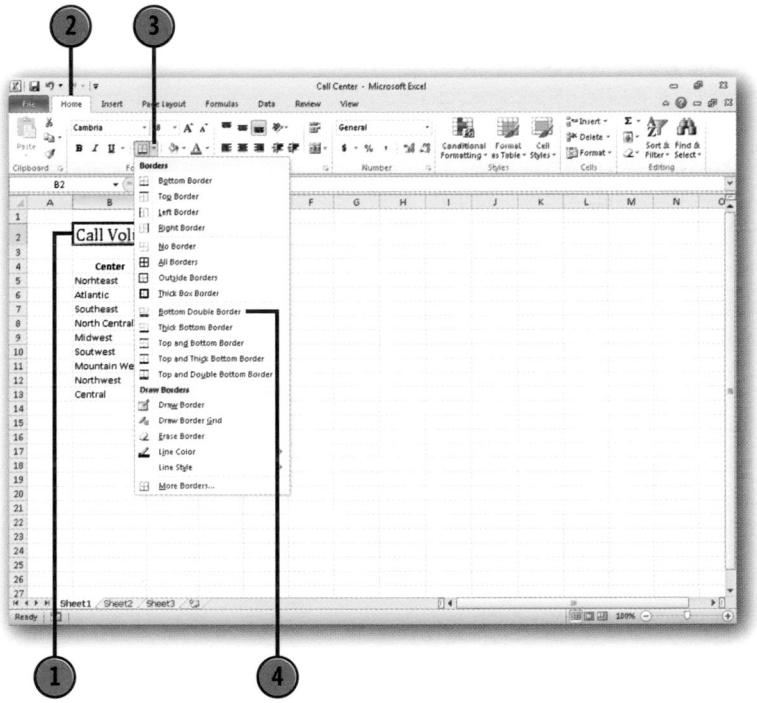

Format Cell Borders

1. Click the cell you want to format.
2. Click the Home tab.
3. Click the Font group's dialog box launcher.
4. Click the Border tab.
5. Select the line style.
6. Click the Color down arrow.
7. Click the color you want to use for the borders.
8. Select the borders you want to use.
9. Click OK.

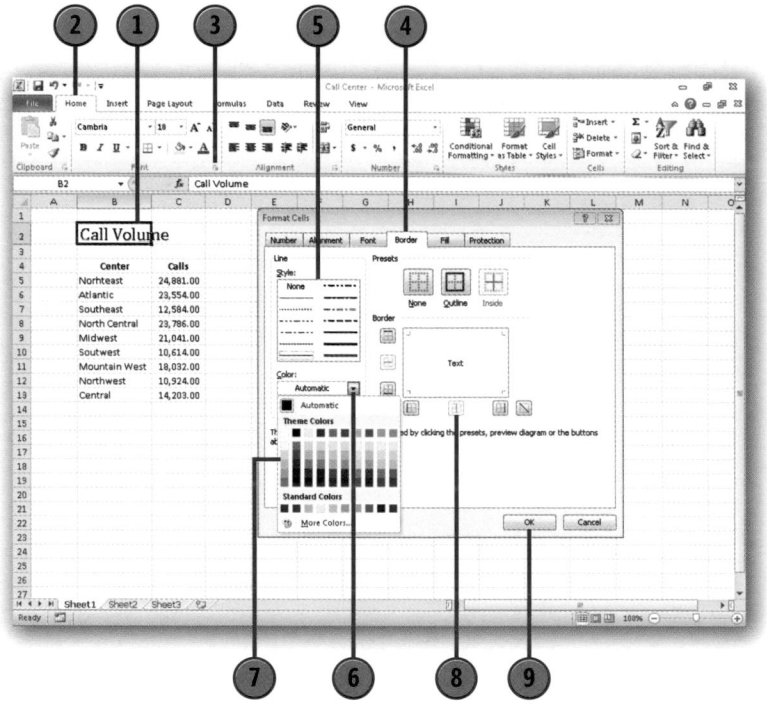

Defining Cell Styles

When you develop a worksheet, you will probably create a set of formats you want to apply consistently to certain parts of it. For example, you might always want your column headings to be slightly larger and in a different font from the body of the worksheet. You can save the formatting you want for a worksheet element as a style, which you then can apply to appropriate parts of your worksheets. Excel 2010 makes using styles much easier than previous versions. Not only do you have more built-in styles from which to choose, it's also no trouble to create a custom style of your own.

Apply a Style

1. Select the cells you want to change.
2. Click the Home tab.
3. In the Styles group, click Cell Styles.
4. Click a style.

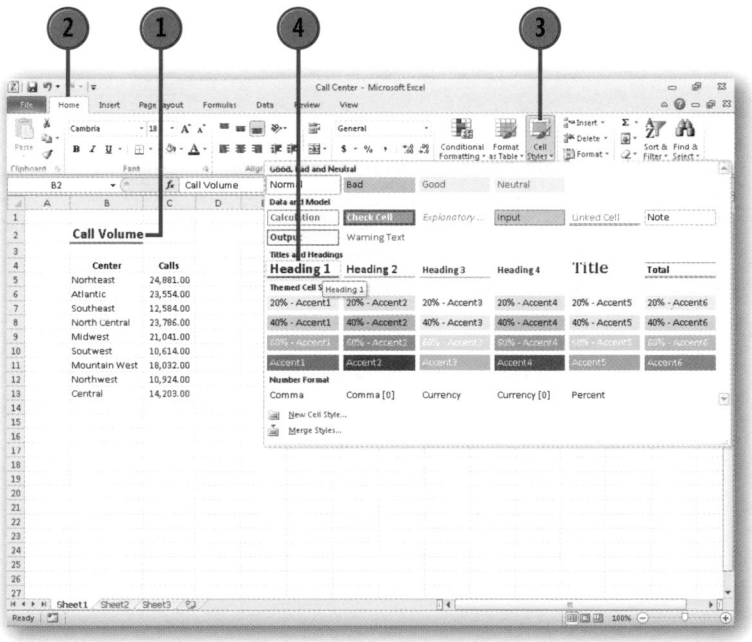

Tip

When you hover the mouse pointer over a style, the selected cells change their appearance to preview how the cells will appear if you apply that style.

Create a Style

1. Click the Home tab.
2. In the Styles group on the ribbon, click Cell Styles.
3. Click New Cell Style.
4. Type a new style name.
5. Click Format.
6. Specify the formatting you want this style to contain.
7. Click OK.
8. Click OK.

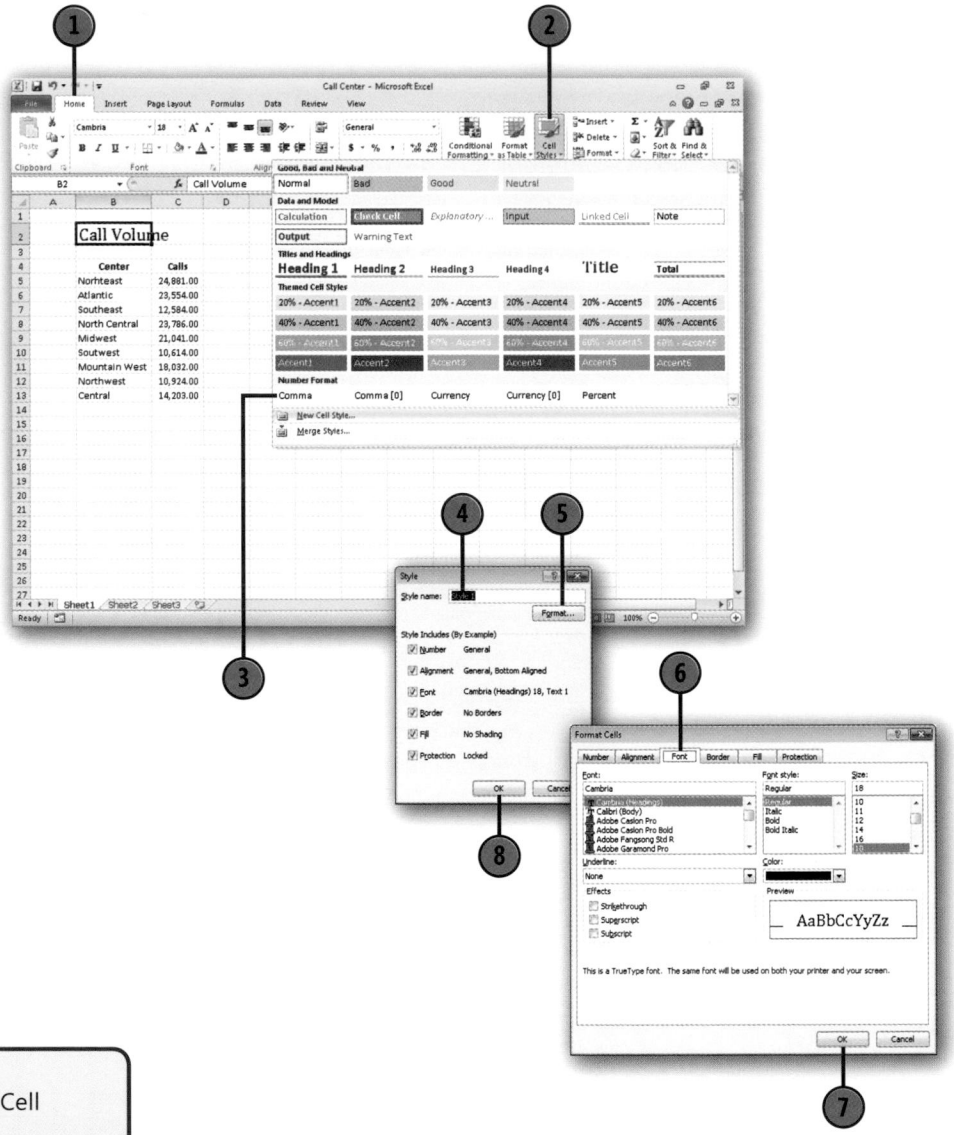

Tip

Any custom styles you create appear at the top of the Cell Styles gallery.

Modify a Style

1. Click the Home tab.
2. In the Styles group on the ribbon, click Cell Styles.
3. Right-click the style you want to modify.
4. Click Modify.
5. Click Format.
6. Specify the formatting you want.
7. Click OK twice.

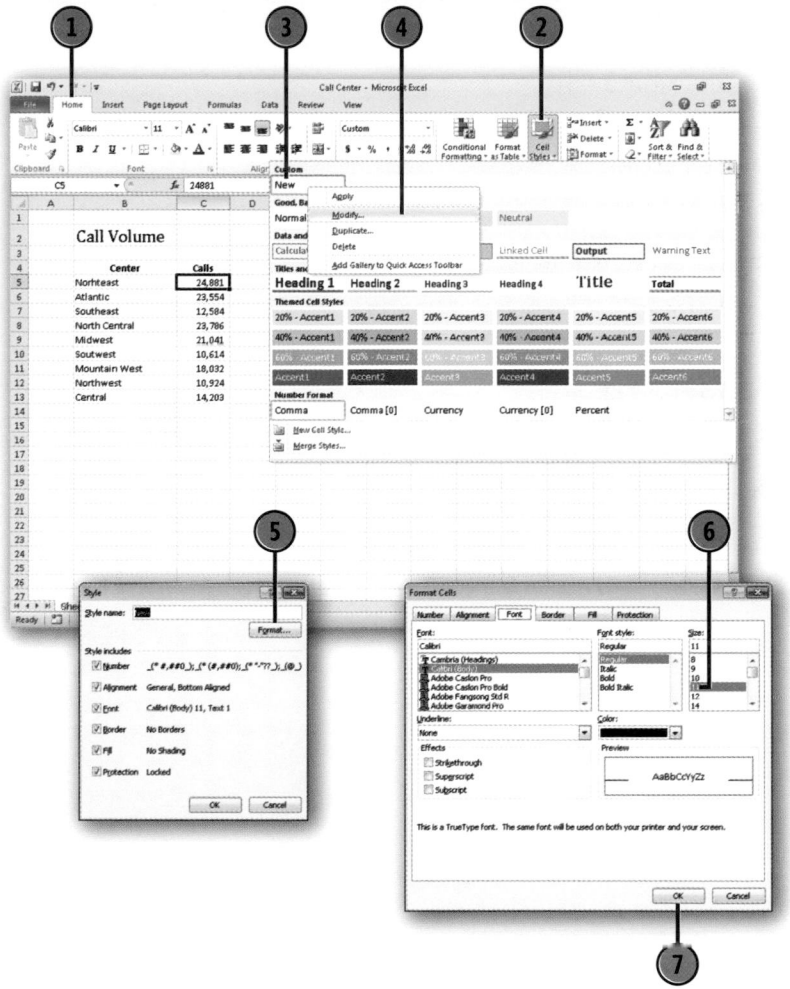

Delete a Style

1. Click the Home tab.
2. In the Styles group on the ribbon, click Cell Styles.
3. Right-click the style you want to delete.
4. Click Delete.

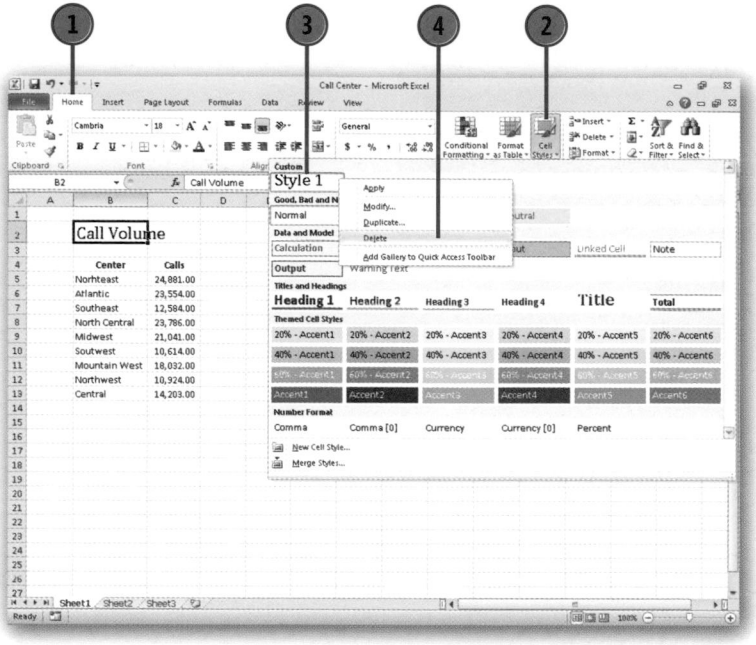

Aligning and Orienting Cell Contents

Most of the time you will want your text to be square with the left edge of a cell, but headings are much easier to read (and stand out better) when they're centered in a cell, and numbers are easier to read when the last digit of every number is flush with the right edge of a column. Similarly, if you want to create a tall, thin cell with text written in a vertical line, you can do so by typing your text in a cell and then changing the content's orientation. When your data doesn't fit neatly within the width of a cell, you can choose to have the text displayed on a new line in the same cell. This setting, called text wrapping, treats a cell like a small text box with narrow margins.

Change Text Alignment

1. Select the cells you want to align.
2. Click the Home tab.
3. Using the controls in the Alignment group on the ribbon, follow any of these steps:
   - Click the Align Left button to align the text with the left edge of the cell.
   - Click the Center button to center the text horizontally within the cell.
   - Click the Align Right button to align the text with the right edge of the cell.
   - Click the Top Align button to align the text with the top of the cell.
   - Click the Middle Align button to center the text vertically within the cell.
   - Click the Bottom Align button to align the text with the bottom edge of the cell.

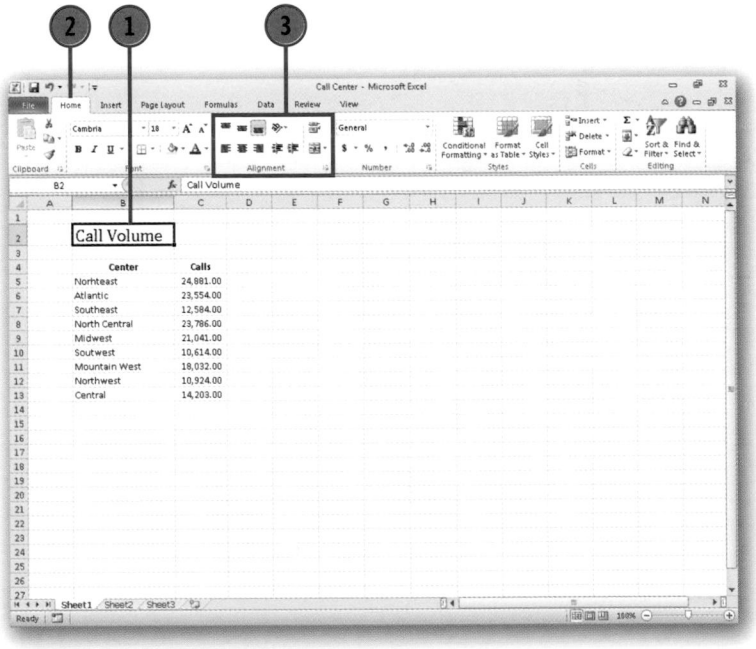

Set Text Orientation and Wrapping

1. Select the cells you want to orient.
2. Click the Home tab.
3. Using the controls in the Alignment group on the ribbon, follow either or both of these steps:
   - Click the Orientation button, and then select the orientation for your cell text.
   - Click the Wrap Text button to wrap the text to fit inside the column width.

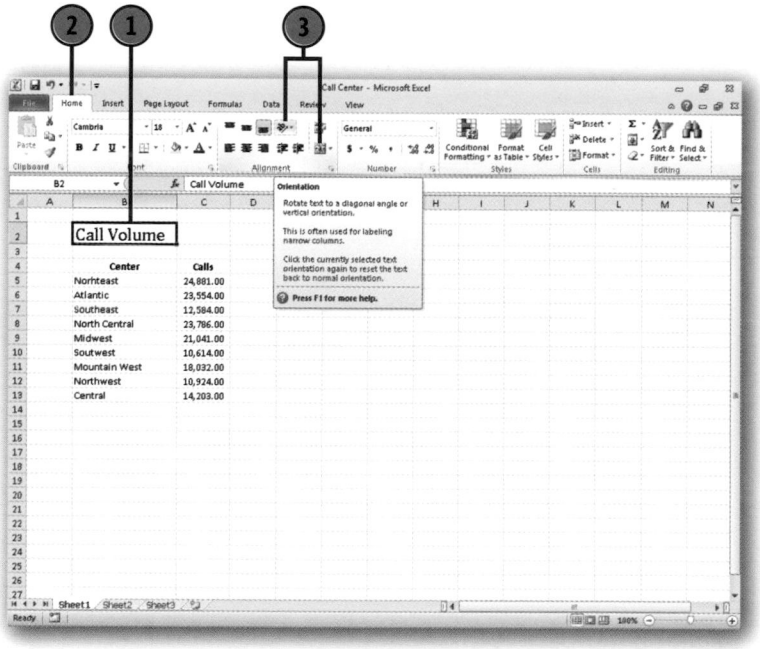

Tip

If you want more control over how to rotate the text within a cell, right-click the cells you want to orient and choose Format Cells from the shortcut menu. In the Format Cells dialog box, click the Alignment tab, type the number of degrees you want to rotate the baseline of your text, and then click OK.

Formatting a Cell Based on Conditions

Another way you can make your data easier to interpret is to change the appearance of your data based on the value in a cell. This kind of formatting is called conditional formatting because the data must meet certain conditions to have a format applied to it. For example, if you use a worksheet to track your customers' credit lines, you could have a customer's outstanding balance appear in red if they are within 10 percent of their credit limit.

Excel 2010 enables you to create an unlimited number of conditions (you were previously limited to three), allows more than one condition to be applied to a cell, and makes it easier for you to manage your conditions.

Change the Format of a Cell Based on Its Value

1. Select the cells you want to change.
2. Click the Home tab.
3. In the Styles group on the ribbon, click Conditional Formatting.
4. Click New Rule.

(continued on next page)

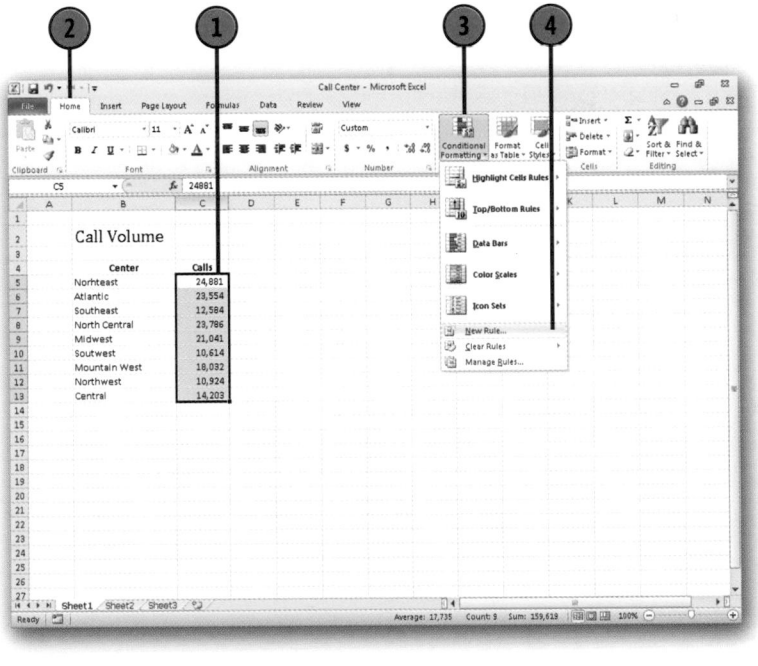

Change the Format of a Cell Based on Its Value *(continued)*

5. Click Format Only Cells That Contain.
6. Click the Comparison Phrase down arrow.
7. Click the comparison phrase you want.
8. Type the constant values or formulas you want evaluated.
9. Click Format.
10. Specify the formatting you want, and click OK.
11. Click OK.

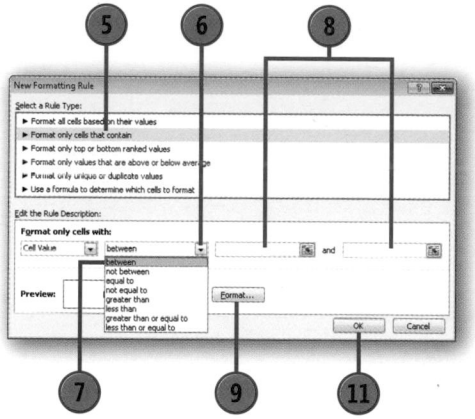

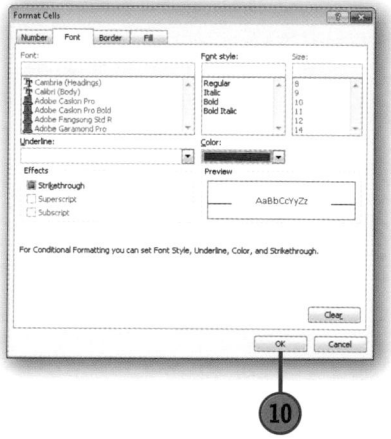

Caution

The layout of the Edit The Rule Description pane changes to reflect the rule type you choose. Don't be surprised if you see a different number of fields than are shown here.

Change the Format of a Cell Based on the Results of a Formula

1. Select the cells you want to change.
2. Click the Home tab.
3. In the Styles group on the ribbon, click Conditional Formatting.
4. Click New Rule.
5. Click Use A Formula to determine which cells to format.
6. Type the formula you want evaluated.
7. Click Format.
8. Specify the formatting you want, and click OK.
9. Click OK.

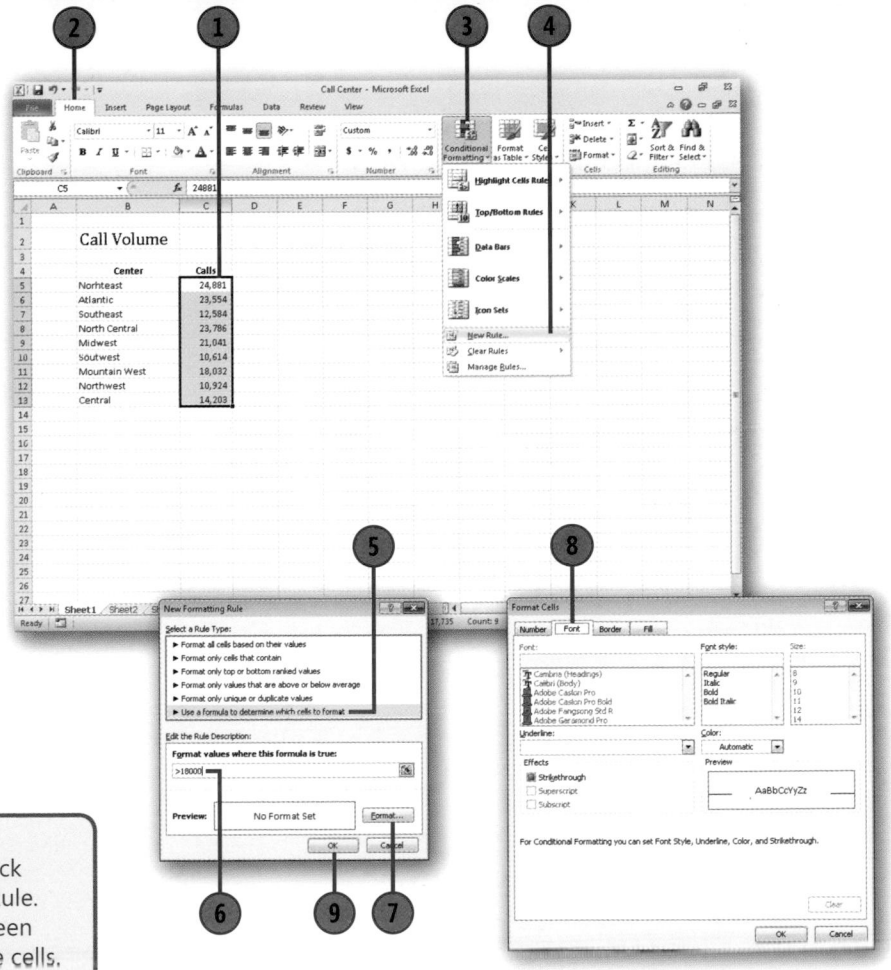

Try This!

In a blank worksheet, click cell A1, click the Home tab, click the Conditional Formatting button, and then click New Rule. Define a condition that applies when a cell value is between 400 and 1,000. Specify bold formatting be applied to the cells. Click OK. Define a second condition that applies when a cell value is less than 400. Specify italic formatting be applied to the cells. Click OK. Type 450 in cell A1, and press Enter. The cell's contents are displayed in bold type. Click cell A1, type 350, and press Enter. The cell's contents are now displayed in italics.

Edit a Conditional Formatting Rule

1. Select the cells that contain the rule you want to edit.
2. Click the Home tab.
3. In the Styles group, click Conditional Formatting.
4. Click Manage Rules.
5. Click the rule you want to change.
6. Click Edit Rule.
7. Use the controls to make your changes.
8. Click OK twice to save your changes.

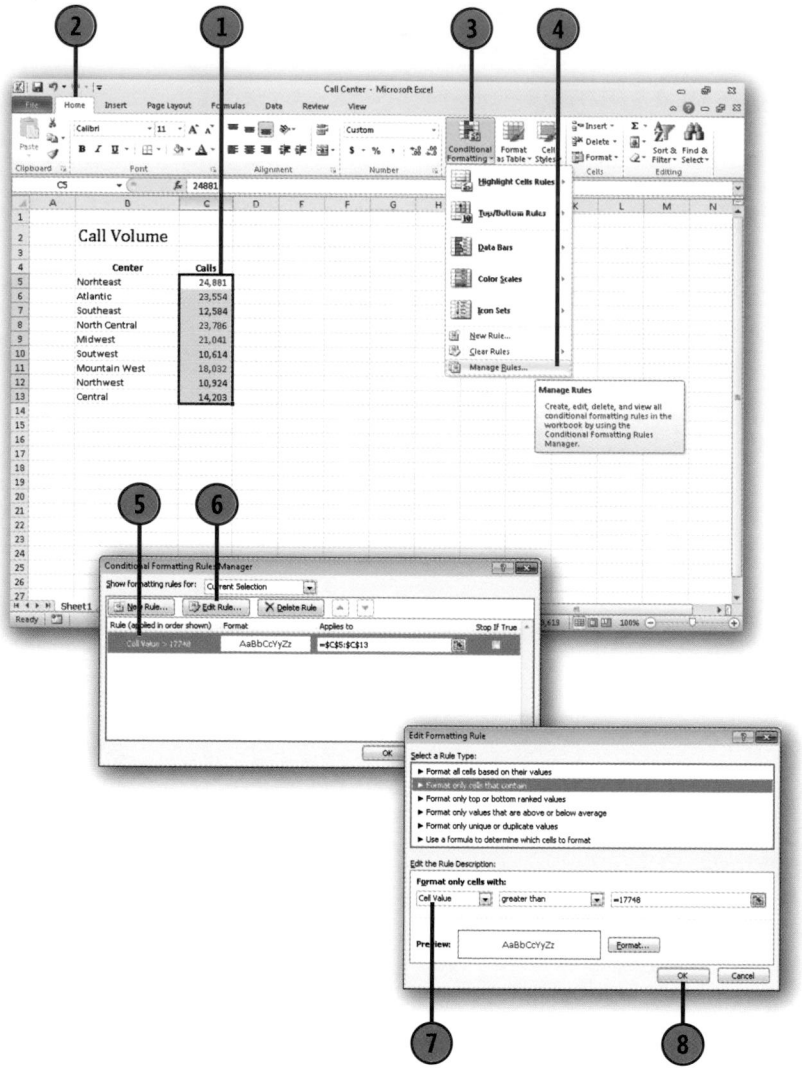

Delete a Conditional Formatting Rule

1. Select the cells that contain the rule you want to edit.
2. Click the Home tab.
3. In the Styles group, click Conditional Formatting.
4. Click Manage Rules.
5. Click the rule you want to delete.
6. Click Delete Rule.
7. Click OK.

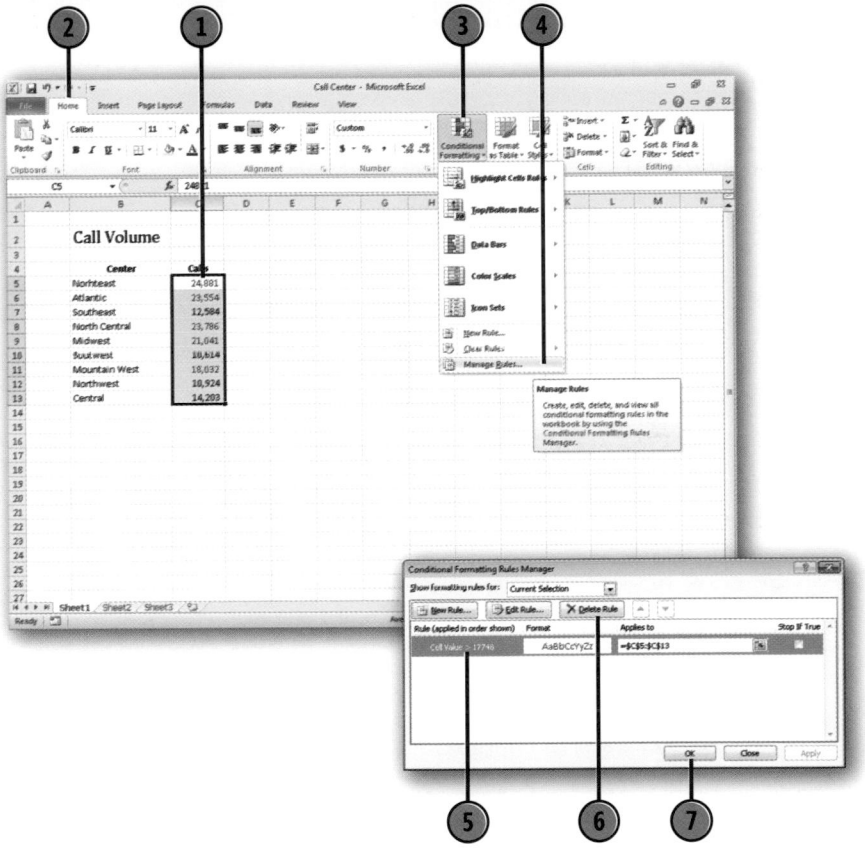

Changing How Conditional Formatting Rules Are Applied

Excel 2010 enables you to create powerful conditional formatting rules, but that's not the only new trick in your conditional formatting bag. In prior versions of the program, when Excel found a condition that applied to your cell data, it stopped checking. That meant that if you had one rule that formatted values of more than 1,000 as bold text and another that formatted values of more than 1,500 as italic text, the value 1,600 would be formatted according only to the first rule applied.

In Excel 2010, you can decide whether Excel should stop after it finds a rule that applies to your data or continue to check other rules. You can also change the order in which Excel checks your conditions to control how Excel applies the rules. Rule order matters only if you choose to have Excel stop after it applies a rule.

Stopping When a Condition Is Met

1. Select the cells that contain the rule you want to edit.
2. Click the Home tab.
3. In the Styles group, click Conditional Formatting.
4. Click Manage Rules.
5. Click the rule you want to change.
6. Select the Stop If True check box.
7. Click OK.

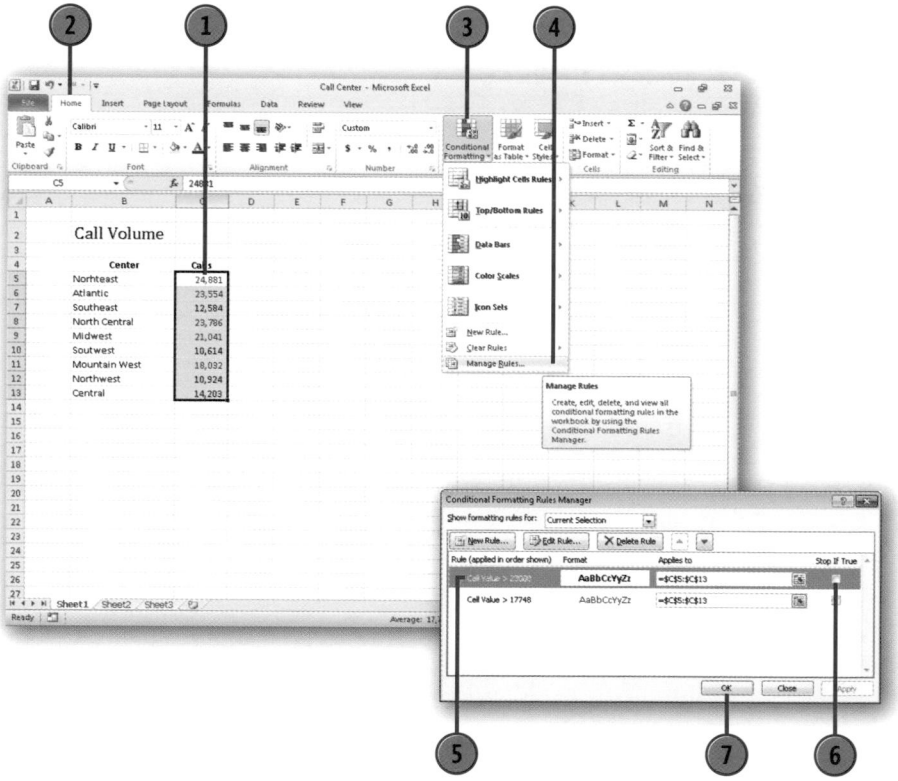

Change the Order of Conditions

1. Select the cells that contain the rules you want to edit.
2. Click the Home tab.
3. In the Styles group, click Conditional Formatting.
4. Click Manage Rules.
5. Click the rule you want to change.
6. Follow either of these steps:
   - Click the Move Up button to move the rule one place higher in the order.
   - Click the Move Down button to move the rule one place lower in the order.
7. Click OK.

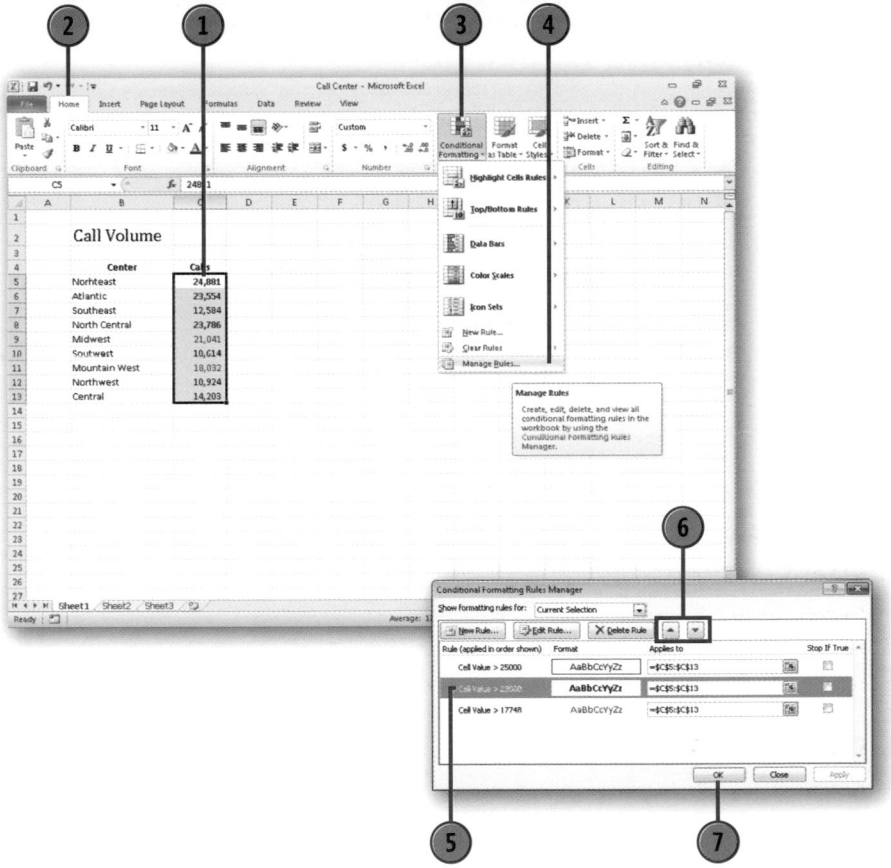

Displaying Data Bars, Icon Sets, or Color Scales Based on Cell Values

Organizations of all kinds track their performance data in Microsoft Excel. The specific numbers are important, of course, but it's also important that you be able to tell how the numbers relate to each other and whether your department is meeting its performance goals. Color scales and data bars show how the data in a cell compares to other data in a selected range. The higher a value is in relation to the other values in the range, the longer the data bar or the more the color is toward the high end of the scale. Icon sets, by contrast, test a value to see whether it is in the top, middle, or bottom third of the values in the range. You can change the tests to determine which icon or color is shown when.

Display Data Bars

1. Select the cells that contain your data.
2. Click the Home tab.
3. In the Styles group on the ribbon, click Conditional Formatting.
4. Point to Data Bars.
5. Click the data bar option you want to apply.

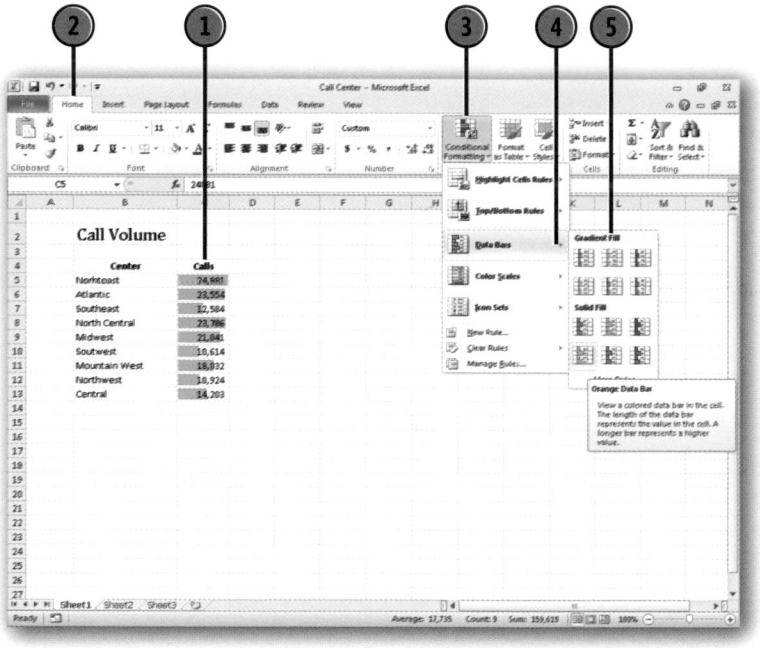

Display Icon Sets

1. Select the cells that contain your data.
2. Click the Home tab.
3. In the Styles group on the ribbon, click Conditional Formatting.
4. Point to Icon Sets.
5. Click the icon set you want to apply.

Display Color Scales

1. Select the cells that contain your data.
2. Click the Home tab.
3. In the Styles group on the ribbon, click Conditional Formatting.
4. Point to Color Scales.
5. Click the color scale pattern you want to apply.

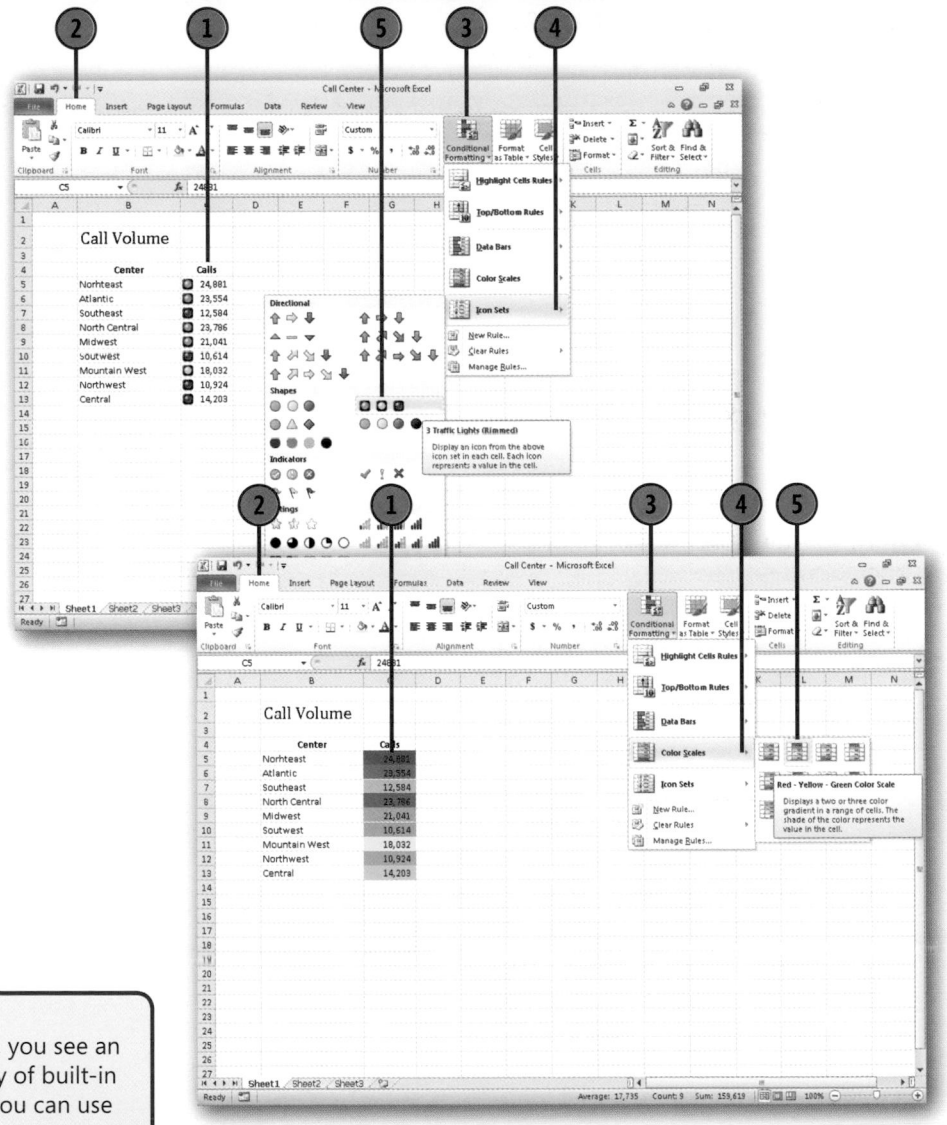

Tip

When you click Data Bars, Icon Sets, or Color Scales, you see an item named More Rules at the bottom of the gallery of built-in formats. Clicking More Rules displays a dialog box you can use to control a format's details.

Deleting Conditional Formats

If you no longer want to use conditional formats to summarize the data in your workbook, you can delete the formats without affecting the underlying data. When you delete a conditional format, you can select whether to do so for the selected cells, the entire sheet, the active PivotTable, or the active Excel table.

Delete Conditional Formats

1. Select the cells with the conditional formatting you want to delete.
2. Click the Home tab.
3. In the Styles group on the ribbon, click Conditional Formatting.
4. Point to Clear Rules.
5. Click the set of rules you want to delete.

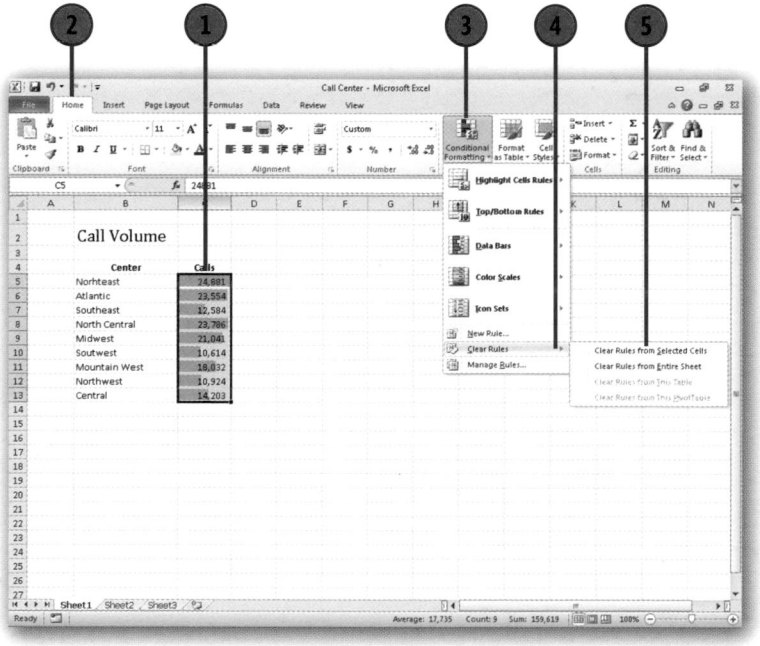

Copying Formats with Format Painter

After you create a format for a cell or group of cells, you can copy the format to another group of cells using Format Painter. Format Painter lets you copy the format quickly, saving you the time and effort it takes to copy the contents of another cell with the formats you want and then changing the data or formula.

Copy Styles with Format Painter

1. Select the cells with the formatting you want to copy.
2. Click the Home tab.
3. In the Clipboard group, click the Format Painter button.
4. Select the cells where you want the formatting applied.

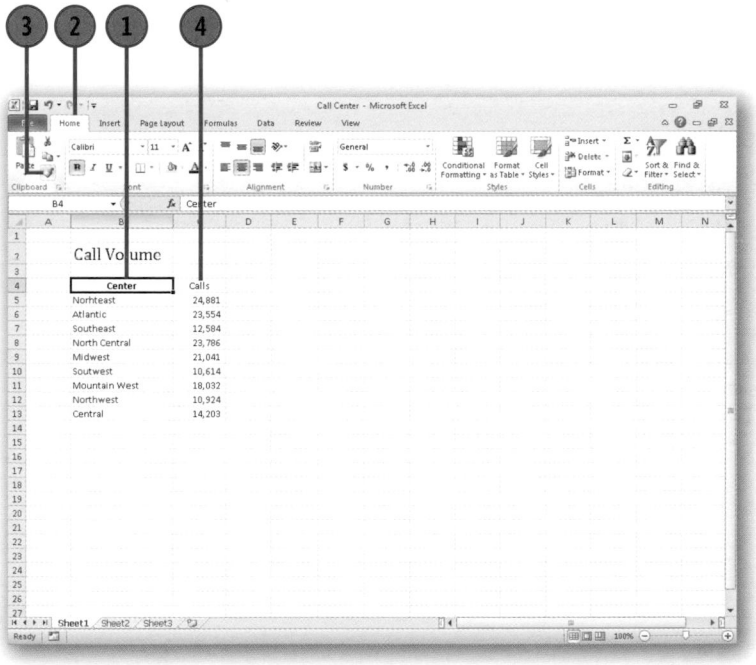

Merging or Splitting Cells or Data

You can change a row's height or a column's width, but this might not be the best way to improve your worksheet's usability. For instance, a label might not fit within a single cell, and increasing that cell's width—or every cell's width—might throw off the worksheet's design. One solution to this problem is to merge two or more cells. Merging cells allows you to treat a group of cells as a single cell as far as content and formatting go.

Merge Several Cells into One

1. Select the cells you want to merge.
2. Click the Home tab.
3. In the Alignment group, click the Merge & Center button.

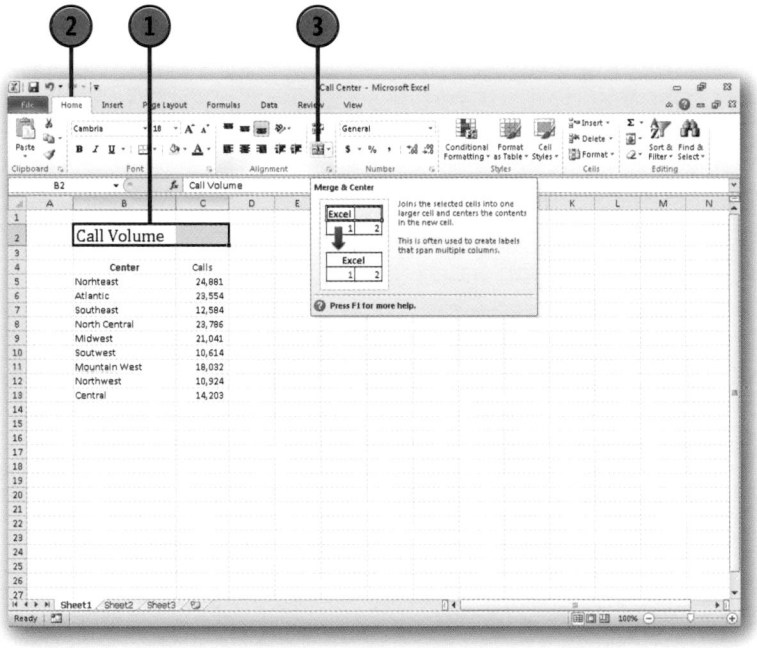

Caution

If the cells you select have data in more than one cell, only the data in the upper-left cell remains after you merge the cells.

Split a Merged Cell

1. Click the merged cell.
2. Click the Home tab.
3. Click the down arrow at the right edge of the Merge & Center button.
4. Click Unmerge Cells.

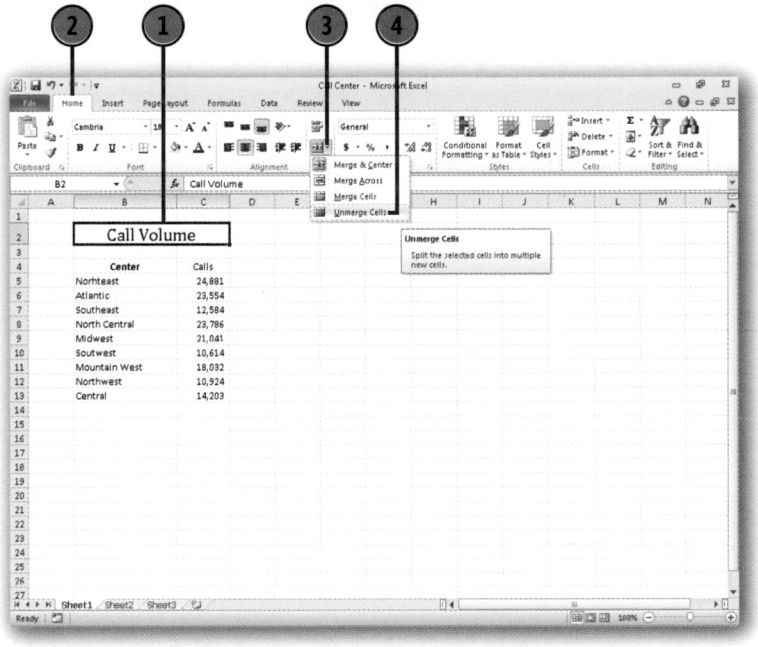

Tip

If you do not want the merged data centered, click a different alignment from the Alignment group on the Home tab.

8 Formatting the Worksheet

In this section:

- Applying Workbook Themes
- Coloring Sheet Tabs
- Changing a Worksheet's Gridlines
- Changing Row Heights and Column Widths
- Inserting, Moving, and Deleting Rows and Columns
- Hiding and Showing Rows and Columns
- Protecting Worksheets from Changes

Microsoft Excel 2010 enables you to change your worksheets' appearance and structure to display your data effectively. For example, you can make rows and columns surrounding your data wider or taller to separate your figures from the worksheet's other contents. You can also move entire rows or columns to different locations in the workbook, such as when a worksheet's data columns are in a different order from those of a related paper form. If you want to call attention to one of your worksheets, perhaps one that contains new data your boss should review, you can change the color of that worksheet's sheet tab so that it stands out within the workbook.

Applying Workbook Themes

Designing attractive Excel worksheets challenges even the most advanced users. Excel 2010 comes with a wide variety of attractive themes that you can apply to your worksheets.

But you're not limited to the themes included when you install Excel! You can create your own themes and find many more themes on the Microsoft Office Online Web site.

Apply a Workbook Theme

1. Click the Page Layout tab.
2. In the Themes group on the ribbon, click Themes.
3. Click the theme you want to apply.

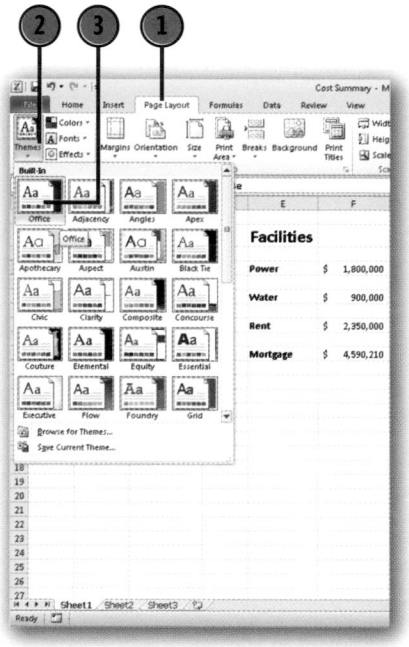

Change Colors Within a Theme

1. Click the Page Layout tab.
2. In the Themes group on the ribbon, click Colors.
3. Click the color scheme you want to apply.

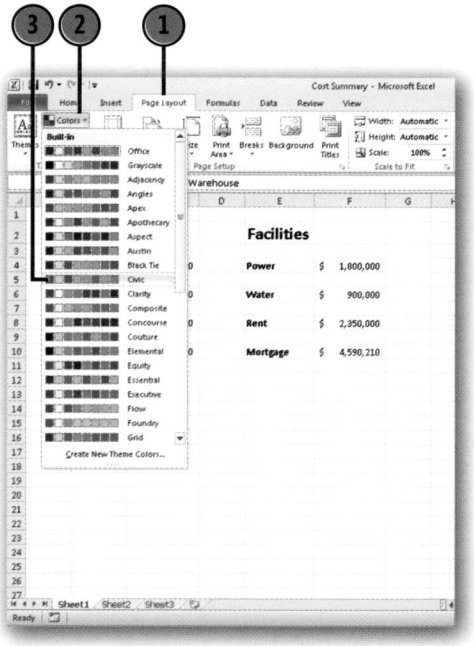

Change Fonts Within a Theme

1. Click the Page Layout tab.
2. In the Themes group on the ribbon, click Fonts.
3. Click the font scheme you want to apply.

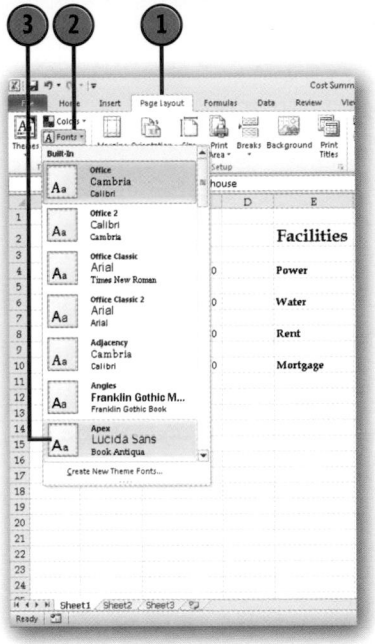

Change Effects Within a Theme

1. Click the Page Layout tab.
2. In the Themes group on the ribbon, click Effects.
3. Click the effects scheme you want to apply.

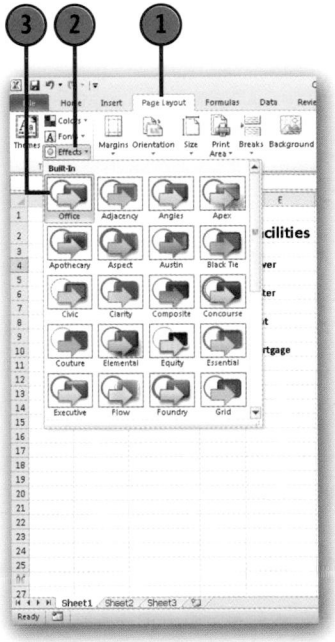

Create a New Workbook Theme

1. Format your worksheet with the colors, fonts, and effects you want to include in your theme.
2. Click the Page Layout tab.
3. In the Themes group on the ribbon, click Themes.
4. Click Save Current Theme.
5. Type a name for your theme.
6. Click Save.

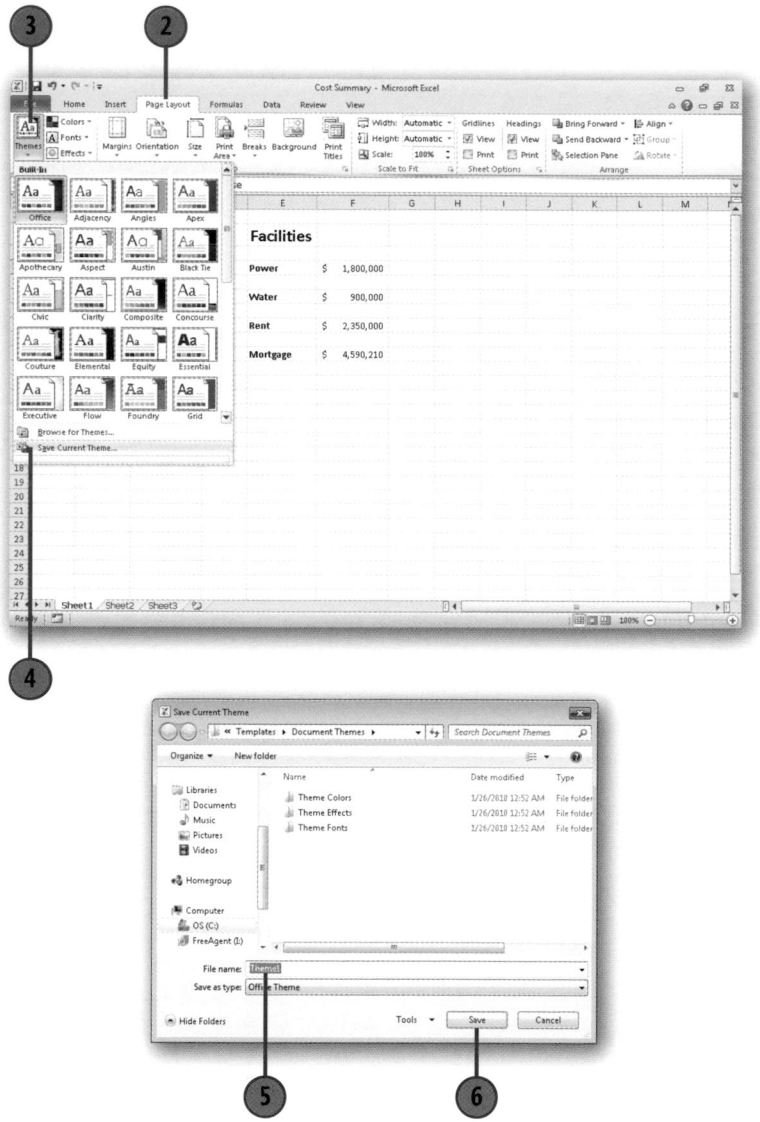

Coloring Sheet Tabs

A great way to make any worksheet element stand out is to change it to a color that contrasts with the other colors used in the worksheet. In Excel 2010, you can change the color of sheet tabs. For example, you can change the color of a sheet tab in a workbook in which you track sales for a year with a worksheet for each month. Rather than move the current worksheet to the front of the list, which would put the worksheets out of order, you can change the color of the sheet tab to make it stand out. When the month ends, you can remove the color from that sheet tab and apply it to the next month's sheet tab.

Color a Sheet Tab

1. Hold down the Ctrl key and click the sheet tabs you want to color.
2. Right-click the selection and point to Tab Color on the shortcut menu.
3. Click the color you want.

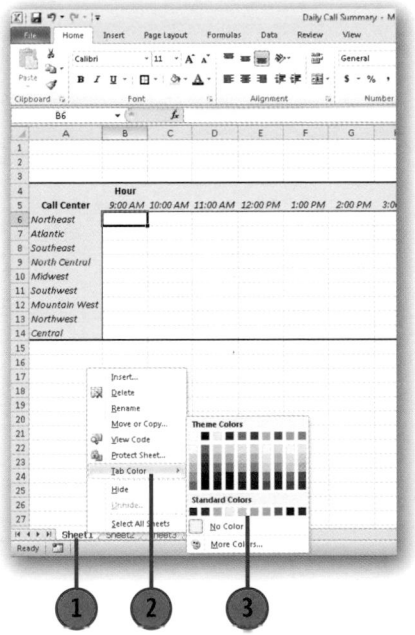

Tip

If you select a sheet tab color from the Theme Colors section of the color palette, changing your workbook's theme will change your sheet tabs' colors.

Changing a Worksheet's Gridlines

Gridlines are the lines on your worksheets that define the cells formed by the intersections of rows and columns. The default gridline color is gray, but not all worksheets work well with this standard setting. Sometimes you'll want to change the color of the cell gridlines or even turn them off. Excel 2010 also makes it easier than previous editions to control whether your gridlines appear when you print a worksheet.

Change the Color of Cell Gridlines

1. Click the File tab.
2. Click Options.
3. Click Advanced.
4. Click the Display Options For This Worksheet down arrow.
5. Select the worksheet, or workbook, to which you want to apply the change.
6. Click the Gridline Color button.
7. Select the color you want to use for the gridlines.
8. Click OK.

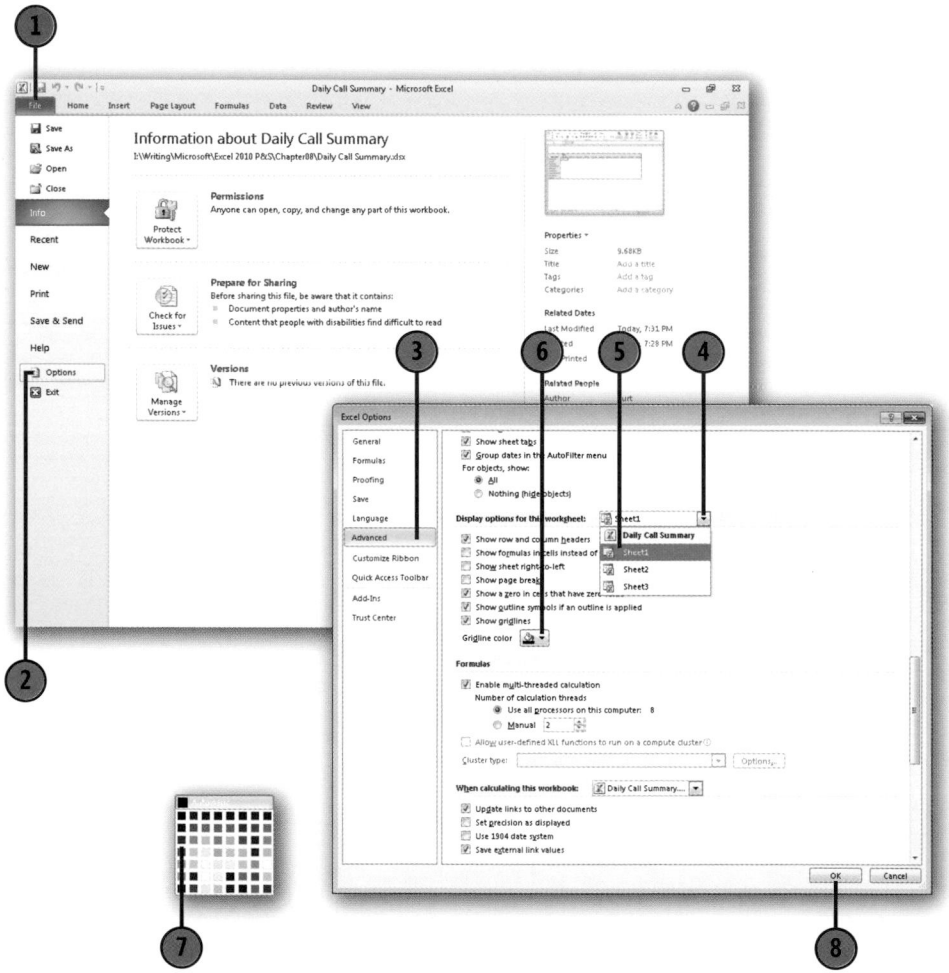

Show or Hide Cell Gridlines

1. Click the Page Layout tab.
2. Using the controls in the Sheet Options group on the ribbon, follow either or both of these steps using the check boxes in the Gridlines section of the group:
   - Select the View check box to show the gridlines as you work in Excel, or clear the View check box to hide the gridlines as you work.
   - Select the Print check box to show the gridlines when you print the worksheet, or clear the Print check box to hide the gridlines when you print.

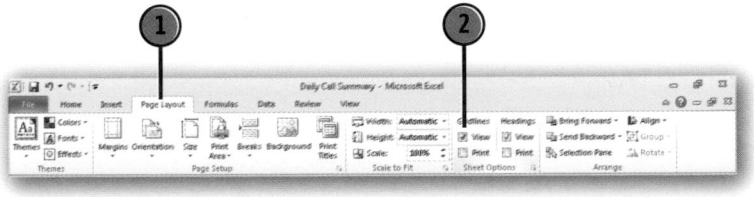

Changing Row Heights and Column Widths

When you create an Excel workbook, the default worksheet rows are tall enough to accommodate text and numbers entered in the standard character format (Calibri, 11 point) and wide enough to display about eight characters. If your text takes up too much space to fit in the cell (because you've changed the font size for a column label, for example), you can widen the column so that the contents of every cell can be seen. You can also increase the height of rows in your worksheet to put some space between values, which makes your data easier to read. If a column is too wide or a row is too high, you can make it narrower or shorter as needed.

Resize a Row

1. Hover the mouse pointer over the lower boundary of the row you want to resize until the mouse pointer turns into a two-headed arrow.
2. Drag the boundary until the row is the height you want.

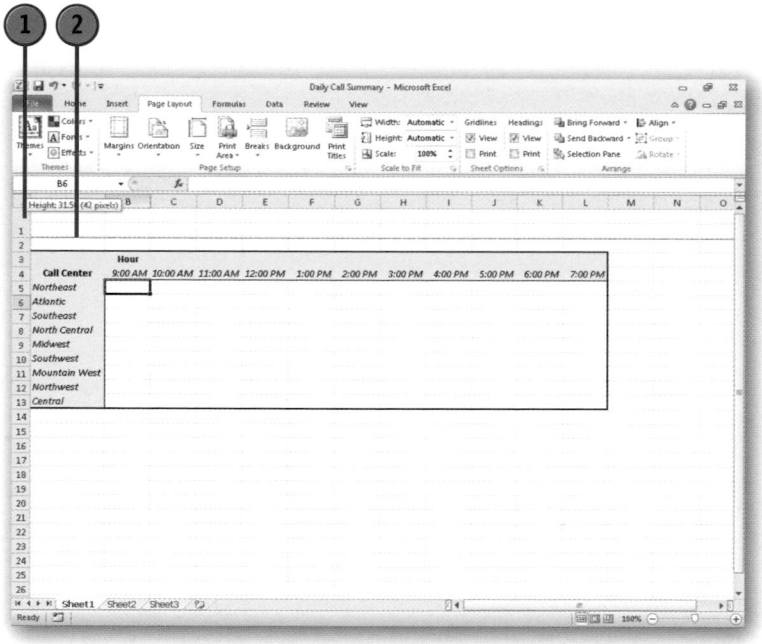

Resize a Column

1. Hover the mouse pointer over the right boundary of the column you want to resize until the mouse pointer turns into a two-headed arrow.
2. Drag the boundary until the column is the width you want.

Resize Multiple Rows or Columns

1. Select the rows or columns you want to resize.
2. Drag the border of any selected column or row to the width or height you want.

Tip

You can resize a column to fit the text of its widest cell by double-clicking the right boundary of the column.

Tip

If you want to set a specific row height or column width, select the rows or columns you want to format, select and right-click any row or column header, and choose either Column Width or Row Height from the shortcut menu. Type the width or height in the dialog box that appears, and click then OK.

Inserting Rows or Columns

After you create a worksheet and begin filling in your data, you might decide to insert a row or column to add data you didn't think to include when you started. For example, a customer might want to add a product to an order. To accommodate this, you can insert a blank row below the last row in the existing order and add the new item there. If you want to add a row in the middle of the existing order data, you can insert a blank row above an existing row. You can perform similar actions with columns: If you want to begin recording a new piece of information about your customers, such as a Web site or e-mail address, you can add a column to store that information. You can even use the Insert Options menu to format the new rows or columns.

Insert a Row in a Worksheet

1. Right-click the row header below where you want the new row to appear.
2. Choose Insert from the shortcut menu.

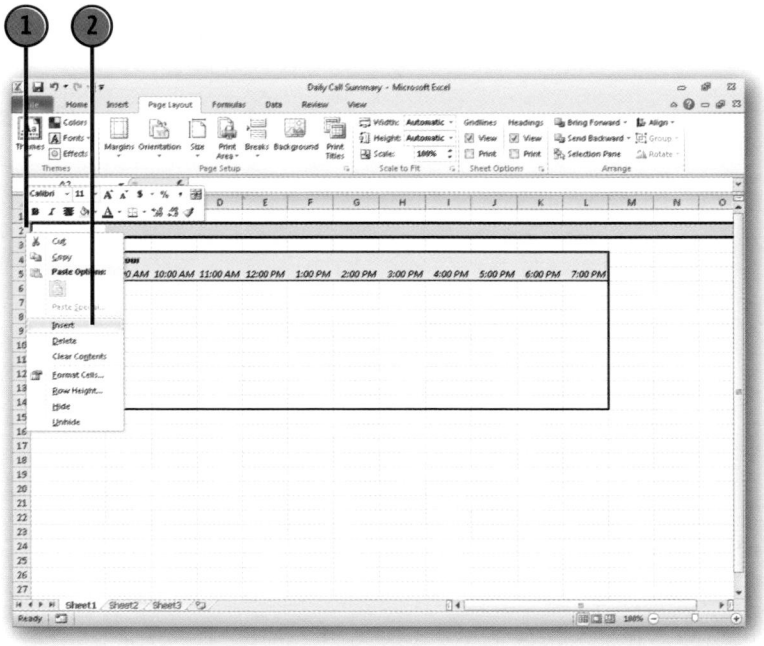

Insert a Column in a Worksheet

1. Right-click the column header to the right of where you want the new column to appear.
2. Choose Insert from the shortcut menu.

Set Insert Options

1. After inserting rows or columns, open the Insert Options menu.
2. Select the type of formatting you want the new cells to have.

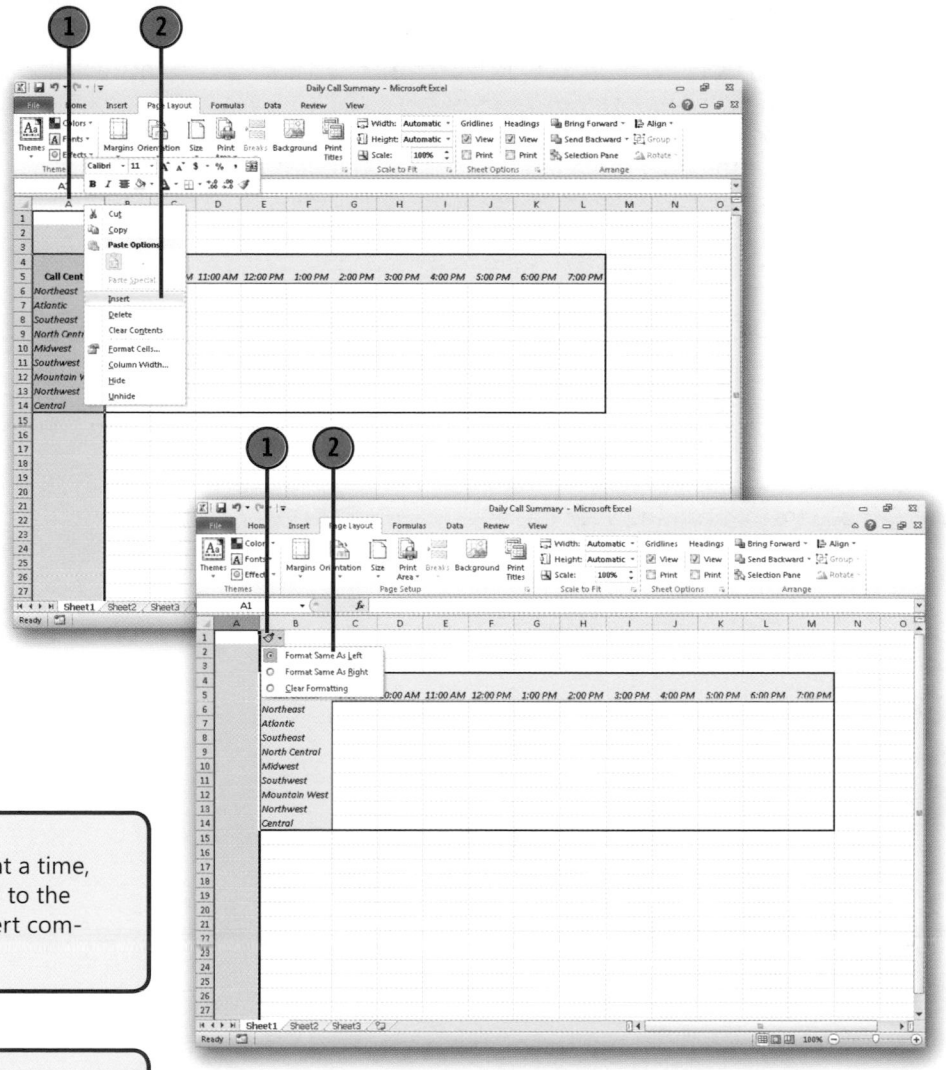

Tip

If you want to insert more than one row or column at a time, select the number of existing rows or columns equal to the number you want to insert and then choose the Insert command from the shortcut menu.

Tip

The Insert Options indicator appears only if the cells above or below the insertion point have special formatting.

Moving Rows and Columns

In many cases, the data in your worksheets is first recorded on paper—for example, when you record times for a race or collect customer responses on survey forms. Sometimes it's easier to type the information into your worksheet so that it looks the same way as it looks on paper. You can move rows and columns to new positions on the worksheet in order to present the information the way you want it to look.

Move One or More Rows

1. Select the rows you want to move.
2. Click the Home tab.
3. In the Clipboard group, click the Cut button.
4. Click the first cell in the row where you want to move the rows.
5. In the Clipboard group, click Paste.

Move One or More Columns

1. Select the columns you want to move.
2. Click the Home tab.
3. In the Clipboard group, click the Cut button.
4. Click the first cell in the column where you want to move the columns.
5. In the Clipboard group, click Paste.

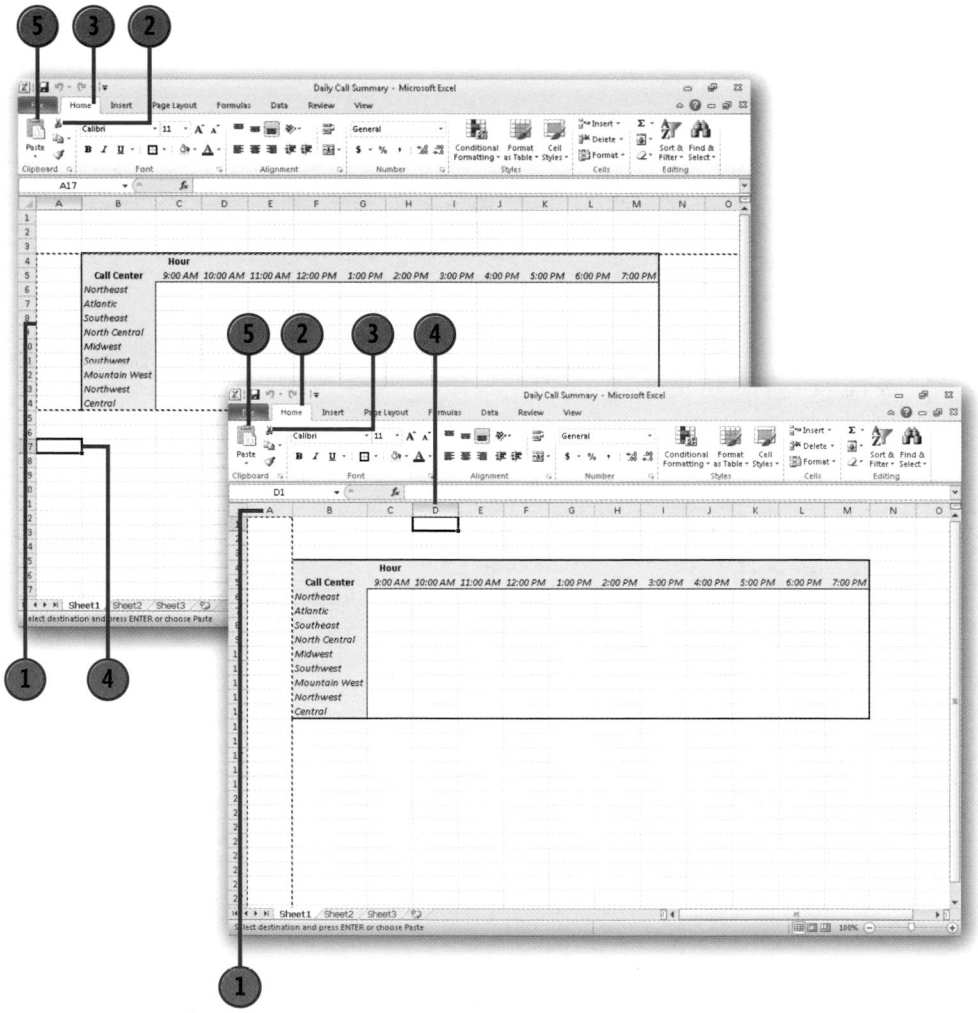

Deleting Rows and Columns

Excel workbooks are a great place to store and manipulate your data, but there might be times when you no longer need to use a particular row or column. Whether you placed an extra column to add some white space between the main body of data and a summary calculation, or a row holds the contact information of a customer who asked to be removed from your list, you can delete a row or column quickly and easily.

Delete a Row or Column

1. Select the row or column you want to delete.
2. Right-click the selection, and choose Delete from the shortcut menu.

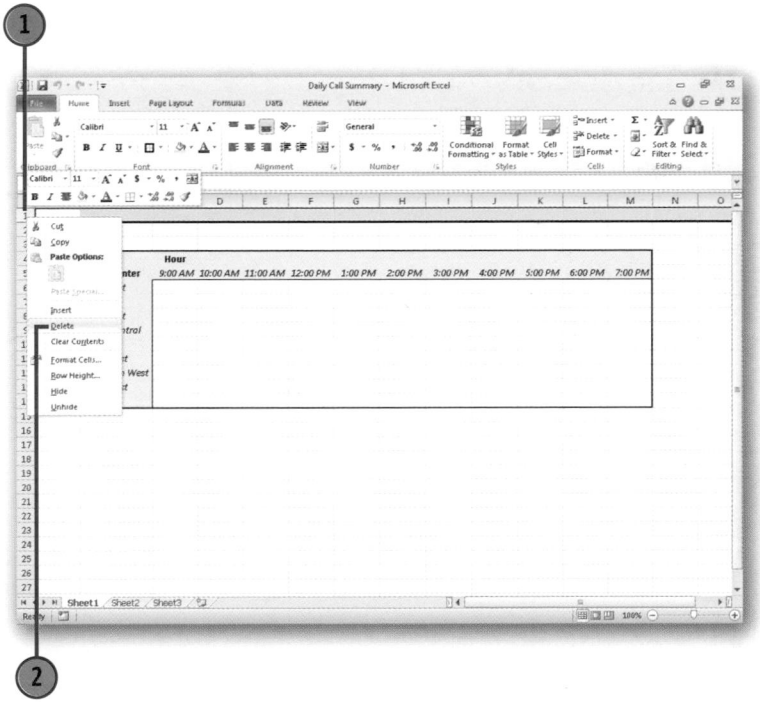

Caution

Formulas that reference cells in the columns or rows you delete will no longer work. The Error indicator tells you that an Invalid Cell Reference Error occurred and gives you options to fix the problem. #REF appears in the damaged cell.

Outlining to Hide and Show Rows and Columns

As you develop worksheets, you'll probably try to keep similar entries together. For example, if you create a worksheet that lists all the products you sell, you can group the products by category. In the case of a garden supply store, all the tools can be together, then the furniture, and then a new category for each type of plant. If you want to hide the rows for one set of products, you can define the rows as a group, and you then have the option to choose which rows you want to display. The rows you hide are gone only temporarily. The data isn't deleted, it's just moved out of your way while you don't need it.

Group Rows and Columns

1. Select the rows or columns you want to group.
2. Click the Data tab.
3. In the Outline group on the ribbon, click Group.

Ungroup Rows and Columns

1. Select the rows or columns you want to ungroup.
2. Click the Data tab.
3. In the Outline group on the ribbon, click Ungroup.

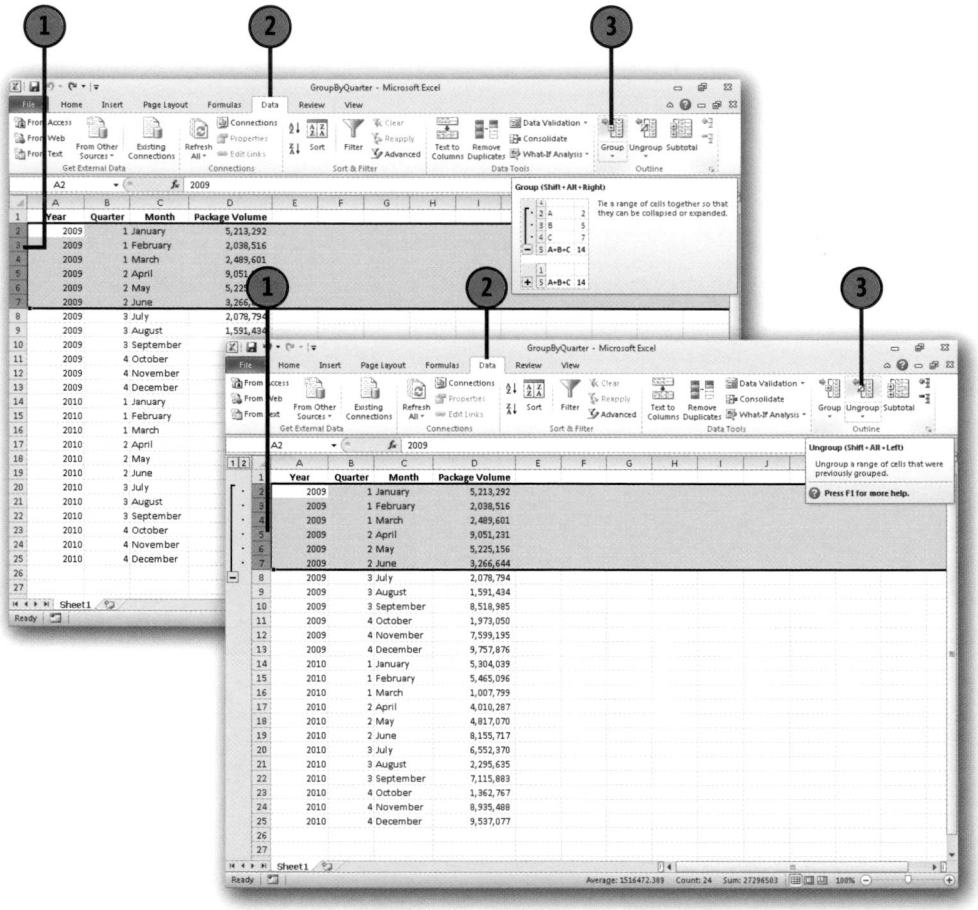

Hide Grouped Rows and Columns

1. Click the Hide Detail button next to the group you want to hide.

Show Grouped Rows and Columns

1. Click the Show Detail button next to the group you want to show.

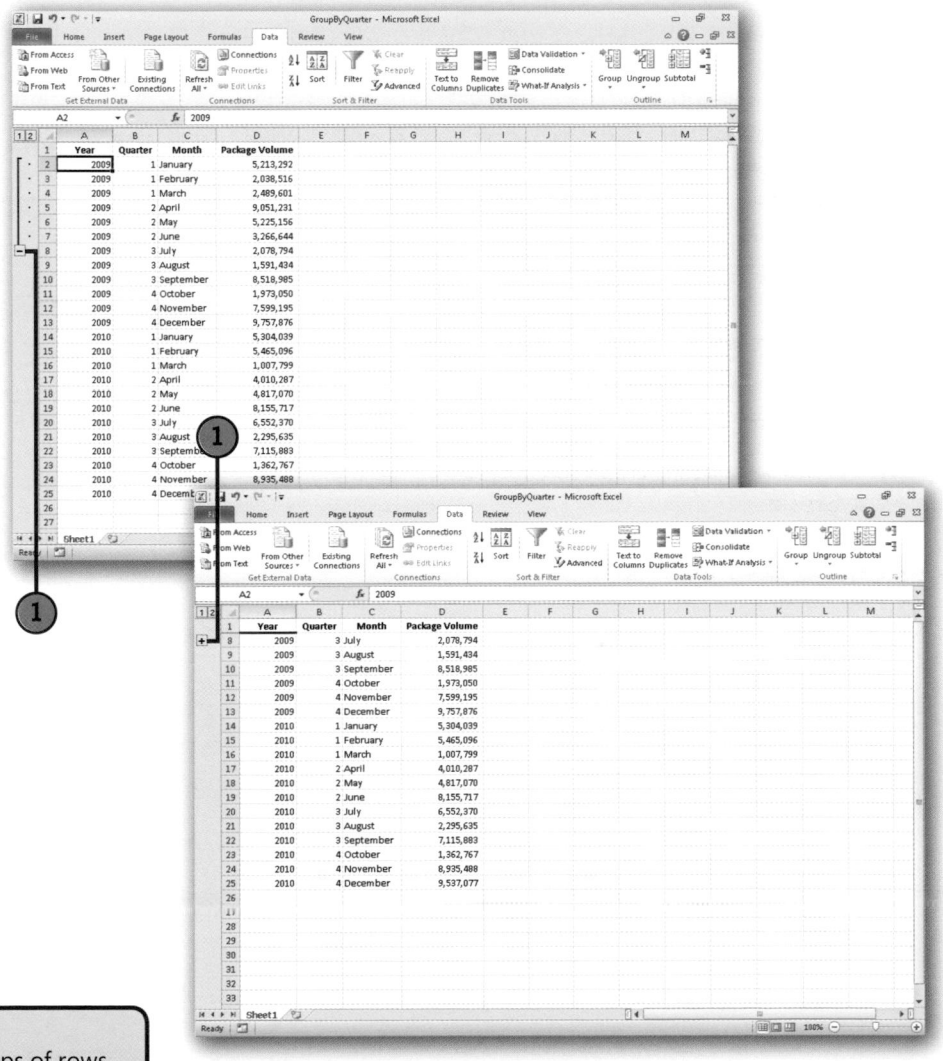

Year	Quarter	Month	Package Volume
2009	1	January	5,213,292
2009	1	February	2,038,516
2009	1	March	2,489,601
2009	2	April	9,051,231
2009	2	May	5,225,156
2009	2	June	3,266,644
2009	3	July	2,078,794
2009	3	August	1,591,434
2009	3	September	8,518,985
2009	4	October	1,973,050
2009	4	November	7,599,195
2009	4	December	9,757,876
2010	1	January	5,304,039
2010	1	February	5,465,096
2010	1	March	1,007,799
2010	2	April	4,010,287
2010	2	May	4,817,070
2010	2	June	8,155,717
2010	3	July	6,552,370
2010	3	August	2,295,635
2010	3	September	7,115,883
2010	4	October	1,362,767
2010	4	November	8,935,488
2010	4	December	9,537,077

See Also

For information about calculating subtotals for groups of rows, see "Summing with Subtotals and Grand Totals" on page 95.

Hiding Rows and Columns

If you're working with a worksheet that contains lots of data, you might need to refer to the contents of rows or columns that aren't close enough on the worksheet to appear on the same screen. Rather than scroll back and forth to access the data you need, you can hide any intervening rows or columns so that everything you need to see is displayed on the screen at the same time. The rows you hide are gone only temporarily. The data isn't deleted, it's just moved out of your way while you don't need it.

Hide Rows or Columns

1. Select the rows or columns you want to hide.
2. Right-click the selection, and choose Hide from the shortcut menu.

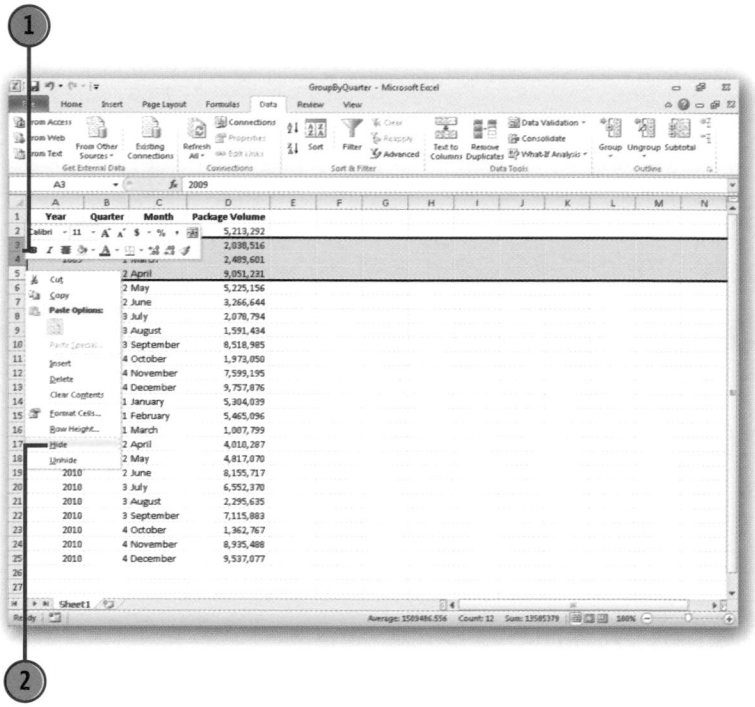

Tip

You can tell that there are hidden rows or columns in a worksheet in two ways. First, whenever rows or columns are hidden, row numbers or column letters are missing. For example, if rows 2 through 4 are hidden, the first two visible rows of the worksheet are labeled row 1 and row 5.

The other way you can tell that a worksheet contains hidden rows or columns is that a thick line appears on the border of the row header or column header where the rows or columns would otherwise appear.

Unhide Rows or Columns

1. Select the rows or columns that surround the rows or columns you want to unhide.
2. Right-click any of the selected row or column headers, and choose Unhide from the shortcut menu.

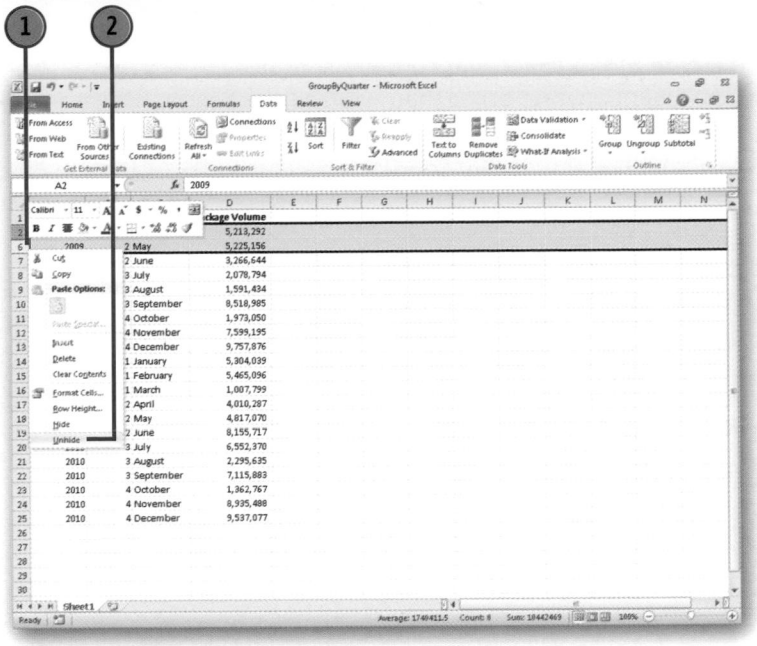

Protecting Worksheets from Changes

When you create a worksheet that contains sensitive data or data you don't want anyone other than yourself to change, you can protect the worksheet from unauthorized changes. In the Protect Sheet dialog box, you can choose the actions you want all users to be able to perform on the worksheet. The options selected by default allow anyone to select a cell but prevent them from deleting rows or columns, changing any formatting, or editing scenarios attached to the worksheet.

Protect a Worksheet

1. Click the Review tab.
2. Click Protect Sheet.
3. Select the protection options you want.
4. Click OK.

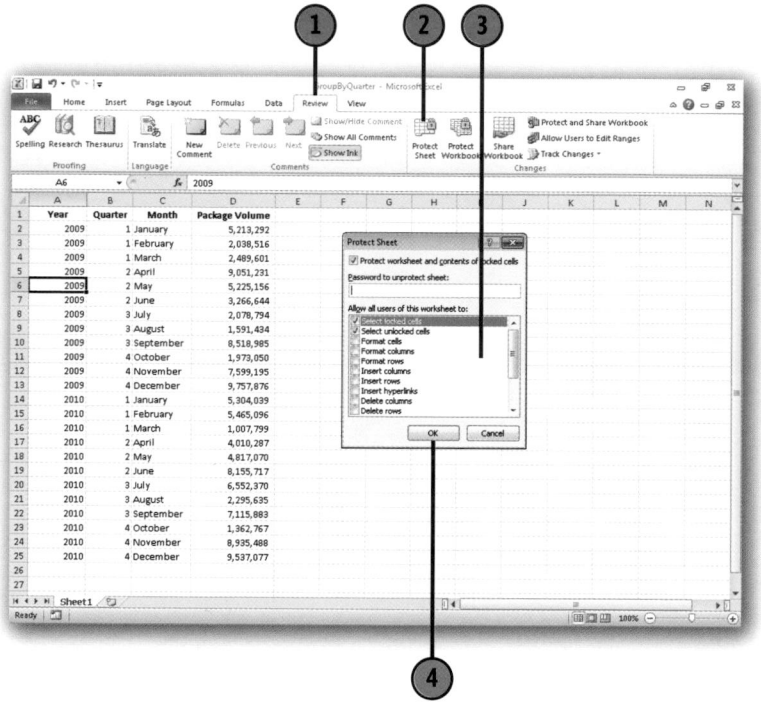

Locking Cells to Prevent Changes

When you protect a worksheet, locking an individual cell prevents it from being changed. This level of protection goes beyond simply protecting a worksheet; it prevents anyone using the worksheet from changing the contents or formatting of the cell. Excel 2010 enables this option by default.

Lock Cells

1. Select the cells you want to lock.
2. Right-click the selection, and click Format Cells on the shortcut menu.
3. Click the Protection tab.
4. Select the Locked check box.
5. Click OK.

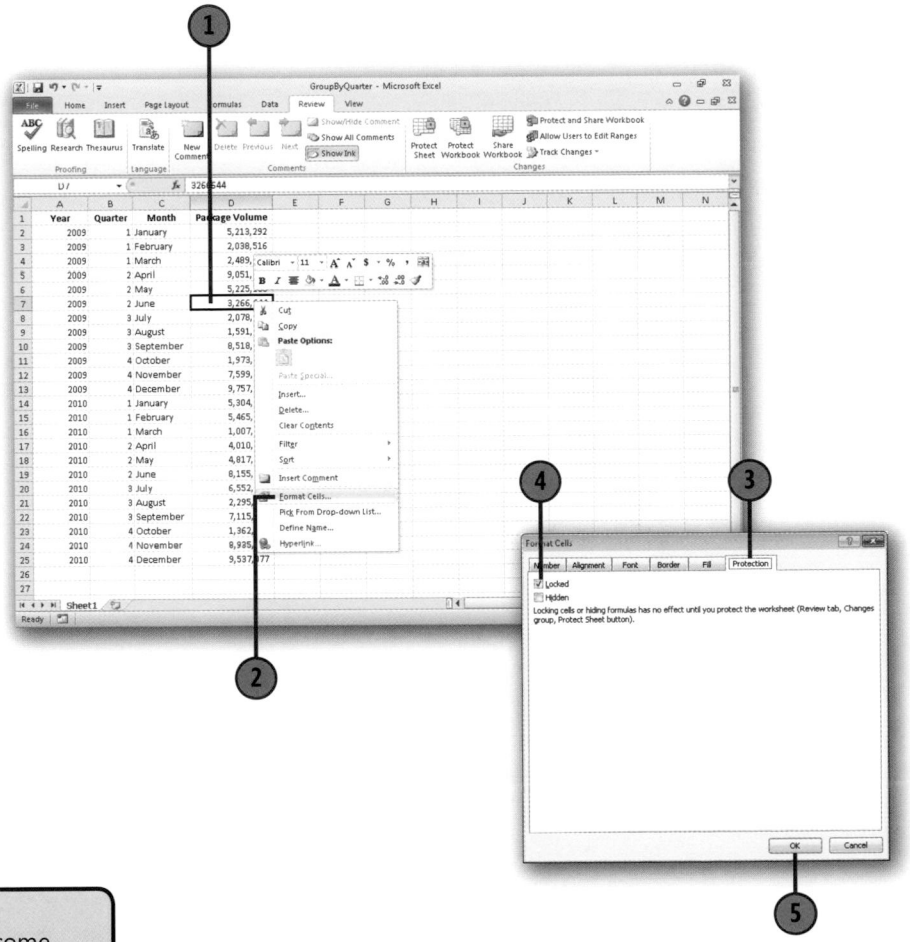

Caution

You must protect your worksheet for cell locking to become effective.

9 Printing Worksheets

In this section:

- Previewing Worksheets Before Printing
- Choosing a Printer and Page Size
- Printing Part of a Worksheet
- Printing Row and Column Headings on Each Page
- Setting and Changing Print Margins
- Setting Page Orientation and Scale
- Creating Headers and Footers
- Adding Graphics to a Header or Footer
- Setting and Viewing Page Breaks

After you create your worksheet, you can print a copy for reference, for backup, or to distribute to your colleagues. Although you might be tempted to print your worksheet as soon as you complete it, it's usually a good idea to check your work first. All you need to do to see how your worksheet will look when it's printed is to display the worksheet in Backstage view. If you want to change how your worksheet will appear on the printed page, you can do anything from changing the orientation of the printout (that is, printing in a vertical format, called portrait mode, or a horizontal format, called landscape mode) to scaling the worksheet to fit within a specific number of pages. It's easy to fine-tune margins, adjust headers and footers, and customize a variety of other print options as well.

Previewing Worksheets Before Printing

Before you print a worksheet, it's helpful to take a step back and look at how your data will appear on the printed page. To do that in Microsoft Excel 2010, you display your worksheet in Backstage view. While you have your workbook open in Backstage view, you can zoom in to see cell contents clearly without altering printing size. Excel 2010 also enables you to view your workbook in Page Layout view, which displays your workbook as it will be printed while still enabling you to edit the workbook's contents easily. You can adjust the widths of any columns or rows in Page Layout view, saving you the trouble of switching between Backstage view and the standard Excel window.

Display a Worksheet in Page Layout View

1. Click the View tab.
2. In the Workbook Views group, click Page Layout.

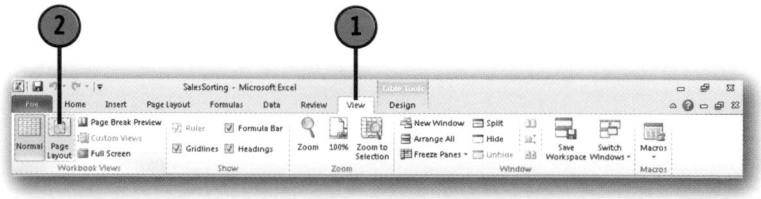

View and Zoom Worksheets in Backstage View

1. Click the File tab.
2. Click Print.
3. Click the Zoom To Page button.
4. Click any tab on the ribbon to exit Backstage View.

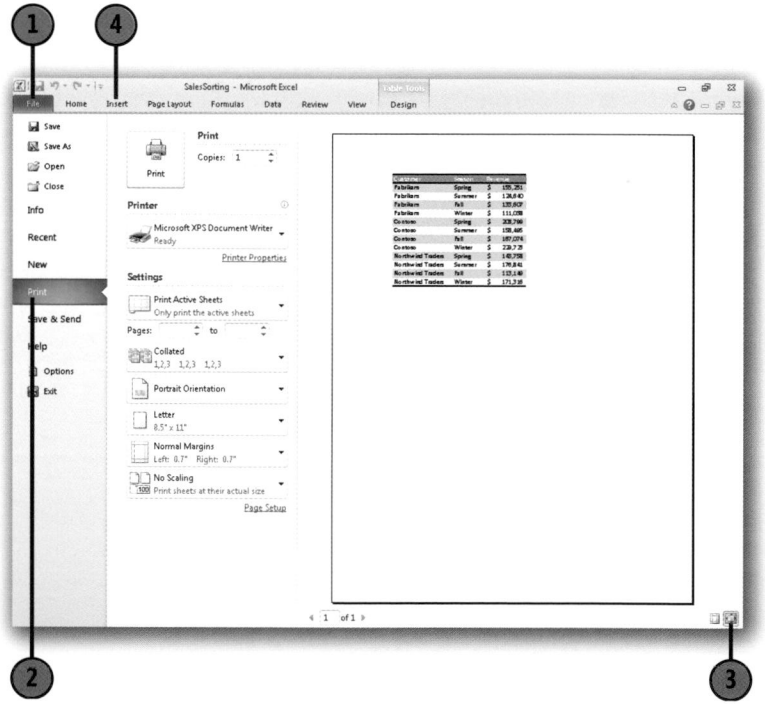

Change Column Widths and Row Heights in Page Layout View

1. Click the View tab.
2. Click Page Layout View.
3. Hover the mouse pointer over the edge of a column or row header until the mouse pointer becomes a two-headed arrow. Drag the edge until the column or row is the size you want.
4. Click Normal to return to Normal view.

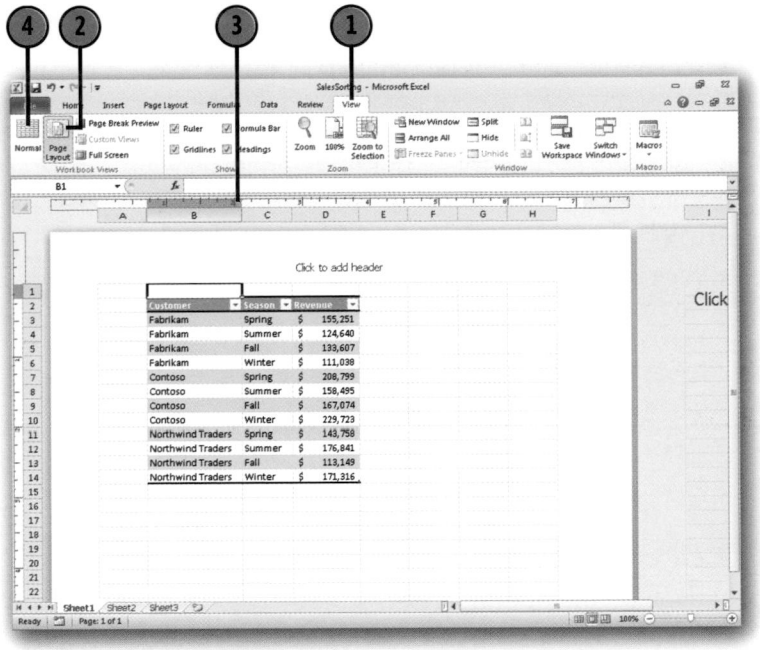

Printing Worksheets with Current Options

After you enter all your data and format your worksheets so that the data is easy to read, you can print your worksheets for distribution to your colleagues, for example. Clicking the File tab, clicking Print, and clicking the Print button prints only the worksheet displayed on the screen—if you want to print more than one worksheet at a time, such as when you want to print several months of sales results and each month is recorded on a separate worksheet, you can do that as well.

Print Multiple Worksheets from the Same Workbook

1. Hold down the Ctrl key, and click the sheet tabs of the worksheets you want to print.
2. Click the File tab.
3. Click Print.
4. Click the Print button.
5. Click any tab on the ribbon to exit Backstage view.

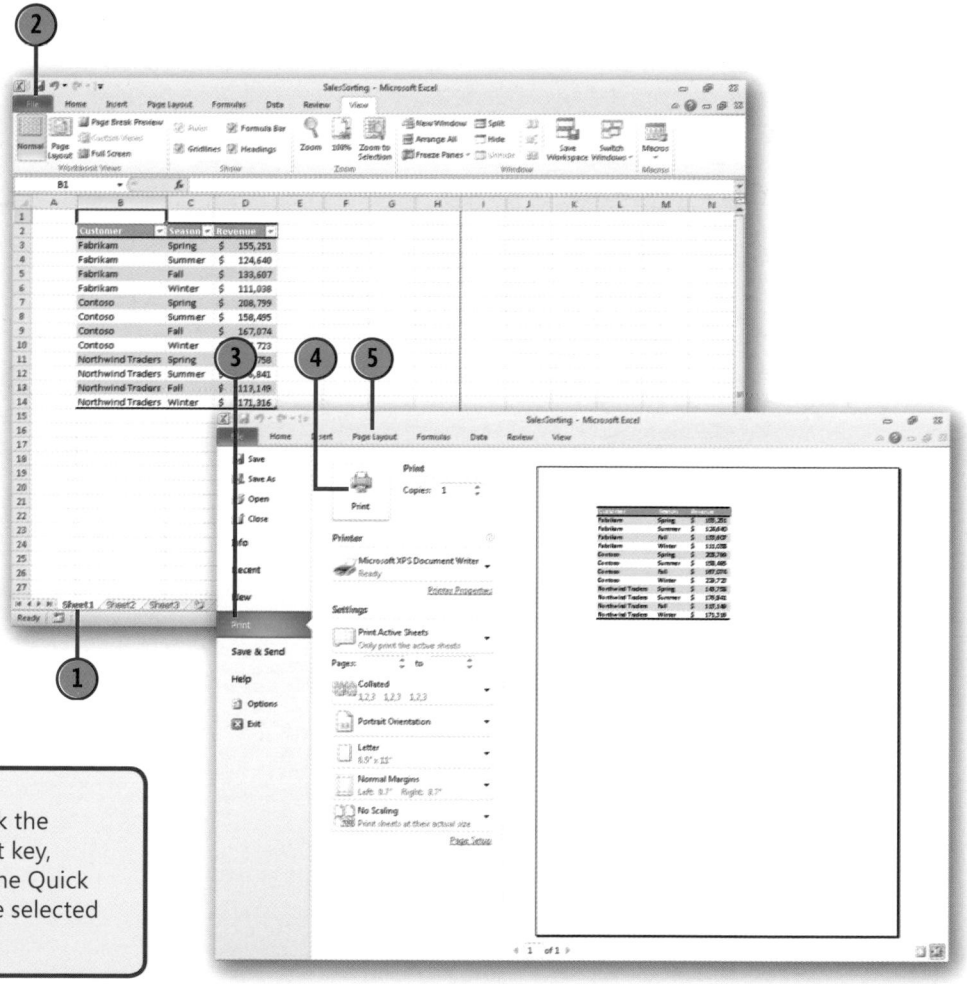

Tip

If all the worksheets in a workbook are adjacent, click the sheet tab for the first worksheet, hold down the Shift key, and click the sheet tab for the last worksheet. Click the Quick Print button on the Quick Access Toolbar to print the selected worksheets.

Choosing Whether to Print Gridlines and Headings

Excel is a spreadsheet program, which means that it generally expects the data you enter in it to be organized into rows and columns. You're not limited to entering just rows and columns of dry figures, of course; you can add images, place text in cells outside your tables, and format your worksheet so that your data looks exactly the way you want it to.

In the spirit of offering you as much control as possible, Excel enables you to choose whether to print your worksheets' gridlines, column headings, and row headings. If you've printed any Microsoft Office document, you've probably noticed that some elements that work very well on your computer screen don't translate well to the printed page. Gridlines, column headings, and row headings are like that. When you're looking at data on a computer screen, those three elements usually help you make sense of your data, but those same elements can clutter your printouts. It's up to you, however; you can choose to print your headings and gridlines or not.

Choose to Print Gridlines

1. Click the Page Layout tab.
2. In the Sheet Options group, under Gridlines, select the Print check box.

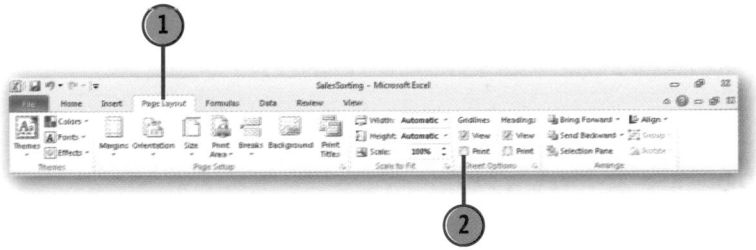

Choose to Print Headings

1. Click the Page Layout tab.
2. In the Sheet Options group, under Headings, select the Print check box.

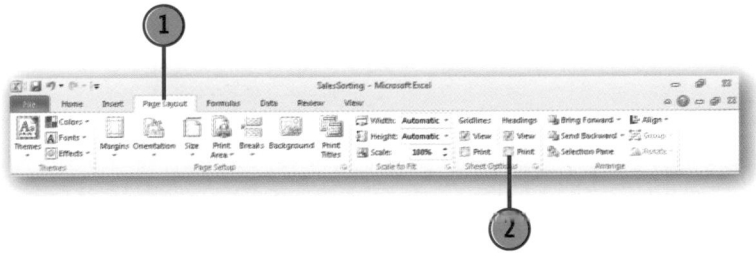

Choosing Printers and Paper Options

You might not want to use the same printer and paper type for everything you print. Standard 8.5-by-11-inch letter-size paper is fine for printing some of your worksheets, but from time to time, you'll probably need to use 8.5-by-14-inch legal size paper. In Excel 2010, you can display a list of every paper size available for your use. You can also select which printer you want to use. Depending on the software available on your computer, you might be able to print your worksheet to a file in another program's format.

Choose a Printer

1. Click the File tab.
2. Click Print.
3. Click the Printer button.
4. Click the printer you want to use.

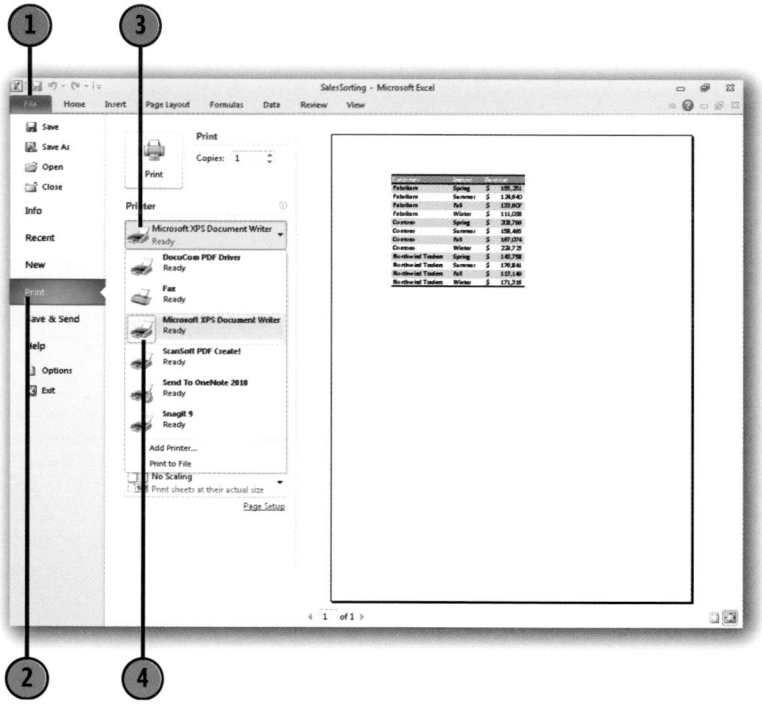

Caution

Depending on your printer and network configuration, you might not see all of the options described in these procedures.

Choose the Paper

1. Click the File tab.
2. Click Print.
3. Click the Paper button.
4. Select the paper size.

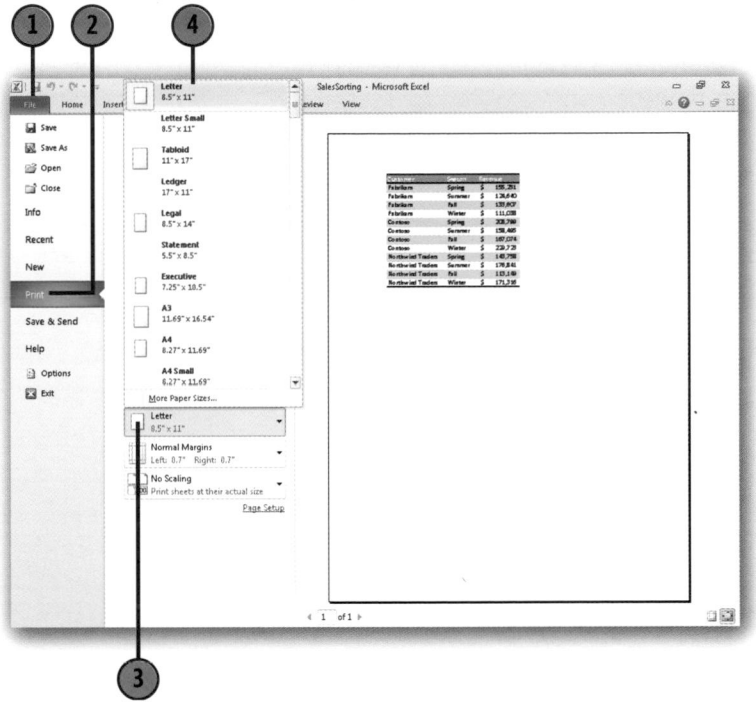

Caution

If you change the paper size for one worksheet, the change is effective only for that worksheet.

Printing Part of a Worksheet

When you create a worksheet containing lots of data, you might want to print just the section of the worksheet with the data relevant to the point you're trying to illustrate. The good news is you can set a print area so Excel prints as much or as little of your worksheet as you like. The print area is outlined with a dashed line, which lets you tell which cells will be printed and which won't. When you set a print area, you can select cells in a single rectangle or select cells located in various areas of your worksheet.

Set a Print Area

1. Select cells you want to print.
2. Click the Page Layout tab.
3. Click Print Area.
4. Click Set Print Area.

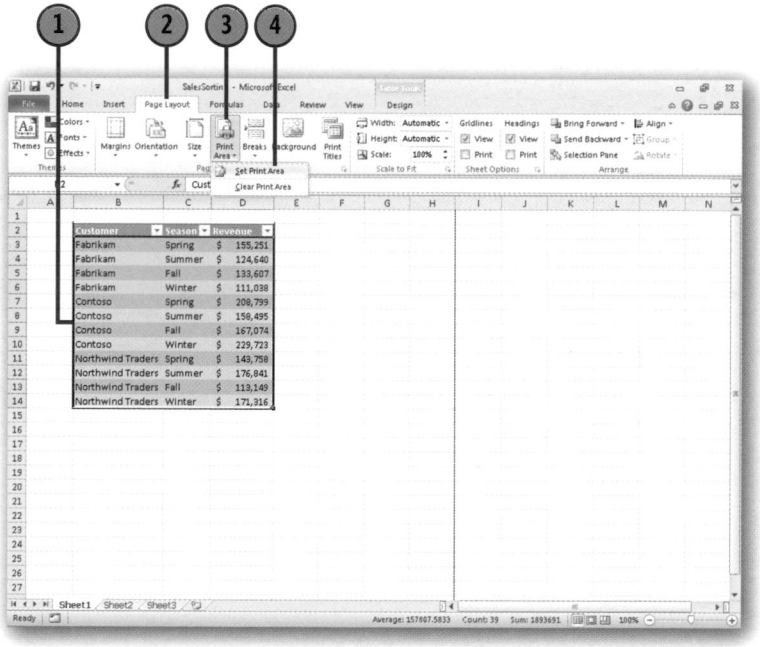

Remove a Print Area

- Click the Page Layout tab.
- Click Print Area.
- Click Clear Print Area.

Caution

Try to arrange your data so that the content to be printed looks the same on the screen as it will on the printed page. You can define print areas composed of multiple parts of the same worksheet, but you should keep that technique in reserve for when your worksheet data appears on more than one page.

Printing Row and Column Headings on Each Page

When you print a worksheet in which the data doesn't fit on a single screen, you might have trouble remembering which data is stored in which column. Rather than having to look back to the top of the worksheet—or even type your headings where you guess the screen transitions occur—you can have Excel print your column and row headings at the top and left of every page. By printing the column and row headings on each page, you save time, improve comprehension, and reduce frustration when dealing with large worksheets.

Identify the Rows and Columns to Repeat

1. Click the Page Layout tab.
2. Click Print Titles.
3. Click the Sheet tab.
4. Click in the Rows To Repeat At Top box.
5. On your worksheet, select the row headings you want to repeat.
6. Click the Columns To Repeat At Left box.
7. On your worksheet, select the column headings you want to repeat.
8. Click OK.

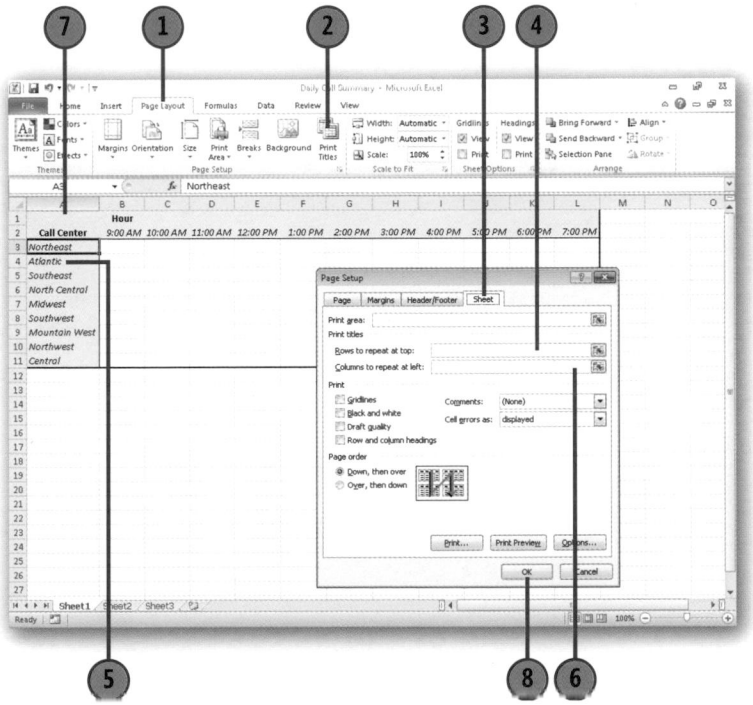

Tip

Repeating rows and columns on every page is useful when your worksheet contains frozen panes and you want to have the frozen panes appear on every page of the printout, just as they appear on the screen.

See Also

For more information about frozen panes, see "View Multiple Parts of a Worksheet by Freezing Panes" on page 79.

Setting and Changing Print Margins

Margins define the boundary areas of the page, which provide a visual border around your printed data. Changing a worksheet's margins increases or decreases the amount of data that can fit on a printed page, which allows you to make room for one last column of data, divide your columns evenly between two pages, or provide for enough room at one edge for the page to be bound in a report or three-ring binder. In Backstage view, margins appear as dark gray lines that you can drag to the positions you want them.

Set Page Margins

1. Click the Page Layout tab.
2. Click Margins, and either click the margin settings you want to use or click Custom Margins.
3. If you selected Custom Margins, type new values for the worksheet's margins in the Top, Bottom, Left, and Right boxes.
4. Click OK.

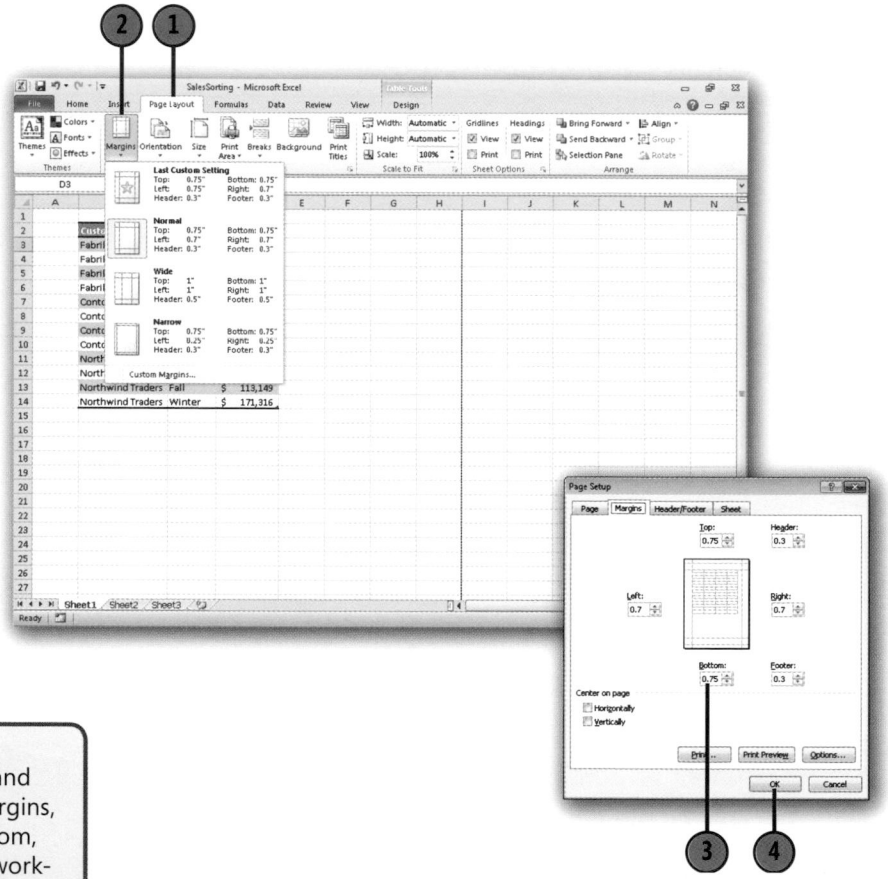

Try This!

Select multiple worksheets by holding down the Ctrl key and clicking the sheet tabs, click the Page Layout tab, click Margins, and then click Custom Margins. Type 0.75 in the Top, Bottom, Left, and Right boxes, and then click OK. All the selected worksheets' margins are changed to three-quarters of an inch.

Adjust Page Margins in Backstage View

1. Click the File tab.
2. Click Print.
3. If necessary, select the Show Margins button to display the margin lines.
4. Hover the mouse pointer over one of the gray lines until the mouse pointer becomes a two-headed arrow. Drag the line until the margin is set the way you want.
5. Click any tab on the ribbon to exit Backstage view.

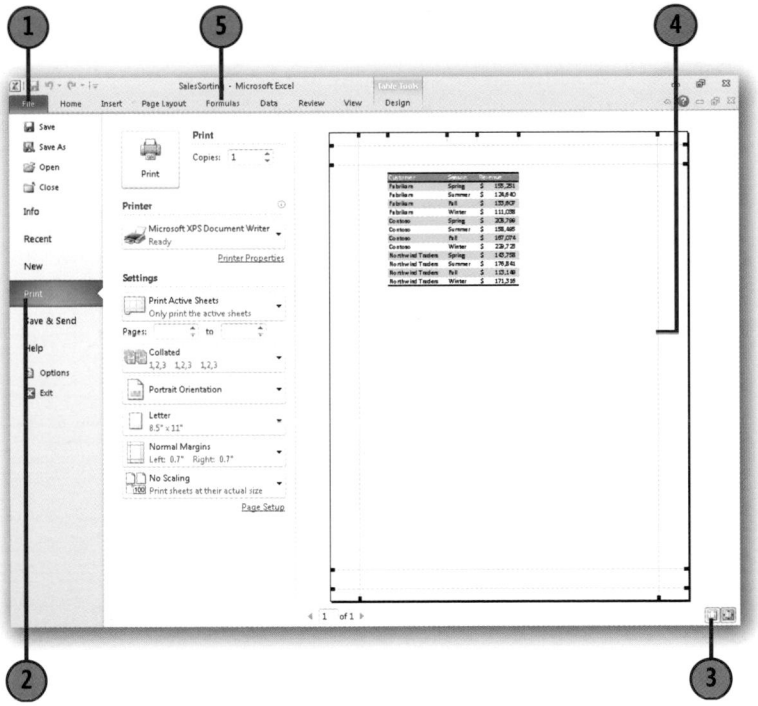

Caution

In Backstage view, it's sometimes difficult to distinguish between margins and header or footer lines. Be sure to keep track of which is which.

Setting Page Orientation and Scale

As you look at your worksheet and think about how you want it to appear on the printed page, be aware that you have the choice of printing in a vertical format (portrait mode) or a horizontal format (landscape mode). Landscape mode is particularly useful when you have a lot of columns in your worksheet, such as in a worksheet storing customer contact or product sales information. You can fit your worksheet onto a specific number of printed pages, which helps if you have been allotted a fixed number of pages in which to present your data in a typeset report.

Set Page Orientation

1. Click the Page Layout tab.
2. Click Orientation.
3. Select either the Portrait or Landscape option.

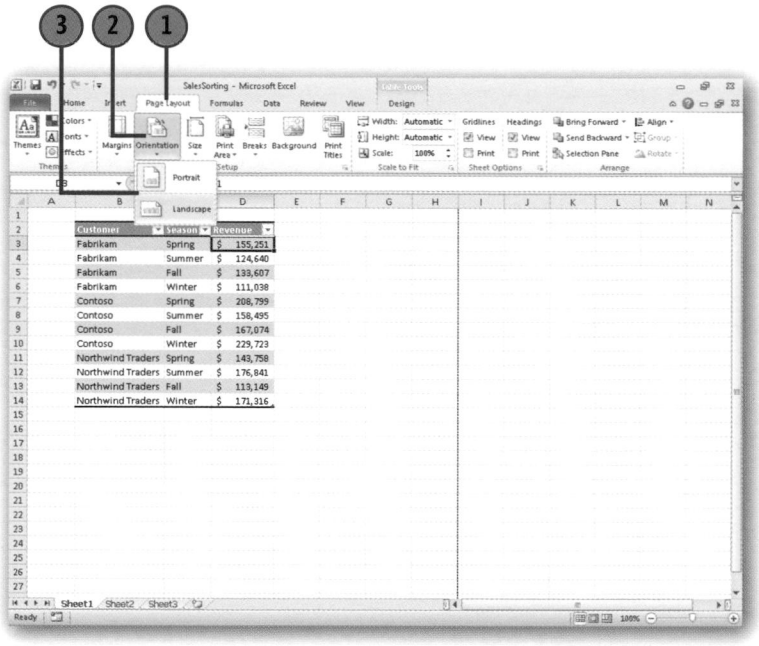

Tip

Select Portrait orientation for long worksheets that are not very wide, or select Landscape orientation for worksheets with many columns.

Scale the Printout to a Fixed Number of Pages

1. Click the Page Layout tab.
2. In the Scale To Fit group, click the Width down arrow and select the number of horizontal pages your worksheet should take up when printed.
3. In the Scale To Fit group, click the Height down arrow and select the number of vertical pages your worksheet should take up when printed.

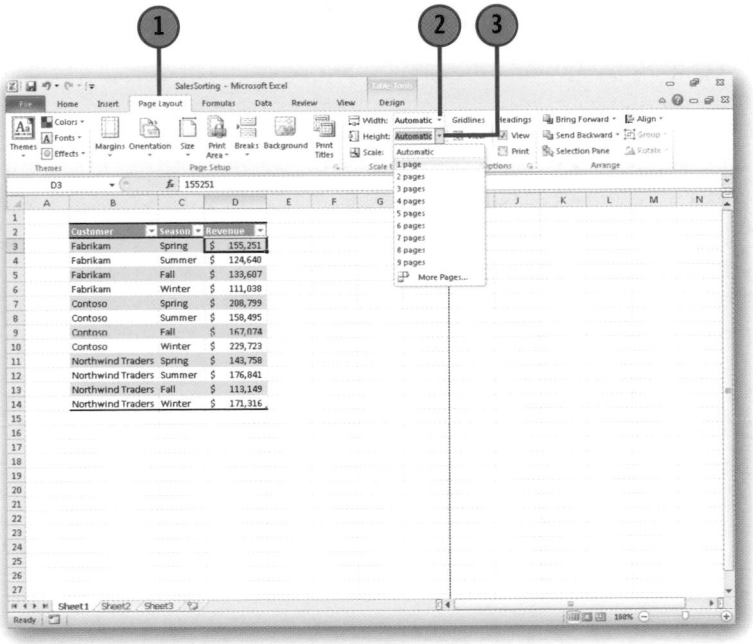

Tip

Click the File tab, and then click Print to see how the document looks after it is forced onto a fixed number of pages.

Tip

The maximum number of pages you can choose from the Width and Height list boxes is 9. If you want to force your worksheet to print on 10 or more pages in either dimension, click the Width or Height control's down arrow, and click More Pages. Then, using the controls on the Page tab of the Page Setup dialog box, select the Fit To option and type the number of pages the rows (pages wide) and columns (tall) your worksheet should be forced to fit on. Click OK.

Try This!

Click the Page Layout tab, and then click the Page Setup group's dialog box launcher. In the Page Setup dialog box, click the Page tab, and then select the Fit To option. Type 1 in the Page(s) Wide box and delete the contents of the Tall box. The worksheet now fits on a single page wide but prints on additional vertical pages if necessary.

Creating Headers and Footers

Headers and footers contain information that appears at the top and bottom of each page of your printed worksheet. You can select a premade header or footer that contains information about your file, or you can create custom headers and footers using predefined text. Excel 2010 comes with a list of expressions you can insert into your headers and footers to display certain information about your worksheet, such as page numbers or file names. Headers might include helpful information such as a workbook name, and footers can include page numbers, file names, or dates.

Add a Premade Header and Footer

1. Click the Insert tab.
2. Click Header & Footer.
3. Click Header.
4. Click the premade header you want to use.
5. If you want to, click Footer, and then click the premade footer to use.

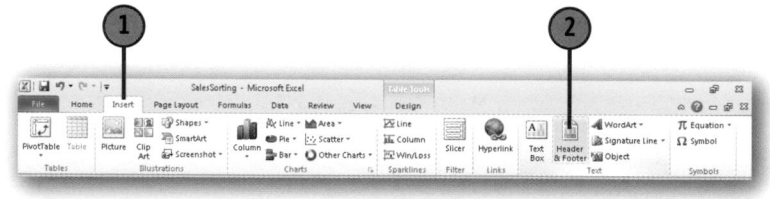

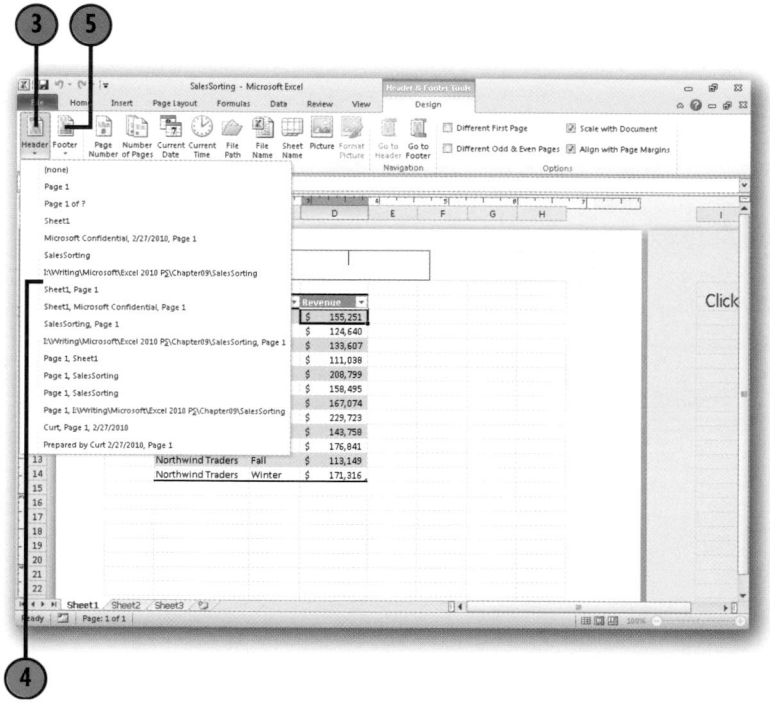

Tip

Click the File tab, and then click Print to preview your headers and footers before you print.

See Also

For more information about how to change the size of your headers, see "Adjust Header and Footer Height" on page 170.

Add Predefined Text to the Header or Footer

1. Click the Insert tab.
2. Click Header & Footer.
3. Click the section of the header or footer where you want your text to appear, and type the text you want.
4. If you want to use predefined text, position the insertion point where you want the text to appear.
5. Click a button to insert the predefined text.

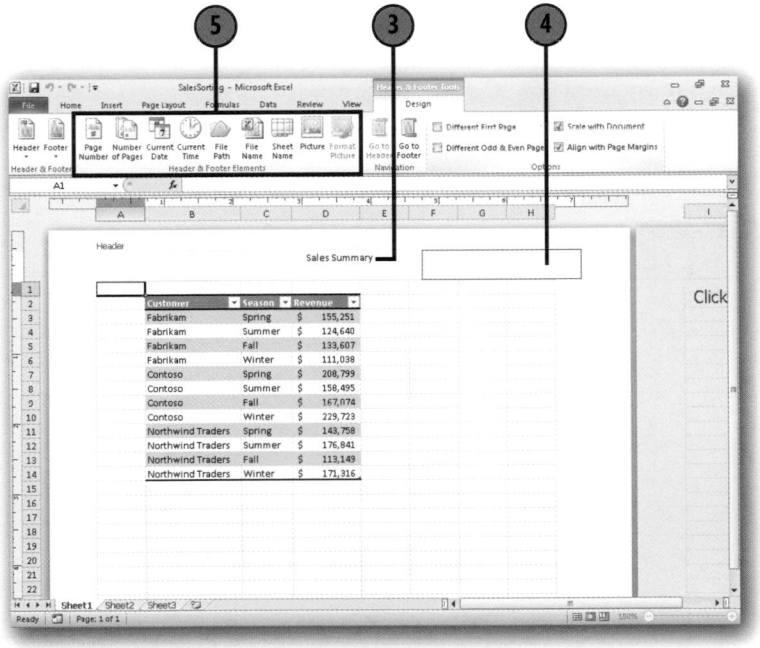

Tip

You can change the appearance of your header and footer text by selecting the text or the code representing the value to be printed (for example, the current time) and then using the controls on the Home tab on the ribbon.

Adjust Header and Footer Height

1. Click the File tab.
2. Click Print.
3. If necessary, click the Show Margins button to display the header and footer lines.
4. Hover the mouse pointer over one of the gray lines until the mouse pointer becomes a two-headed arrow. Drag the line until the header or footer is the height you want.
5. Click any tab on the ribbon to exit Backstage view.

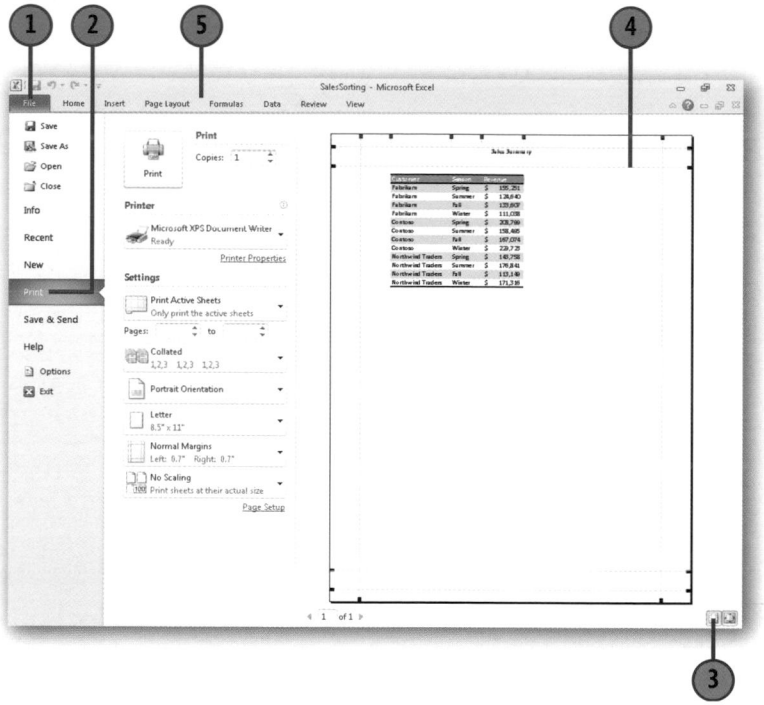

Tip

The directions of the arrowheads show you in which direction you can move the line.

Adding Graphics to a Header or a Footer

Creating attractive and professional looking printouts helps you communicate your message better. Often, the addition of a simple graphic to a header or footer gives your worksheet a truly professional appearance. You might want to create printouts that include your company's letterhead or logo or a graphic related to the information on your worksheet. An excellent way to include graphics on every printed page is to place them into the header and footer of your worksheet.

Include a Graphic in a Header or Footer

1. Click the Insert tab.
2. Click Header & Footer.
3. Click in the section of the header or footer where you want your graphic to appear.
4. Click the Picture button.
5. Navigate to the folder that contains the picture you want to insert.
6. Double-click the image.

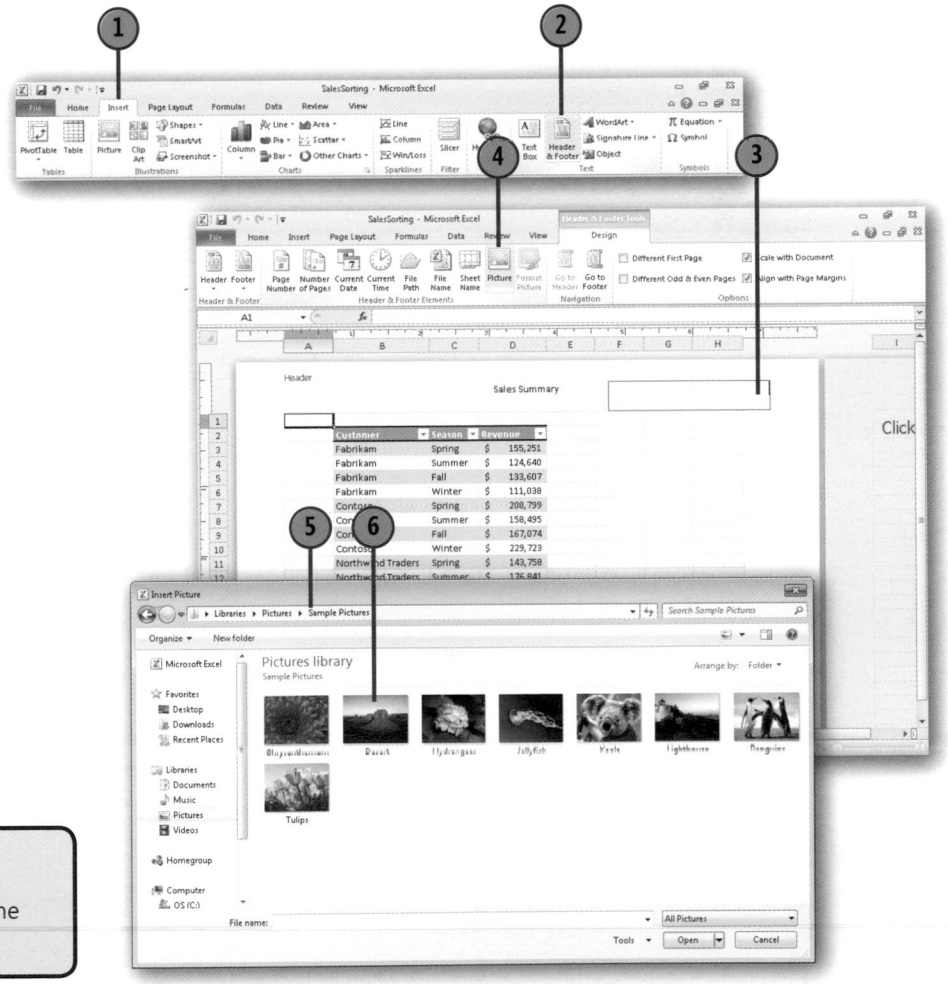

Caution

If the graphic is larger than the area allotted for the header or footer, the image will cover up some of the worksheet data.

Format a Graphic in a Header or Footer

1. Click the Insert tab.
2. Click Header & Footer.
3. Select the text *& [Picture]*.
4. Click the Format Picture button.
5. Click the Size and Picture tabs and specify the options you want.
6. Click OK.

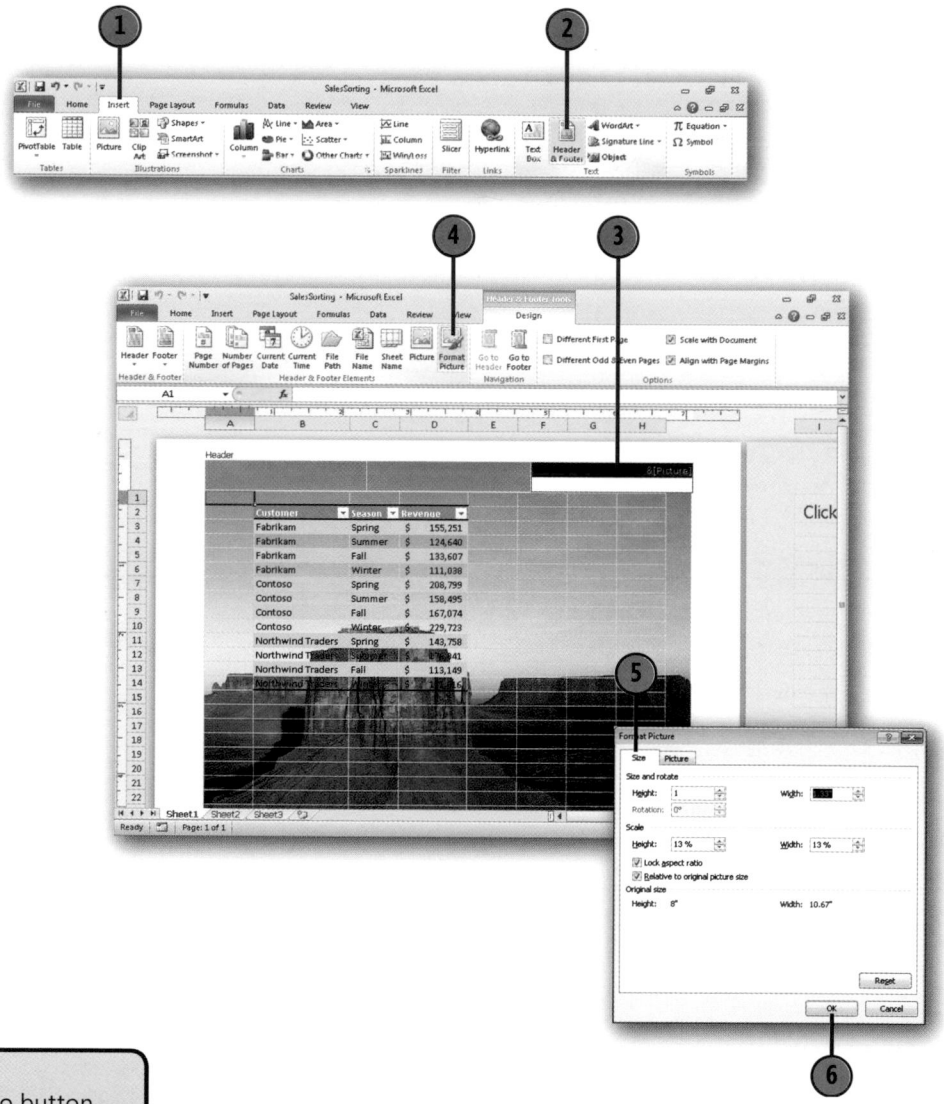

Caution

When using Format Picture, you cannot use the Undo button to reverse your actions after they are complete.

Setting and Viewing Page Breaks

Excel determines where one printed page ends and the next begins based on the page size, margins, and orientation; however, the page breaks Excel sets might not work for a particular worksheet. You might want to place a chart or table on its own sheet, or you might want to force two separate tables onto one printed page. You can display all existing page breaks by opening your worksheet in Page Break Preview mode, which displays the page breaks as blue lines. If the blue lines are dashed, they represent an automatic page break; if the blue lines are solid, they represent a manually set page break. While in Page Break Preview mode, you can change the location of any existing page breaks to ensure that your worksheets print exactly the way you want.

View Current Page Breaks

1. Click the View tab.
2. Click Page Break Preview.

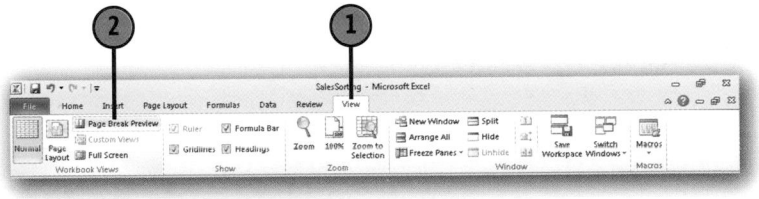

Set Manual Page Breaks

1. Click the cell the below and to the right of where you want to insert a page break.
2. Click the Page Layout tab.
3. Click Breaks.
4. Click Insert Page Break.
5. If necessary, on the status bar, click the Normal button to exit Page Break Preview.

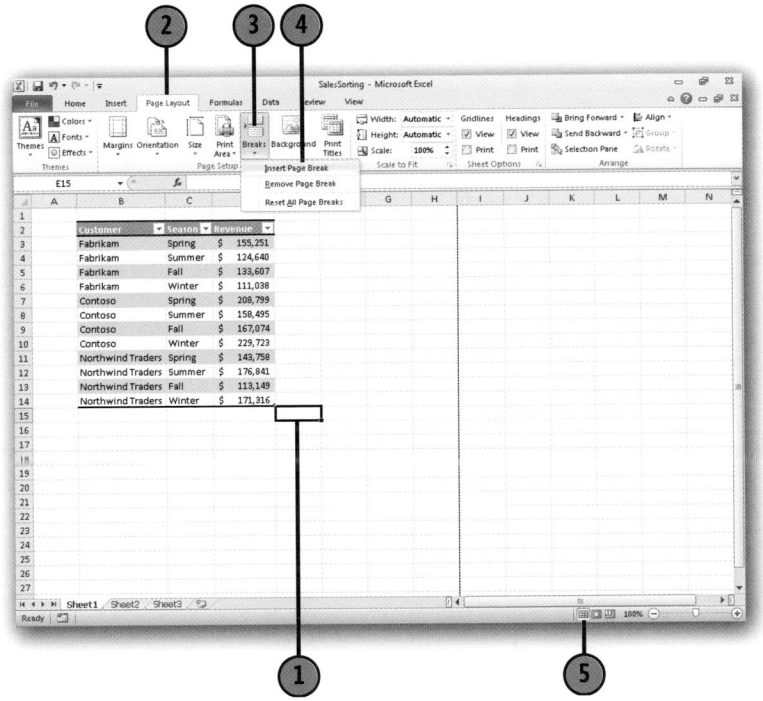

Change Manual Page Breaks

1. Click the View tab.
2. Click Page Break Preview.
3. Hover the mouse pointer over one of the blue lines until the mouse pointer becomes a two-headed arrow. Drag the line until the page break is where you want it.

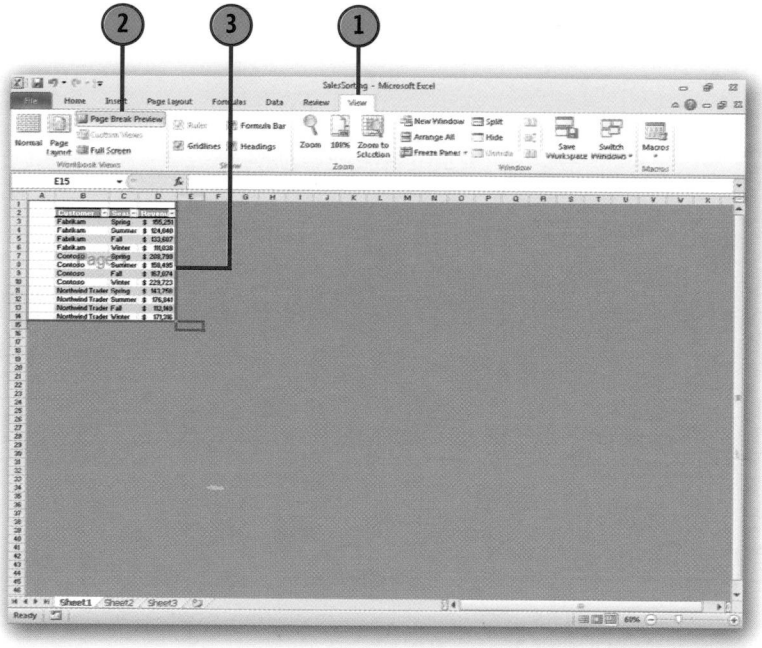

10 Customizing Excel to the Way You Work

In this section:

- Creating and Modifying Templates
- Modifying the Quick Access Toolbar
- Modifying the Ribbon User Interface
- Controlling Which Error Messages Appear
- Creating and Deleting AutoCorrect Entries
- Controlling Worksheet Gridline Appearance

Microsoft Excel 2010 gives you lots of ways to work with your data, with literally hundreds of commands at your disposal. If you find that it takes several mouse clicks to reveal a command you use all the time, you can add that command to the Quick Access Toolbar so that you can activate it with a single click. Excel 2010 also enables you to create custom tabs on the ribbon.

Another way to make your life easier is to create templates. A template is a workbook you use as a pattern for other workbooks. When you open a template, which is a separate Excel file type, you have the outline you need to create frequently used workbooks quickly.

You also have a great deal of control over how Excel handles the data you enter in your worksheets. Excel tries to be helpful by identifying formulas it thinks are mistakes, probably because the formula isn't consistent with other formulas near it or because it leaves out cells in a range. Sometimes those mistakes are exactly what you intended. The same is true for potential misspellings. Excel identifies and corrects the most common misspellings, but if a word Excel thinks is misspelled is actually correct, you can prevent Excel from making that change without turning off the corrective behavior entirely.

Opening Ready-to-Use Workbook Templates

When you decide on the type of data you want to store in a workbook and what that workbook should look like, you will probably want to create similar workbooks without adding all the formatting and formulas again. For example, you might have settled on a design for your monthly sales-tracking workbook. When you settle on a design for your workbooks, you can save one of the workbooks as a pattern, or template, for similar workbooks you create in the future.

Create a Workbook from a Template

1. Click the File tab.
2. Click New.
3. If necessary, click a template category.
4. Double-click the template you want to use to create your workbook.
5. Click the Save button.
6. Type a name for the file.
7. Click Save.

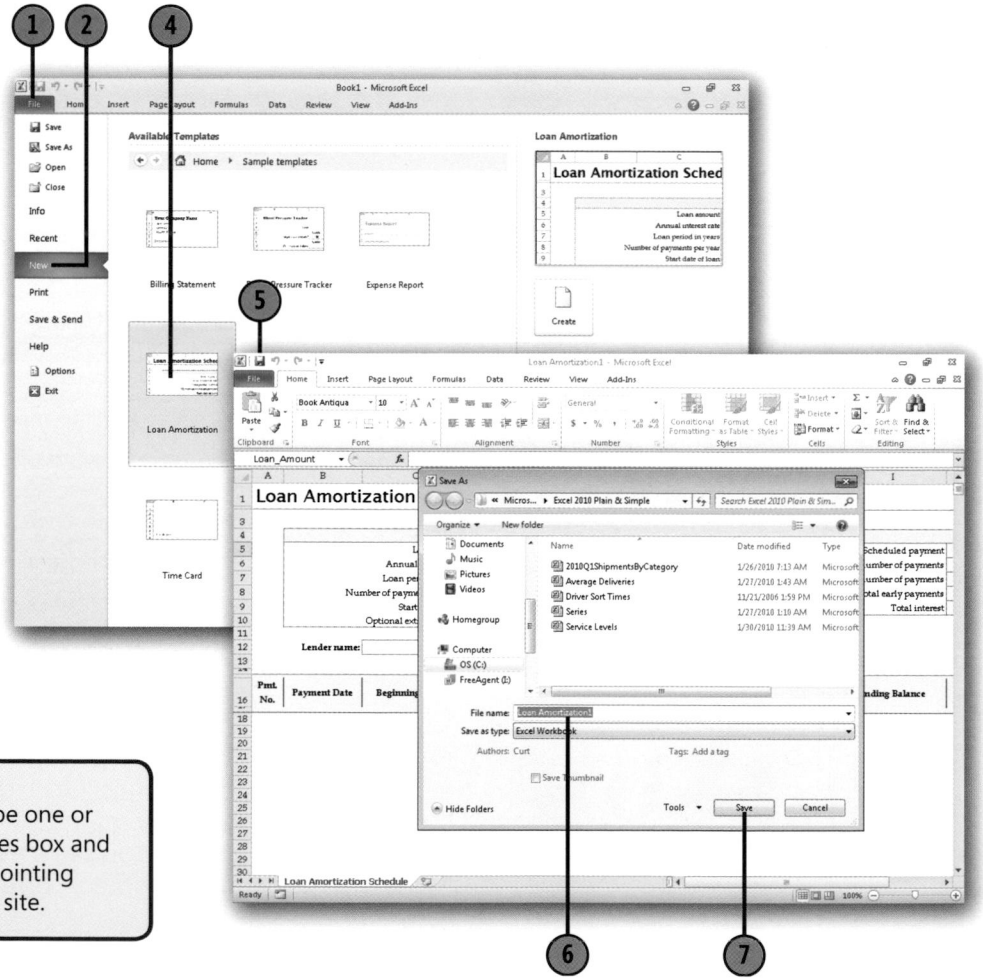

Tip

If you have an active Internet connection, you can type one or more keywords in the Search Office.com For Templates box and click the Start Searching button (it looks like a right-pointing arrow) to look for templates on the Office.com Web site.

Save a Workbook As a Template

1. Click the File tab.
2. Click Save As.
3. Click the Save As Type down arrow.
4. Click Excel Template.
5. Type the name you want for the template.
6. Click Save.

Caution

Be sure you don't change the directory where Excel offers to save your template. If you do change it, your template won't show up in the list of available templates. You can still open it by navigating to the folder in which you save it, of course.

Tip

You should remove any existing data from a workbook you save as a template, both to avoid data entry errors and to remove any confusion as to whether the workbook is a template. The one exception to this rule is when your template contains formulas that result in an error if you delete all data from the worksheet. In that case, you should enter some obviously incorrect data that future users know to replace.

Modify a Template

1. Click the File tab.
2. Click Open.
3. Click the template you want to modify.
4. Click Open.
5. Make the changes you want.
6. Click the Save button.

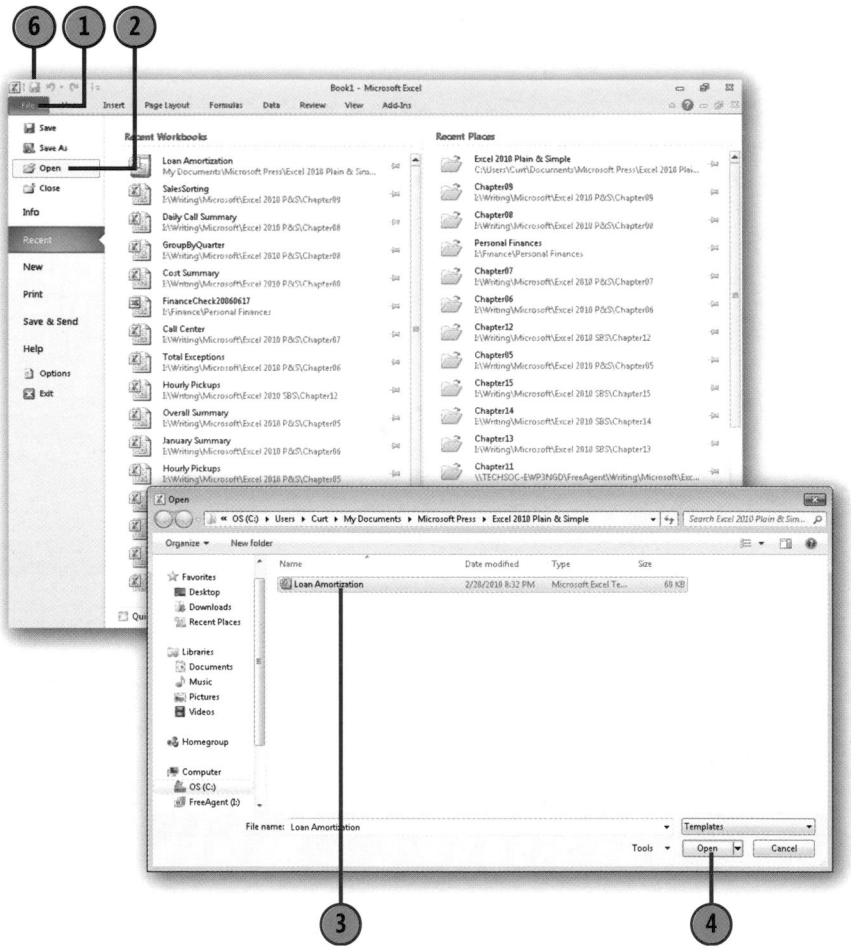

Tip

You can always change a workbook's file type to Excel Template, so don't worry if you accidentally try to create a regular workbook instead of saving your changes to the template.

Adding Commands to the Quick Access Toolbar

The vast majority of commands you use in Excel 2010 appear on the ribbon, but some of the commands require you to move through one or two levels of the user interface (for example, click the correct ribbon tab and then click a button to open a dialog box). If there's a specific command you use all the time, you can make that command easier to find by adding it to the Quick Access Toolbar. If you later find that you don't use the command as much as you used to, you can always remove the command and make room for the commands you do use.

Add a Command to the Quick Access Toolbar

1. Right-click any command on the Quick Access Toolbar.
2. Click Customize Quick Access Toolbar.
3. Click the Choose Commands From down arrow.
4. Click the category from which you want to choose the command.
5. Click the command you want to add.
6. Click Add.
7. Click OK.

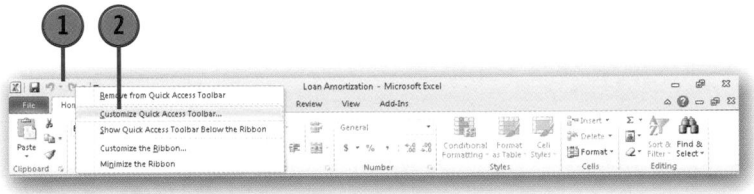

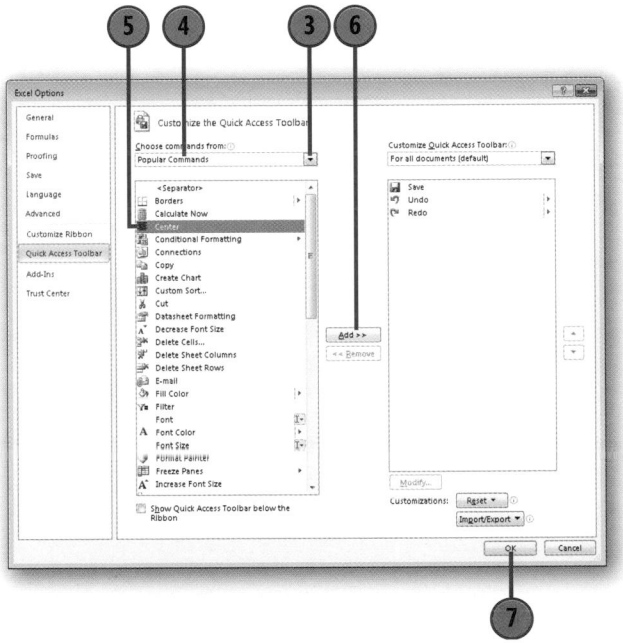

Remove a Command from the Quick Access Toolbar

1. Right-click any command on the Quick Access Toolbar.
2. Click Remove From Quick Access Toolbar.

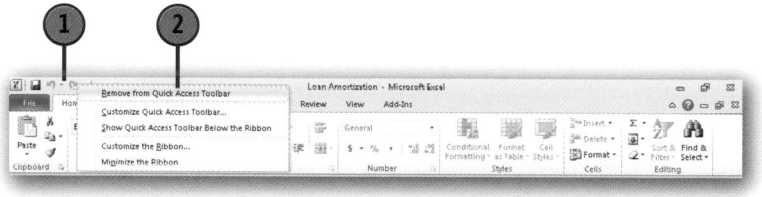

Move the Quick Access Toolbar

1. Right-click any command on the Quick Access Toolbar.
2. Click Show Quick Access Toolbar Below The Ribbon.

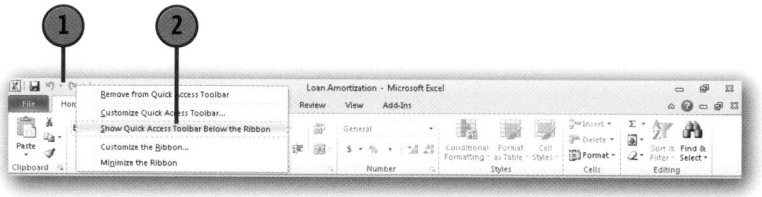

Tip

You can change the order of the buttons on the Quick Access Toolbar by displaying the Quick Access Toolbar page of the Excel Options dialog box, clicking the command you want to move, and then clicking the Move Up or Move Down button.

Tip

You can also add a button on the ribbon to the Quick Access Toolbar by right-clicking the button and choosing Add To Quick Access Toolbar.

Modifying the Ribbon User Interface

Excel 2010 enhances your ability to customize the entire ribbon user interface. The ribbon consists of several elements: tabs, which are designated by the clickable words at the top of the ribbon (for example, Home, Insert, and Page Layout); groups, which are named collections of commands (such as the Font group on the Home tab); and commands, which are individual items within a group (such as the Bold button in the Home tab's Font group.)

In Excel 2010, you can hide and display ribbon tabs; reorder tabs, groups, and commands displayed on the ribbon; customize existing tabs (including Tool tabs, which appear when specific items are selected); and create custom tabs.

Add a Command to a Ribbon Tab

1. Right-click any ribbon tab.
2. Click Customize The Ribbon.
3. Click the Choose Commands From down arrow.
4. Click the category from which you want to choose the command.
5. Click the command you want to add.
6. Click Add.
7. Click OK.

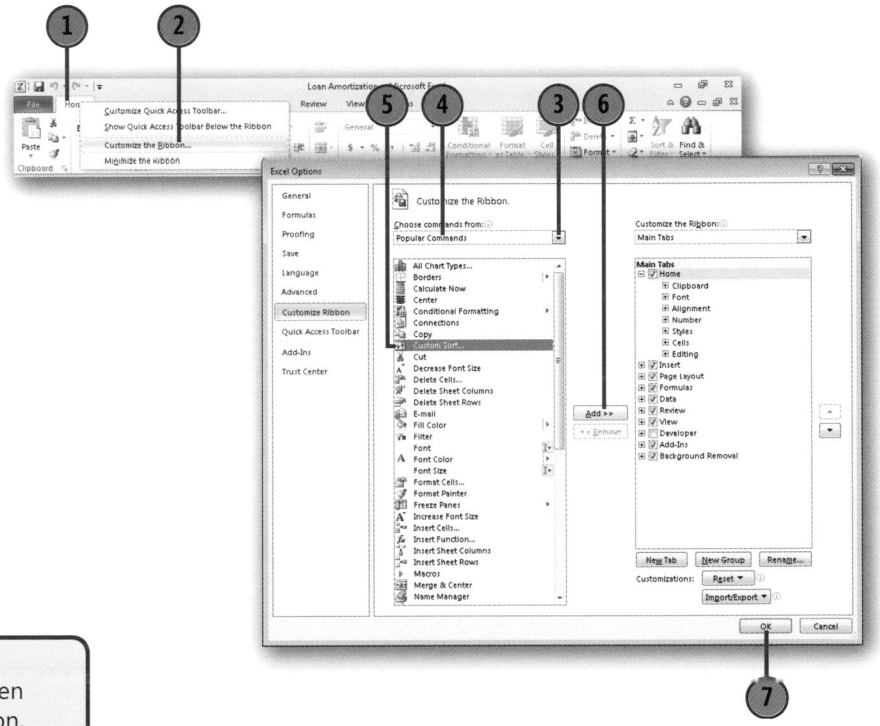

Tip

To restore the ribbon to the same configuration it had when you installed Excel 2010, right-click anywhere on the ribbon, click Customize The Ribbon, click Reset, click Reset All Customizations, and then click OK. If you just want to remove the changes from a specific ribbon tab, click that tab in the right-hand pane, click Reset, click Reset Only Selected Ribbon Tab, and then click OK.

Tip

To have Excel 2010 display just the names of the ribbon tabs, press Ctrl+F1. To restore the ribbon, press Ctrl+F1 again.

Reorder Commands on a Ribbon Tab

1. Right-click any ribbon tab.
2. Click Customize The Ribbon.
3. Click the command, group, or tab you want to move.
4. Click the Move Up or Move Down button.
5. Click OK.

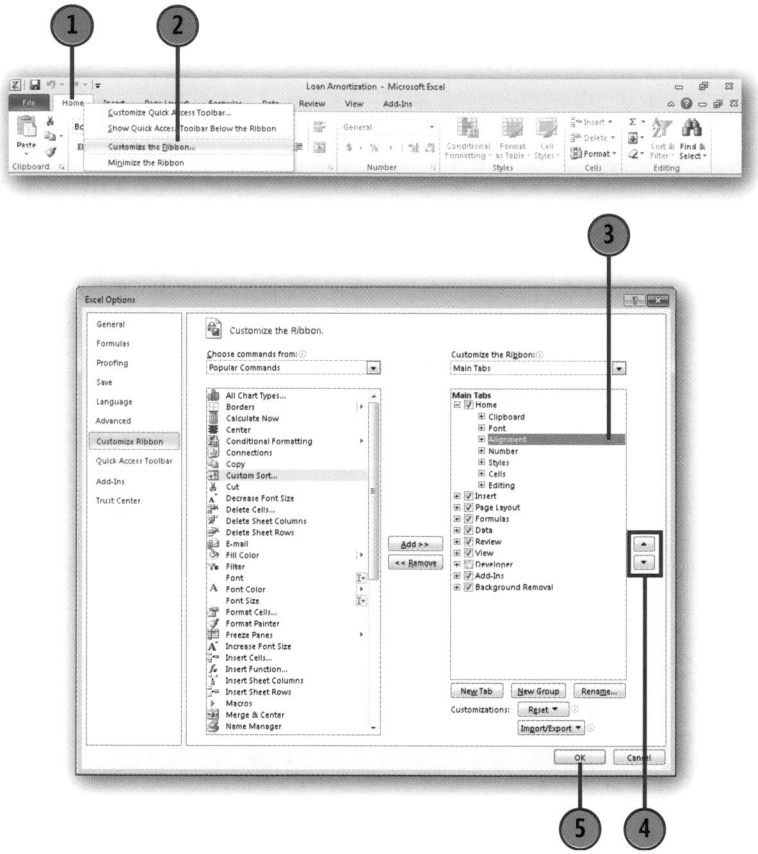

Tip

If a command is in the last position on a tab and you click the Move Down button, Excel 2010 places the command in the first position of the next tab.

Remove a Ribbon Element

1. Right-click any ribbon tab.
2. Click Customize The Ribbon.
3. Click the command, group, or tab you want to remove.
4. Click Remove.
5. Click OK.

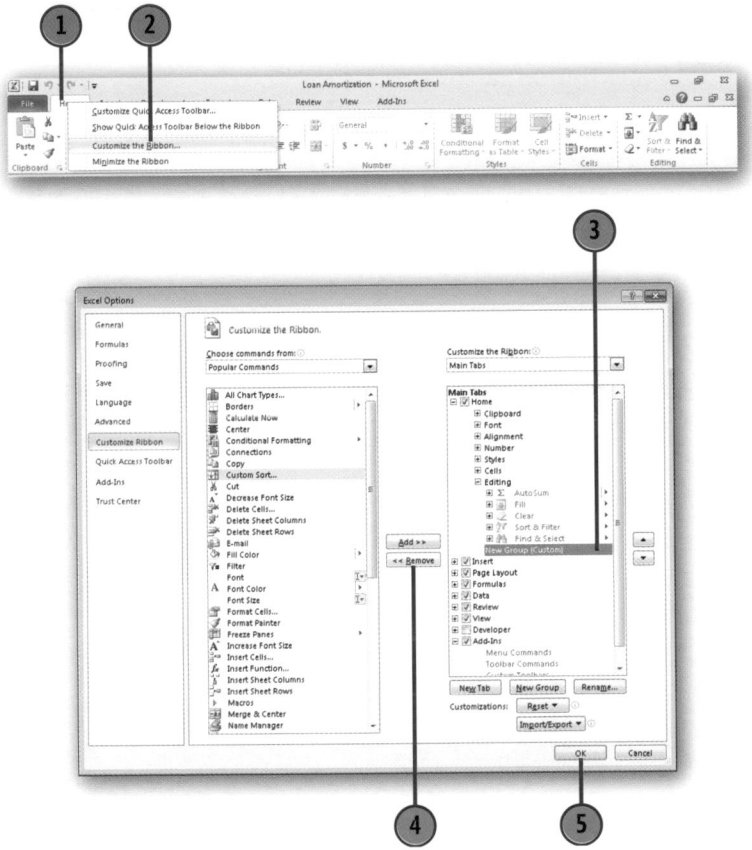

Caution

Removing a custom tab or group deletes that element. If you want the element to remain available for use, hide it instead of removing it.

Create a Custom Ribbon Tab

1. Right-click any ribbon tab.
2. Click Customize The Ribbon.
3. Click the tab above where you want the new tab to appear.
4. Click New Tab.
5. Click OK.

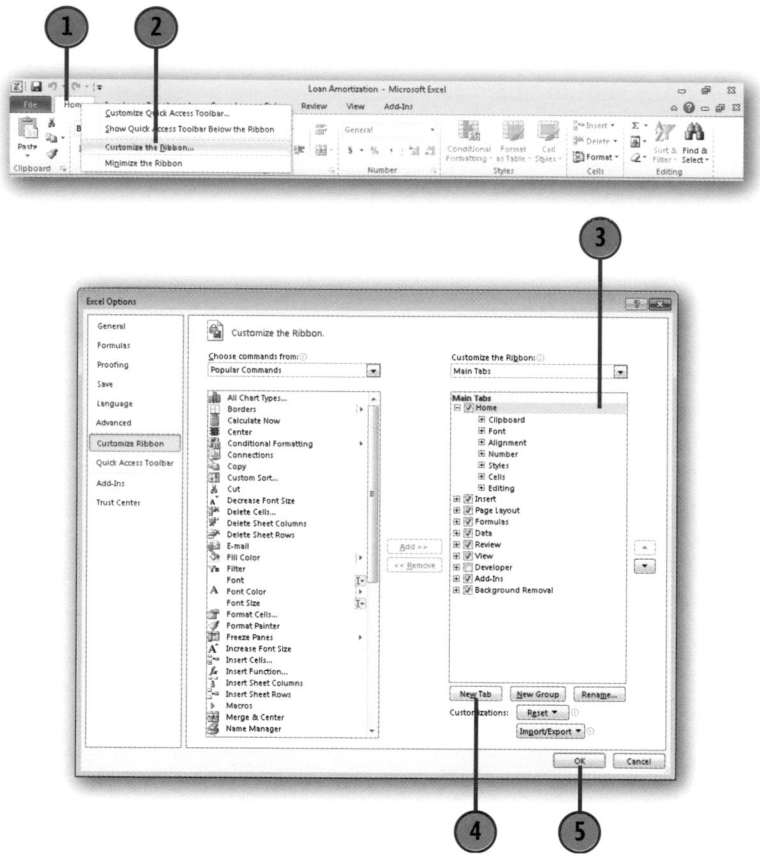

Try This!

Right-click anywhere on the ribbon, and then click Customize The Ribbon. In the right-hand pane, click the Insert tab, and then click New Tab. Then, from the command list in the left-hand pane, click Font, and then click Add. When you click OK to close the Excel Options dialog box, a tab named New Tab appears on the ribbon. When you click the New Tab tab, you'll see that it contains a group named New Group, which in turn contains the Font command.

Add a New Group to a Ribbon Tab

1. Right-click any ribbon tab.
2. Click Customize The Ribbon.
3. Click the group or tab name above where you want the new group to appear.
4. Click New Group.
5. Click OK.

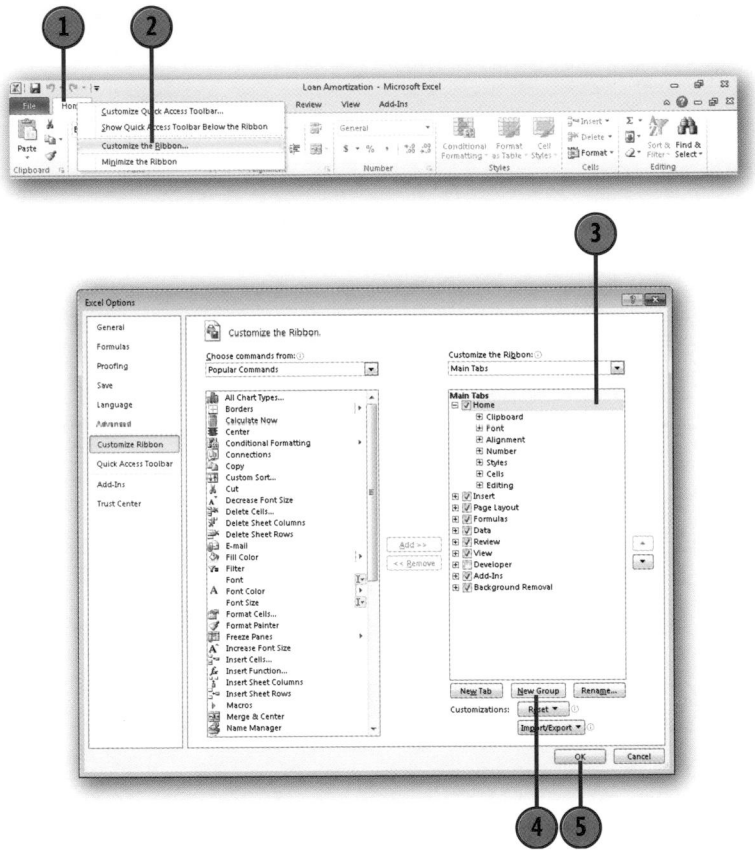

Tip

Don't feel the need to fill up your custom ribbon tab. If you use five groups of commands and they fit in the left half of the tab, you should leave the rest of the custom tab empty.

Rename a Ribbon Element

1. Right-click any ribbon tab.
2. Click Customize The Ribbon.
3. Click the element you want to rename.
4. Click Rename.
5. Type a new name for the element.
6. Click OK.
7. Click OK.

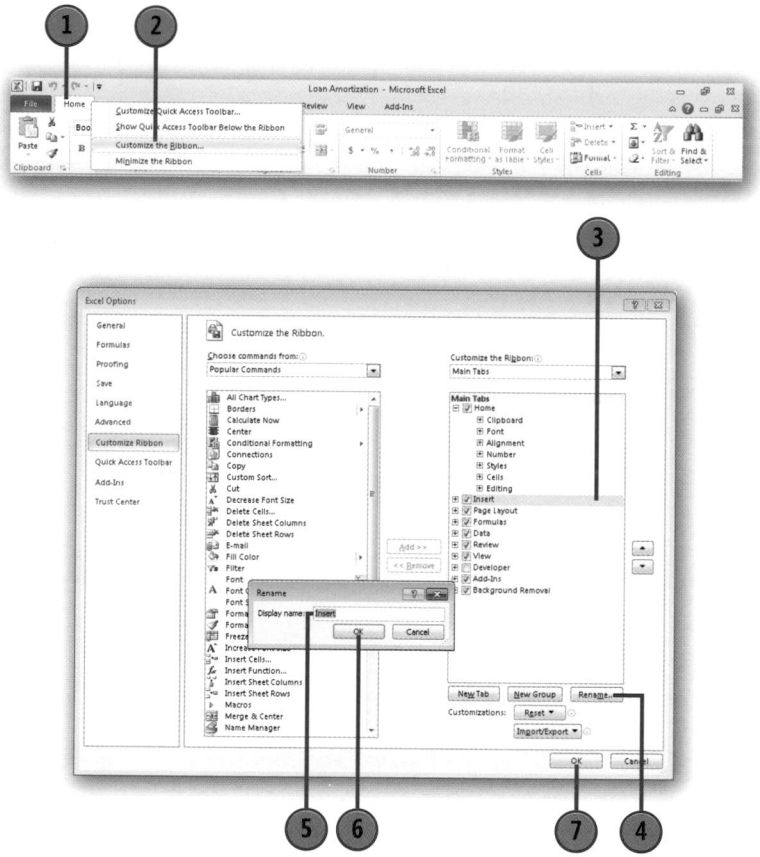

Tip

When you rename a custom ribbon command, the Rename dialog box displays a set of icons. Selecting one of the icons helps you identify the element visually.

Hide a Ribbon Element

1. Right-click any ribbon tab.
2. Click Customize The Ribbon.
3. Clear the check box next to the item you want to hide.
4. Click OK.

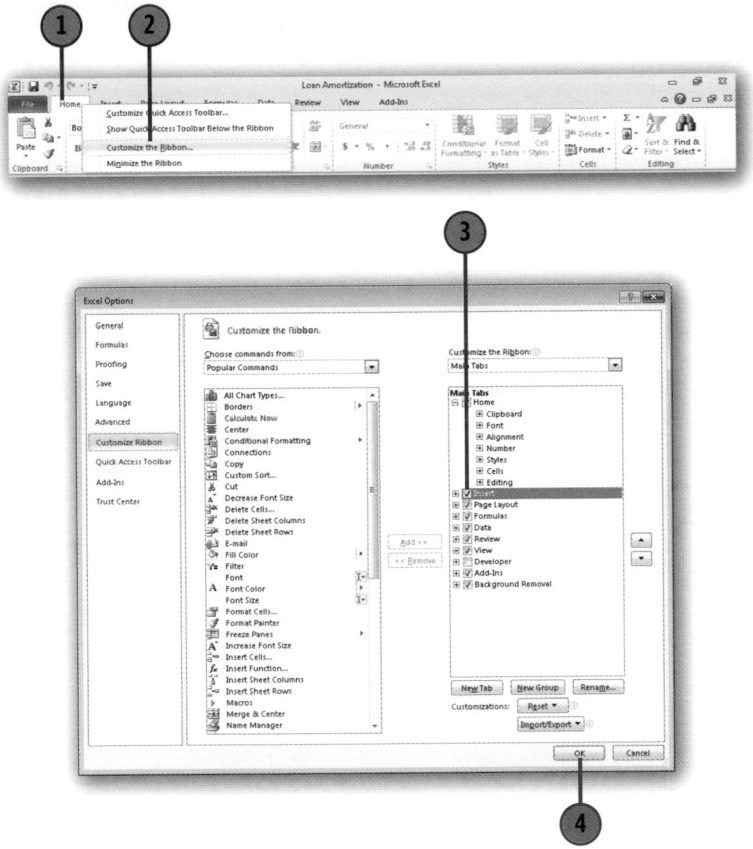

Redisplay a Hidden Ribbon Element

1. Right-click any ribbon tab.
2. Click Customize The Ribbon.
3. Select the check box next to the item you want to display.
4. Click OK.

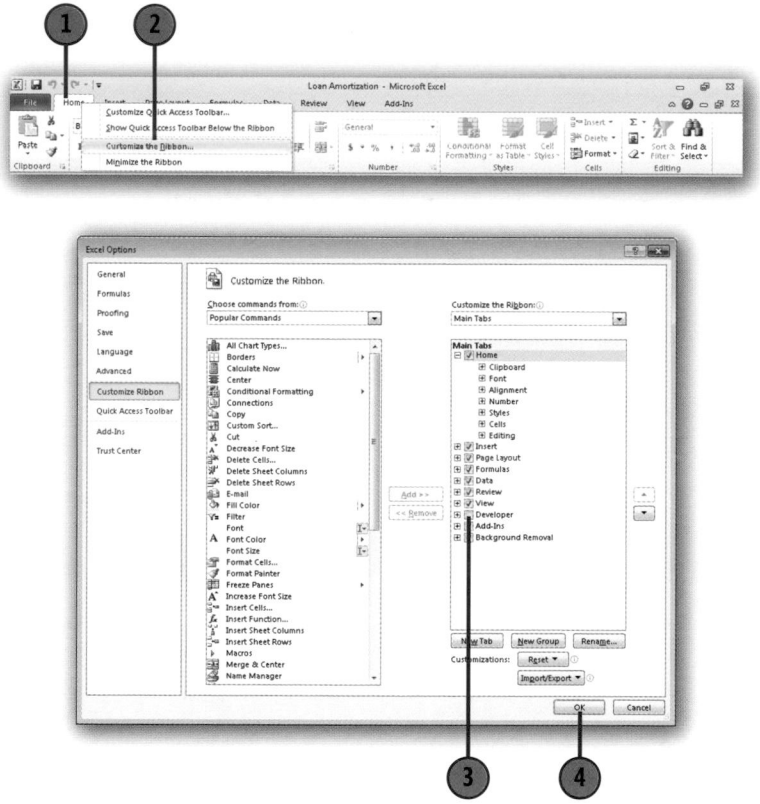

Controlling Which Error Messages Appear

We all make mistakes, but some of those mistakes are easier to recover from than others. If you create a formula that tries to have Excel divide a value by zero or use a value from a cell that's currently blank, Excel displays an error flag indicating that it thinks you made a mistake. If the error is that no value is in a cell you refer to in a formula, you can fix the problem by putting a value in that cell.

At times, though, Excel identifies a formula as an error when, in fact, it's exactly what you intended. For example, if you create a worksheet that contains five columns of data, and you find the sum of each of those columns, Excel identifies the pattern inherent in those formulas. If you put a different type of formula (such as a formula that finds the maximum value in all five rows) in the cell next to those five consistent formulas, Excel displays an error indicating that the formula is inconsistent. Fortunately, you can choose to turn several types of error indicators on or off, saving you and your colleagues from worrying about errors that don't exist.

Choose Which Error Messages Appear

1. Click the File tab.
2. Click Options.
3. Click Formulas.
4. Clear the check boxes next to the errors you want Excel to ignore.
5. Click OK.

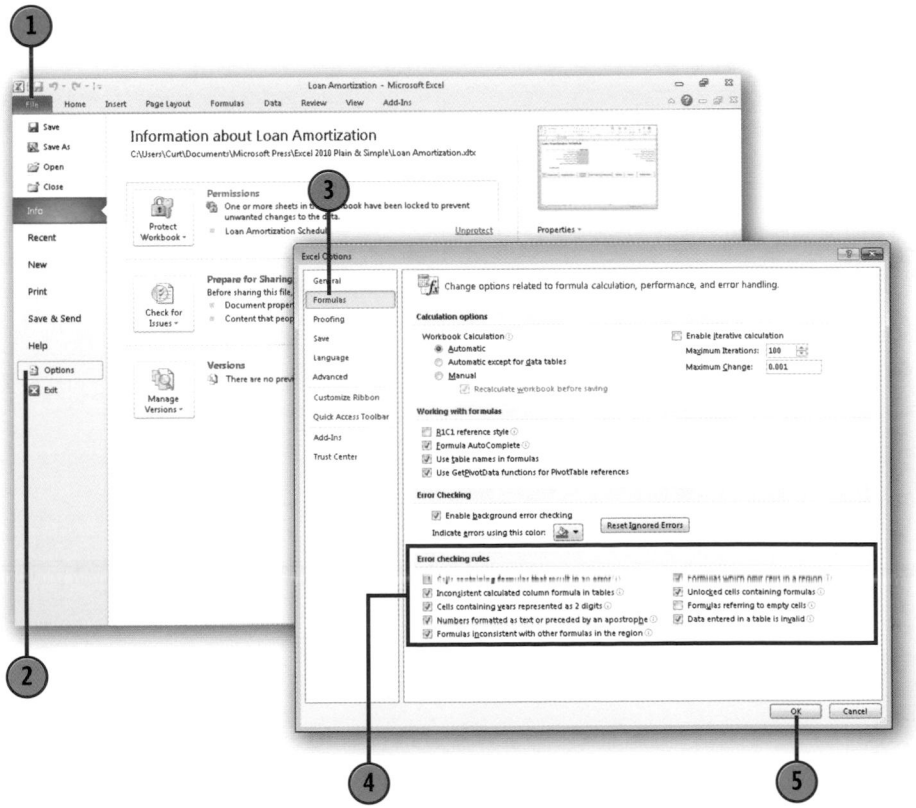

Tip

The most common errors you'll want to ignore are formulas that are inconsistent with other formulas in the region and formulas that omit cells in a region.

Reset Ignored Errors

1. Click the File tab.
2. Click Options.
3. Click Formulas.
4. Click Reset Ignored Errors.
5. Click OK.

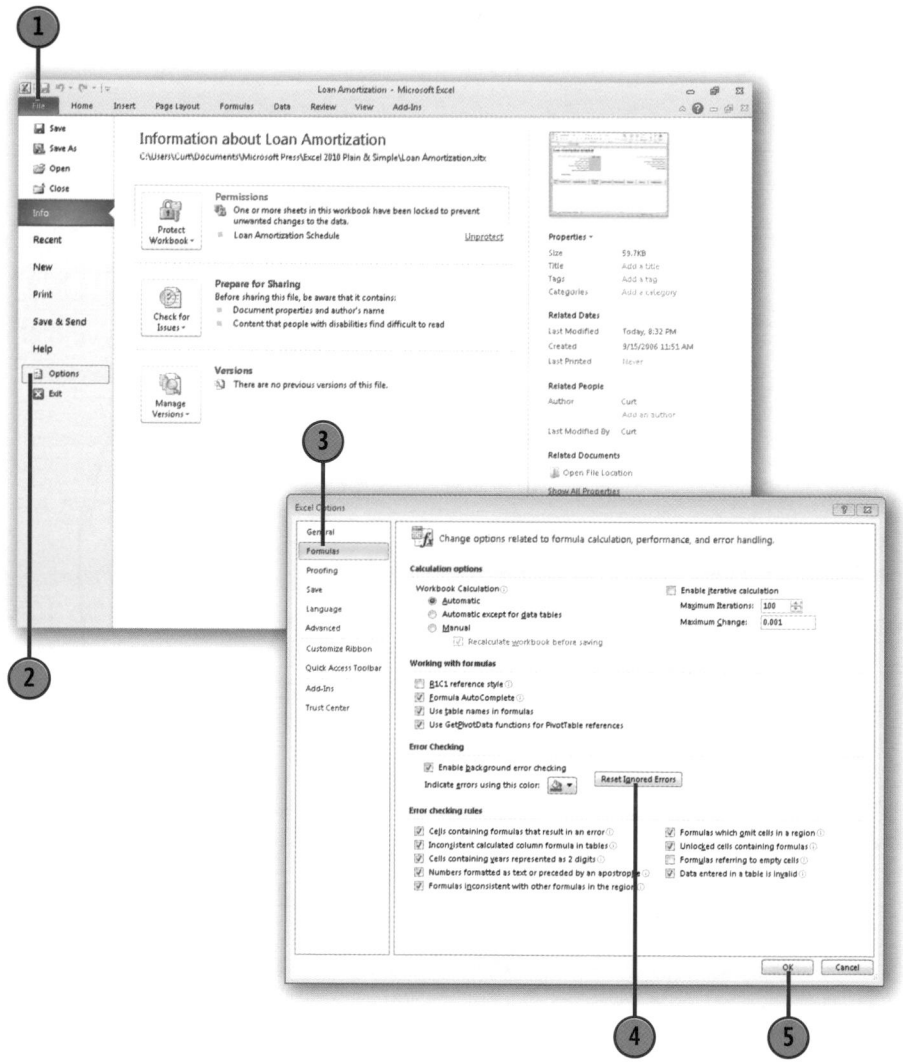

Select the Color in Which Excel Displays Errors

1. Click the File tab.
2. Click Options.
3. Click Formulas.
4. Click Indicate Errors Using This Color.
5. Click the color you want to use.
6. Click OK.

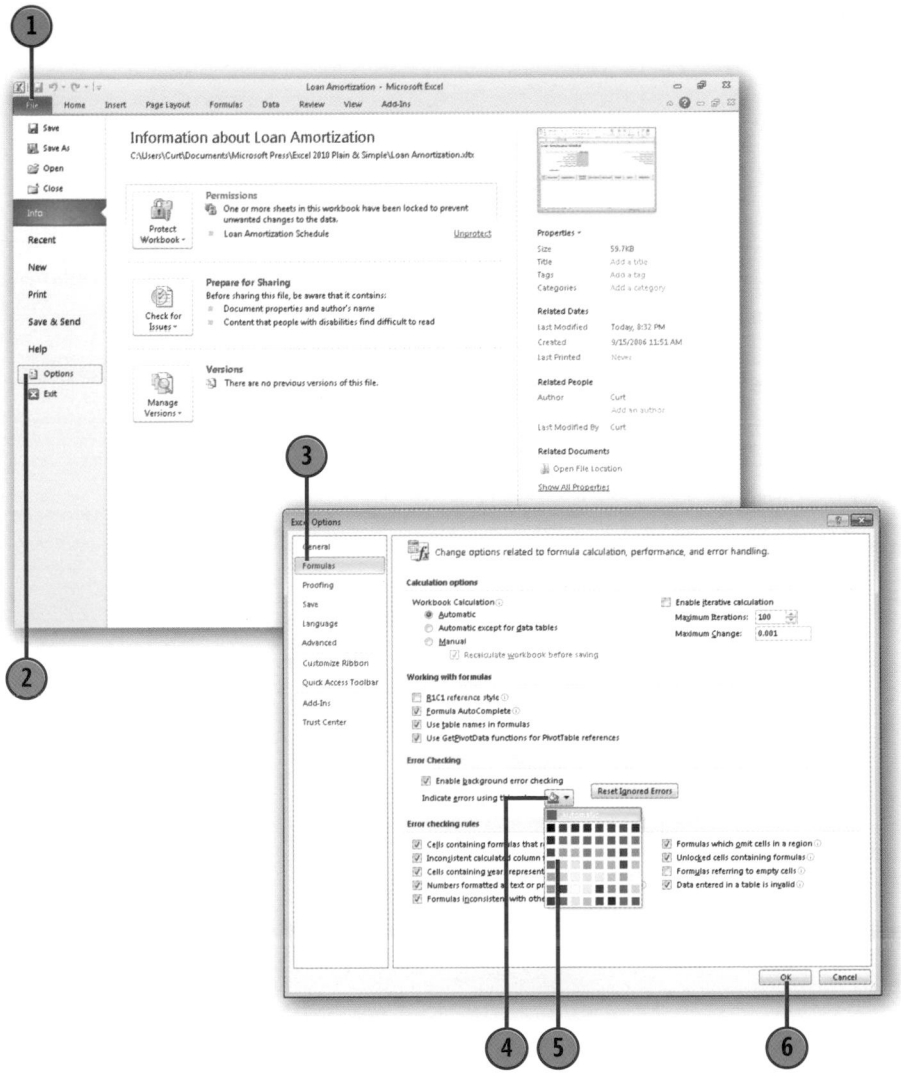

Defining AutoCorrect and AutoFormat Entries

You're bound to make typing mistakes when you spend a lot of time at the keyboard. In fact, slowing down doesn't help; the more slowly you go, the more likely you are to hit the wrong keys.

Over the years, many Excel users have allowed the programming team to monitor their typing, which means that the Excel team has been able to identify the most common mistakes resulting from popular misspellings, letter transpositions, and errors that are the result of not pressing the Spacebar fast enough to put a space between words. If one of the words Excel identifies as an error is actually correct (for example, you work with a client corporation named Idae, a popular misspelling of the word idea), you can delete that entry from the AutoCorrect list.

Create an AutoCorrect Entry

1. Click the File tab.
2. Click Options.

(continued on next page)

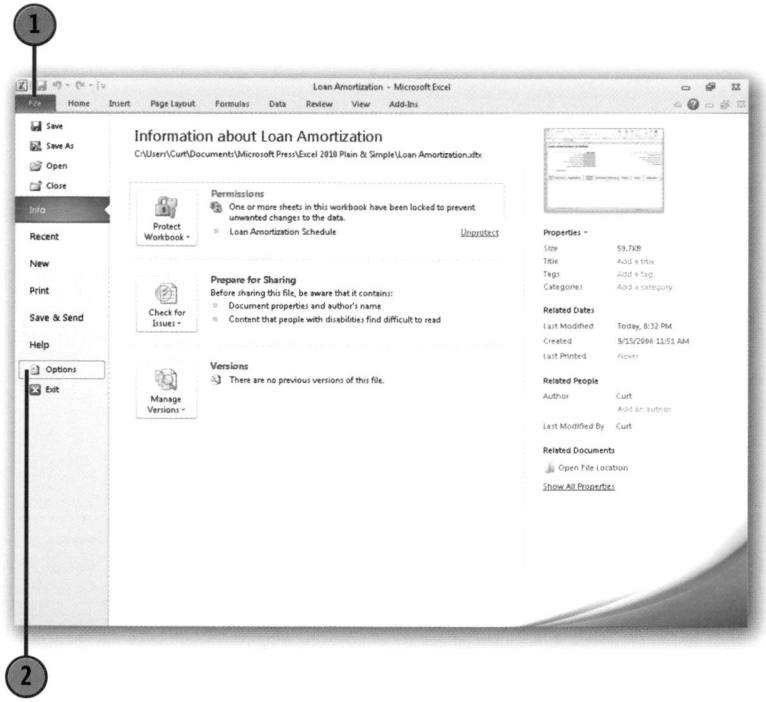

Create an AutoCorrect Entry

(continued)

3. Click Proofing.
4. Click AutoCorrect Options.
5. Type the text to be replaced.
6. Type the text with which to replace the previous entry.
7. Click Add.
8. Click OK.
9. Click OK.

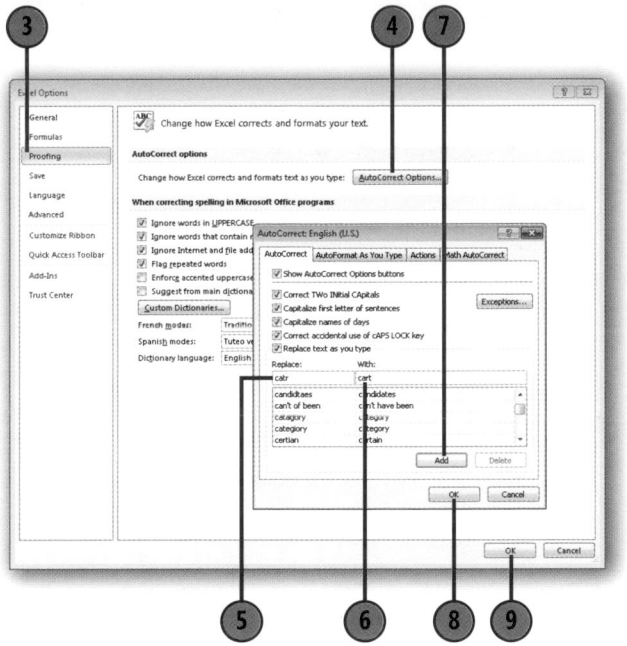

Tip

To undo an AutoCorrect correction, press Ctrl+Z.

Tip

Many users type the same text frequently, such as "Payment is due within 30 days. If payment is made within 10 days, you may deduct 2% from the total amount due." If you often type this text, you could create an AutoCorrect entry that replaces the phrase Net30/2 with the text describing the payment terms already listed.

Delete an AutoCorrect Entry

1. Click the File tab.
2. Click Options.
3. Click Proofing.
4. Click AutoCorrect Options.
5. Click the entry to be removed.
6. Click Delete.
7. Click OK.
8. Click OK.

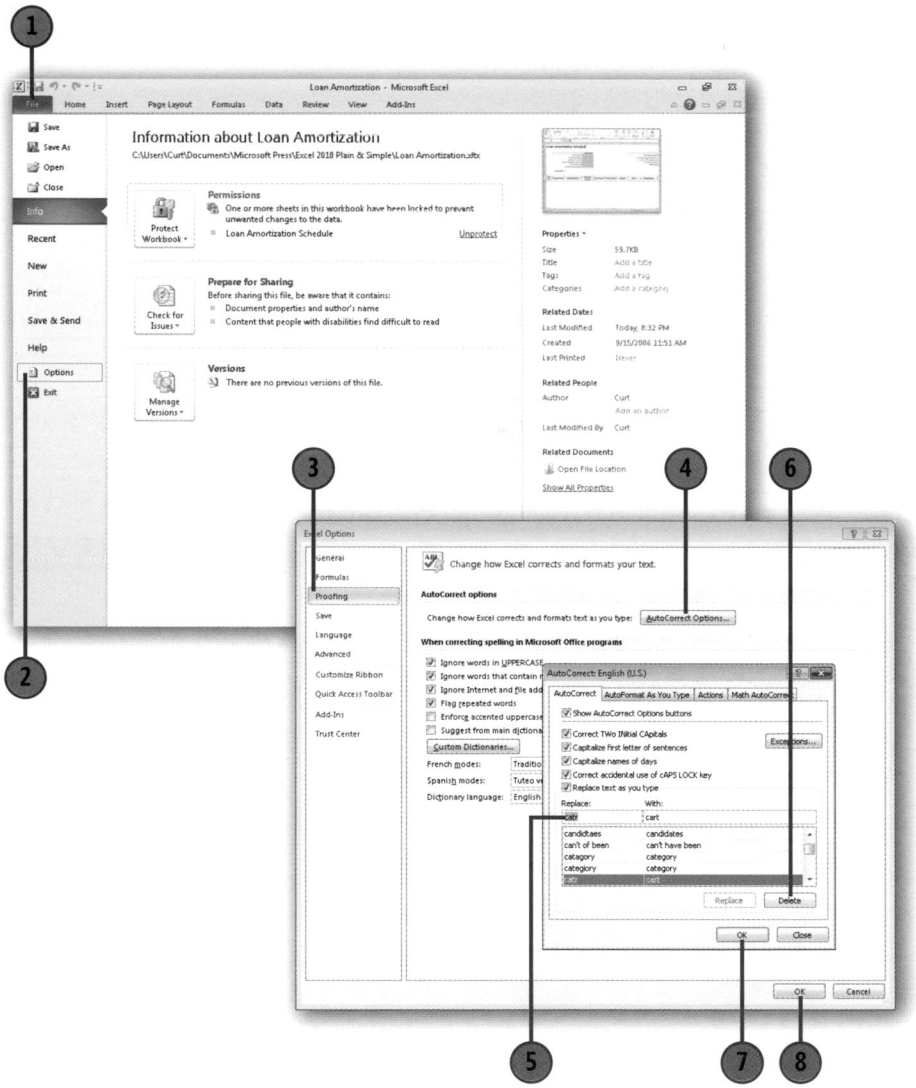

Control AutoFormat Rules

1. Click the File tab.
2. Click Options.
3. Click Proofing.
4. Click AutoCorrect Options.
5. Click the AutoFormat As You Type tab.
6. Clear the check boxes next to the rules you want to turn off, or select the check boxes next to the rules you want to turn on.
7. Click OK.
8. Click OK.

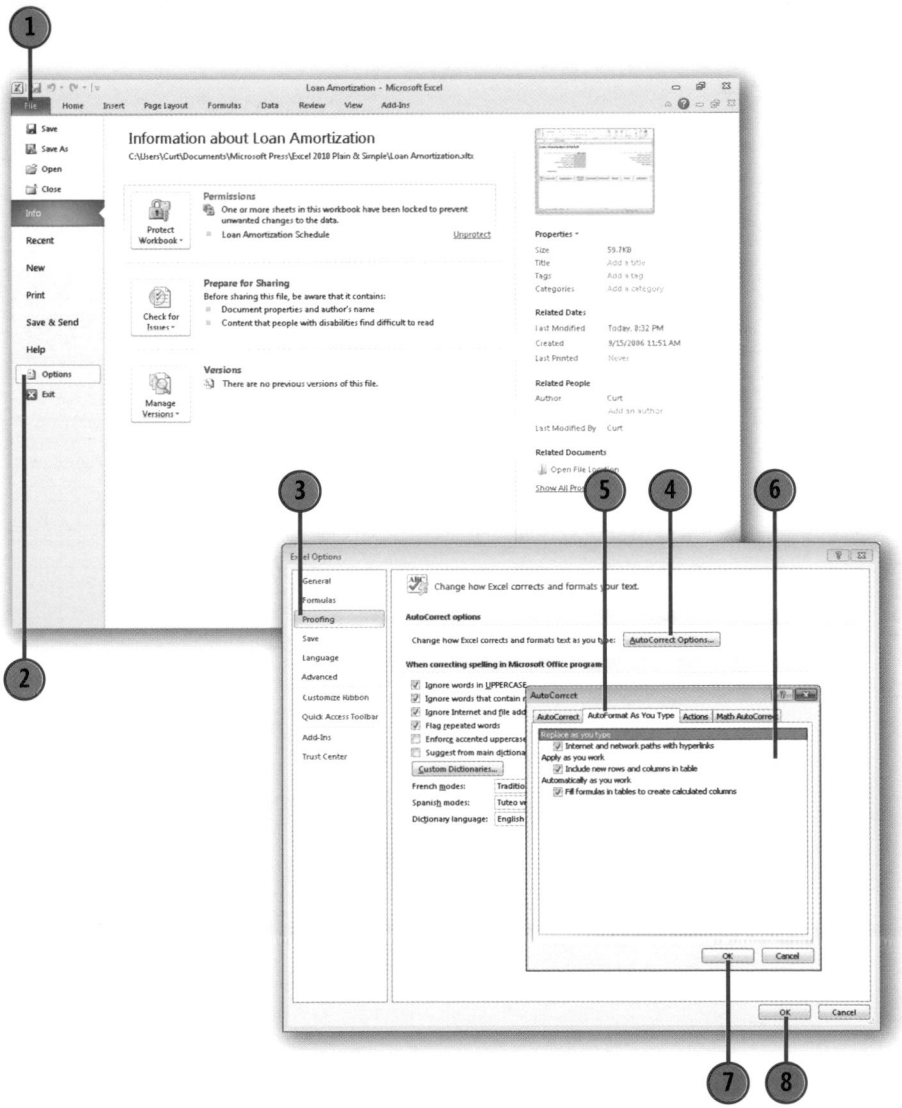

11 Sorting and Filtering Worksheet Data

In this section:

- Sorting Worksheet Data Using Single Column and Multicolumn Sorts
- Defining Custom Lists and Sort Using Those Lists
- Limiting Worksheet Data Using Filters
- Guiding Data Entry with Validation Rules

After you add data to your worksheets, you might want to change the order in which the worksheet rows are displayed. For example, if you have a worksheet listing orders for a week, you might want to list the orders for each customer or perhaps reorder the rows in your worksheet so that the most expensive orders are at the top of the list and the least expensive at the bottom. You can also hide any rows that don't meet your criteria, which is particularly useful if you work with a large data set.

Just as you can change or limit how your worksheet data is displayed, you can control what data is entered in your worksheets. By setting validation rules for groups of cells, you can check each value, and if the value you or your colleague enters falls outside the accepted range, you can display an error message informing you or your colleague what went wrong and what sort of value should be entered.

Sorting Worksheet Data

You can sort a group of rows in a worksheet in a number of ways, but the first step is identifying the column that includes the values by which to sort the rows. After you select the column by which you want to sort the worksheet, you can choose whether to display the sorted values in ascending or descending order. For example, if you have a list of products your company sells with each product's sales in the same row, you could sort the worksheet by the contents of the sales column in descending order to discover which products generated the most revenue for your company. You could sort the worksheet rows in ascending order to put the lowest-revenue products at the top of the list. If you want to sort by the contents of more than one column, you can create a multicolumn sort. One handy use for a multicolumn sort is to sort your products by category and then by total sales.

Sort Data in Ascending or Descending Order

1. Click any cell in the column by which you want to sort your data.
2. Click the Data tab.
3. Follow either of these steps:
   - Click the Sort Ascending button in the Sort & Filter group on the ribbon.
   - Click the Sort Descending button in the Sort & Filter group on the ribbon.

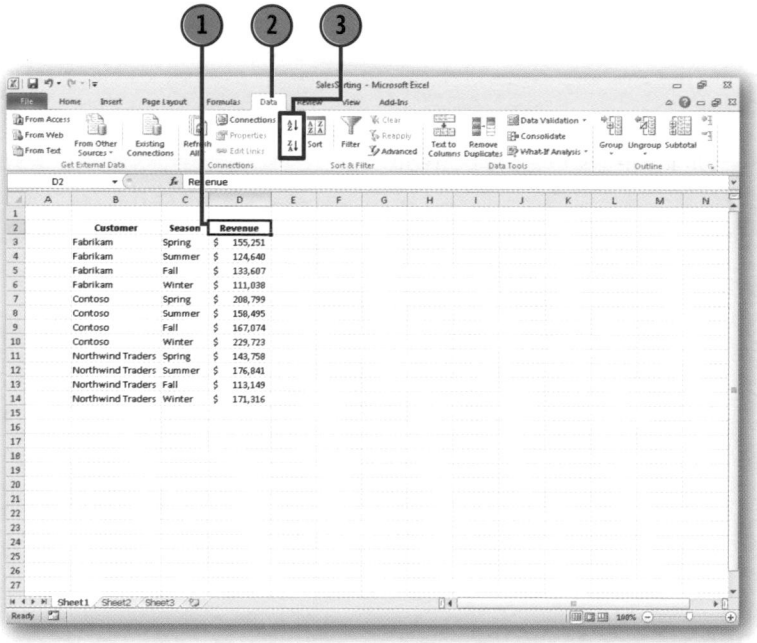

Tip

The names of the sorting buttons in the Data tab's Sort & Filter group change to reflect the type of data in the column to be sorted. If the column contains numbers, the buttons are named Sort Smallest To Largest and Sort Largest To Smallest; for text, the buttons are named Sort A To Z and Sort Z To A; for dates, they are named Sort Oldest To Newest and Sort Newest To Oldest.

Create a Multicolumn Sort

1. Select a cell in the data list or Excel table you want to sort.
2. Click the Data tab.
3. Click Sort.
4. Click the Sort By down arrow, and then click the first column by which you want to sort.
5. Click the Sort On down arrow, and then click the criteria by which you want to sort.
6. Click the Order down arrow.
7. Select the A to Z item or the Z to A item to indicate the order in which the column's values should be sorted.
8. Click Add Level.
9. If necessary, repeat steps 4–8 to set the columns and order for additional sorting rules.
10. Click OK.

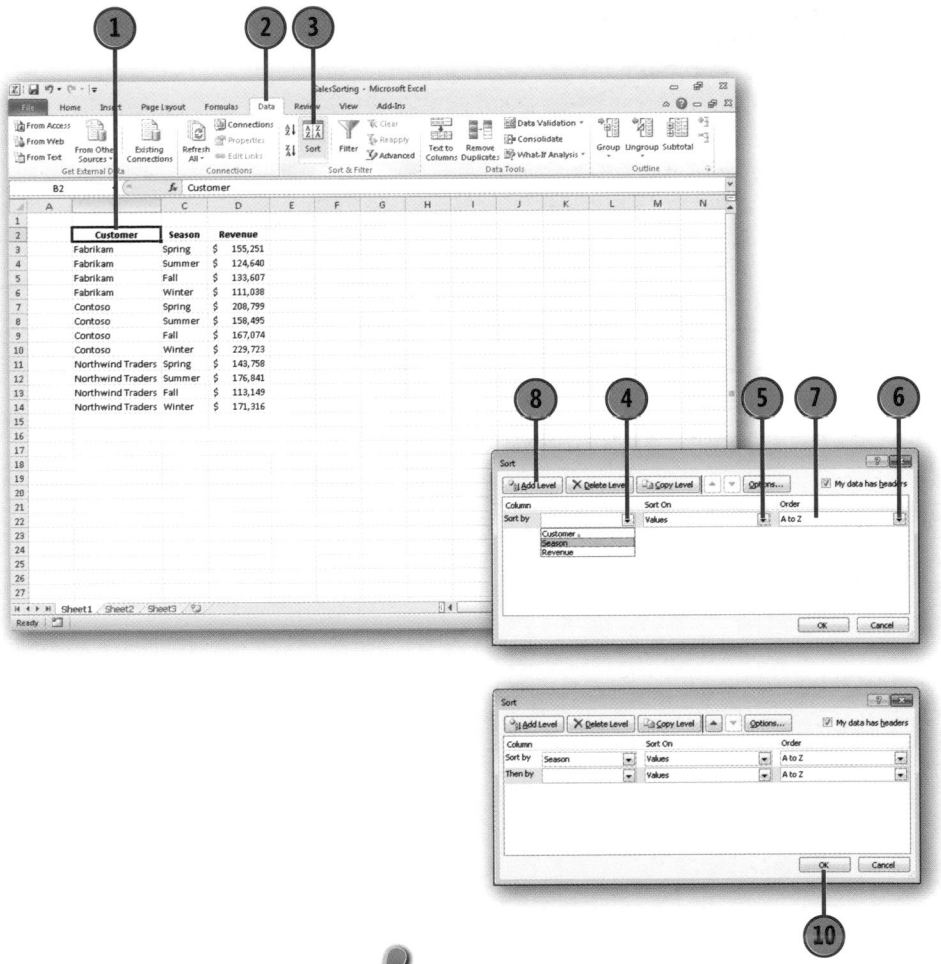

Tip

In Microsoft Excel 2010, you can sort by the values in as many as 64 columns if you need to.

Caution

If you don't have a column with a unique value in each cell, such as a product number or customer identification number, you might not be able to put your worksheet back to its original order.

Creating a Custom Sort List

When you sort column data, Excel sorts numbers according to their values and words in alphabetical order, but that pattern doesn't work for some sets of values. For example, sorting the months of the year in alphabetical order puts February in front of January. To avoid those errors, Excel comes with four custom lists: days of the week, abbreviations for days of the week, months, and abbreviated month names. You can have Excel sort based on those lists, or if you want to create a custom list of your own, you can do so. Because the day and abbreviated day name lists begin with Sunday, you could create a new list beginning with Monday to reflect your business schedule.

Define a Custom List of Values

1. Click the File tab.
2. Click Options.
3. Click Advanced.
4. In the General section of the Advanced page, click Edit Custom Lists.
5. Click New List.
6. Type the custom list you want. Separate each entry by pressing Enter.
7. Click Add.
8. Click OK twice to close the Custom Lists dialog box and the Excel Options dialog box.

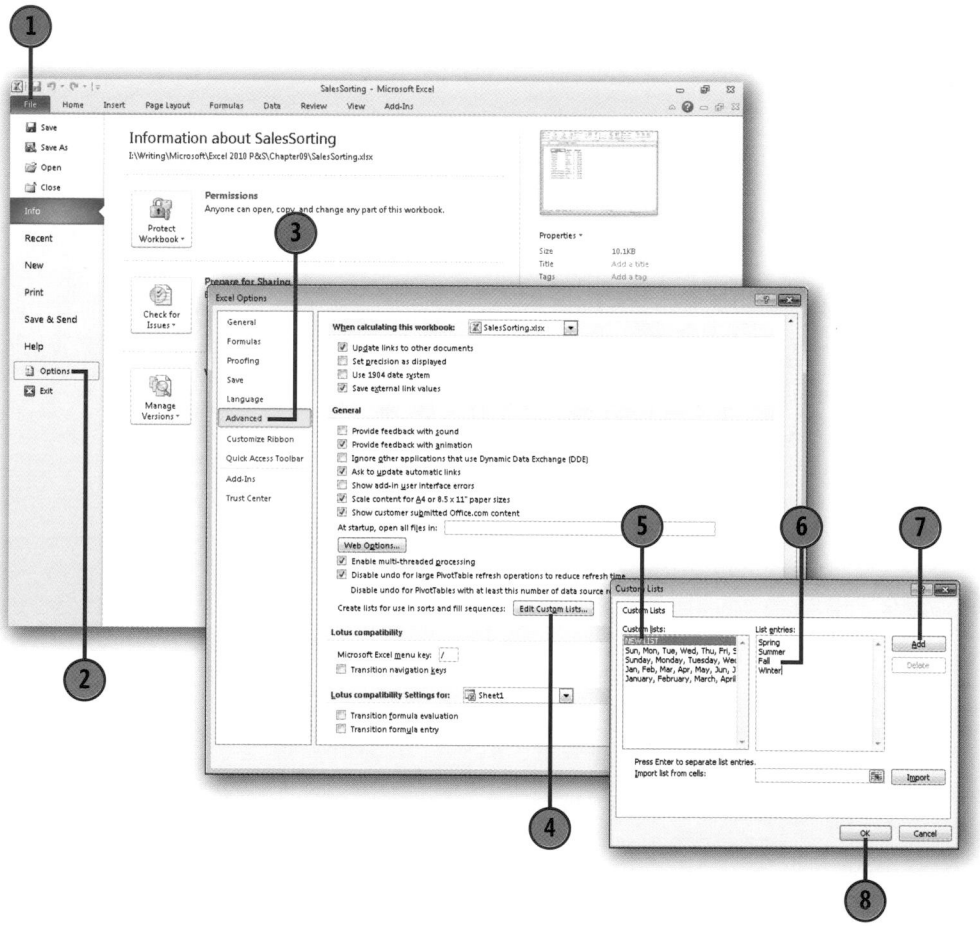

Sort Using a Custom List

1. Click any cell in the list you want to sort.
2. Click the Data tab.
3. Click Sort.
4. Click the Sort By down arrow, and then click the column you want to sort by.
5. Click the Sort On down arrow, and then click the criteria you want to sort by.
6. Click the Order down arrow, and then click Custom List.
7. Click a custom list.
8. Click OK to close the Custom Lists dialog box.
9. Click OK to sort the data list.

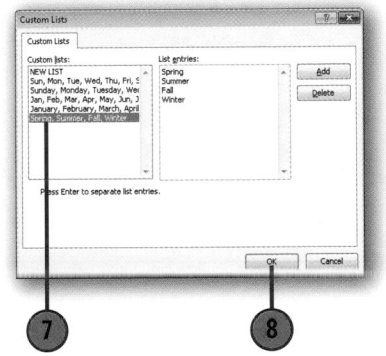

Tip

In earlier versions of Excel, you could use a custom list to sort only one column of your worksheet data, and that column had to be the first by which you sorted your data. In Excel 2010, you can sort any number of columns according to the values in a custom list.

Filtering Data Quickly with AutoFilter

An important aspect of working with large amounts of data is the ability to zero in on the most important data in a worksheet, whether that data represents the best 10 days of sales in a month or slow-selling product lines you might need to re-evaluate. In Excel 2010, you have a number of powerful, flexible techniques you can use to limit the data displayed in your worksheet. One of those techniques is to filter the contents of a worksheet. You can filter a data list or Excel table by selecting individual values, creating a rule, or by searching for values within a field.

Create a Selection Filter

1. Click any cell in the range you want to filter.
2. Click the Data tab.
3. Click Filter.
4. Click the filter arrow for the column by which you want to filter your worksheet.
5. Select the check boxes next to the values by which you want to filter the list.
6. Click OK.

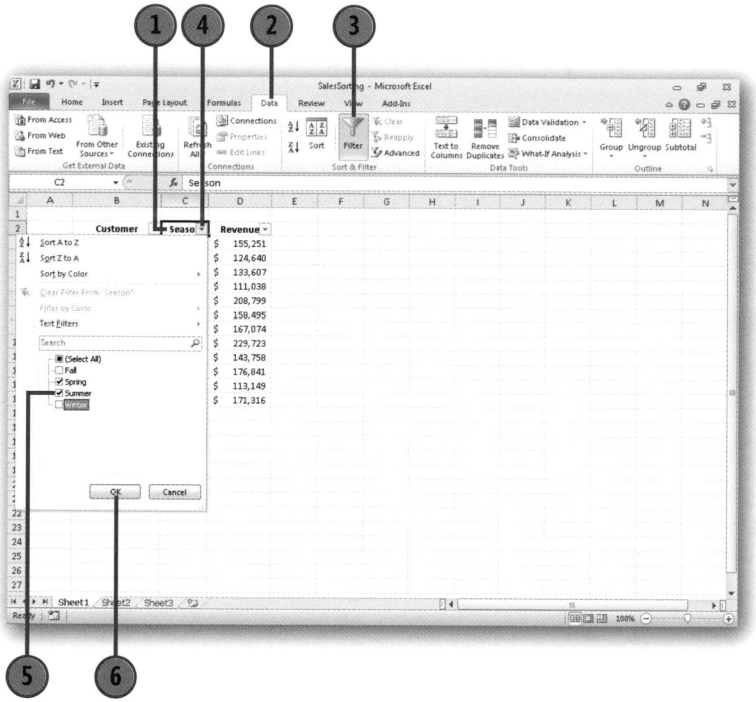

Tip

When you create a custom AutoFilter, the menu item changes to reflect the type of data in the column (date, text, number, and so on).

Tip

If you create an Excel table to store your data, the filter arrows appear on the table's header row by default.

Create a Filtering Rule

1. Click any cell in the list you want to filter.
2. Click the Data tab.
3. If necessary, click Filter to display the filter arrows.
4. Click the filter arrow of the column for which you want to create a custom filter.
5. Point to Text Filters.
6. Click Custom Filter.
7. Click the Comparison Operator down arrow.
8. Click the comparison you want to use.
9. Type the value with which you want to compare the values in the selected column.
10. Click OK.

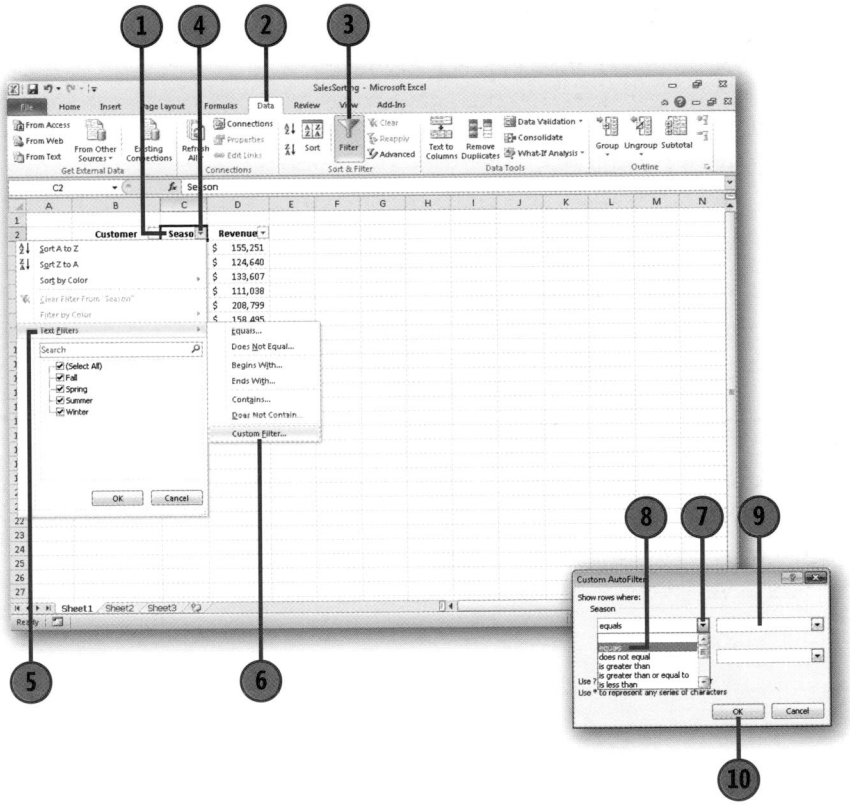

Tip

When a column is filtered, the filter arrow that appears to the right of the filtered list header is replaced by a filter icon.

Create a Search Filter

1. Click any cell in the list you want to filter.
2. Click the Data tab.
3. If necessary, click Filter to display the filter arrows.
4. Click the filter arrow of the column for which you want to create a search filter.
5. In the Search box, type the character string for which you want to search.
6. Use the check boxes to include or exclude specific values.
7. Click OK.

Clear a Filter from a List

1. Click the filter arrow of the filtered column.
2. Click Clear Filter.

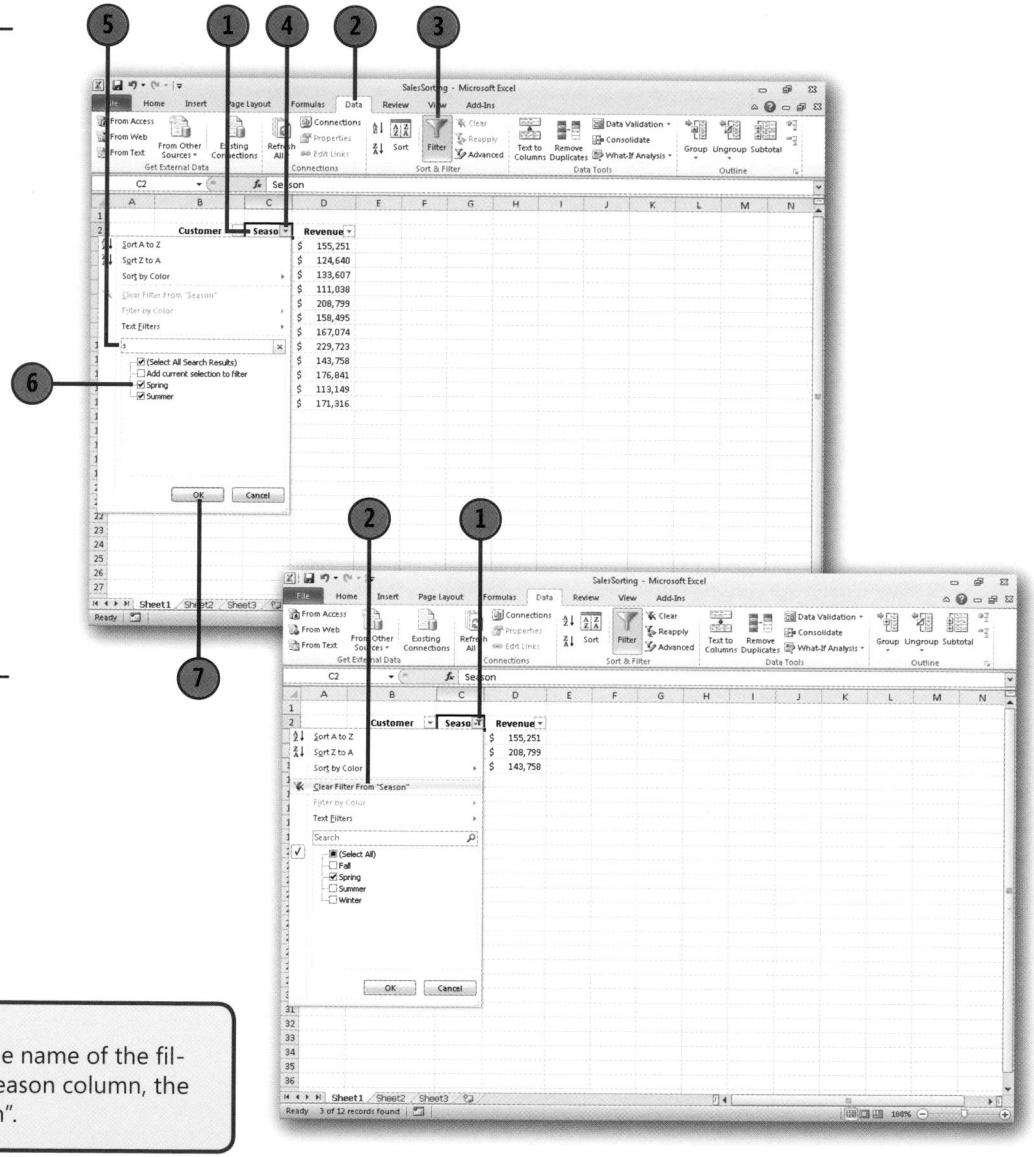

Tip

The Clear Filter menu item changes to reflect the name of the filtered column. For example, if you filtered the Season column, the menu item would read Clear Filter from "Season".

Creating an Advanced Filter

When you create a filter using AutoFilter, you can create complex rules to filter the contents of the worksheet. The limitation is that the rules used to filter the worksheet aren't readily discernable. If you want the rules used to filter a column's values to be displayed in the body of the worksheet, you can write each rule in a cell and identify those cells so that Excel knows how to filter the worksheet. If you ever want to change the rules used to filter your data, all you need to do is change a rule and reapply the filter.

Build an Advanced Filter

1. Copy the column titles of the list you want to filter.
2. Paste the titles into another spot on your workbook.
3. Under their respective titles, type the criteria you want the filter to meet.
4. Select a cell in the list you want to filter.
5. Click the Data tab.
6. In the Sort & Filter group on the ribbon, click Advanced.
7. Click the List Range box.
8. If necessary, select the entire list you want to filter, including the column headers.
9. Click the Criteria Range box.
10. Select the cells on which you want to base the filter, including the column headers.
11. Click OK.

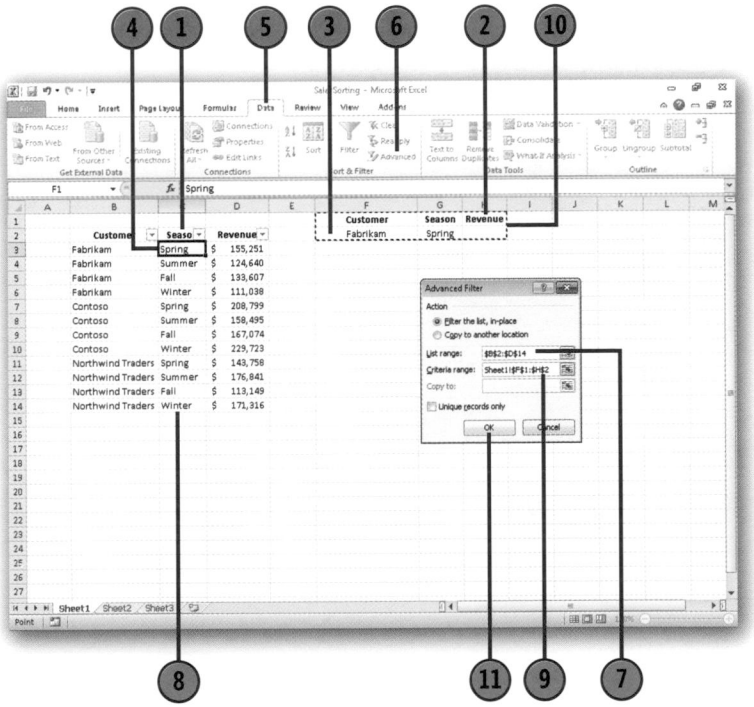

Tip

If you want to copy the results of the filter to another cell range, select the Copy To Another Location option and then specify the range of cells into which you want Excel to copy the filtered list.

Remove an Advanced Filter

1. Select a cell in the range from which you want to remove the filter.
2. Click the Data tab.
3. In the Sort & Filter group on the ribbon, click Clear.

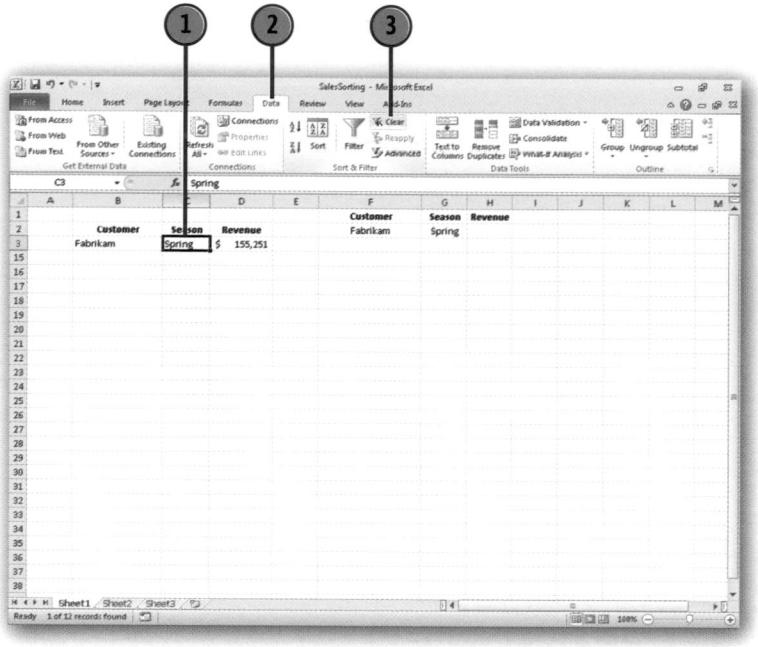

Validating Data for Correctness During Entry

Just as you can limit the data displayed by your worksheets, you can limit the data entered into them. Setting validation rules for data entered into cells lets you catch many of the most common data-entry errors, such as entering values that are too small or too large, or attempting to enter a word in a cell that requires a number. When you create a validation rule, you can also create a message to inform you and your colleagues what sort of data is expected for the cell.

Create a Validation Rule

1. Select the cells you want to validate.
2. On the Data tab, click the Data Validation button's down arrow.
3. Click Data Validation.
4. Click the Allow down arrow.
5. Click the type of data you want to allow.
6. Click the Data down arrow, and then click the condition you want to validate.
7. Type the appropriate values in the boxes.
8. Click the Input Message tab.

(continued on next page)

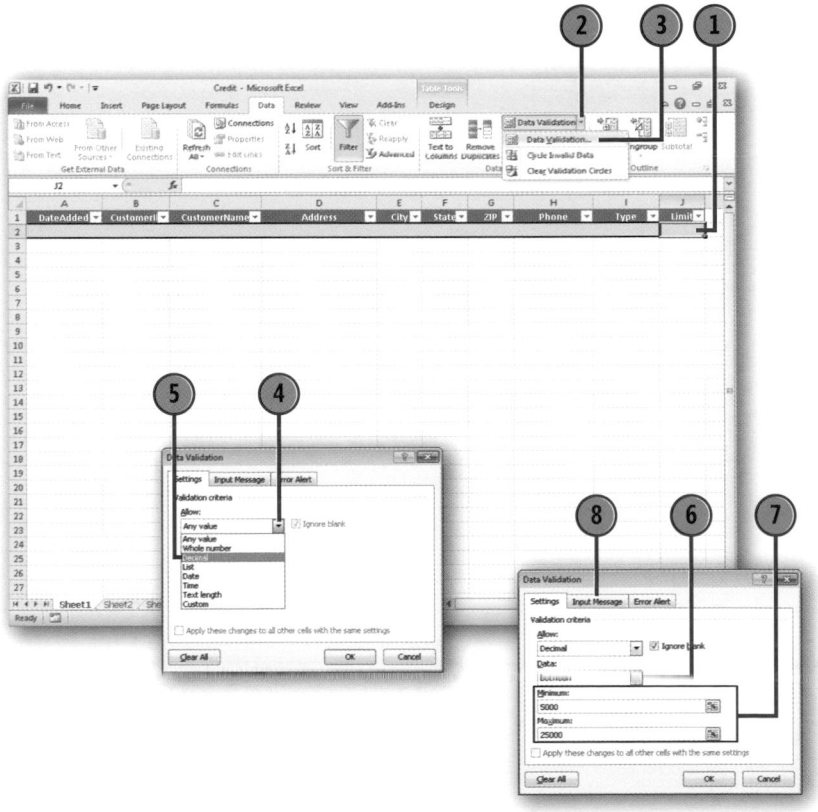

Create a Validation Rule *(continued)*

9. Select the Show Input Message When Cell Is Selected check box.
10. Type a title for the Input Message box.
11. Type the message you want Excel to display when the cell is clicked.
12. Click the Error Alert tab.
13. Select the Show Error Alert After Invalid Data Is Entered check box.
14. Click the Style down arrow.
15. Click the icon you want to appear next to your message.
16. Type a title for the error message box.
17. Type the error message you want.
18. Click OK.

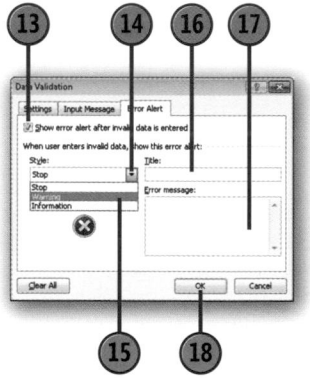

Tip

If you want to highlight all of the cells in your worksheet that have validation criteria, click the Home tab on the ribbon, click Find & Select, and then click Data Validation.

Validate Data According to a List in a Worksheet Range

1. Select the cells that you want to validate.
2. On the Data tab, click the Data Validation button's down arrow.
3. Click Data Validation.
4. Click the Settings tab.
5. Click the Allow down arrow.
6. Click List.
7. Click the Source box.
8. Select the cells that contain the values you want in your list.
9. Click OK.

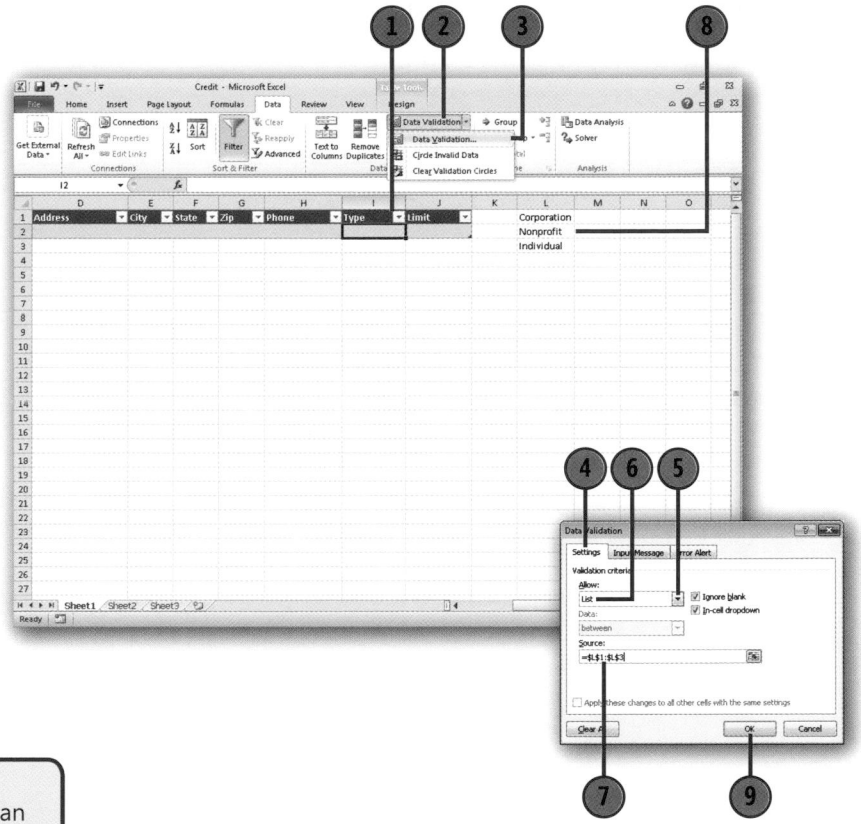

Tip

On the Settings tab of the Data Validation dialog box, you can clear the In-Cell Dropdown check box so that a drop-down arrow does not appear next to the cell with the available options.

Tip

To validate the entire workbook, hold down the Ctrl key and press the A key to select the entire workbook. Then apply the data validation criteria.

Tip

If you don't want to display the list items in your workbook, you can type them in the dialog box. Be sure to separate each item with a comma (,).

12 Summarizing Data Visually Using Charts

In this section:

- Creating a Chart Quickly
- Changing a Chart's Appearance
- Formatting Chart Legends and Titles
- Changing the Body of a Chart
- Customizing Chart Data
- Working with Common and Uncommon Charts
- Adding a Trend Line to a Chart
- Summarizing Data Using Sparklines

Microsoft Excel 2010 gives you lots of ways to change how your numeric data is displayed. You can change the color or font of data you want to emphasize, make your labels bold to set them apart from the body of data in your worksheets, and add graphics to establish your corporate identity. You can use totals and subtotals to summarize your data, making it easier for you and your colleagues to compare values for entire categories of data.

The limitation of working with numbers, even in summary, is that it can be difficult to keep track of several numbers at a time. If you've worked for several years in a package delivery company, you might know that November and December are the busiest months of the year and that February and March show the lowest package volume. If you're presenting results to colleagues or potential investors who are less familiar with your business, you can use charts and graphs to summarize your data visually. By summarizing your data using a chart, you make it much easier for your colleagues to see patterns and relationships.

Displaying Data Graphically

When you enter data into a Microsoft Excel worksheet, you create a record of important events, whether they are individual product sales, sales for an hour of a day, or the price of a product. What a list of values in cells can't communicate easily, however, are the overall trends in your data. The best way to communicate trends in large data collections is through charts and graphs, which summarize data visually.

As an example of how charts and graphs can help present your data more effectively, consider the following Excel table, which lists the number of transactions generated by a small company's Web site.

	A	B	C	D
1	Month	Transactions	Goal	Difference
2	January	5,000	2,500	2,500
3	February	2,715	2,500	215
4	March	2,767	2,500	267
5	April	4,557	2,500	2,057
6	May	3,613	2,500	1,113
7	June	4,348	2,500	1,848
8	July	2,267	2,500	(233)
9	August	1,092	2,500	(1,408)
10	September	3,962	2,500	1,462
11	October	3,551	2,500	1,051
12	November	1,555	2,500	(945)
13	December	1,339	2,500	(1,161)

In a sense, the data does speak for itself. The total transactions and goals for each month are listed so that you and your colleagues can compare them. Each number must be comprehended, remembered, and compared to the other results individually. When you present the results in a chart or graph, as in the following line chart, you can compare the values more readily.

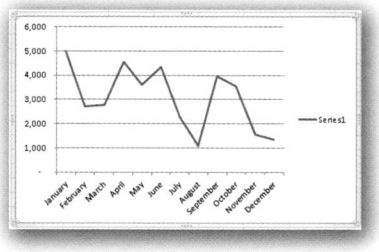

If you have trouble deciding which type of chart or graph you should create, you can experiment while you build a chart. The following table explains which types of data each chart type can be used to represent effectively, but feel free to experiment!

Standard Excel Chart Types and Uses

Chart Type	Use
Column	Compares categories of data in vertical format.
Bar	Compares multiple values in horizontal format.
Line	Displays trends in data over time.
Pie	Compares data as part of a contribution to a whole.
Scatter Plot	Compares pairs of values in a dot format.
Area	Compares the trend of values over time or categories.
Doughnut	Compares multiple series of data in a percent format.
Radar	Displays changes in values relative to a center point.
Surface	Displays trends in values across two dimensions.
Bubble	Compares sets of three values.
Stock	Displays a chart to compare stock prices.
Cylinder	Same as a column or bar chart, but a cylinder is used instead.
Cone	Same as a column or bar chart, but a cone is used instead.
Pyramid	Same as a column or bar chart, but a pyramid is used instead.

Creating a Chart Quickly

To present your Excel data graphically, select the cells you want to summarize, click the Insert tab, and then use the controls in the Chart gallery to select the chart type that's best for your data and the message you want to get across. The cells with the data to be represented in the chart are part of one or more data series. A series is a collection of related data, such as all sales for a particular product or the sales for each day of a month. A bar chart could contain just one series; a line chart, which might display monthly sales for several years, can have many series.

It's easy to create attractive charts in Excel 2010. Not only can you create the chart quickly by using the controls on the ribbon, but you can use the same controls to choose your chart's overall layout and style. After you set your chart's general appearance, you can make changes with no trouble at all.

Create a Chart

1. Click a cell in the data list you want to summarize.
2. Click the Insert tab.
3. Click the type of chart you want to create.
4. Click the chart subtype you want to use.

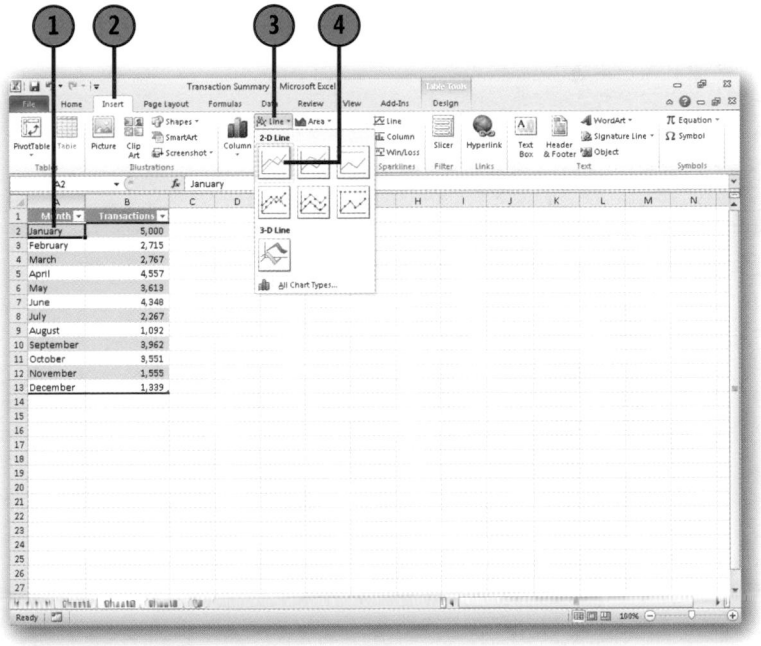

Tip

Pressing F11 creates a chart of the default type (a column chart, unless you've changed it), with the default layout and formatting, on a new workbook sheet.

Change a Chart's Layout

1. Click the chart you want to change.
2. Click the Design tab.
3. In the Chart Layouts group on the ribbon, click the new layout.

Change a Chart's Style

1. Click the chart you want to change.
2. Click the Design tab.
3. In the Chart Styles group on the ribbon, click the new style.

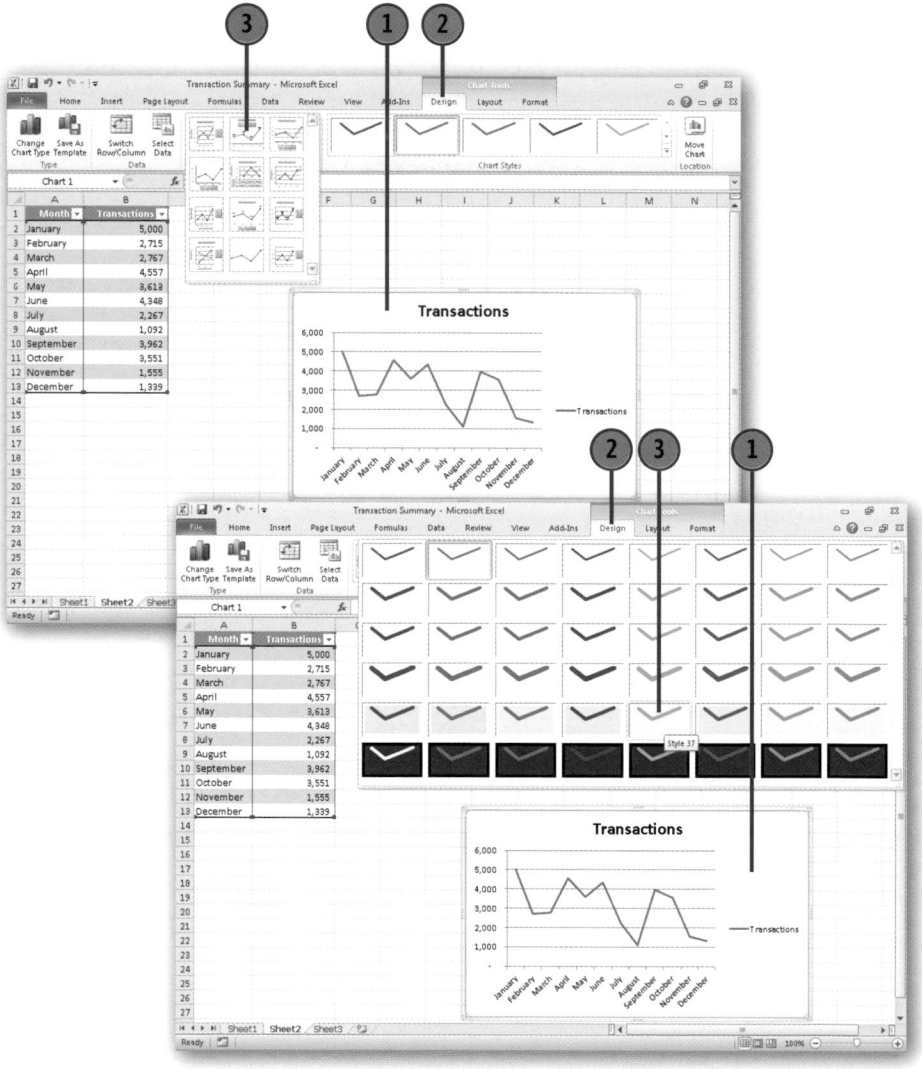

Changing a Chart's Appearance

After you create a chart, you can change any part of its appearance, including the chart's type! If you display monthly sales data as a series of columns and decide that you want to show the data as a line rising and falling as it moves from month to month, you can change the chart's type at will. You can also change the color, font, and other properties of any chart element. If you want your chart's title to be displayed in your company's official font, you can format the title easily.

Change a Chart's Type

1. Click the chart you want to change.
2. Click the Design tab.
3. Click Change Chart Type.
4. Click the type of chart you want.
5. Click the chart subtype you want.
6. Click OK.

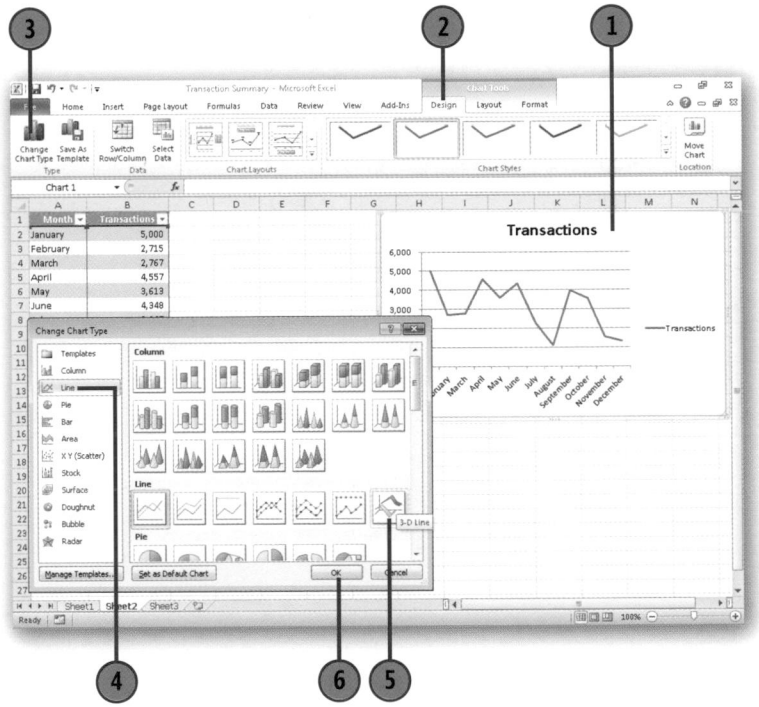

Change the Formatting of a Chart Element

1. Click the chart element you want to change.
2. Click the Format tab.
3. Use the controls in the Shape Styles group to format the chart element.

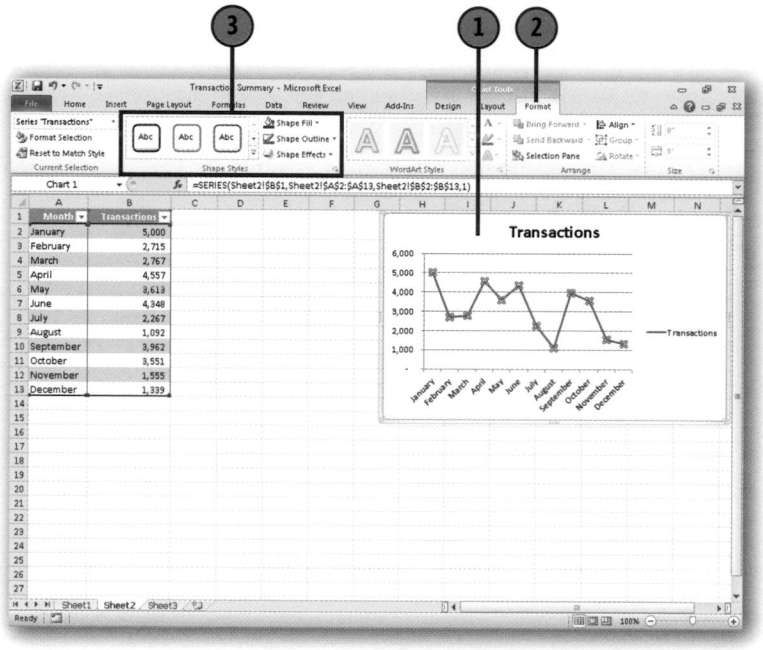

Formatting Chart Legends and Titles

An important part of creating an informative, easily read chart is to describe the contents of the chart. Some of the chart elements you can add to describe your Excel charts are legends, titles, data labels, and annotations. A legend is an index of categories in a chart and the color used to describe them. A sales chart comparing monthly sales for several years, for example, might display the first year in yellow, the second year in blue, and the third year in red. The legend identifies those relationships so that you can read the chart accurately. Titles, data labels, and annotations describe specific parts of a chart and, in the case of annotations, also give general information about the data the chart displays.

Show or Hide a Chart Legend

1. Click the chart you want to format.
2. Click the Layout tab.
3. Click Legend.
4. Click a legend display option.

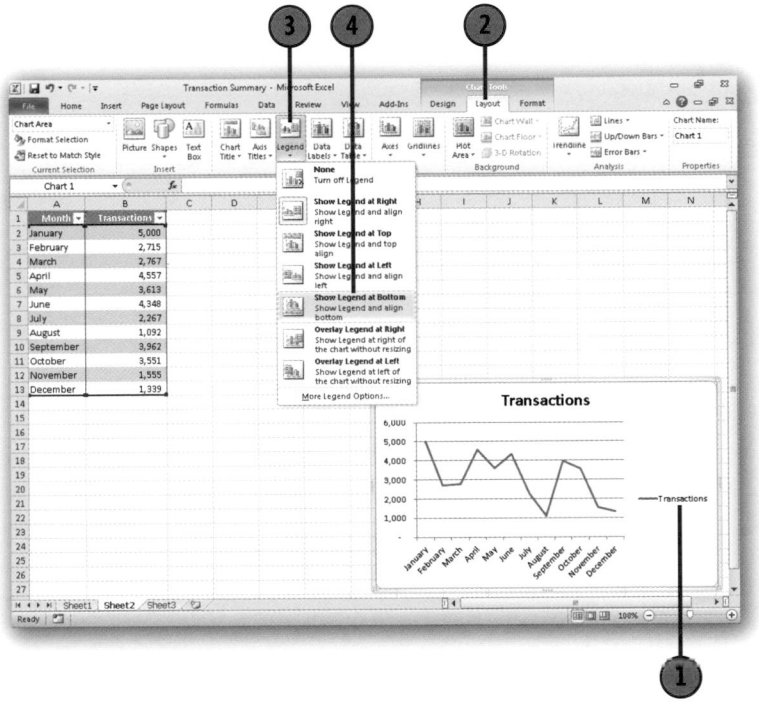

Add Titles

1. Click the chart you want to format.
2. Click the Layout tab.
3. Click Chart Title.
4. Click the title display option you want.
5. Click the title, and then type the new title for the chart.

Add and Remove Data Labels

1. Click the chart you want to format.
2. Click the Layout tab.
3. Click Data Labels.
4. Click a data label option.

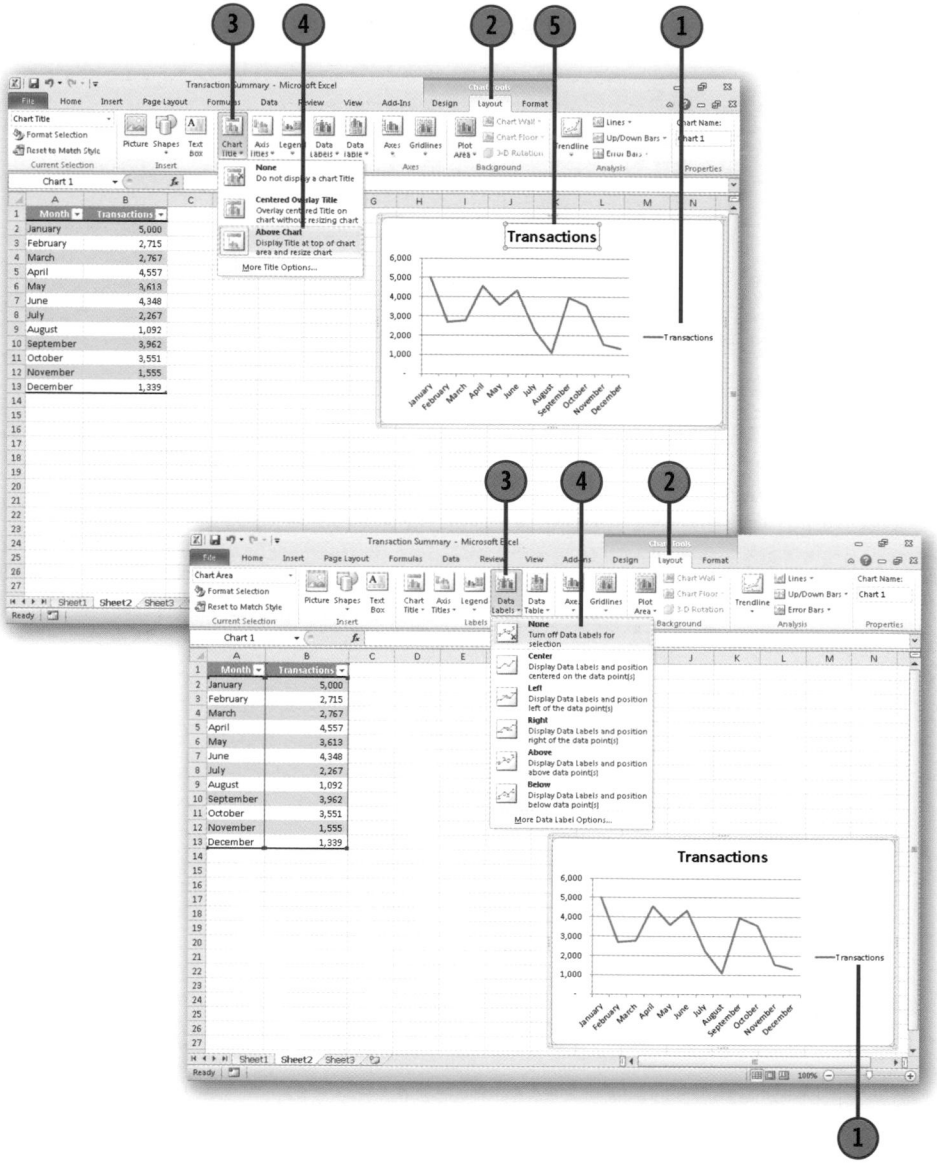

Changing the Body of a Chart

When you add labels, a legend, or annotations to a chart, you change the periphery of the chart, but you don't affect how the data is displayed. If you do want to change how the data is displayed in the body of the chart, such as by showing or hiding gridlines or changing the scale of the chart, you can do so. Adding gridlines can help viewers make fine distinctions between values, even if they're viewing the chart from the other end of a conference table, while changing the scale of the chart lets you heighten or downplay the differences among the chart's values.

Show or Hide Chart Gridlines

1. Click the chart you want to format.
2. Click the Layout tab.
3. Click Gridlines.
4. Click the set of gridlines you want to change.
5. Click a gridline display option.

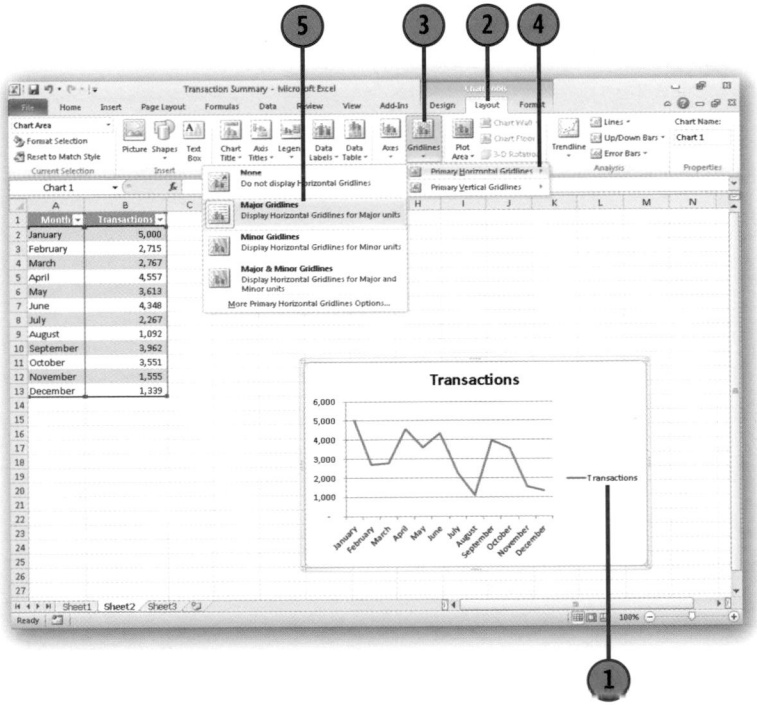

Change the Scale on the Value Axis

1. Click the chart you want to format.
2. Click the Layout tab.
3. Click Axes.
4. Click Primary Vertical Axis.
5. Click More Primary Vertical Axis Options.
6. Click Axis Options.
7. Click the Minimum row's Fixed option, and then type a value for the minimum value on the vertical axis.
8. Click the Maximum row's Fixed option, and then type a value for the maximum value on the vertical axis.
9. Click the Major Unit row's Fixed option, and then type a value for the major units to be displayed on the vertical axis.
10. Click the Minor Unit row's Fixed option, and then type a value for the minor units to be displayed on the vertical axis.
11. Click Close.

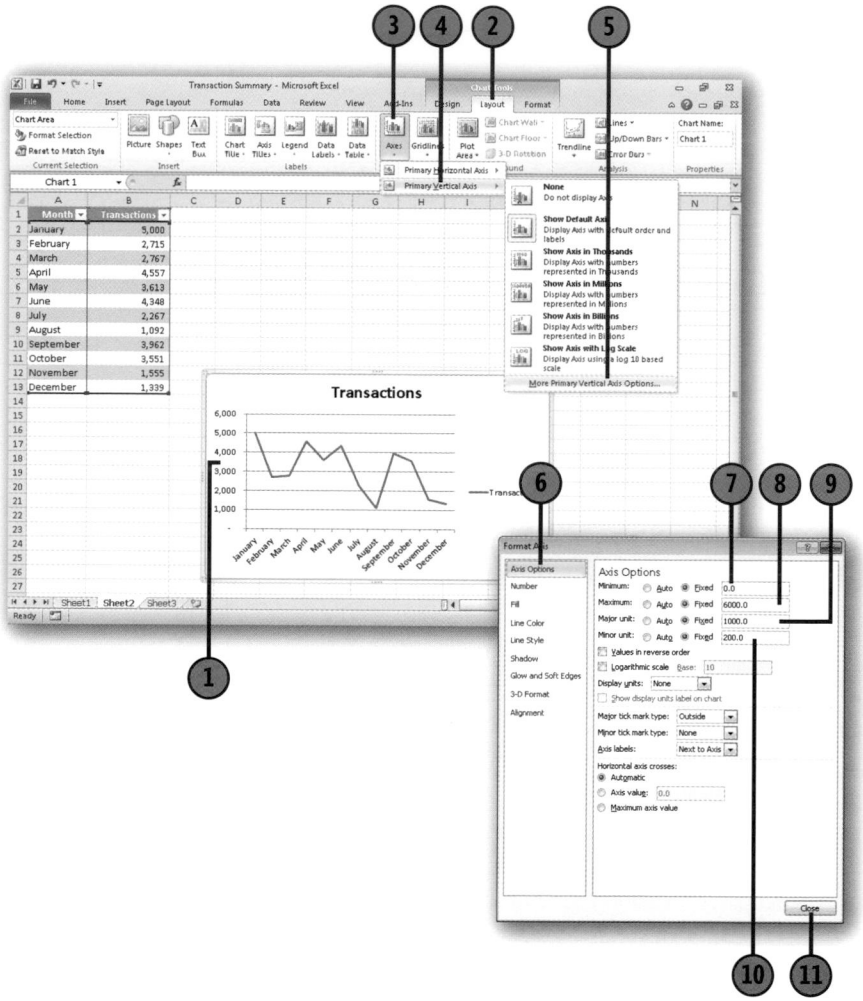

Change the Scale on the Category (X) Axis

1. Click the chart you want to format.
2. Click the Layout tab.
3. Click Axes.
4. Click Primary Horizontal Axis.
5. Click More Primary Horizontal Axis Options.
6. If necessary, click the Axis Options tab.
7. Enter how often you want the tick marks to appear.
8. Select the Specify Interval Unit option.
9. Enter how often you want the tick mark labels to appear.
10. Select or clear the other options.
11. Click Close.

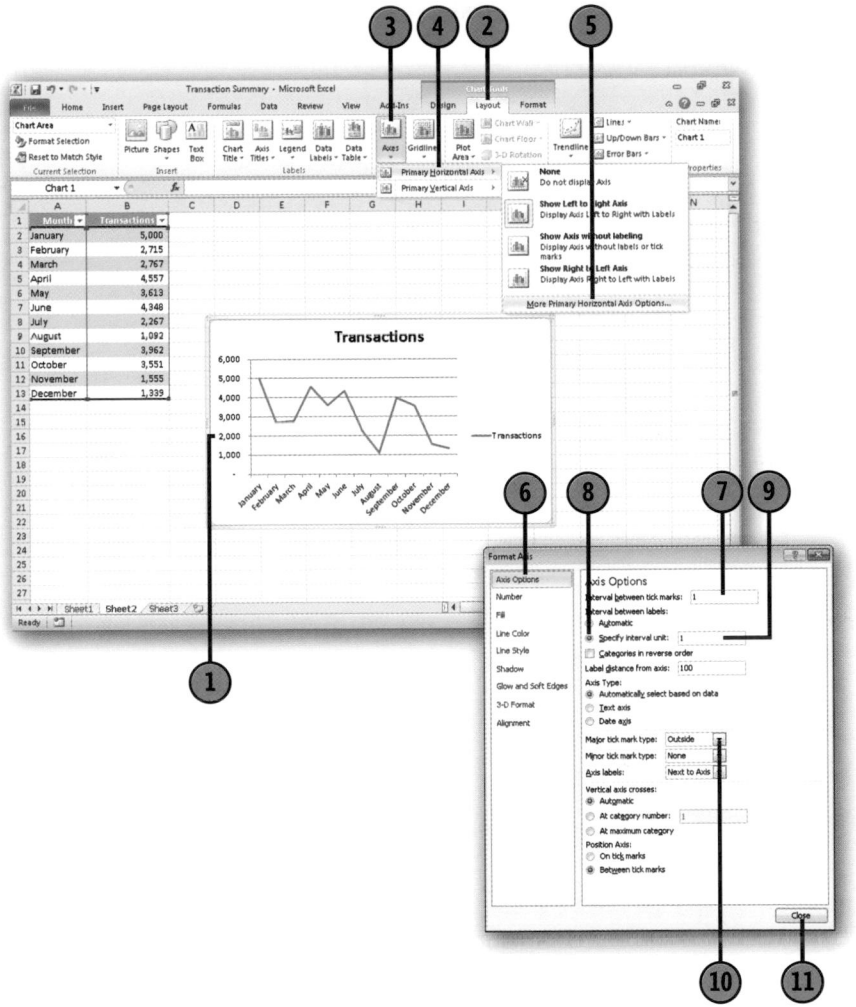

Customizing Chart Data

Whenever you create a chart for a business, there's always the possibility that the data displayed in the chart will change. Whether those changes reflect continuing sales, updated values that account for returns and inventory charges, or investment projections revised to match market conditions, you can update your chart by identifying a new data source. The data can be in any workbook on your computer or network—all you need to do is identify the cells with the data, and Excel does the rest.

Change the Source Data for Your Chart

1. Click the chart you want to change.
2. Click the Design tab.
3. Click Select Data.
4. Click in the Chart Data Range field.
5. Select the cells you want to provide the new source data.
6. Click OK.

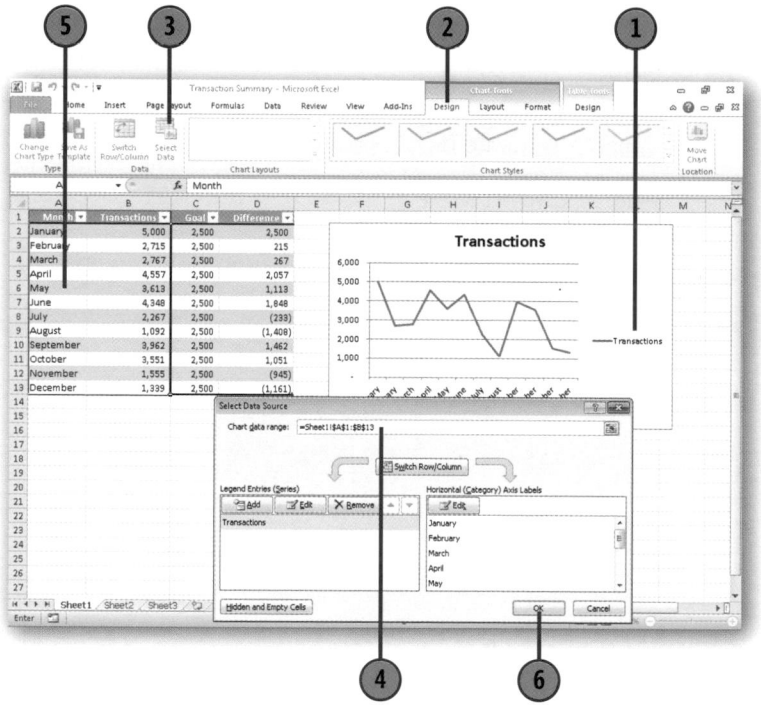

Add a New Series

1. Click the chart you want to change.
2. Click the Design tab.
3. Click Select Data.
4. Click Add.
5. Type the name you want to assign to the series.
6. Click in the Series Values field.
7. Select the cells you want to add.
8. Click OK.
9. Click OK.

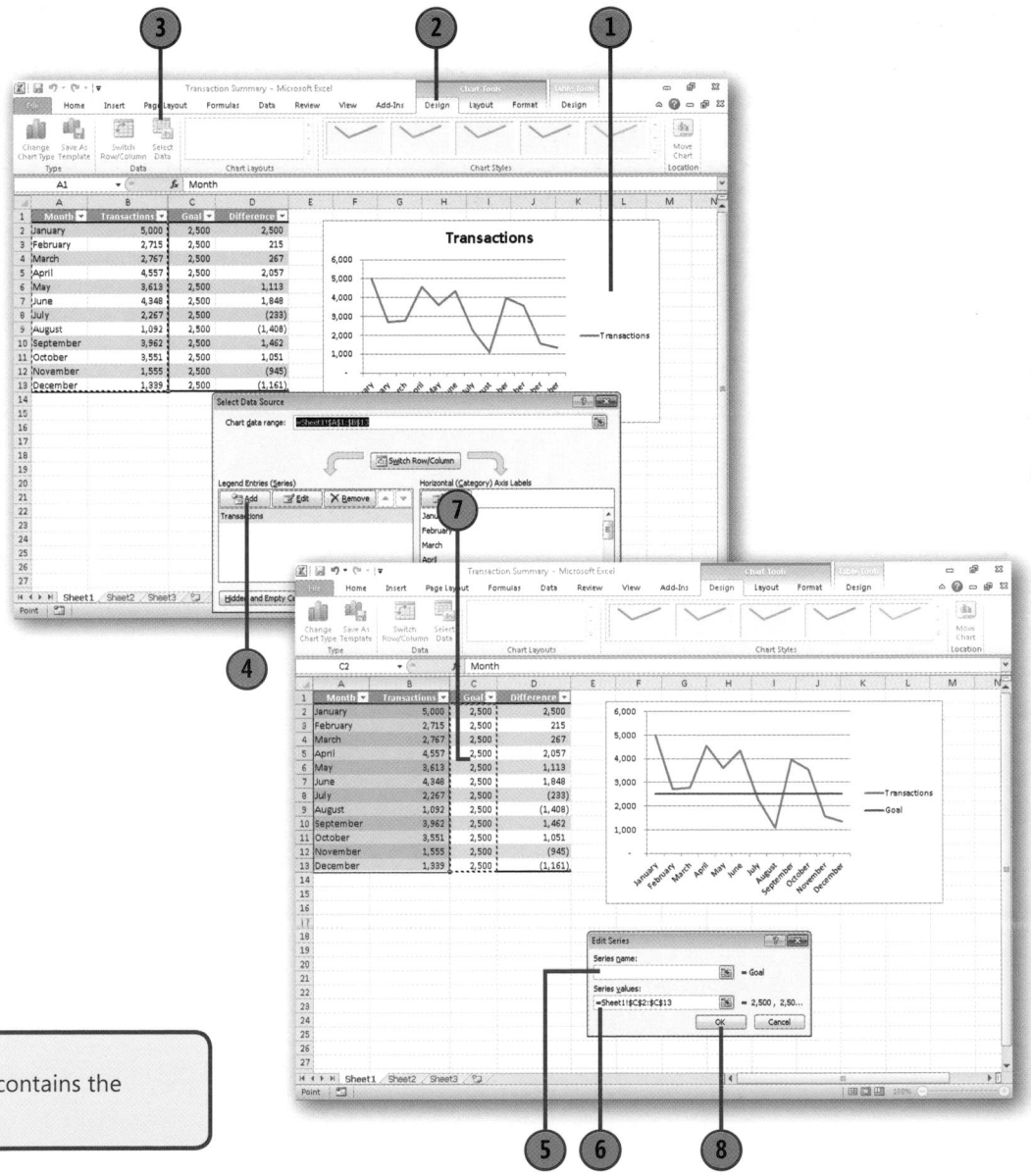

Tip

You can also type the address of the cell that contains the series name you want to use in the chart.

Delete a Series

1. Click the chart you want to change.
2. Click the Design tab.
3. Click Select Data.
4. Click the name of the series you want to delete.
5. Click Remove.
6. Click OK.

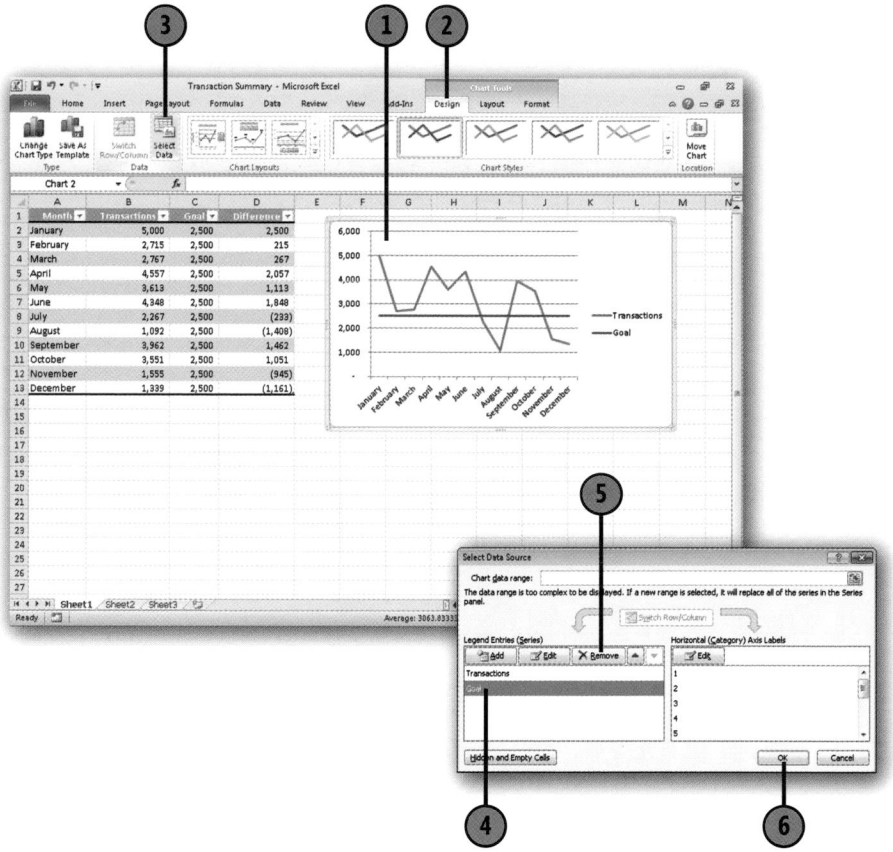

Working with Common Charts

One chart type you'll probably work with quite frequently is the pie chart, which displays the contribution of a series of values to the total of those values. Each section represents a category of data, such as a month in a year or a category of product. One way you can extend the capabilities of a basic pie chart and emphasize part of the data is to pull one section of the pie away from the rest of the chart. You can also change how you look at a three-dimensional chart, moving closer or farther away from the chart and changing your perspective.

Pull a Slice Out of a Pie Chart

1. Click the body of the pie chart you want to change.
2. Click the piece of data you want to separate.
3. Drag the piece away from the pie.

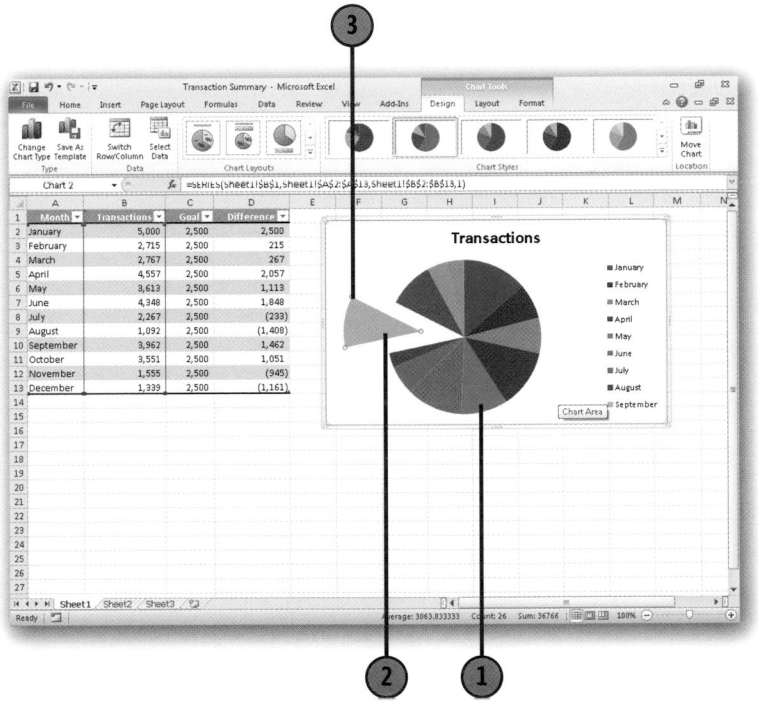

Create a 3-D Exploded Pie Chart

1. Click a cell in the data list you want to summarize in the pie chart.
2. Click the Insert tab.
3. Click Pie.
4. Click the second chart type under the 3-D Pie heading.

Change the Way You View 3-D Charts

1. Click the chart element you want to format.
2. Click the Format tab.
3. Click Shape Effects.
4. Click Shadow.
5. Click the shadow setting you want.

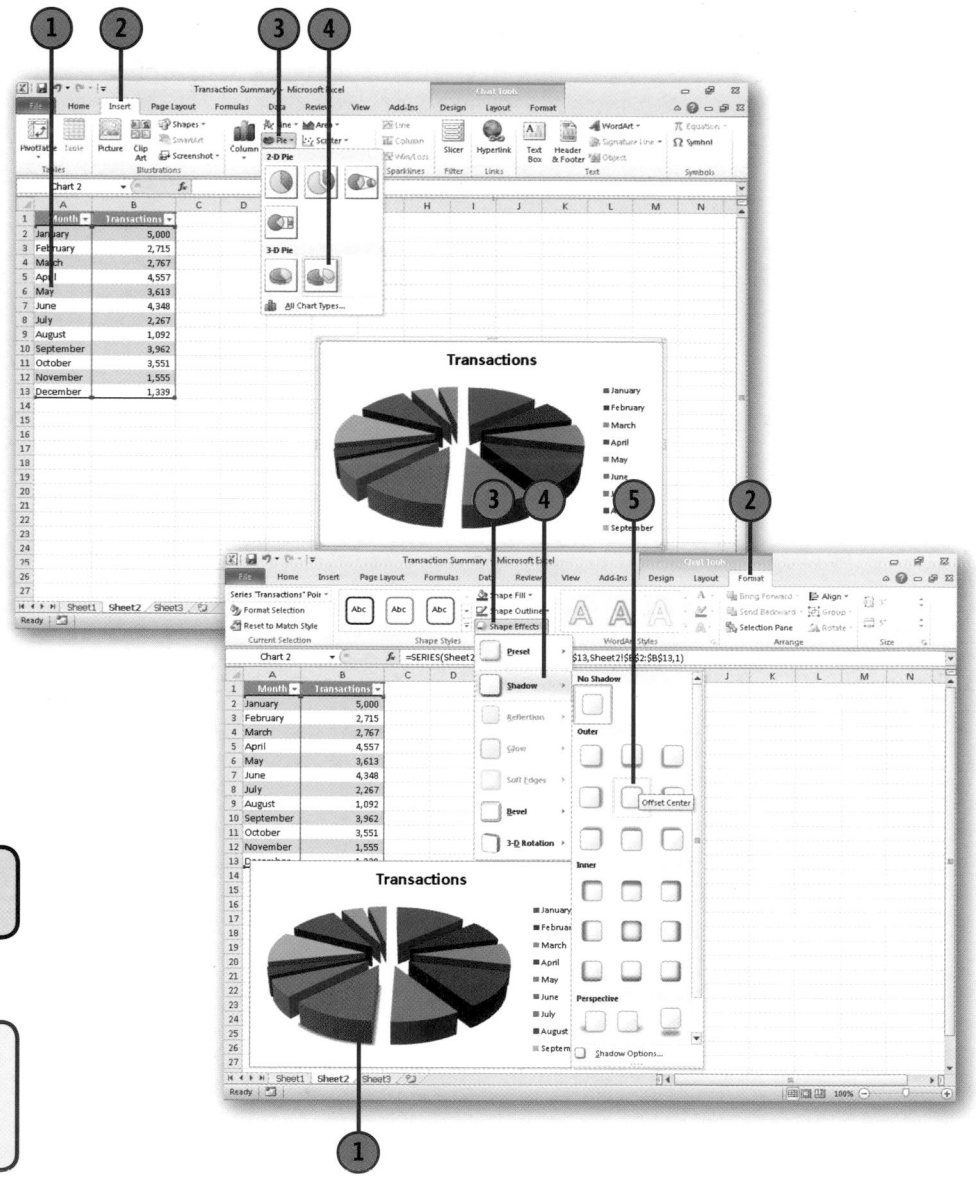

Caution

Not all 3-D options are available for all chart types.

Tip

If you want to remove the explosion effect from a pie chart, drag the data of the pie chart toward the center of the pie.

Working with Uncommon Charts

When you pick a type of chart or graph to present your data, you'll probably consider pie charts, line graphs, and bar charts. Those chart types are used most often because of their familiarity and their straightforward presentation of the relationships between elements of a data series. You can use other types of charts, however, when appropriate. One of those chart types is the stock chart, which you can use to present stock market data.

Create a Stock Chart

1. Select the stock data you want to chart. Be sure the data is formatted as shown in the figure.
2. Click the Insert tab.
3. Click Other Charts.
4. Click a Stock chart subtype.

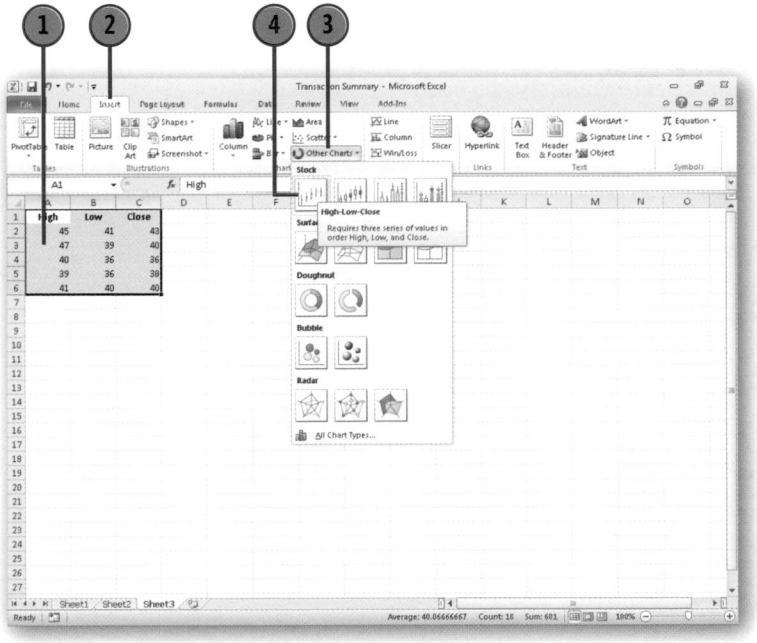

Tip

Several stock chart subtypes are available, each of which requires a different set of data columns. When you hover your mouse pointer over a chart subtype, Excel displays information about the subtype and the data it requires.

Adding a Trendline to a Chart

You can use the data in your Excel workbooks to analyze past performance, but you can also have Excel make its best guess as to future performance if current trends continue. For example, if you create a chart that represents your company's sales for the past five years, you can have Excel analyze the data and add a trendline to the chart to represent how much sales would increase if the current trend holds true for the next year.

Add a Trendline to a Data Series

1. Click the chart to which you want to add a trendline.
2. Click the data series to which you want to add a trendline.
3. Click the Layout tab.
4. Click Trendline.
5. Click Linear Forecast Trendline.

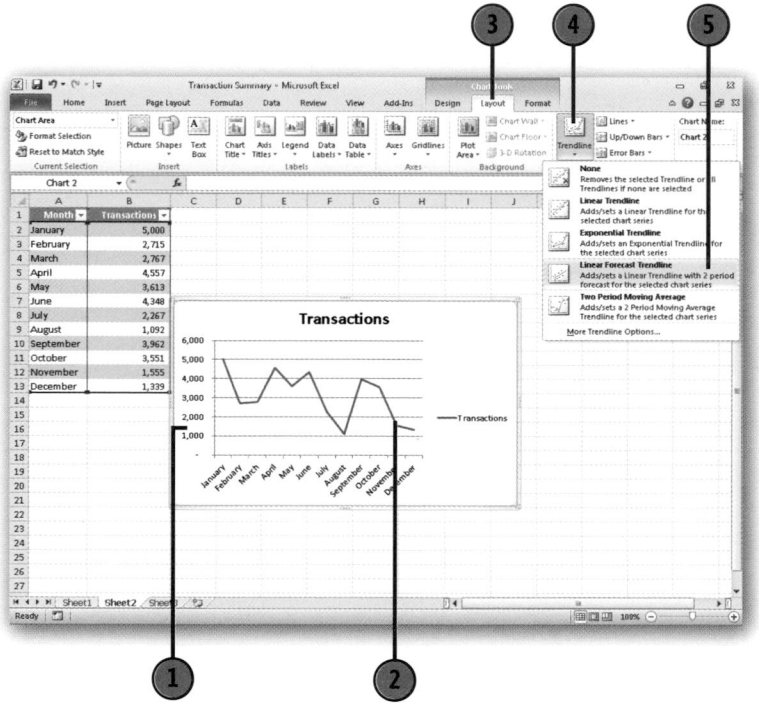

Tip

If you want more control over your trendline, such as by choosing a different mathematical procedure to extend the line (although the default Linear option works the vast majority of the time) or by choosing the number of units by which to extend the line, click Trendline and then click More Trendline Options to display the Format Trendline dialog box.

Caution

Unless you're working with certain types of scientific data and you know that your trendline requires a logarithmic, exponential, or other regression type, select the Linear Trendline option. If you don't, you won't get accurate results!

Summarizing Data Using Sparklines

Creating charts in Excel 2010 workbooks enables you to summarize your data visually, using legends, labels, and colors to highlight aspects of your data. It is possible to create very small charts to summarize your data in an overview worksheet, but you can also use sparklines, which are new in Excel 2010, to create compact, informative charts that provide valuable context for your data.

Edward Tufte introduced sparklines in his book *Beautiful Evidence*, with the goal of creating charts that imparted their information in approximately the same space as a word of printed text. In Excel 2010 a sparkline occupies a single cell, which makes it ideal for use in summary worksheets. You can create three types of sparklines: line, column, and win/loss. The line and column sparklines are compact versions of the standard line and column charts. The win/loss sparkline indicates whether a cell value is positive (a win), negative (a loss), or zero (a tie).

Create a Line Sparkline

1. Select the cells you want to summarize.
2. Click the Insert tab.
3. In the Sparklines group, click Line.
4. Click the Location Range box.
5. Click the cell where you want the sparkline to appear.
6. Click OK.

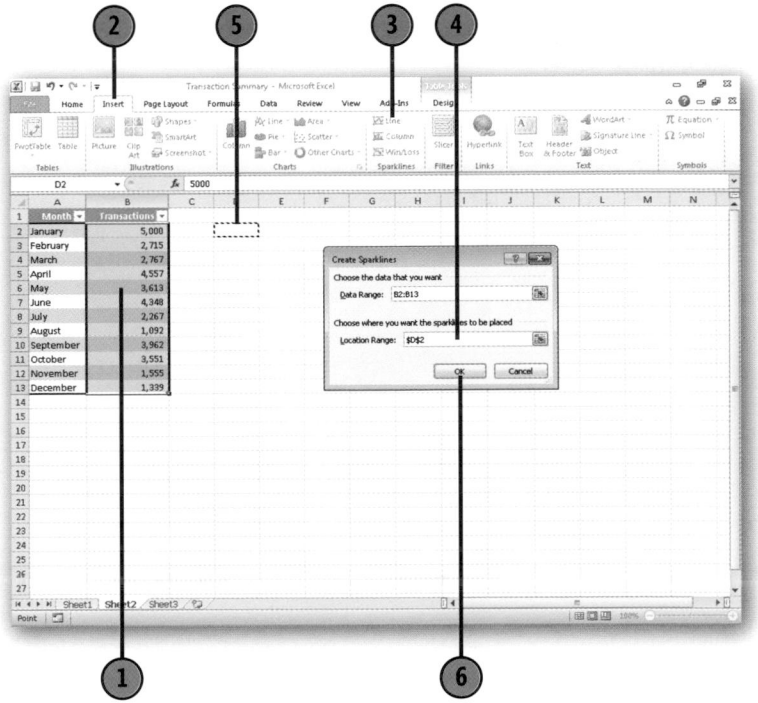

Tip

A sparkline fits into a single worksheet cell, which leaves no room for labels. For that reason, you have to select just the data to be summarized, not the category labels.

Create a Column Sparkline

1. Select the cells you want to summarize.
2. Click the Insert tab.
3. In the Sparklines group, click Column.
4. Click the Location Range box.
5. Click the cell where you want the sparkline to appear.
6. Click OK.

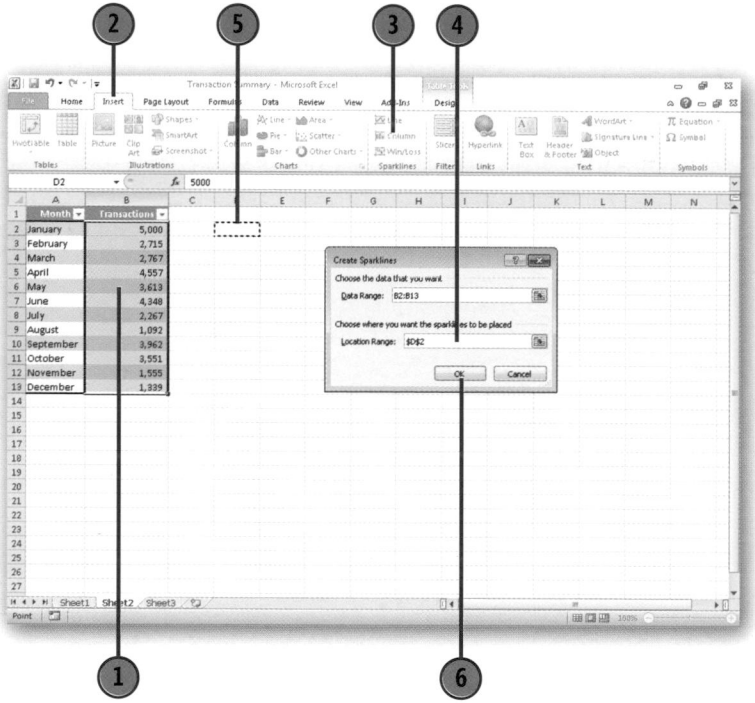

Create a Win/Loss Sparkline

1. Select the cells you want to summarize.
2. Click the Insert tab.
3. In the Sparklines group, click Win/Loss.
4. Click the Location Range box.
5. Click the cell where you want the sparkline to appear.
6. Click OK.

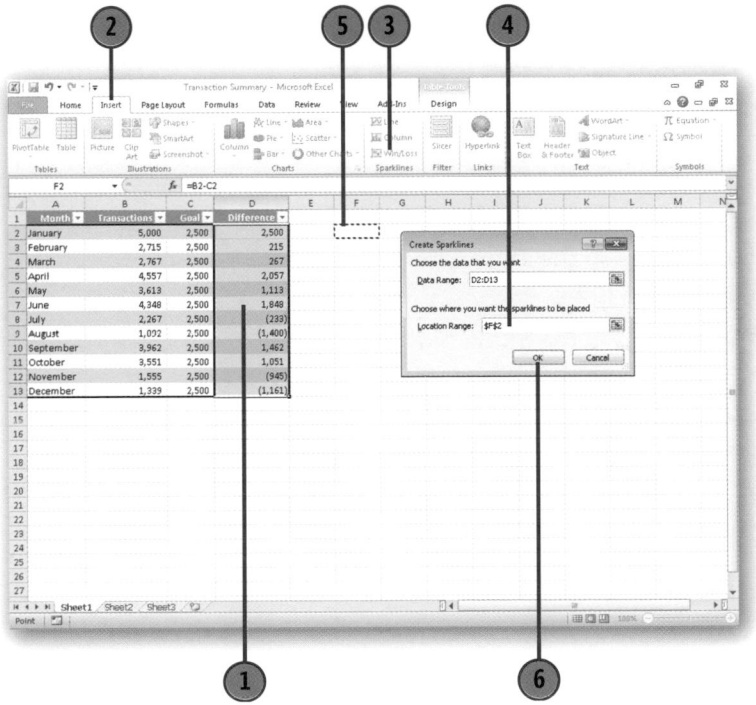

Caution

A win/loss sparkline distinguishes between positive, negative, and zero values. Summarizing a series of monthly sales values using a win/loss sparkline won't provide any useful information. Comparing the sales figures to each month's goal, however, would be appropriate for a win/loss sparkline.

Format a Sparkline

1. Select the sparkline you want to change.
2. Click the Design tab.
3. Use the controls in the Sparkline group to change which data the sparkline summarizes.
4. Use the controls in the Type group to change the sparkline's type.
5. Use the controls in the Show group to determine which sparkline elements to show.
6. Use the controls in the Style group to change the sparkline's style, color, and marker color.
7. Use the controls in the Group group to reformat the sparkline's axes.

Delete a Sparkline

1. Select the cell that contains the sparkline you want to delete.
2. Click the Design tab.
3. Click the Clear button.

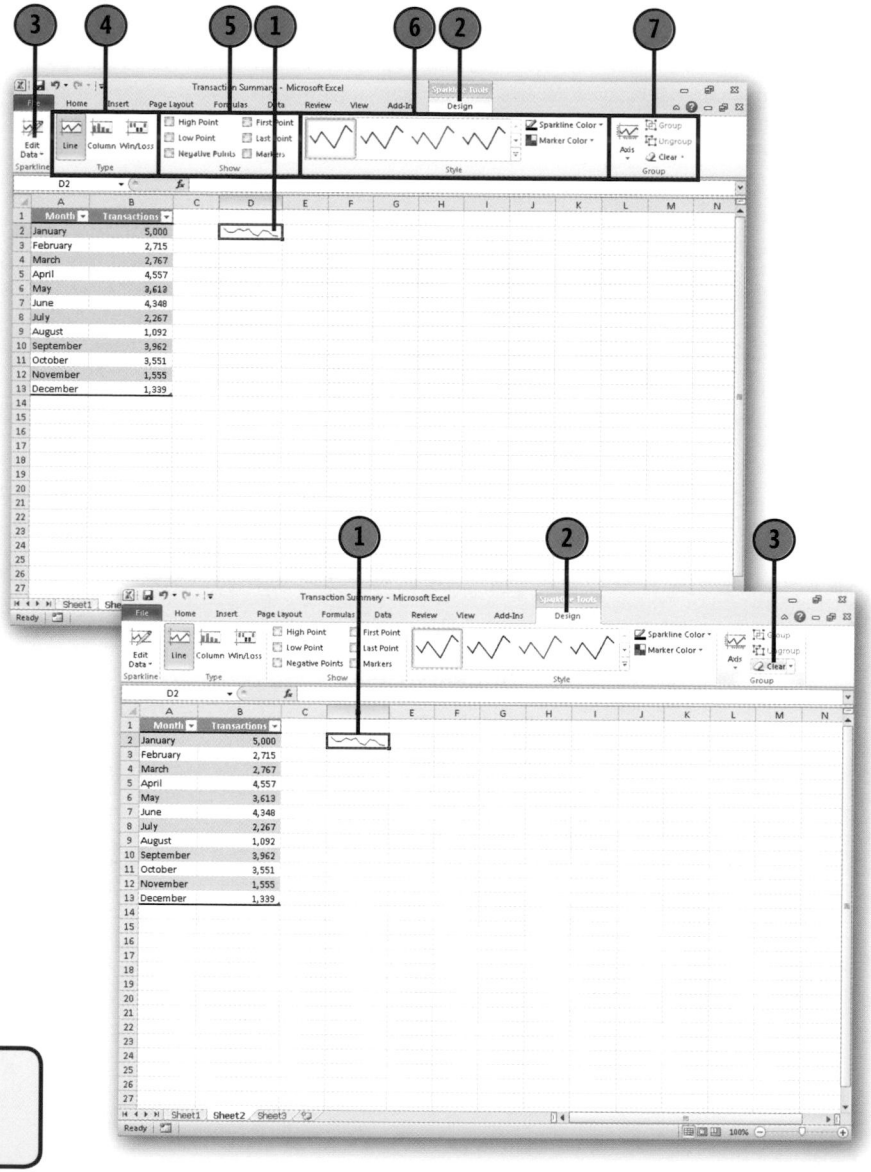

Tip

You can make a sparkline larger or smaller by changing the cell's column height and row width.

13 Enhancing Your Worksheets with Graphics

In this section:

- Adding an Image to a Worksheet
- Creating and Edit Drawing Objects
- Adding Text to Drawing Objects
- Changing the Appearance of Drawing Objects
- Aligning and Grouping Drawing Objects
- Adding WordArt to a Worksheet
- Inserting Clip Art into a Worksheet
- Creating Common Business Diagrams
- Creating an Organization Chart

When you create a worksheet, your first consideration is to ensure that the data is stored in an understandable format and that all the formulas produce the expected results. After you take care of the worksheet's structure, however, you should ensure that you and your colleagues can comprehend the data easily. One way that you can help you and your colleagues understand the data in your worksheet is to add drawing objects—such as boxes, stars, and banners—to make your annotations and labels stand out.

Another way you can present business data in an Excel worksheet is to create a diagram. In Excel, diagrams encompass common business items such as Venn diagrams, which show the intersection of several data sets, and organization charts, which describe the hierarchy of a company or other organization.

Working with Graphics in Your Worksheets

When you add graphics to your worksheets, you go through the Insert tab on the ribbon. The buttons on the Insert tab let you add lines, shapes of many different types, and images to your worksheets. After you create a drawing object, you can change its line color or, if the object has an interior space, fill that space with a color or pattern of your choosing. Another way you can make your images and drawing objects stand out is to add a shadow so that the objects appear to float above the surface of the worksheet. Hard shadows, which you create with black lines, mark the shadowed object as separate from the surrounding items. A softer shadow, one created with a lighter shade of gray, makes the shadowed object appear as part of the collection of objects on the worksheet. You can also add a reflection to an image, adding depth to the image and implying that the worksheet contains a reflective surface.

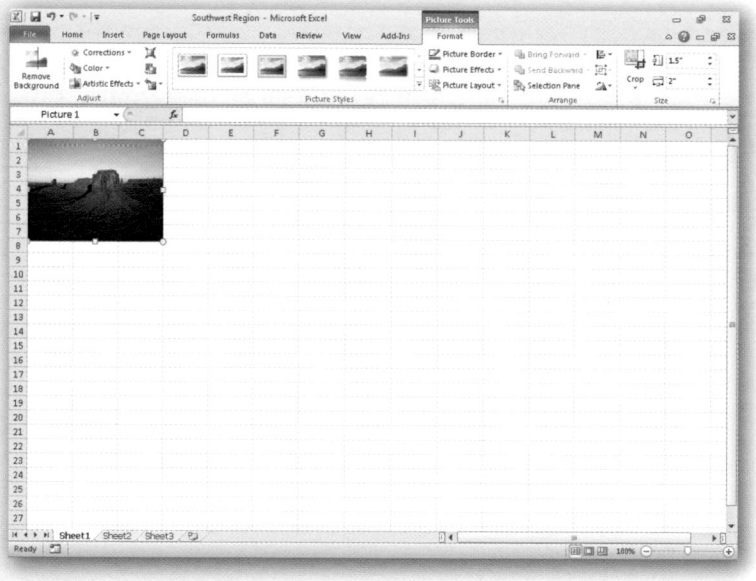

Adding Graphics to Worksheets

After you create a worksheet, you can add graphics to enhance the data on the worksheet. If your worksheet details the sales of a specific product, you can add a photograph of the product to the worksheet. Adding a visual representation of the item described in the worksheet makes the results you offer much more memorable. Not only do you and your colleagues have numbers to work with; you also have something solid with which to associate the data, enhancing recall.

Add a Picture

1. Click the Insert tab.
2. Click Picture.
3. Navigate to the folder with the picture you want to insert.
4. Double-click the picture you want to insert.

Delete a Picture

1. Click the picture you want to delete.
2. Press the Delete key.

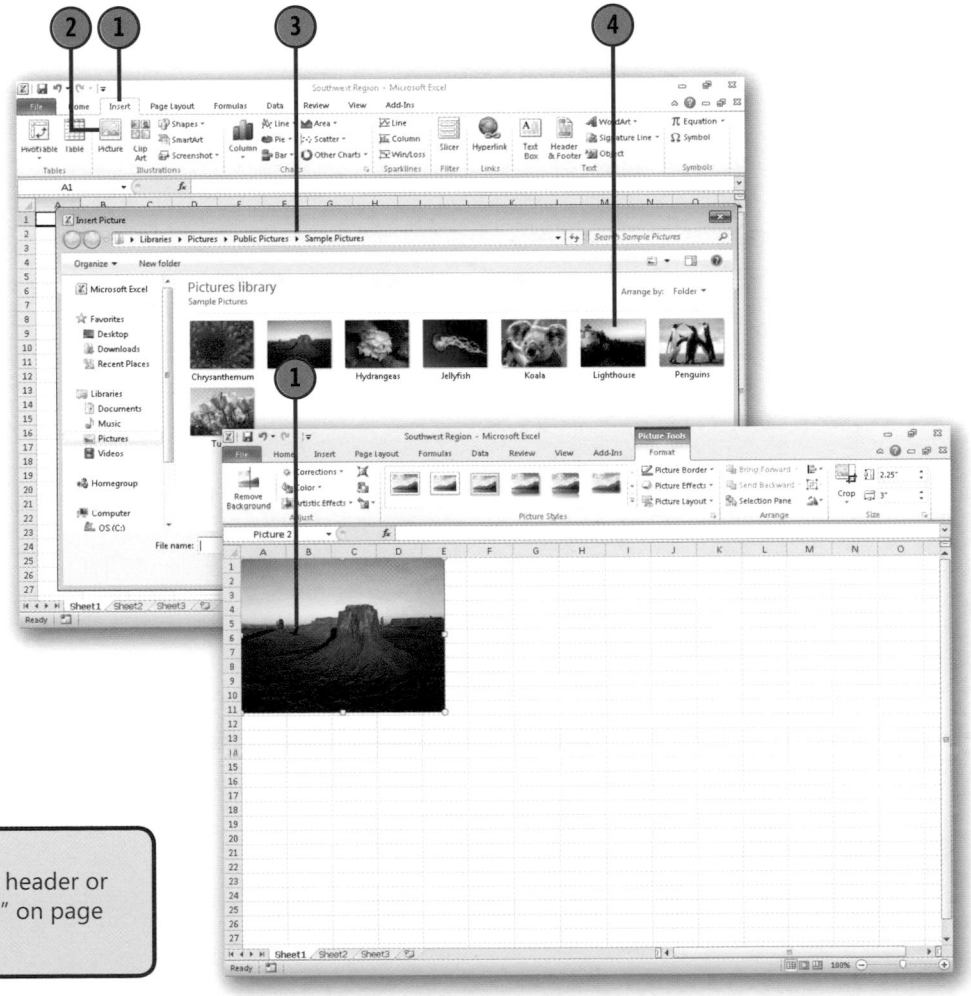

See Also

For information on adding a picture to a worksheet header or footer, see "Include a Graphic in a Header or Footer" on page 171.

Adding Drawing Objects to a Worksheet

Adding graphics or pictures of items described in your worksheets makes it easier to understand the data in those worksheets, but you're not limited to adding images from other sources. If you want, you can add drawing objects to your worksheets. For example, you can add shapes such as rectangles and circles to your worksheets, with the rectangles holding explanatory text and the circles displaying a one-word or two-word caption describing the contents of a cell.

Add a Simple Shape

1. Click the Insert tab.
2. In the Illustrations group, click Shapes.
3. Click the button representing the shape you want to add.
4. Drag where you want your shape to appear.

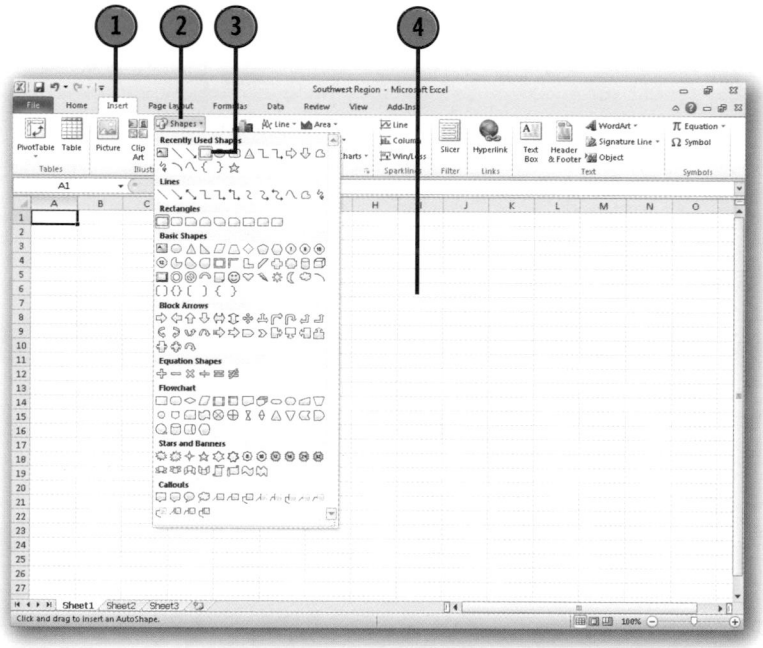

Tip

To create a circle or square instead of an oval or rectangle, hold down the Shift key while you drag the mouse pointer.

Add Text to Any Shape

1. Click the shape.
2. Type the text you want, and then click outside the shape.

Format Text in a Shape

1. Click the shape.
2. Click the Home tab.
3. Using the controls in the Font and Alignment groups on the ribbon, follow any of these steps:
   - Click the Font down arrow and then click the font you want to use.
   - Click the Font Size down arrow and then click the font size.
   - Click the Font Color down arrow and then click a color.
   - Use the other controls to assign bold, italic, underline, and other formatting options.

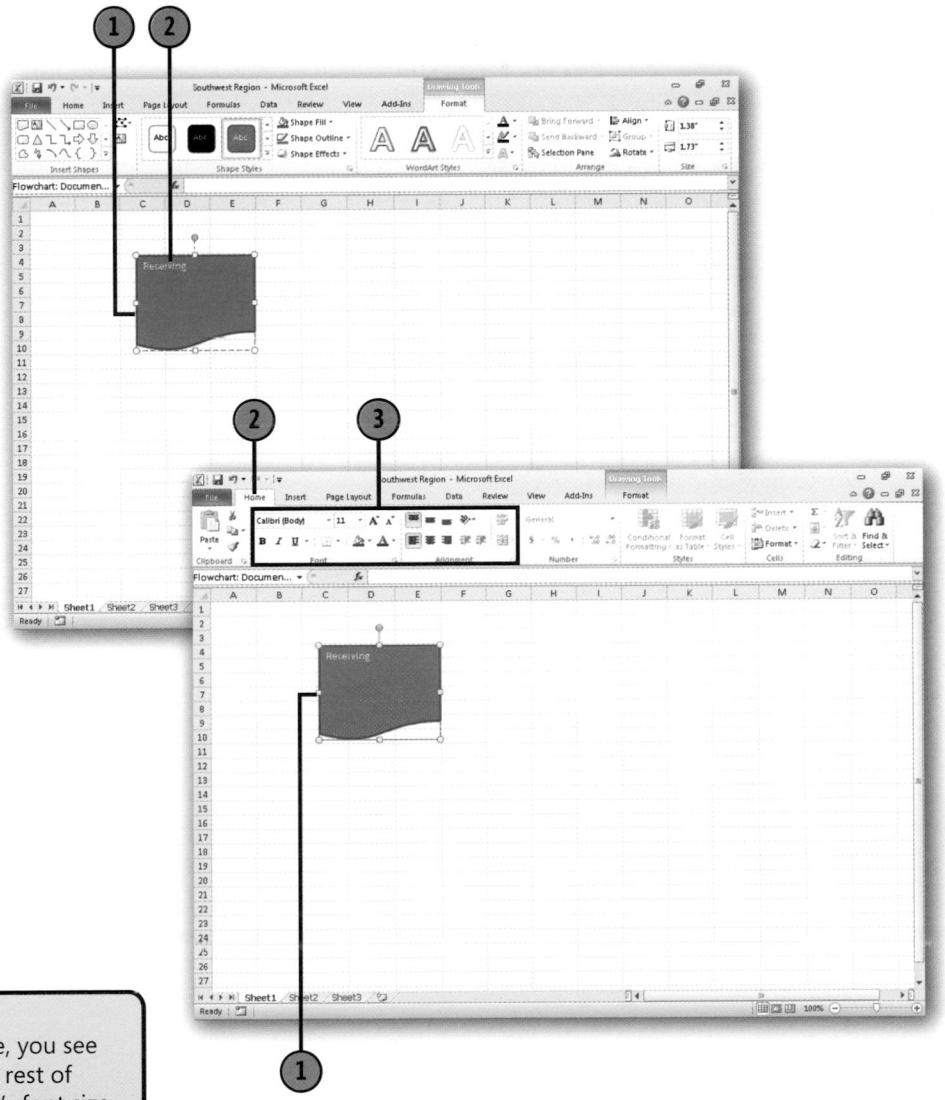

Caution

If the text you add to a shape doesn't fit in the shape, you see only the first part of the text you added. To view the rest of the text, you can enlarge the shape or make the text's font size smaller.

Adding Fills to Drawing Objects

When you create a drawing object in Excel, you create a default version of the object, meaning that the object has the program's usual color or pattern filling its interior. If you want to change the object's appearance, you can select from a series of built-in styles that control the image's fill color, outline, and text color. You can change these colors or patterns to bring the object's appearance in line with your company's color scheme or to make an object stand out from its surroundings.

Apply a Shape Style

1. Click the object you want to format.
2. Click the Format tab.
3. In the Shape Styles group on the ribbon, click the style you want to apply.

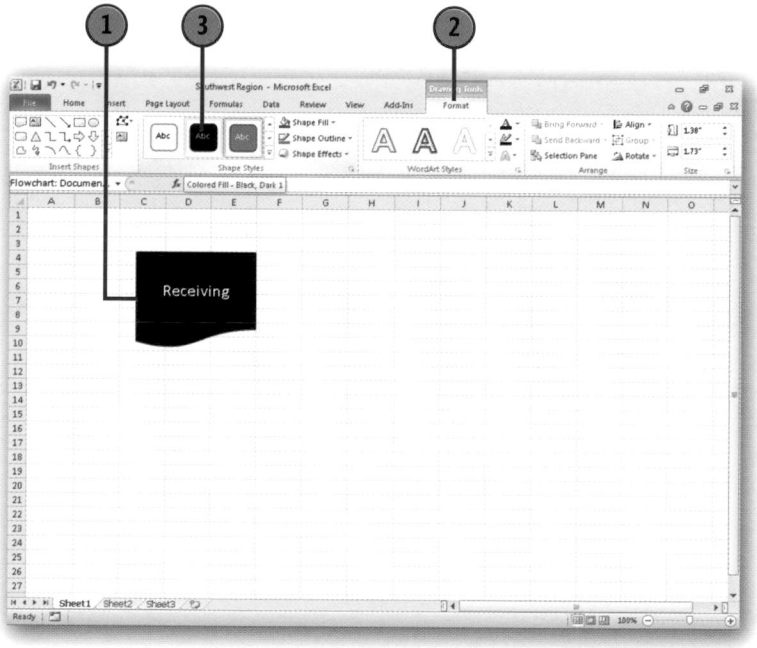

Tip

You can display the entire Shape Styles gallery by clicking the gallery's More button.

Apply a Fill

1. Click the shape you want to fill.
2. Click the Format tab.
3. Click the Shape Fill down arrow, and use the controls on the menu that appears to pick a fill color, gradient, or texture.
4. Click the color with which you want to fill the object.

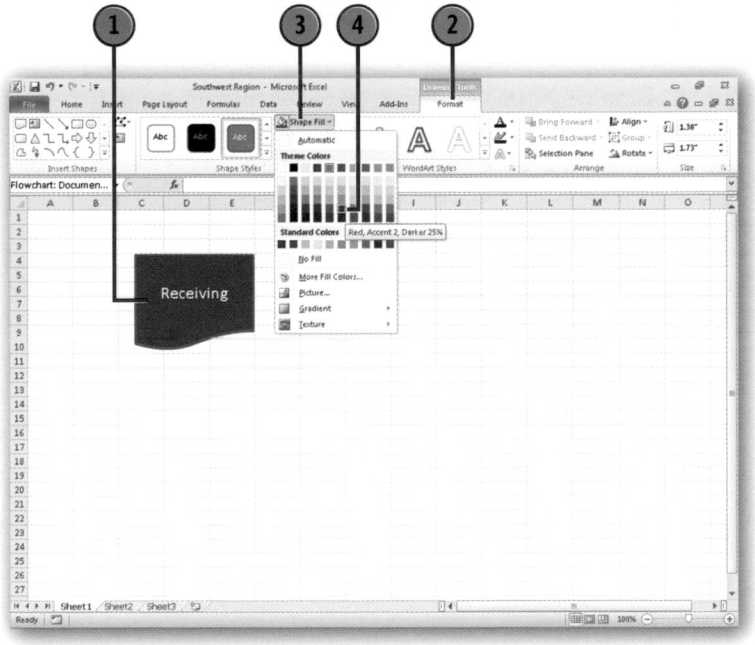

Tip

Textures are a great way to apply a gentle, overall pattern to an object without interfering with any text or image already positioned in the object.

Fill an Object with a Picture

1. Click the object you want to fill.
2. If necessary, click the Format tab.
3. Click Shape Fill.
4. Click Picture.
5. Navigate to where the picture you want is located.
6. Double-click the picture you want.

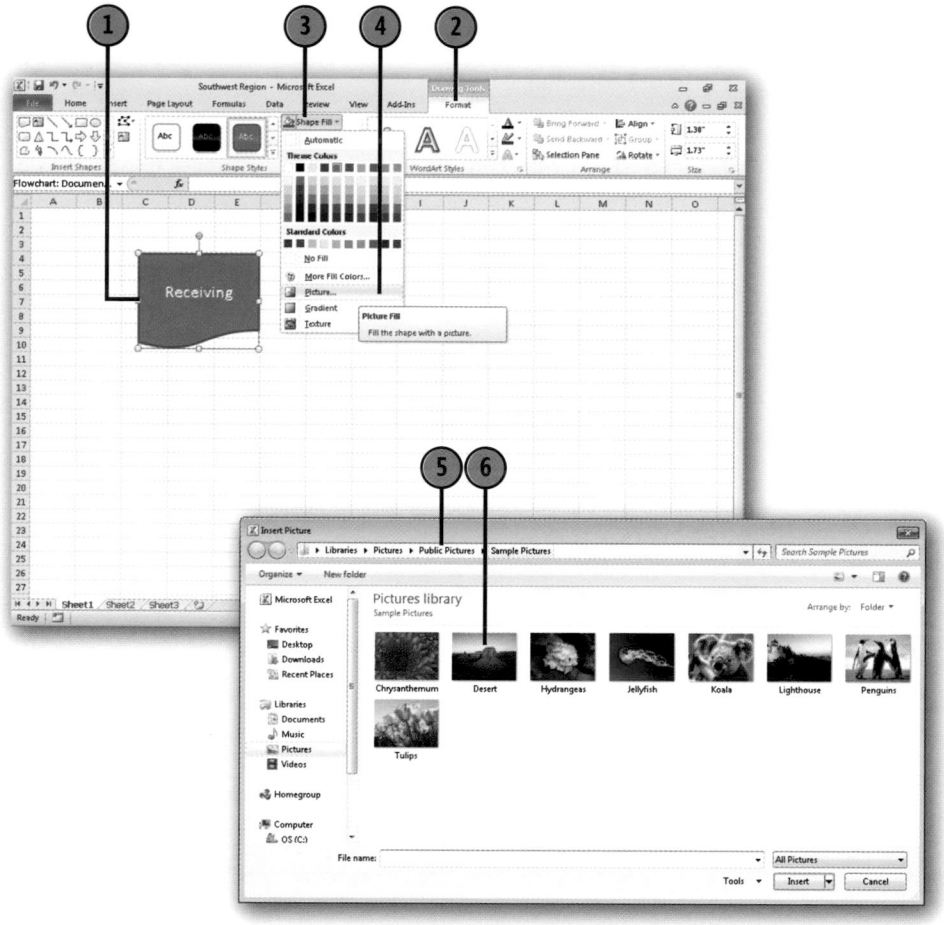

Adding Effects to Drawing Objects

When you add a drawing object to a worksheet, you can add text or color to the object to make it stand out from the rest of the worksheet's contents. Other options you have to make drawing objects stand out are to add a shadow to the object, which makes it appear that the object is raised off the surface of the worksheet, and to make the object appear as though it is three-dimensional. Excel knows how to make its drawing objects appear three-dimensional—all you need to do is describe how you want the object to look!

Add or Edit an Object's Shadow

1. Click the object you want to edit.
2. If necessary, click the Format tab.
3. Click Shape Effects.
4. Click Shadow.
5. Click the shadow style you want for your object.

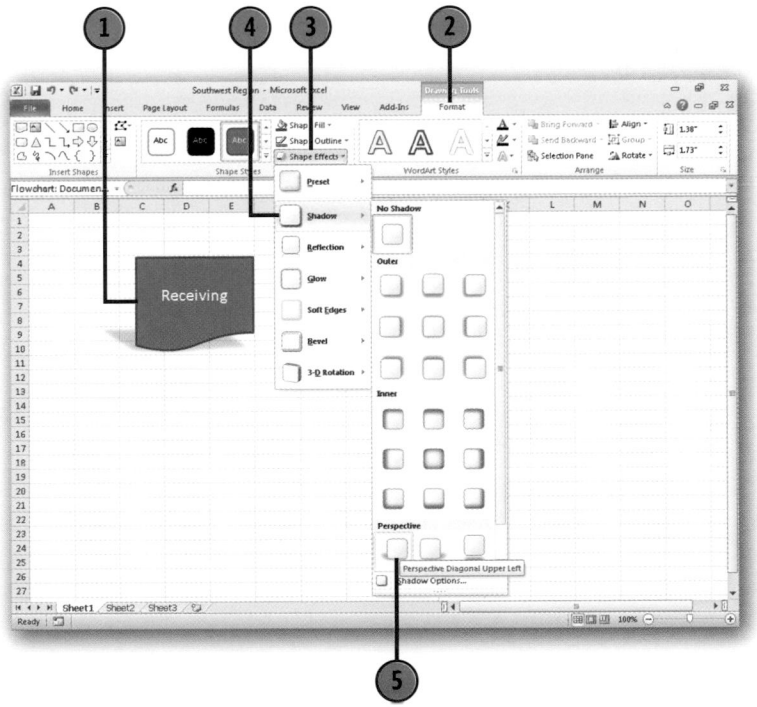

Rotate an Object in Three Dimensions

1. Click the object you want to edit.
2. If necessary, click the Format tab.
3. Click Shape Effects.
4. Click 3-D Rotation.
5. Click the 3-D rotation you want for your object.

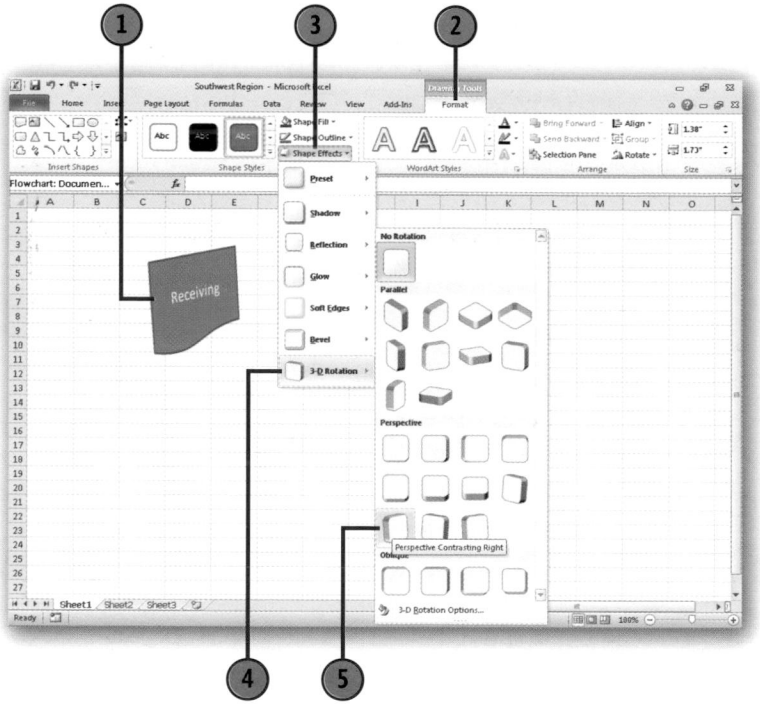

Customizing Pictures and Objects

After you add a picture or drawing object to a worksheet, you can change the object's size to have it take up more or less space on the sheet. You can also rotate the object to change its orientation on the page. Rotating an image a little to one side can imply action or fun, while turning an image upside down indicates something a bit more crazy. Of course, if your image is upside down when you add it to your worksheet, you can rotate it to its "normal" position. Also, if you find that you want to work only with the foreground element of the image, Excel 2010 provides a new background removal tool you can use to edit the image.

Resize a Picture or Object

1. Click the object you want to resize.
2. Hover over one of the white handles surrounding the object, and drag the handle to the size you want.

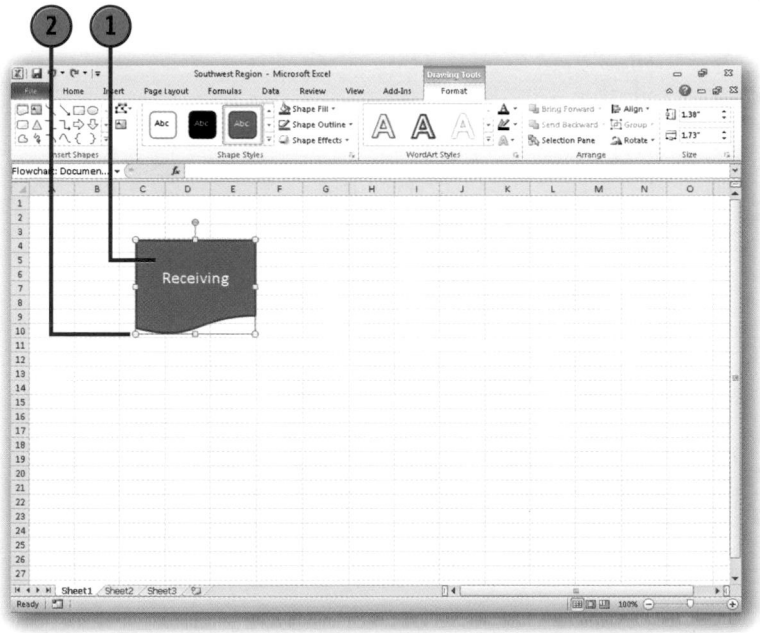

Rotate a Picture or Object

1. Click the object you want to rotate.
2. If necessary, click the Format tab.
3. Follow either of these steps:
   - In the Arrange group, click Rotate, and then select how you want to rotate the object.
   - Hover over the rotation handle (the green dot), and then drag the dot to rotate the object to the angle you want.

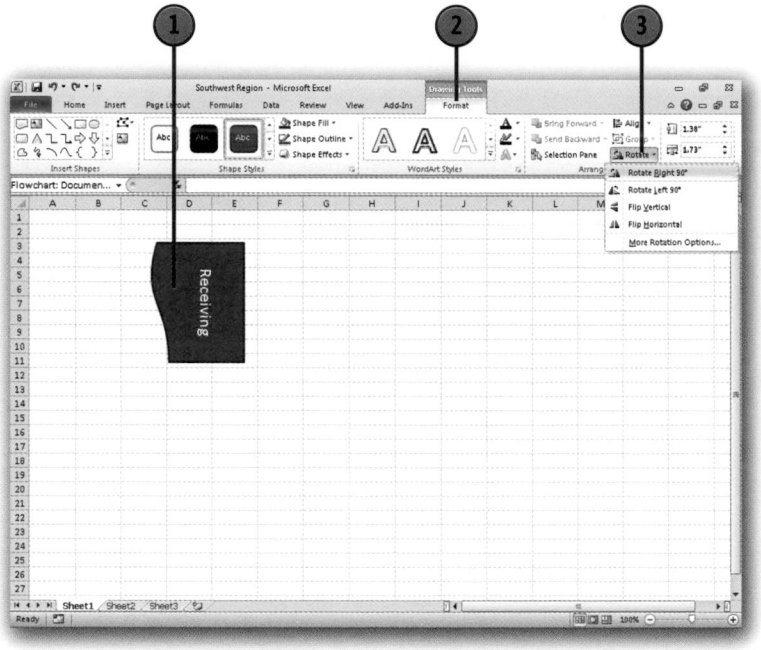

Tip

When you select an object, your object's size dimensions appear in the Size group on the Format tab on the ribbon. If you want to resize your object to a specific size, such as 1.53" wide by 1.77" high, you can type those values directly into the group's fields. You can also click the spin control at the right edge of the fields to increase or decrease a dimension by 0.1" per click.

Remove the Background from a Picture

1. Click the picture you want to edit.
2. If necessary, click the Format tab.
3. Click Remove Background.
4. If necessary, drag the handles at the corners and edges of the interior box to identify the image background.
5. Click Keep Changes.

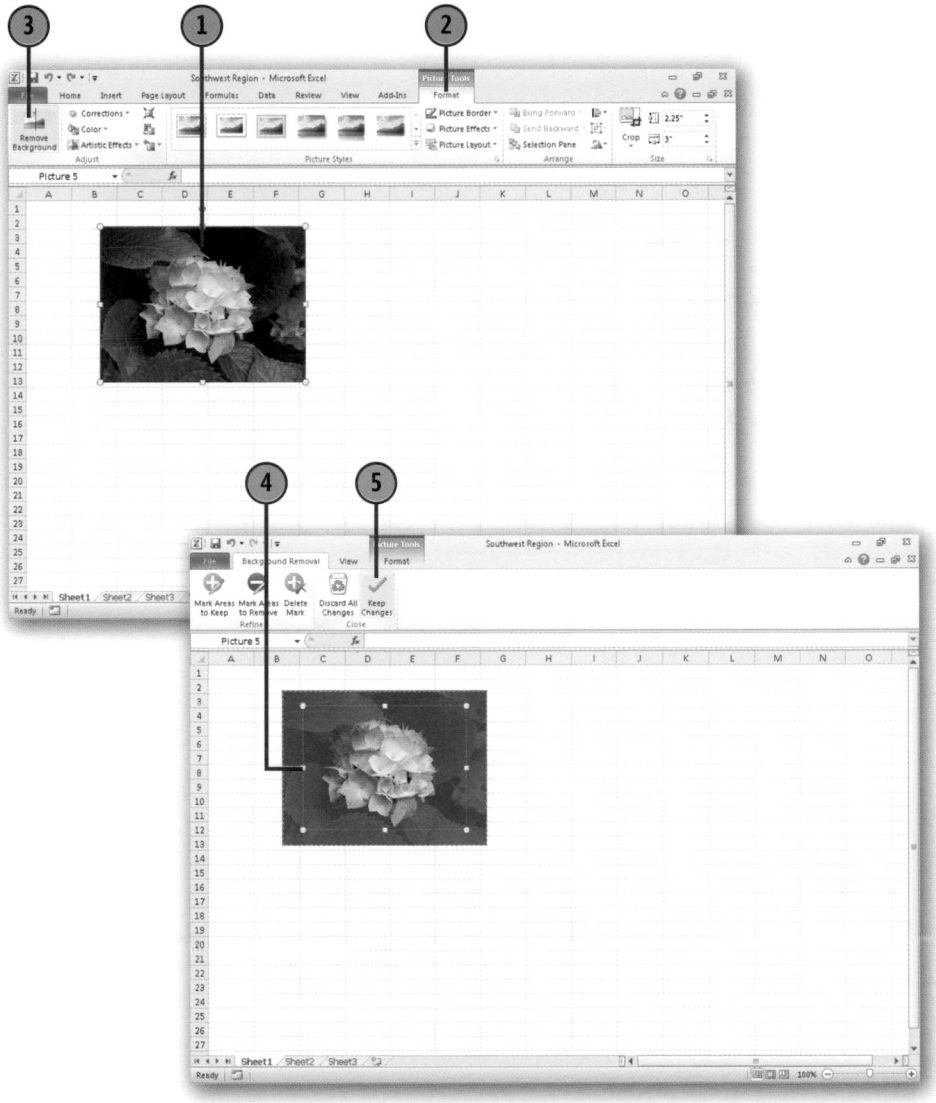

Aligning and Grouping Drawing Objects

One important design element is ensuring that any objects you add to your worksheets are aligned properly, both in relation to the edges of the worksheet and any other objects. If you want a number of your objects to line up with each other, such as aligning all objects with the left edge of the page, you can do so. In a similar manner, if you want to work with a set of objects as a single unit, such as three text boxes you want to appear together regardless of position, you can define the objects as a group and work with them as a single entity.

Align Objects

1. Hold down the Ctrl key, and click the objects you want to align.
2. If necessary, click the Format tab.
3. Click Align.
4. Click how you want to align your objects.

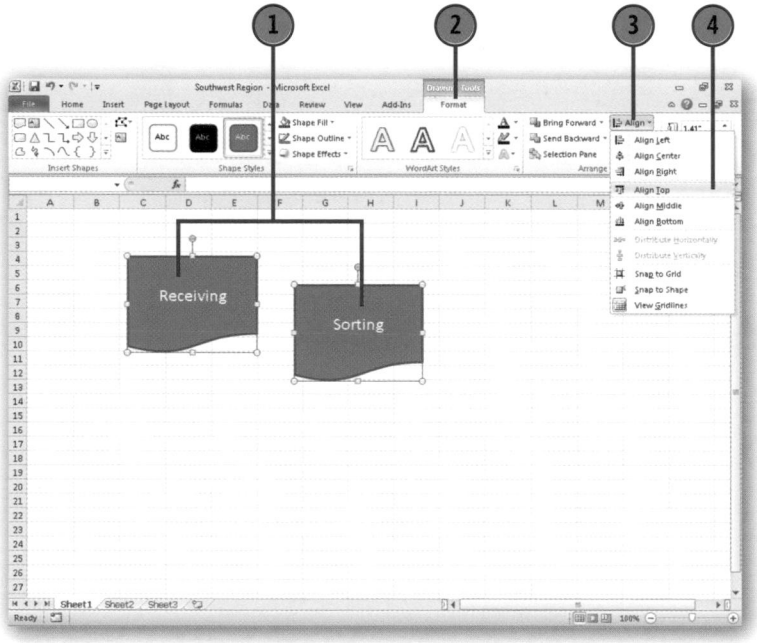

Group or Ungroup Objects

1. Hold down the Ctrl key, and click the objects you want to group.
2. If necessary, click the Format tab.
3. Click the Group button.
4. Click the Group menu item.

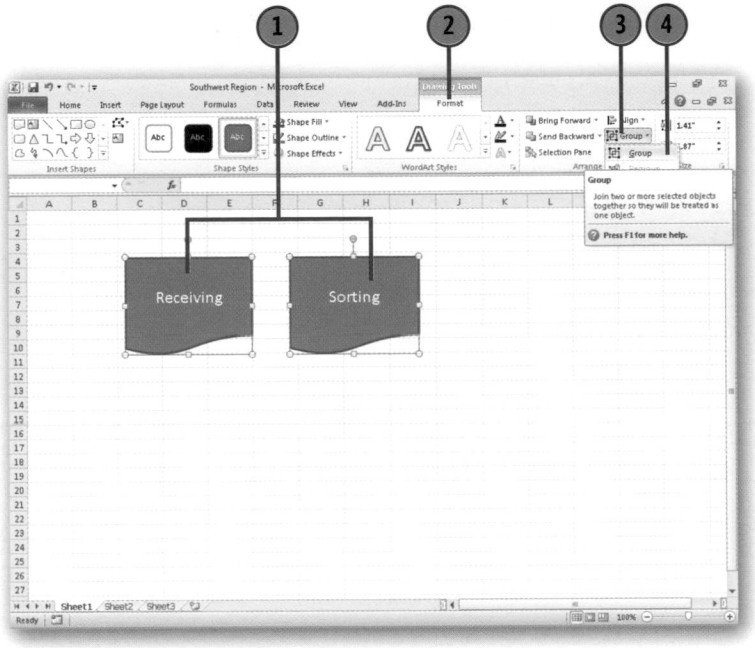

Tip

Right-click any object in a group you want to ungroup, and click Group, Ungroup. If you have many objects grouped together and then ungroup them, you might want to regroup them in the same way. You can do this quickly and easily by right-clicking one of the objects you want to regroup, clicking Group, and then clicking Regroup.

Tip

If you want to apply a format to more than one object, you can group the objects and apply the formatting to all objects at once!

Change the Order of Objects

1. Click the object you want to move.
2. If necessary, click the Format tab.
3. Follow either of these steps:
   - Click the Bring Forward down arrow, and then select whether to bring the object to the front of the stack or to move it up one place.
   - Click the Send Backward down arrow, and then select whether to send the object to the back of the stack or to move it back one place.

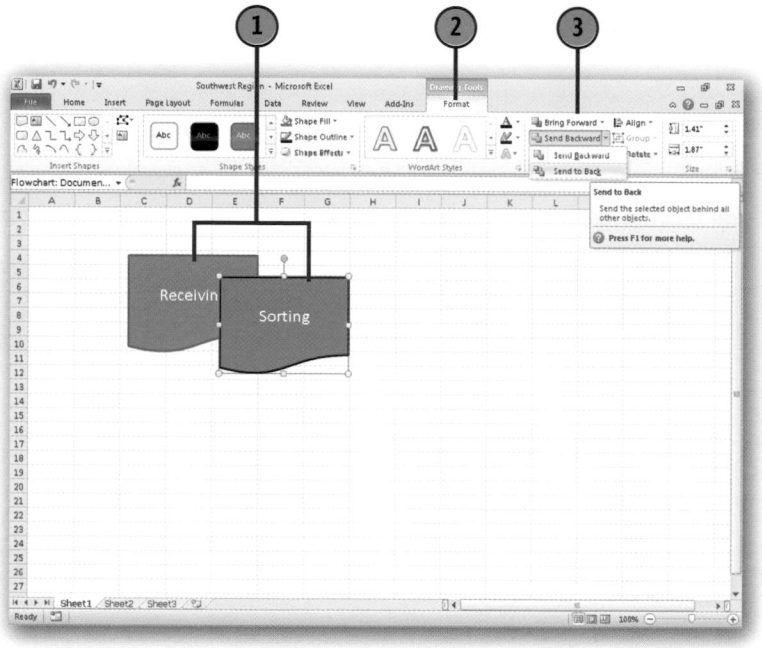

Using WordArt to Create Text Effects in Excel

One of the benefits of working with Excel 2010 is that you can take advantage of the capabilities of Microsoft Office 2010 to enhance your worksheets. One of those capabilities is WordArt, which lets you select from a wide range of styles to add exciting two- and three-dimensional text to your worksheets. Every style comes with a predefined color scheme, but you can change the color, size, and alignment of your WordArt by using the tools on the ribbon's Home tab.

Add WordArt Text

1. Click the Insert tab.
2. Click WordArt.
3. Click the WordArt style you want.
4. Type the text you want to style.
5. Click the border of the WordArt text.
6. Click the Home tab.
7. Click the Font down arrow.
8. Click the font you want.

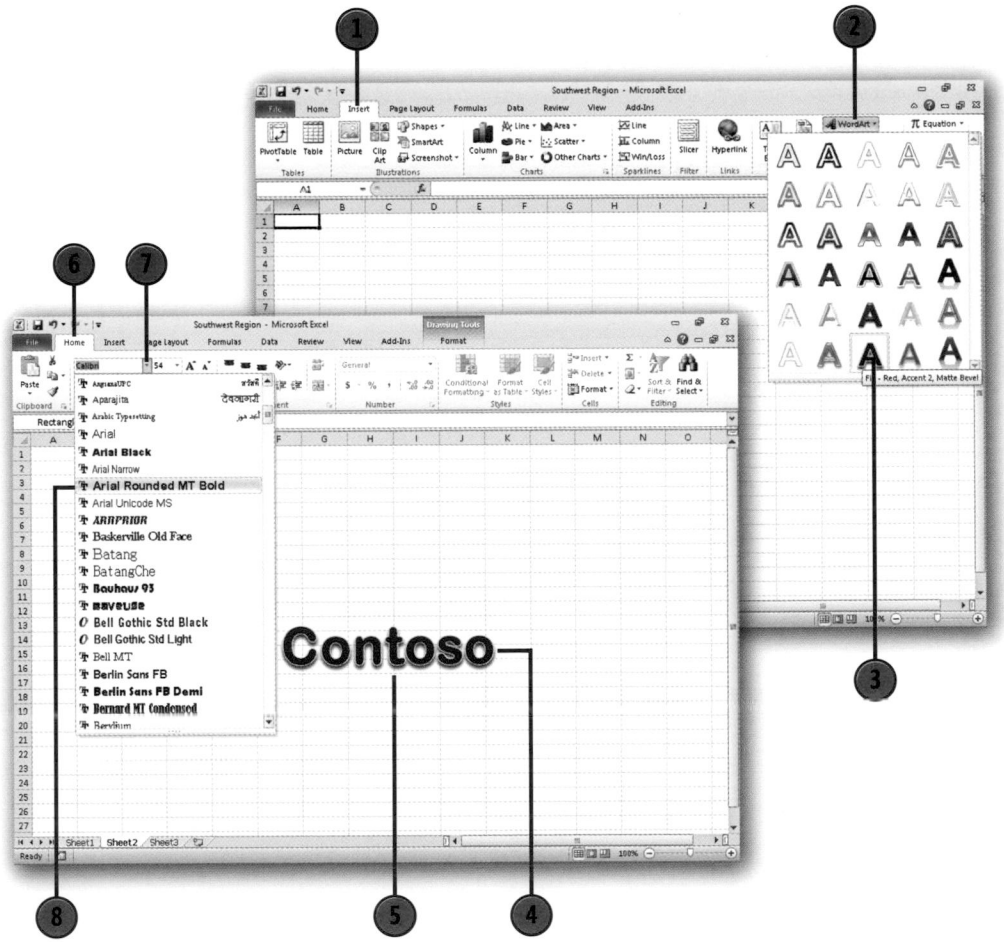

Change WordArt Text Colors

1. Click the border of the WordArt you want to format.
2. Click the Home tab.
3. Click the Font Color down arrow.
4. Click the color you want.

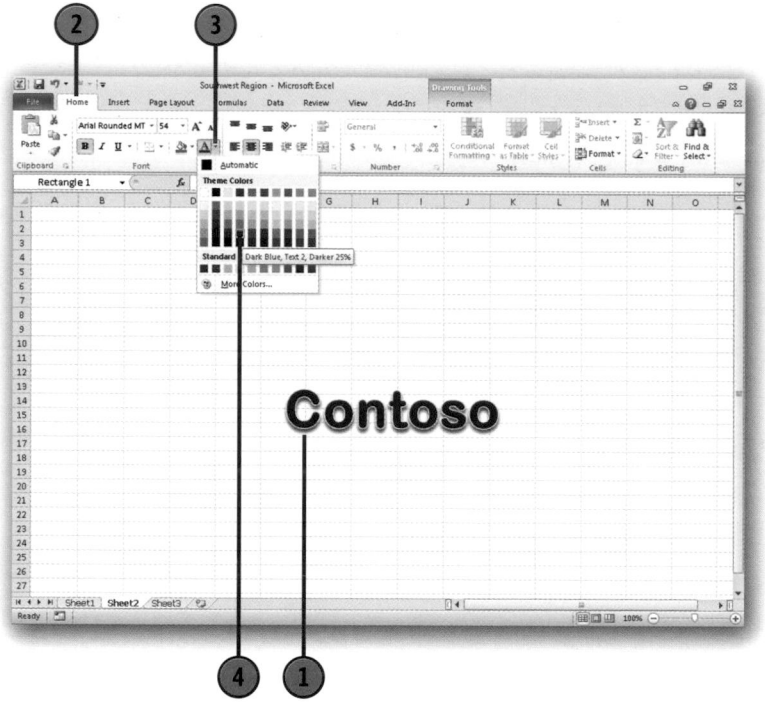

Inserting Clip Art into a Worksheet

If you want to include a worksheet in a presentation you give to your colleagues or in a report you make available on your company's Web site, you can add images from the clip art collection that comes with Office to accent your worksheet.

You can manage your clip art by using the Clip Art task pane, whether that means searching for clip art on your computer or on the Web.

Add Clip Art

1. Click the Insert tab.
2. Click Clip Art.
3. Type a description of the clip art you want.
4. Click Go.
5. Click the clip art you want to insert.

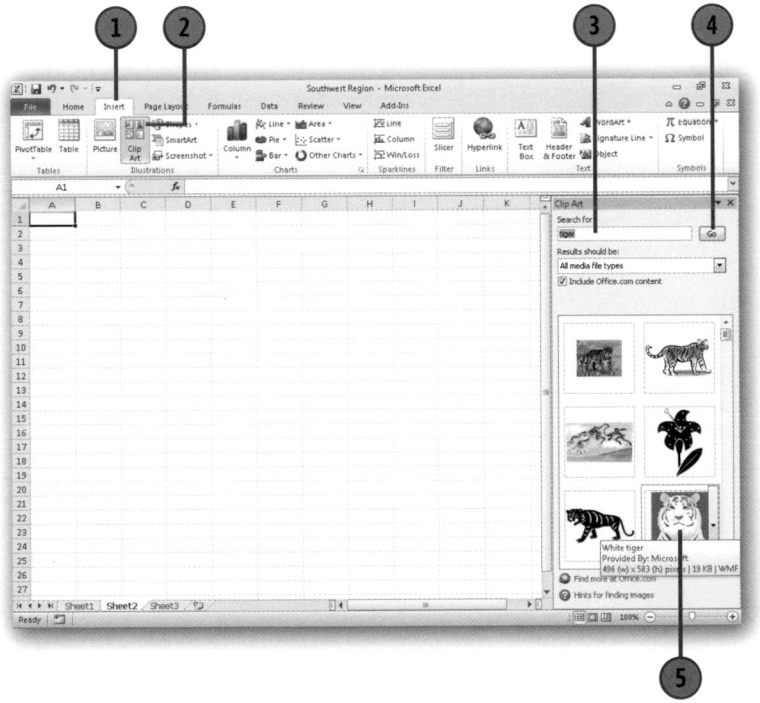

Tip

If you want to find additional clip art, click the Insert tab, and then click Clip Art. In the Clip Art task pane, click Find More At Office.com, and you are directed toward the Microsoft Office Images site, where you can search a large number of clips.

Inserting and Changing a Diagram

A number of diagram types are probably familiar to most business people: the pyramid, which shows a hierarchical relationship; the target, which uses a ring of concentric circles to display the approach to a target; the Venn diagram, which shows the intersection of items in various sets; and the cycle, which displays the steps in a repeating process. Rather than create these diagrams on your own, you can have Excel create the basic diagram, and then you fill in the details. After you create the diagram, you can apply an AutoFormat to alter its appearance.

Insert a Diagram

1. Click the Insert tab.
2. Click SmartArt.
3. Click the category of SmartArt you want to create.
4. Click the specific diagram you want to add to your worksheet.
5. Click OK.
6. Click a text box to add text to your diagram.

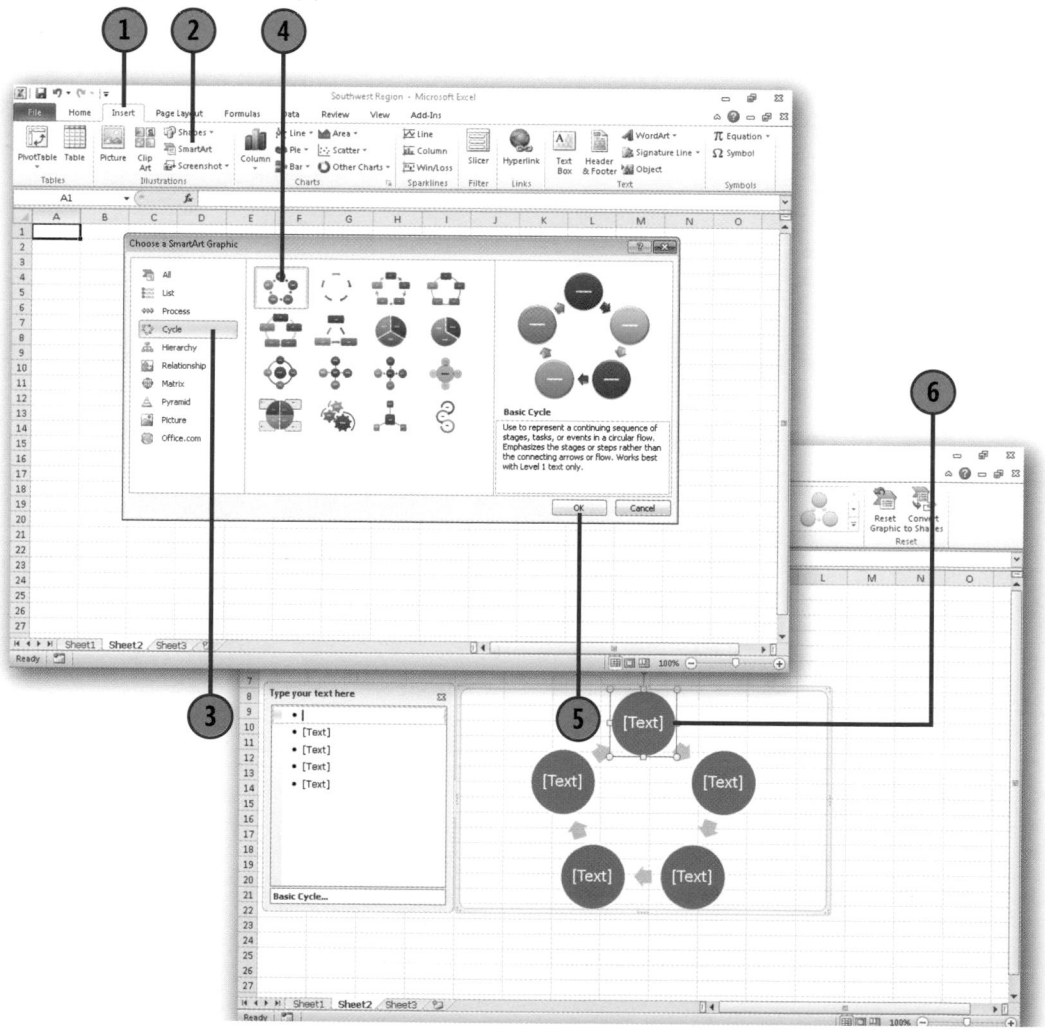

Change the Style of a Diagram

1. Click the diagram you want to change.
2. Click the Design tab.
3. In the Layouts group on the ribbon, click the layout you want to apply to the diagram.

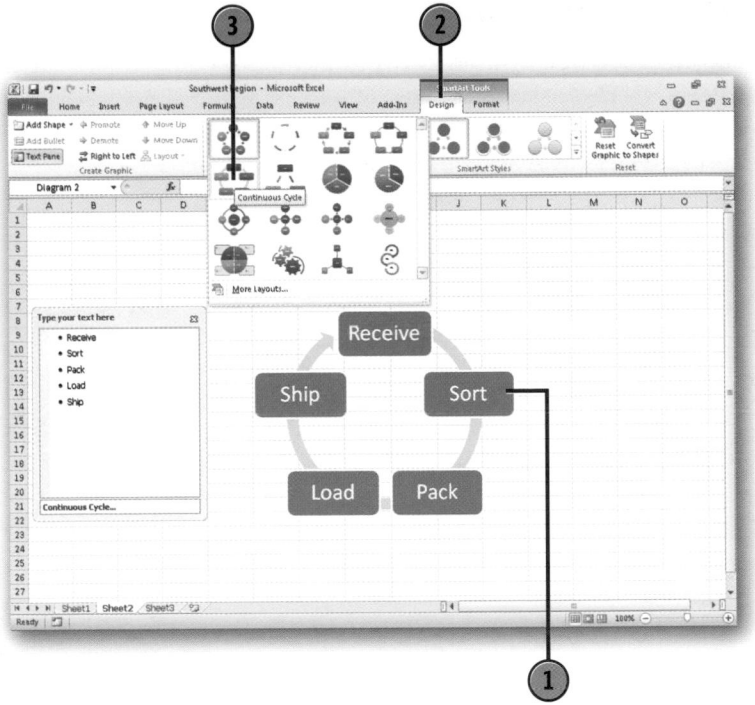

Tip

A preview of the new format appears when you hover the mouse pointer over a layout in the Layouts gallery—feel free to experiment!

Creating an Organization Chart

One of the most important tools in any business is the organization chart, which shows the reporting relationships between employees and their supervisors. Creating the base of an organization chart is simple, as is adding employees to the chart.

After you create the chart, you can change the chart's direction so that the relationships run from left to right and not up and down. You can also apply an AutoFormat to the chart.

Create an Organization Chart

1. Click the Insert tab.
2. Click SmartArt.
3. Click Hierarchy.
4. Click the first graphic in the Hierarchy group.
5. Click OK.

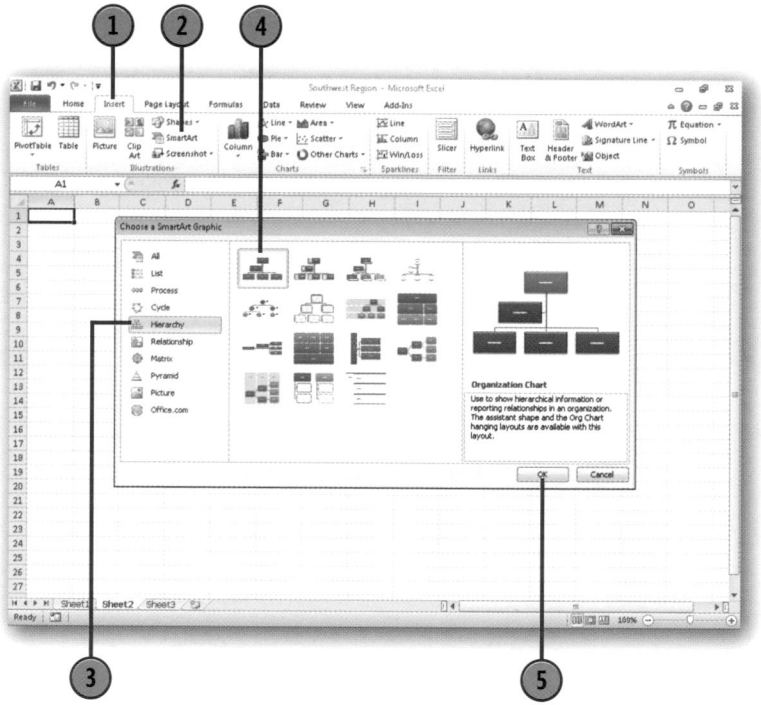

Add a Shape

1. Click the shape you want to add a shape above, under, or next to.
2. If necessary, click the Design tab.
3. Click Add Shape.
4. Click the option that reflects where you want to add the shape in the chart.

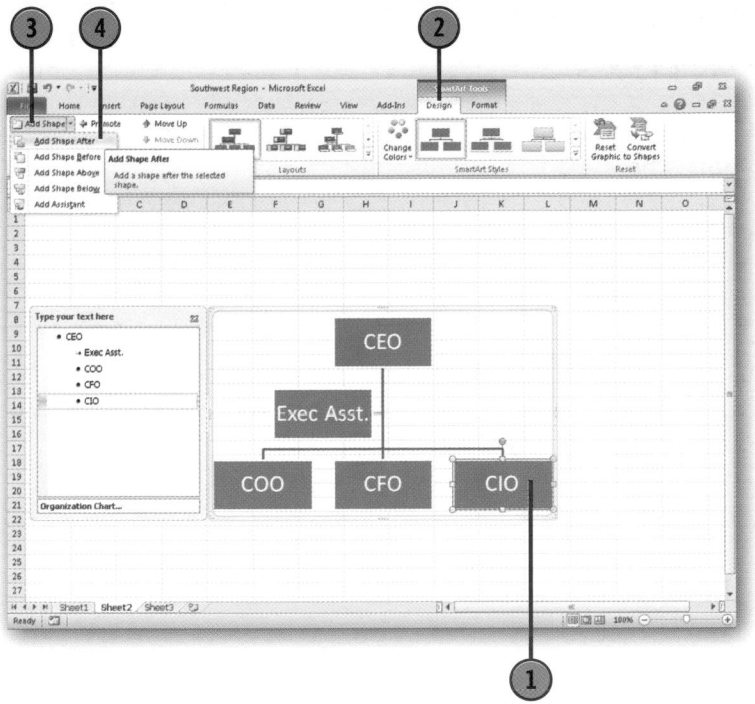

Tip

Click Add Assistant to place the shape below the current shape with an elbow connector.

Alter the Layout of Your Organization Chart

1. Click the organization chart.
2. Click the Design tab.
3. Click a new layout for your organization chart.

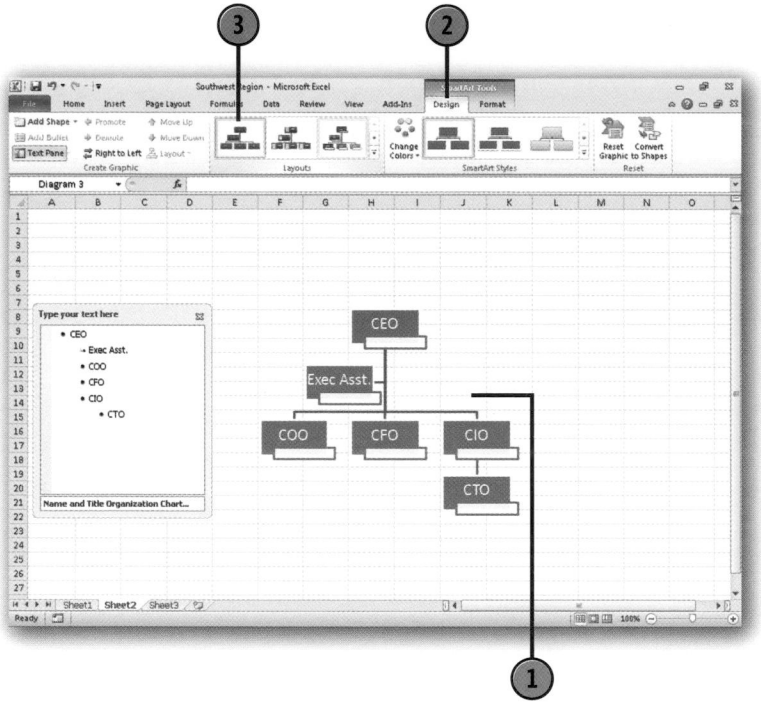

Change the Design of Your Organization Chart

1. Click the organization chart you want to change.
2. Click the Design tab.
3. Click Change Colors.
4. Click the color scheme you want.

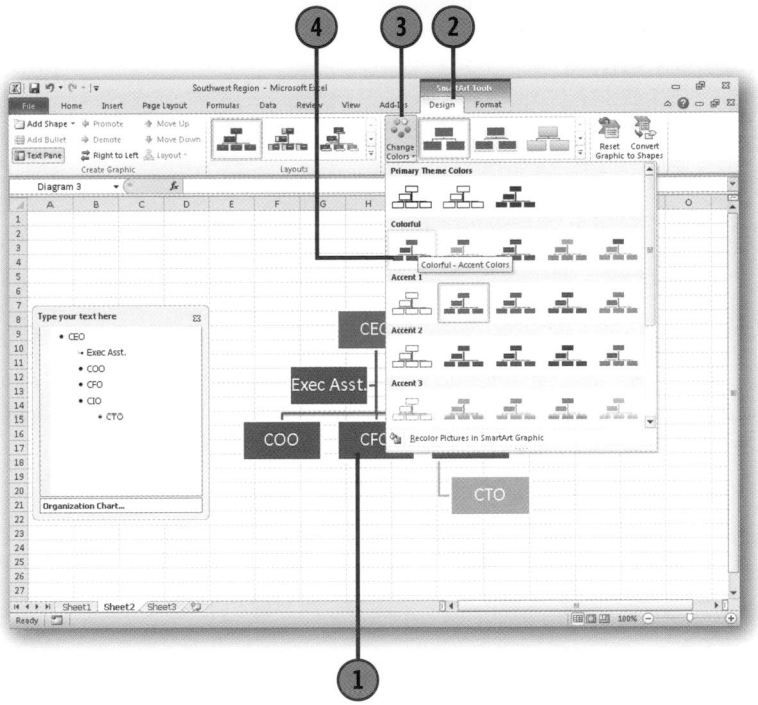

Tip

You can format individual shapes in a SmartArt graphic by clicking the shape you want to format and then clicking the Format tab that appears under SmartArt Tools at the top of the Excel window.

Adding an Equation to a Shape

You can use Excel 2010 to analyze your data in many ways, but it can be difficult to understand exactly how your formulas calculate their values. If you want to display the equation you use to calculate a value, you can add that mathematical equation to the interior of a shape. To add an equation to a shape, click the shape, and then click the Insert tab. In the Symbols group, click Equation, and then click the Equation Tools Design tab on the ribbon to display the equation-editing interface.

Add a Model Equation

1. Click the shape to which you want to add the equation.
2. Click the Insert tab.
3. Click Equation.
4. If necessary, click the Design tab.
5. Click the Equation button's down arrow.
6. Click the equation you want to add.

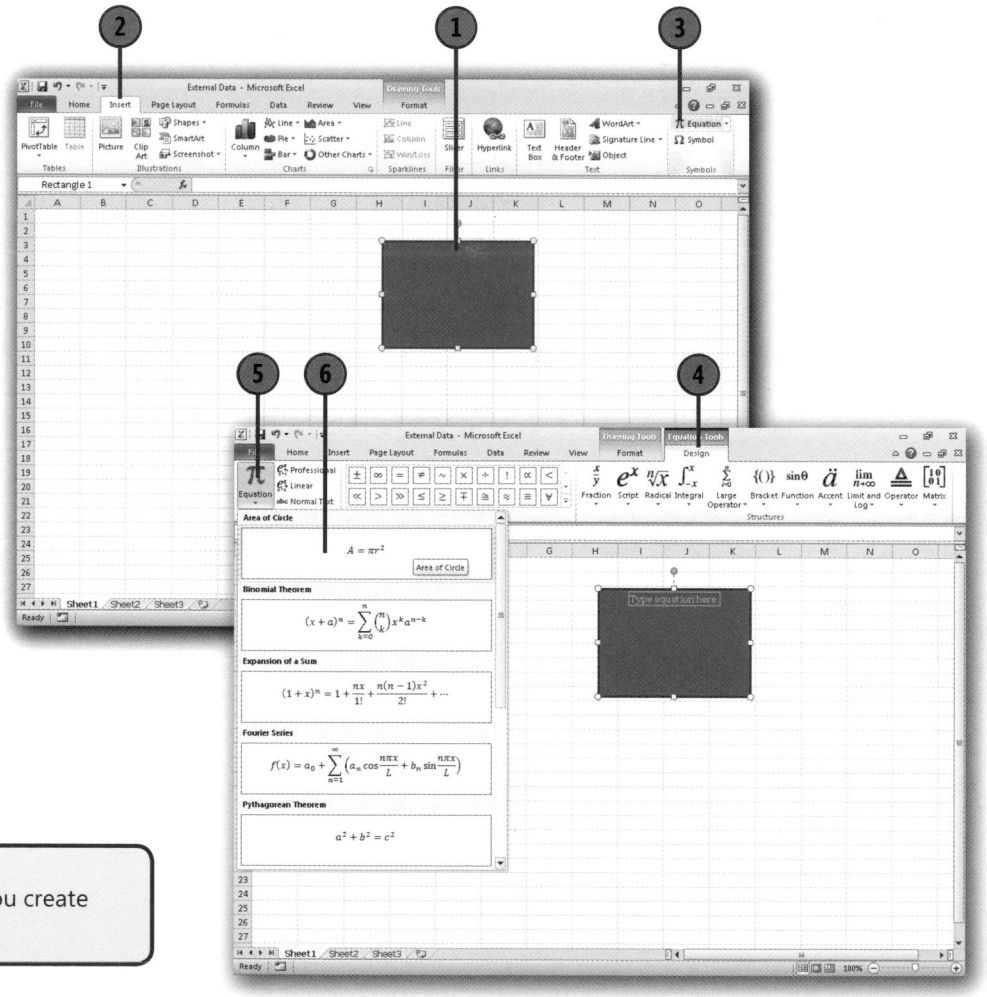

Tip

You can edit the model equation's elements after you create the equation.

Add a Custom Equation

1. Click the shape to which you want to add the equation.
2. Click the Insert tab.
3. Click Equation.
4. If necessary, click the Design tab.
5. Click the type of equation structure you want to create.
6. Click the specific structure to use for your equation.
7. Type the equation elements into the structure's boxes.

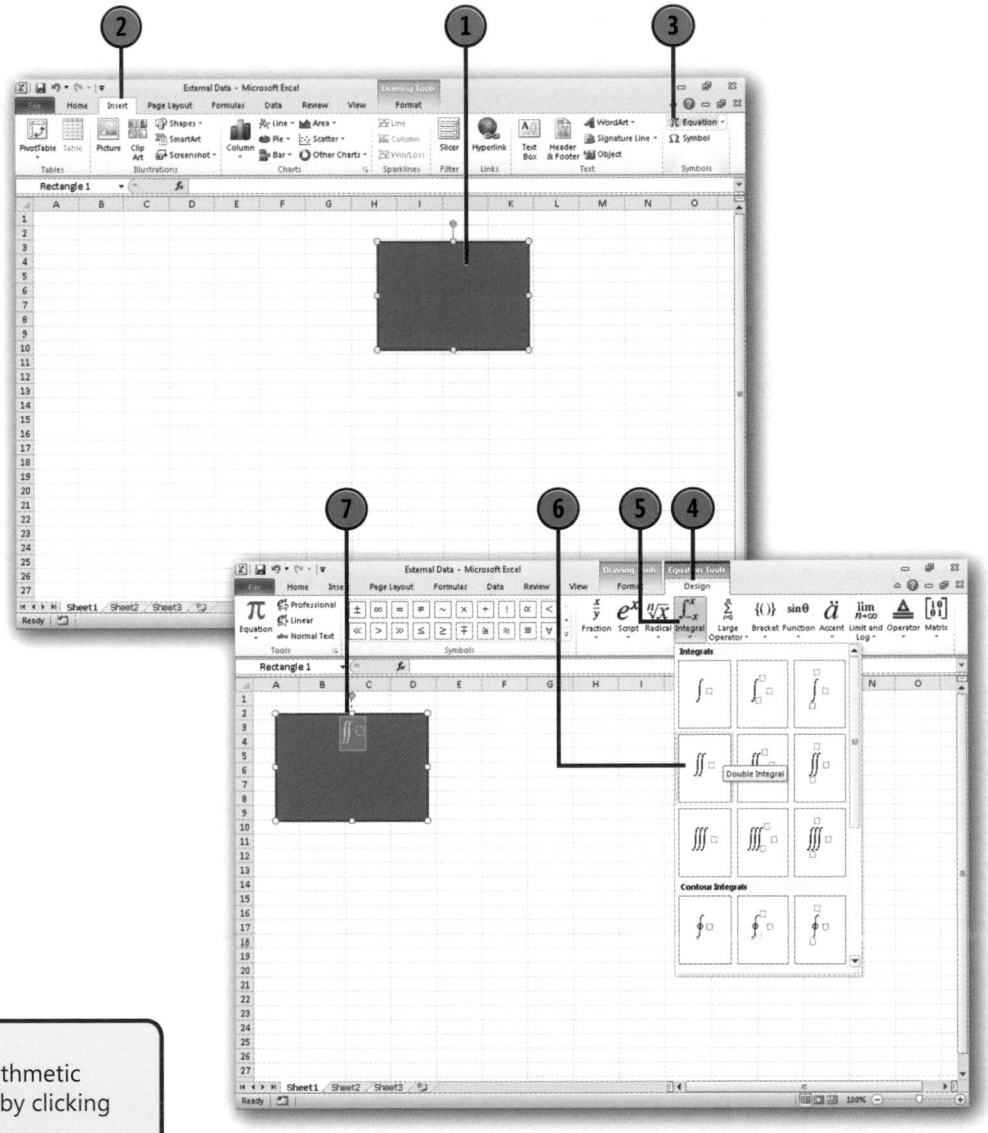

Tip

You can add symbols such as the infinity sign or arithmetic operators such as plus, minus, multiply, and divide by clicking the symbol or operator in the Symbols gallery.

14 Sharing Excel Data with Other Programs

In this section:

- Linking and Embedding Other Files
- Exchanging Table Data Between Excel and Word
- Copying Excel Charts and Data into PowerPoint
- Exchanging Data Between Access and Excel
- Importing a Text File

Microsoft Excel 2010 is a powerful program, but it doesn't try to do everything. Other Microsoft Office 2010 programs have complementary strengths: Microsoft Access 2010 is ideal for working with large data collections, Microsoft PowerPoint 2010 lets you create attractive presentations to print or project onto a screen, and Microsoft Word 2010 is great for creating text documents. You can include files created in other programs in your Excel workbooks or create links to them. Also, if a colleague uses a database or spreadsheet program that can write its data to a text file, there's a very good chance you can bring that data into Excel.

Introducing Linking and Embedding

Excel works wonderfully as a stand-alone program, but it really shines when you use it in combination with other programs. One way to use Excel in conjunction with other programs is to include in your worksheets files created in other programs, such as graphics, Word documents, or PowerPoint presentations. You can add these objects to your workbooks through linking and embedding.

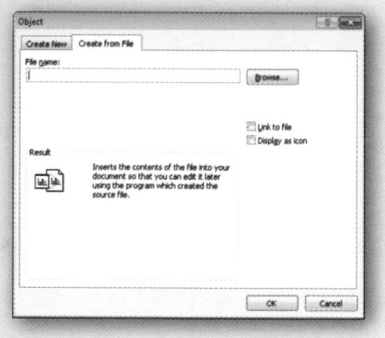

Keep in mind several important things when you consider whether to link to an object or embed it in a worksheet. As the name implies, embedding an object in a worksheet stores a copy of the object in the workbook. For example, if you want to add a company logo to an invoice generated from table data, you can identify the graphic and indicate that you want to embed it in the file. The advantage of embedding an object in an Excel file is that you don't have to worry about the graphic, chart, or image not being available because the person who created the workbook didn't include the graphic. If you create a workbook with embedded files, you can open your workbook anywhere and be certain that your graphics are available.

A disadvantage of embedding objects in workbooks is that the embedded files can be large and can dramatically increase the size of your workbooks. Although a single low-resolution logo meant to be viewed on a computer monitor probably won't have much of an impact on your file's size, the same image rendered at a resolution suitable for printing might double the size of the workbook. If you embed more than one image—or more than one copy of the same image—you might make your file unworkably large.

When you want to include more than one image or external file in an Excel workbook, you should consider creating a link to the files. For example, rather than embed many copies of a high-resolution logo in your worksheets, you can save the logo file on your hard disk and link to the file's location on your computer. Excel uses the reference to find the file and display it as part of the workbook. The workbook will be no larger than it was originally, and you won't need multiple copies of the same file if you link to it more than once. The advantage of linking is that you save disk space, but the disadvantage is that moving the workbook from computer to computer can be difficult unless you have the extra files when you travel or distribute the workbook to colleagues.

In general, embedding an object in an Excel workbook works best if you use the object only once in the workbook and you have room to store the workbook with the embedded object. Otherwise, such as when you use the same file multiple times in the same workbook, you need to link to the file instead.

Linking and Embedding Other Files

Excel workbooks can hold a lot of data, and you can make your data even more meaningful when you include files created with other programs. For example, you might have a Word document with important background information or a PowerPoint presentation that puts your data into context for your colleagues. You can include those files in your worksheets by linking or embedding the files as objects.

Embed a File in a Worksheet

1. Click the Insert tab.
2. In the Text group, click Object.
3. Click Create From File.
4. Click Browse.
5. Navigate to the folder that contains the file you want to embed.
6. Double-click the file you want to embed in your worksheet.
7. Click OK.

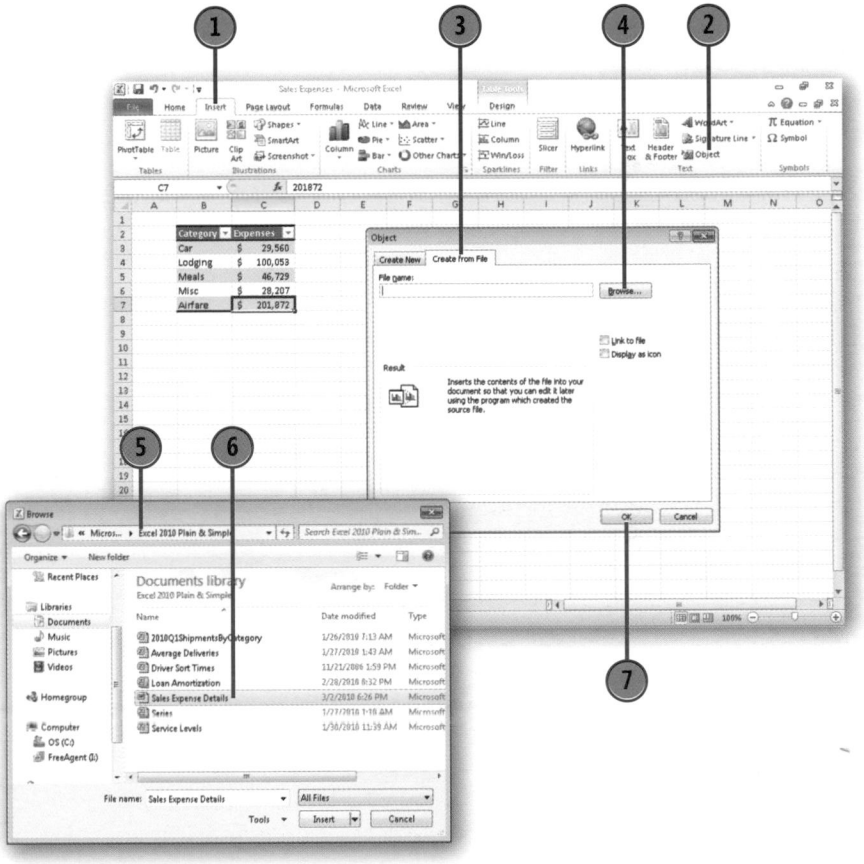

Tip

If you want the file you've linked to or embedded to take up as little room as possible in your workbook, select the Display As Icon check box in the Object dialog box.

Link to a File

1. Click the Insert tab.
2. In the Text group, click Object.
3. Click Create From File.
4. Click Browse.
5. Navigate to the folder that contains the file you want to link to.
6. Double-click the file you want to link to.
7. Select the Link To File check box.
8. Click OK.

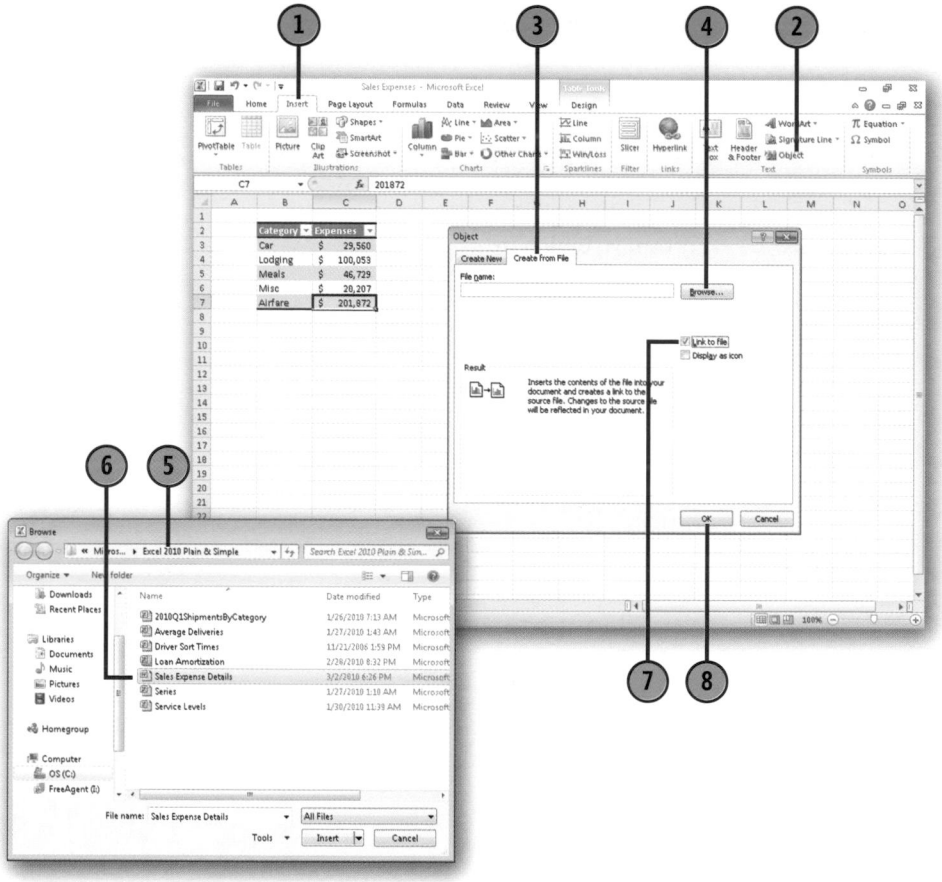

Exchanging Table Data Between Excel and Word

Just as you can create workbooks to store and manipulate financial and other data in Excel, you can use Word to create reports and other text documents to interpret and provide valuable context for your worksheet data. Word documents can also present data in tables, which are arranged in rows and columns like a worksheet. For example, if you receive a report from a traveling colleague in which she created a table listing the prices of popular products at a competitor's store, you can copy the data from the Word document to an Excel worksheet for direct comparison. You can also go in the opposite direction, copying Excel data to a table in Word.

Bring Word Data into Excel

1. In Word, select the table you want to import into Excel.
2. Click the Home tab.
3. Click the Copy button.
4. In Excel, click the cell in which you want the upper-left table cell to appear.
5. Click the Home tab.
6. Click Paste.

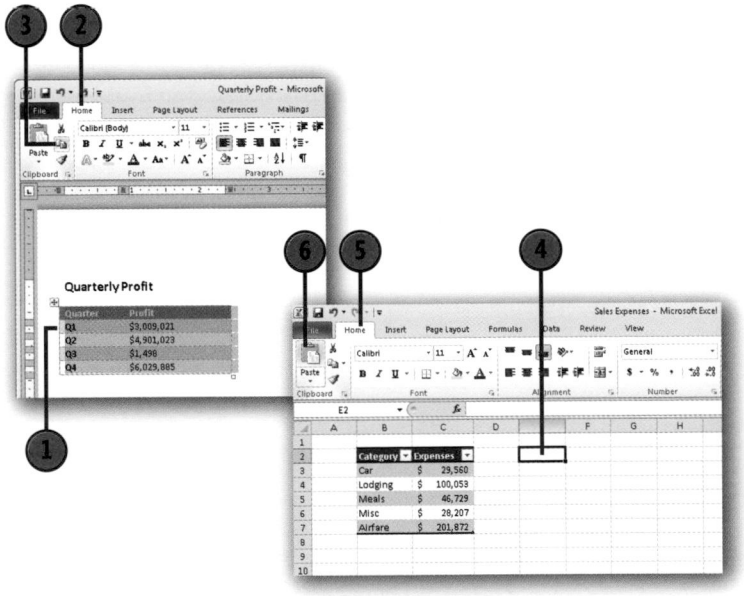

Copy Excel Data to Word

1. In Excel, select the cells you want to export.
2. Click the Home tab.
3. Click the Copy button.
4. In Word, click the location where you want the pasted cells to appear.
5. Click the Home tab.
6. Click Paste.

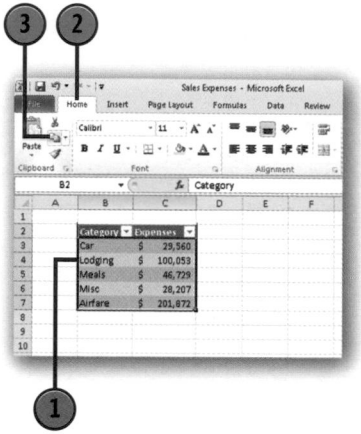

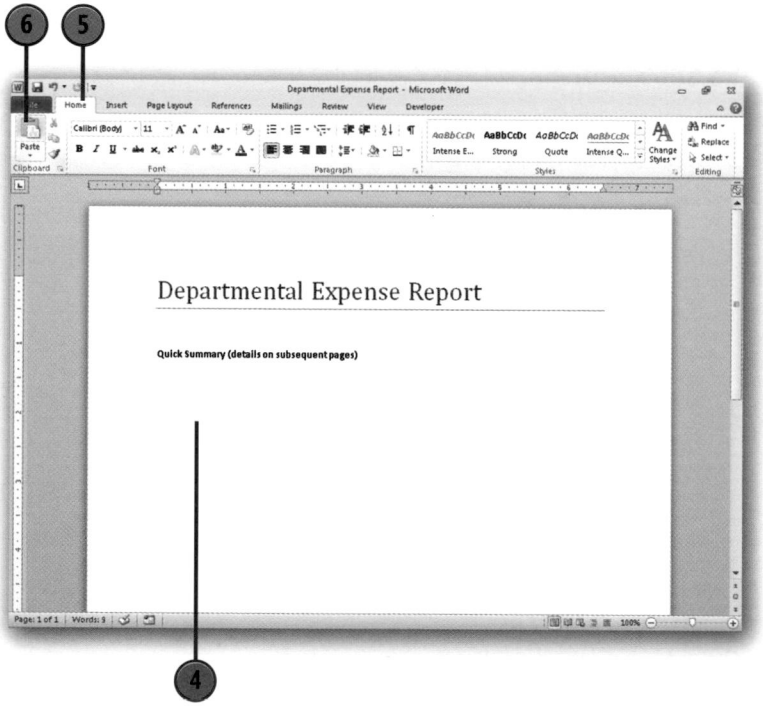

Copying Excel Charts and Data into PowerPoint

It's possible to present Excel data to your colleagues using Excel exclusively, but if you're developing a formal presentation, you might want to use PowerPoint. Because presentations often contain graphical representations of numerical data, it's easy to include your Excel data in a PowerPoint presentation.

When you copy an Excel chart into a PowerPoint presentation, you can select how you want PowerPoint to manage the chart and its data. If you don't make any changes, PowerPoint creates the chart and maintains a link to the workbook from which it came. You can also choose to paste the entire workbook into PowerPoint or paste a picture of the chart's current state.

Move Excel Data to PowerPoint

1. In Excel, select the cells you want to export.
2. Click the Home tab.
3. Click the Copy button.
4. In PowerPoint, click the location where you want the pasted cells to appear.
5. Click the Home tab.
6. Click Paste.

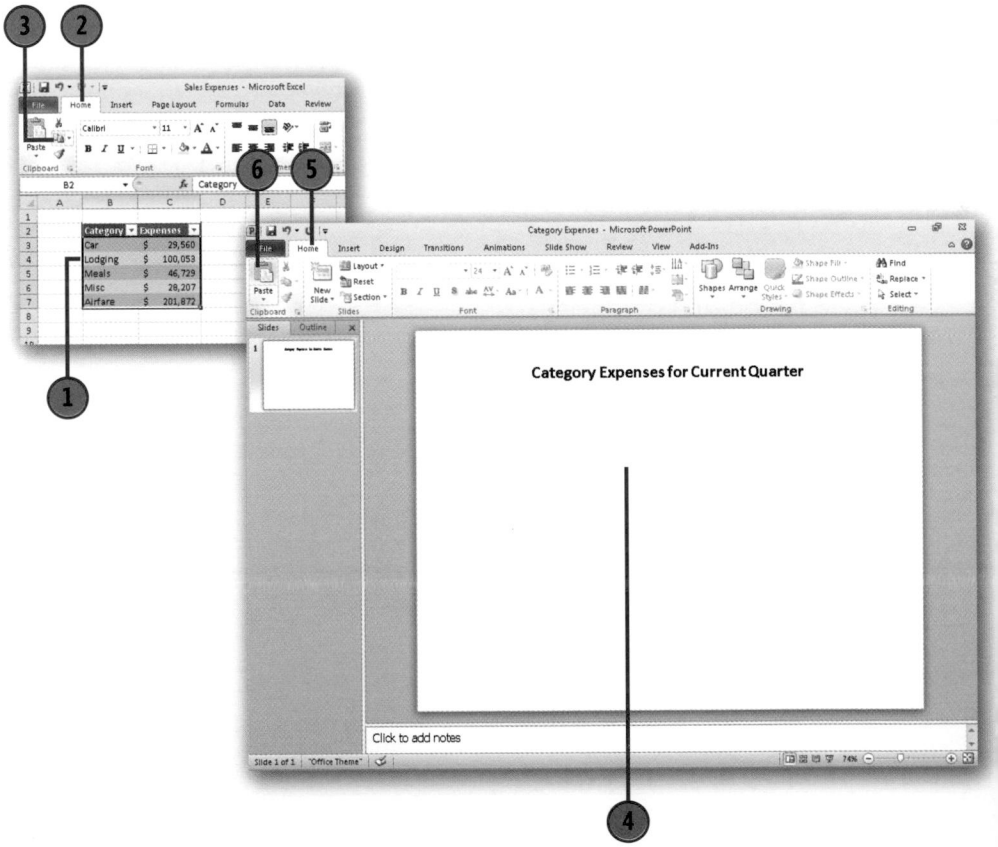

Copy an Excel Chart to PowerPoint

1. In Excel, select the chart you want to export.
2. Click the Home tab.
3. Click the Copy button.
4. In PowerPoint, click the location where you want the pasted chart to appear.
5. Click the Home tab.
6. Click the Paste button's down arrow.
7. Follow any of these steps:
   - Click the Chart (Linked To Excel Data) option to paste the chart into the presentation and retain a live link to the source workbook.
   - Click the Excel Chart (Entire Workbook) option to paste the chart and a copy of the workbook to the presentation.
   - Click the Paste As Picture option to paste an image of the chart into the presentation.

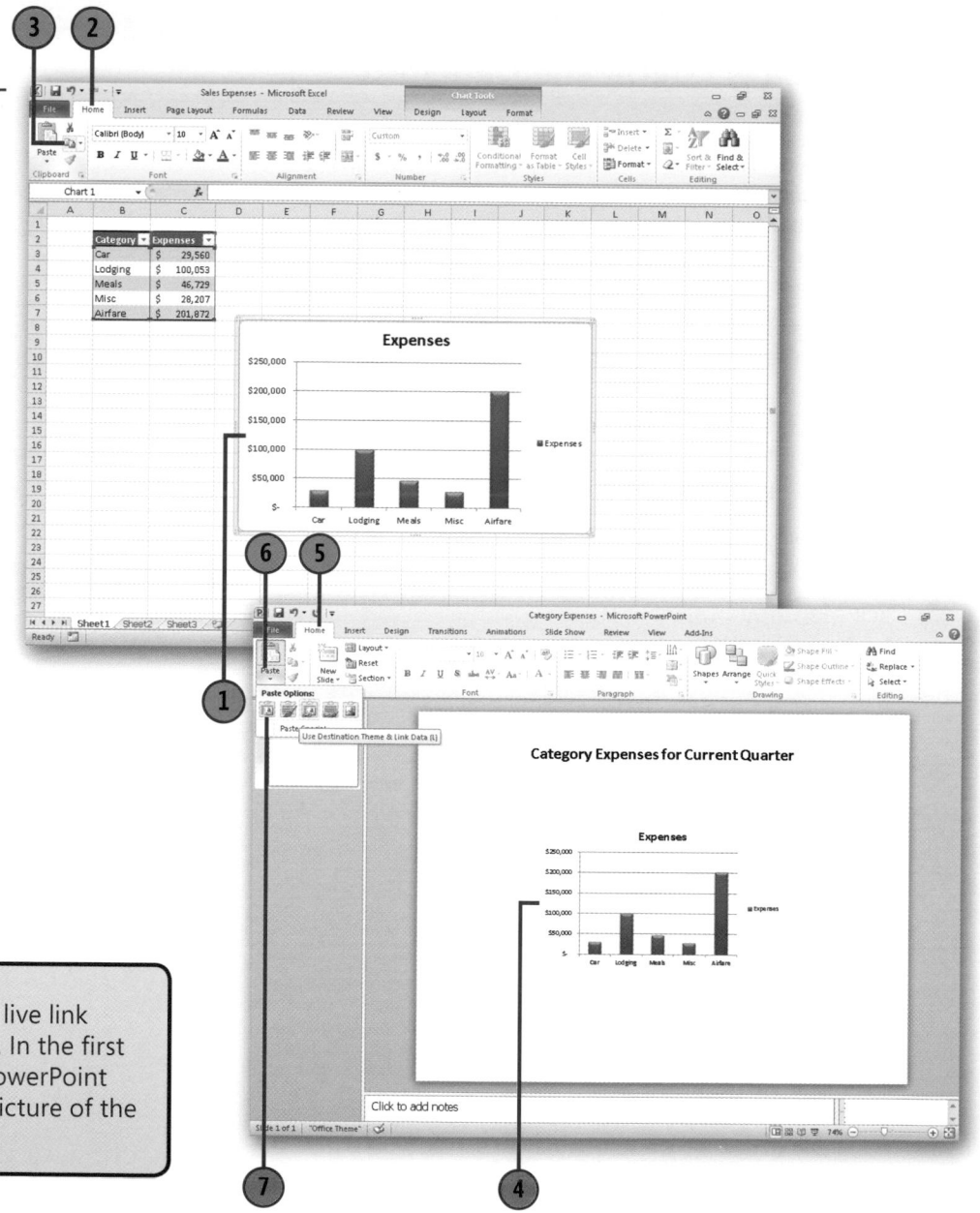

Caution

Neither of the latter two options maintains a live link between the chart and its original workbook. In the first case, you paste a copy of the data into the PowerPoint presentation; in the second, you just take a picture of the chart and paste that into the presentation.

Exchanging Data Between Access and Excel

No other Microsoft Office 2010 programs have as much in common as Access and Excel, but each program retains its unique strengths. Where Excel offers a wide range of data analysis and presentation tools you can use to summarize your data, Access is designed to let you store, manipulate, and ask questions about large data collections. You can also use Access queries to locate and summarize table data. Although it is possible to look up data in an Excel worksheet, it's much easier to do in Access.

Bring Access Table Data into an Excel Worksheet

1. In Access, display the table from which you want to copy the data.
2. Select the table cells you want to copy.
3. Click the Home tab.
4. Click Copy.
5. In Excel, click the cell where you want the first table cell to appear.
6. Click the Home tab.
7. Click the Paste button's down arrow.
8. Click the Match Destination Formatting icon.

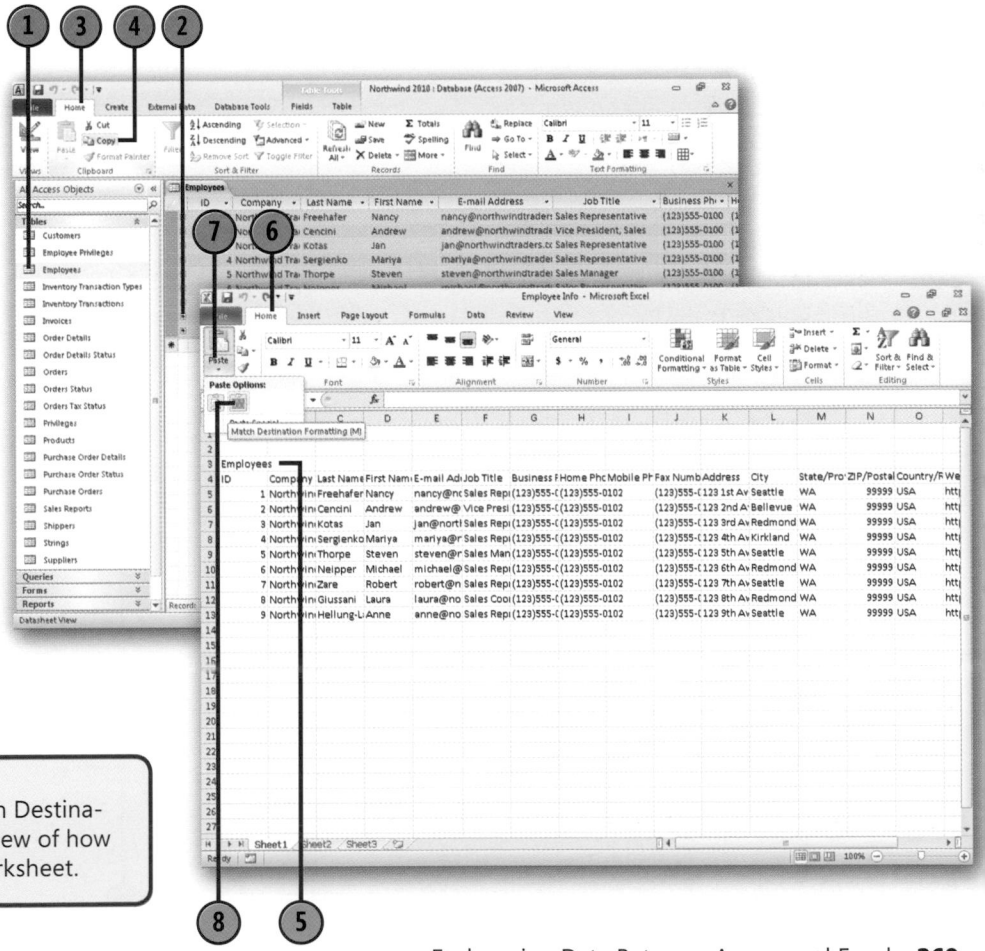

Tip

When you hover your mouse pointer over the Match Destination Formatting icon, Excel 2010 displays a live preview of how the data will appear when you paste it into your worksheet.

Send Excel Data to Access

1. In Excel, select the cells you want to copy.
2. Click the Home tab.
3. Click the Copy button.
4. In Access, display the table that you want to receive the pasted data.
5. In the (New) record row, select as many cells as there are columns of data to be pasted.
6. Click the Home tab.
7. Click Paste.
8. Click Yes to acknowledge that you want to paste the worksheet data into the table.

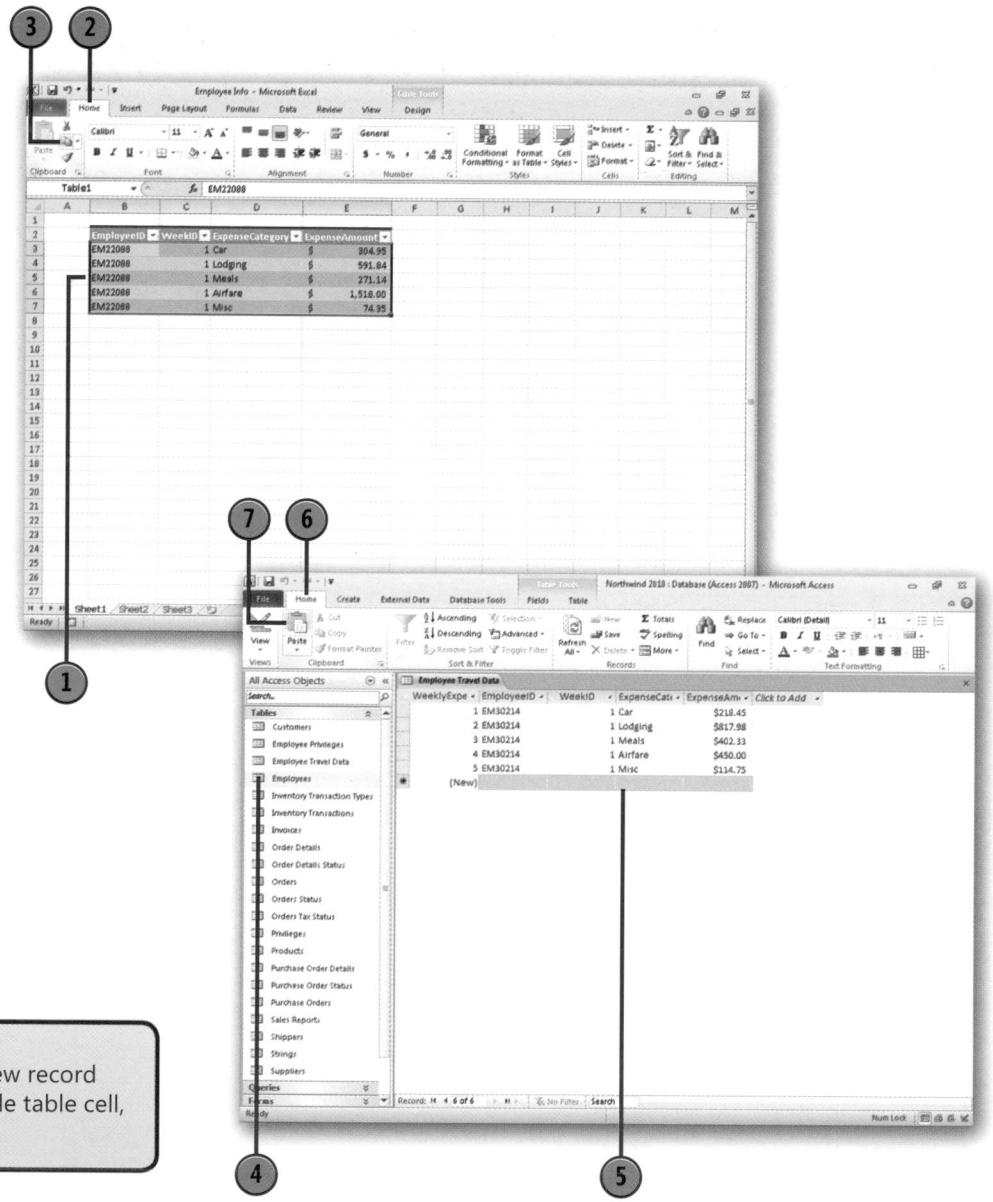

Caution

If you click only a single cell in the Access table's New record row, you'll paste all your worksheet data into a single table cell, making the new data worthless.

Importing a Text File

Excel can read data from quite a few other spreadsheet and database programs, but you may have a colleague who uses a spreadsheet or database program that creates files you can't read with Excel. If that's the case, you can ask your colleague to save the file as a text file, using a comma, tab, or other character (called a delimiter) to mark the end of each cell's data. Even if you can't transfer data any other way, you can always read spreadsheet data if it's presented to you in a text file. Any formatting and formulas are lost, but the data will be there for you to analyze.

Bring Text into Excel

1. Click the Data tab.
2. In the Get External Data group, click From Text.
3. Navigate to the folder that contains the text file you want to import.
4. Double-click the text file.
5. Select the Delimited option.
6. Click Next.

(continued on next page)

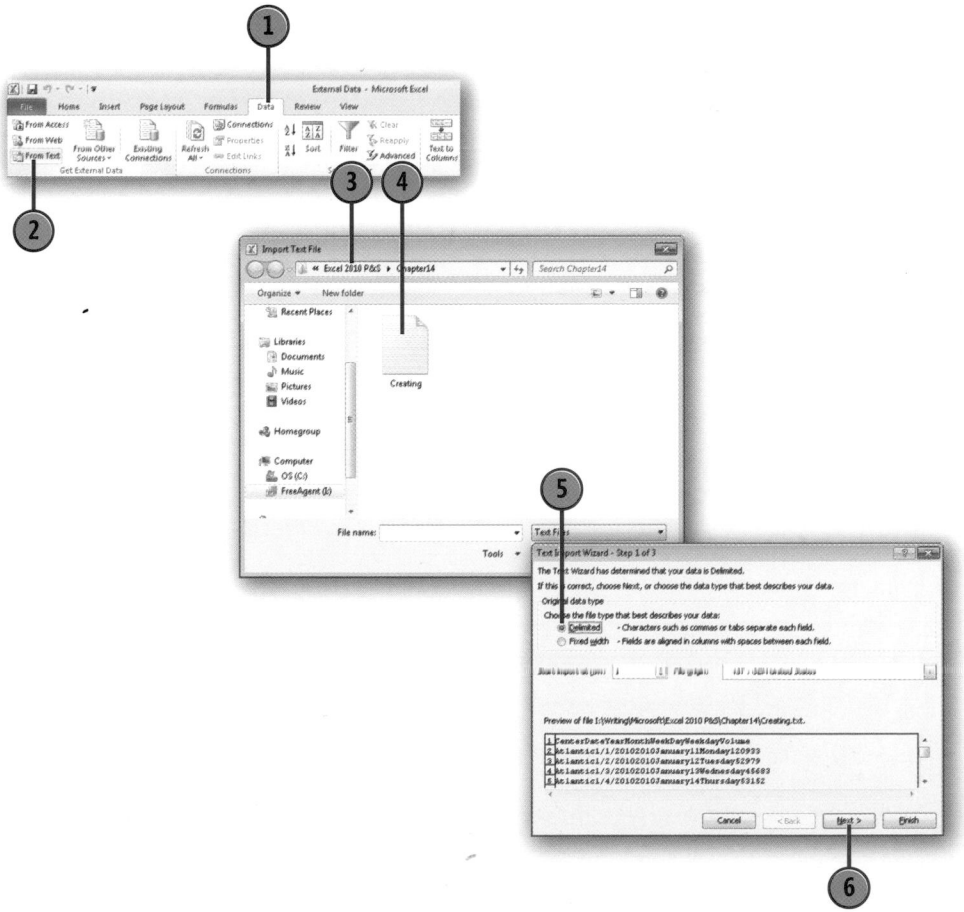

Bring Text into Excel *(continued)*

7. Select the file's delimiter character.
8. Verify that the data appears correctly in the Data Preview pane.
9. Click Finish.
10. Click OK.

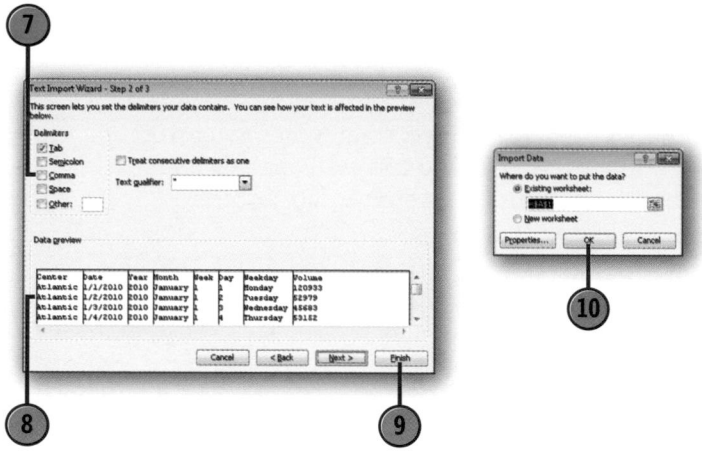

Tip

If you can choose whether to have a text file created so that it contains fixed-width or delimited values, ask for the delimited values. Character delimiters are much easier for Excel to detect, which means less work for you when you want to import the data.

Tip

If your text file contains data where each data column always contains the same number of characters, select the Fixed Width option on the first Text Import Wizard page, click Next, and then use the following wizard pages to define each field's width.

15 Using Excel in a Group Environment

In this section:

- Sharing Workbooks in Excel
- Commenting in Cells
- Tracking Changes in Workbooks
- Accepting or Rejecting Changes
- Saving Worksheets to the Web
- Dynamically Updating Worksheets Published to the Web
- Retrieving Web Data from Excel
- Modifying Web Queries
- Interacting over the Web with XML

Even though single individuals might be in charge of managing a company's financial data and related information, there is usually a group of folks who either enter data into workbooks or have input into future revenue or growth projections. You and your colleagues can add comments to workbooks to describe their contents and to offer insights into how certain values are derived. If you and your colleagues need to open or edit a workbook at the same time but from different computers, you can turn on workbook sharing so that more than one person can have the workbook open at a time. You can view any changes your colleagues make and then accept or reject those changes to produce a final version of a workbook.

Microsoft Excel 2010 also takes full advantage of XML (the Extensible Markup Language). XML is a content markup language, meaning that an XML file has information about the data contained within it, not just how the data should be displayed. Not only is the Excel 2010 file format based on XML, but you can also save your Excel workbooks as SpreadsheetML (Spreadsheet XML) files, which means that your Excel data can be read by a wide range of programs, not just those programs listed in the Save As dialog box's Save As Type drop-down list.

Sharing Workbooks in Excel

When you want to enable more than one individual to work with a workbook simultaneously, you must turn on workbook sharing. Workbook sharing is perfect for mid-sized businesses in which employees need to look up customer, sales, and product data frequently. In larger companies, turning on workbook sharing makes it possible for coworkers at different offices to add values to a workbook that's used to develop a cost estimate or maintain expense reports.

Turn on Workbook Sharing

1. Click the Review tab.
2. Click Share Workbook.
3. Select the Allow Changes By More Than One User... check box.
4. Click OK to close the dialog box.
5. Click Save to save the workbook.

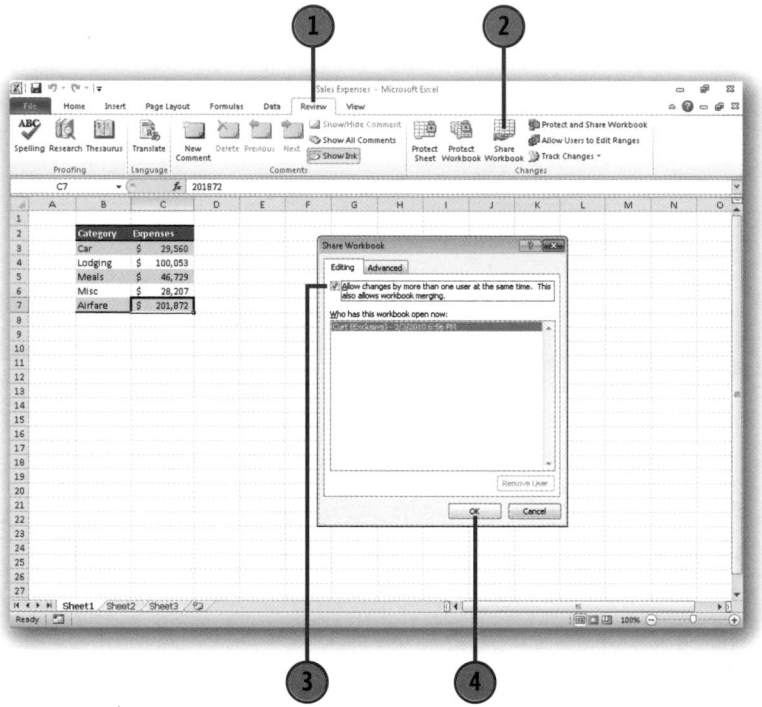

Caution

You can't share a workbook that contains an Excel table. If you want to share a workbook that contains an Excel table, you must convert the table to a normal range. The error message that appears explains how to convert the Excel table to a normal range.

Commenting in Cells

When you and your colleagues share responsibility for creating a workbook, you might want to add comments to some cells to suggest modifications to a formula, ask whether a cell's contents might be formatted differently, or provide an updated value for a workbook's owner to add after the owner verifies the data. Excel 2010 marks cells that contain comments by placing a red flag at the top-right corner, making it easy for you and your colleagues to identify which cells have additional information available. For example, you could add a comment to a sales worksheet explaining that two exceptionally large purchases pushed one hour's sales way beyond the norm.

Add a Comment

1. Click the cell to which you want to add a comment.
2. Click the Review tab.
3. Click New Comment.
4. Type the comment you want.
5. Click anywhere outside the comment to stop adding text.

View a Comment

- Hover the mouse pointer over a cell with a red triangle in the top-right corner.

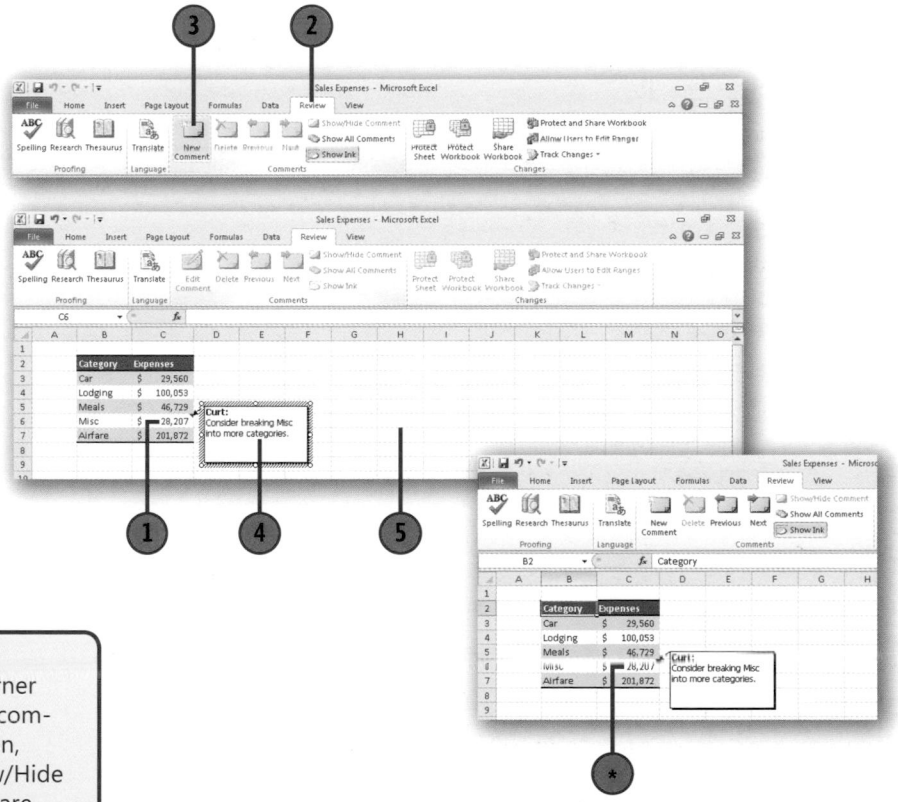

Tip

By default, Excel displays the red flag at the top-right corner only for cells that contain comments. If you want a cell's comments to be shown the entire time your workbook is open, right-click the cell with the comment and then click Show/Hide Comments from the shortcut menu. If a cell's comments are shown the entire time, you can return to just the indicator by right-clicking the cell and then clicking Hide Comment.

Edit a Comment

1. Select the cell that contains the comment.
2. Click the Review tab.
3. Click Edit Comment.
4. Edit the comment text.
5. Click anywhere outside the comment box to stop editing.

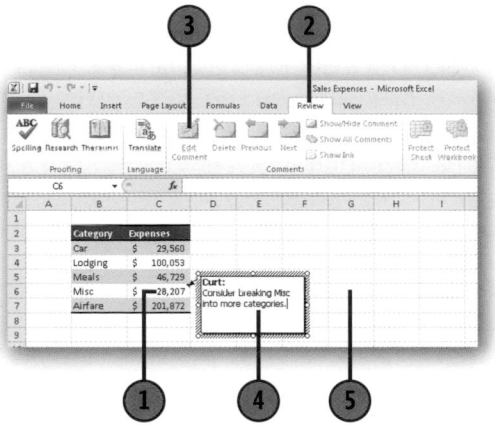

Delete a Comment

1. Select the cell that contains the comment.
2. Click the Review tab.
3. Click Delete.

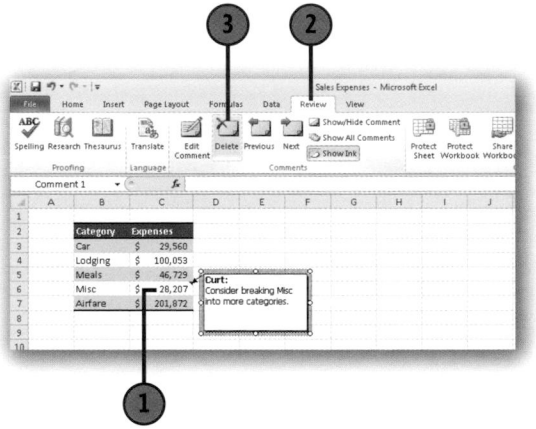

Caution

Note that the name attributed to a comment may not be the same as the person who actually created it. Instead, a comment reflects the name of the person who was logged on to the computer on which the comment was made.

Tracking Changes in Workbooks

Whenever you collaborate with a number of your colleagues in producing or editing a document, you should consider tracking the changes each user makes. When you turn on Track Changes, Excel 2010 highlights any changes made to the workbook in a color assigned to the user who made the changes. When you have a question about a change, you can quickly identify who made it and verify that it is correct.

Turn on Track Changes

1. Click the Review tab.
2. Click Track Changes.
3. Click Highlight Changes.
4. Select the Track Changes While Editing check box.
5. Click OK.

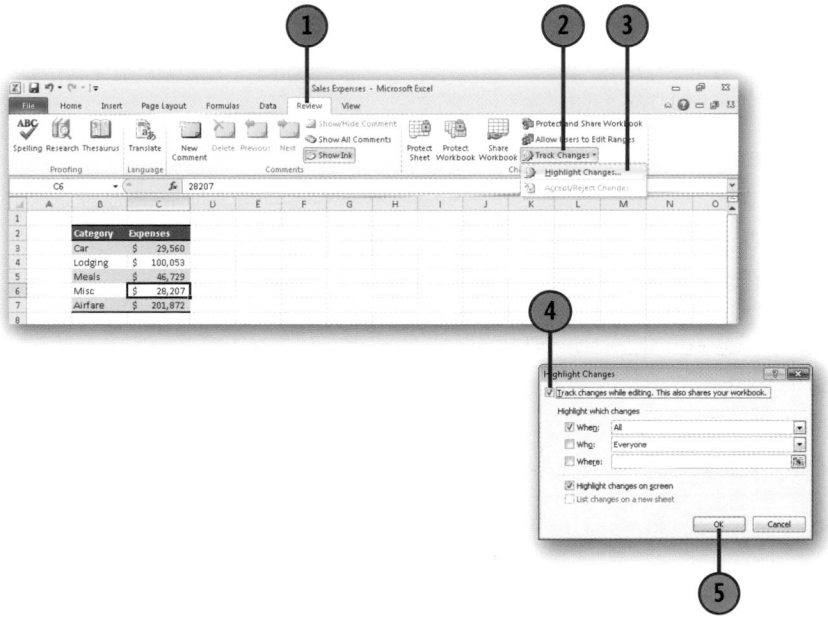

Tip

If your workbook's changed cells aren't marked, you can have Excel display them by clicking the Review tab, clicking Track Changes, clicking Highlight Changes, selecting the Highlight Changes On Screen check box, and clicking OK.

Accepting or Rejecting Changes

When you and your colleagues have made your changes to a workbook, you can go through the workbook and accept or reject those changes. The best way to accept or reject changes is to move through them one at a time. Examining each change in a large document can be tedious, but it's far less of a hassle to take an hour to finalize a workbook than it is to spend a day reconstructing a workbook after you accidentally accept every change. If you want to keep track of every change, you can have Excel create a new worksheet named History and list every change made since you last saved. Whenever you save your workbook, Excel deletes the History worksheet.

View a Change

- Hover over a cell with a blue triangle in the top-left corner.

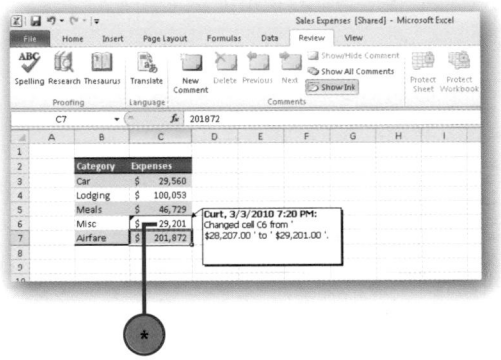

Review Changes

1. Click the Review tab.
2. Click Track Changes.
3. Click Accept/Reject Changes, and then click OK to save your workbook.
4. Select the Who check box.
5. Click the Who down arrow.
6. Click Everyone.
7. Click OK.

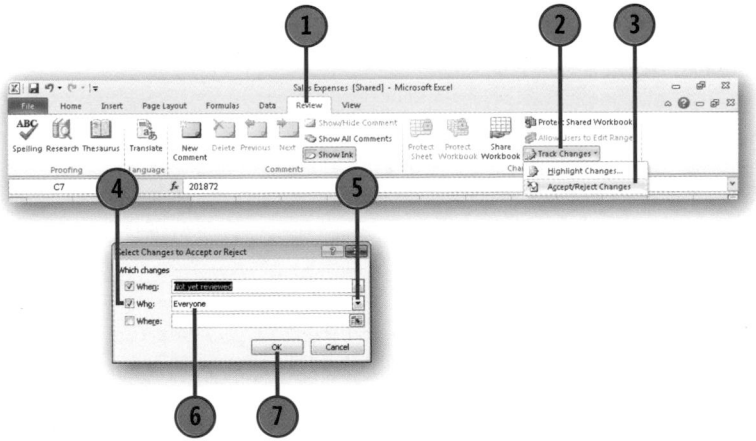

(continued on next page)

Review Changes *(continued)*

8. Do any of the following:
   - Click Accept to accept the current change.
   - Click Reject to reject the current change.
   - Click Accept All to accept all the changes.
   - Click Reject All to reject all the changes.
   - Click Close to stop reviewing changes.

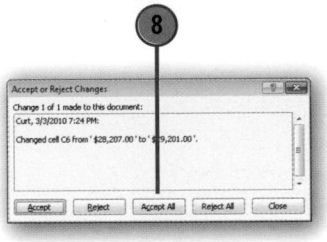

Create a Change History

1. Make changes to a workbook that has change tracking turned on.
2. Click the Review tab.
3. Click Track Changes.
4. Click Highlight Changes.
5. Select the List Changes On A New Sheet check box.
6. Click OK.

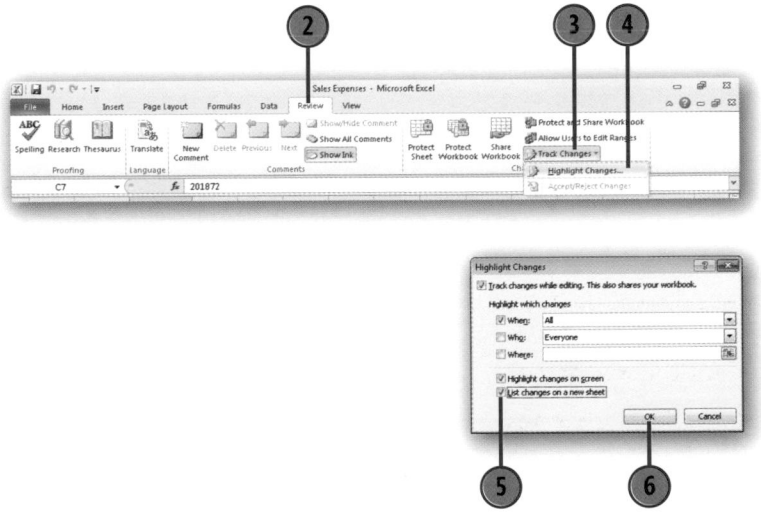

Tip

You should consider making a backup copy of your workbook before accepting any changes. Having a record of what changes were made in case something goes wrong is never a bad idea.

Tip

If you want to review only those changes made after a specific date, click the When down arrow in the Highlight Changes dialog box, click Since Date, and type the date in the When box.

Saving Worksheets to the Web

Exchanging data with traveling colleagues presents a real challenge to all organizations. Writing the data to a Web page means that you don't have to send the entire workbook to travelers. In fact, your colleagues don't even need Excel on their machines! Saving workbooks as Web pages also enables you to make data available over a corporate network (an intranet). So long as your company's network supports Web connections, you can make your data available to any authorized user.

Save a Workbook to the Web

1. Click the File tab.
2. Click Save As.
3. Click the Save As Type down arrow.
4. Click Web Page.
5. Navigate to the folder where you want to save your workbook.
6. Type the file name you want.
7. Click Save.

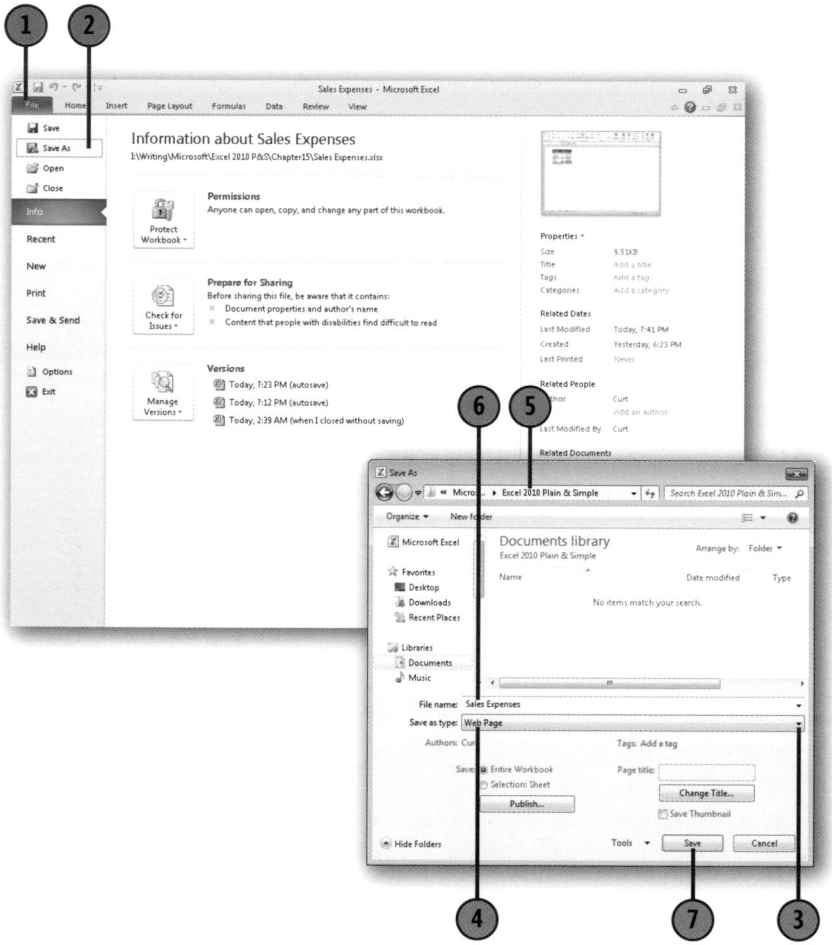

Tip

Excel saves each worksheet as a separate file. You can move from worksheet to worksheet using the representation of the sheet tabs at the bottom left of each page.

Tip

You can change the text that appears on the title bar of the Excel document's Web page by clicking the Change Title button in the Save As dialog box.

Dynamically Update Worksheets Published to the Web

One advantage of working with Excel over the Web is that you and your colleagues can interact with Excel worksheets you have published on the Web. By adding interactivity to your worksheet, you and your colleagues can edit cell values, sort the values in the worksheet, apply a filter, or create formulas. You can also use interactivity to update an Excel-based Web page whenever there is a change in the workbook on which the file is based.

Update Worksheets Published to the Web

1. Click the File tab.
2. Click Save As.
3. Click the Save As Type down arrow.
4. Click Web Page.
5. Click Publish.
6. Click the Choose down arrow.
7. Click the sheet that contains the data you want to update.
8. Click the element you want to publish.
9. Select the AutoRepublish Every Time This Workbook Is Saved check box.
10. Click Publish.

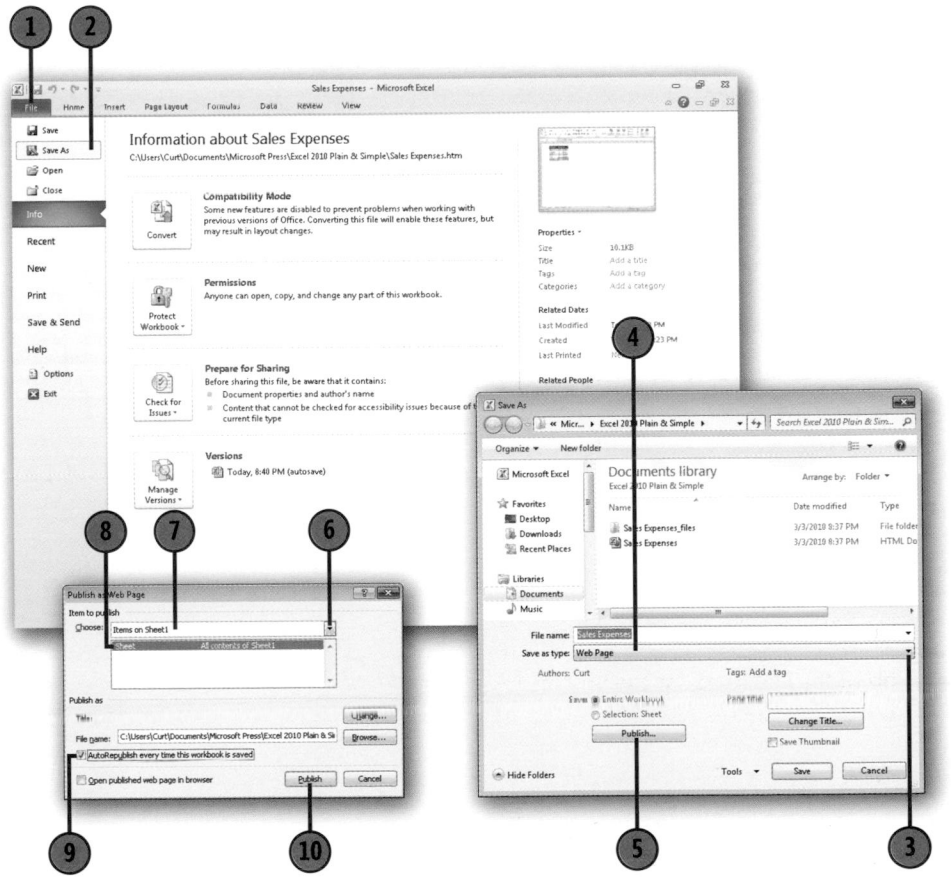

Retrieving Web Data Using Excel

The World Wider Web is a great source of information. From stock quotes to product descriptions, many companies publish useful information on their Web sites. The most common structure used to present financial information is the table, which, like a spreadsheet, organizes the data into rows and columns. Excel 2010 makes creating a Web query easy by letting you copy data directly from a Web page into Excel and then create a query to retrieve data from the table you copied.

Retrieve Data from Web Pages

1. Click the Data tab.
2. Click From Web.
3. Type the address of the Web page you want.
4. Click Go.
5. Click the yellow boxes with black arrows to specify which tables you want to import.
6. Click Import.
7. Click OK.

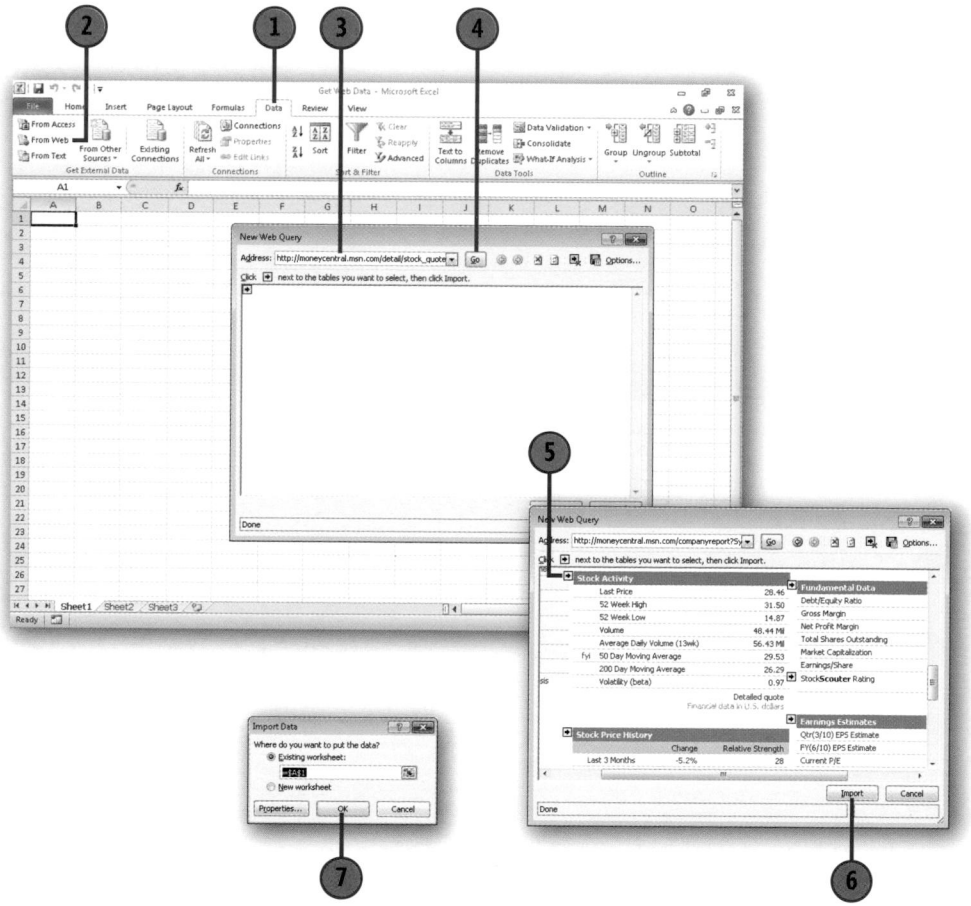

Copy Data from the Web to Excel

1. In your Web browser, type the URL you want to visit.
2. Select the data you want to copy into Excel.
3. Press Ctrl+C to copy the data to the Clipboard.
4. In Excel, click the cell where you want to paste the data.
5. Click the Home tab.
6. Click Paste.

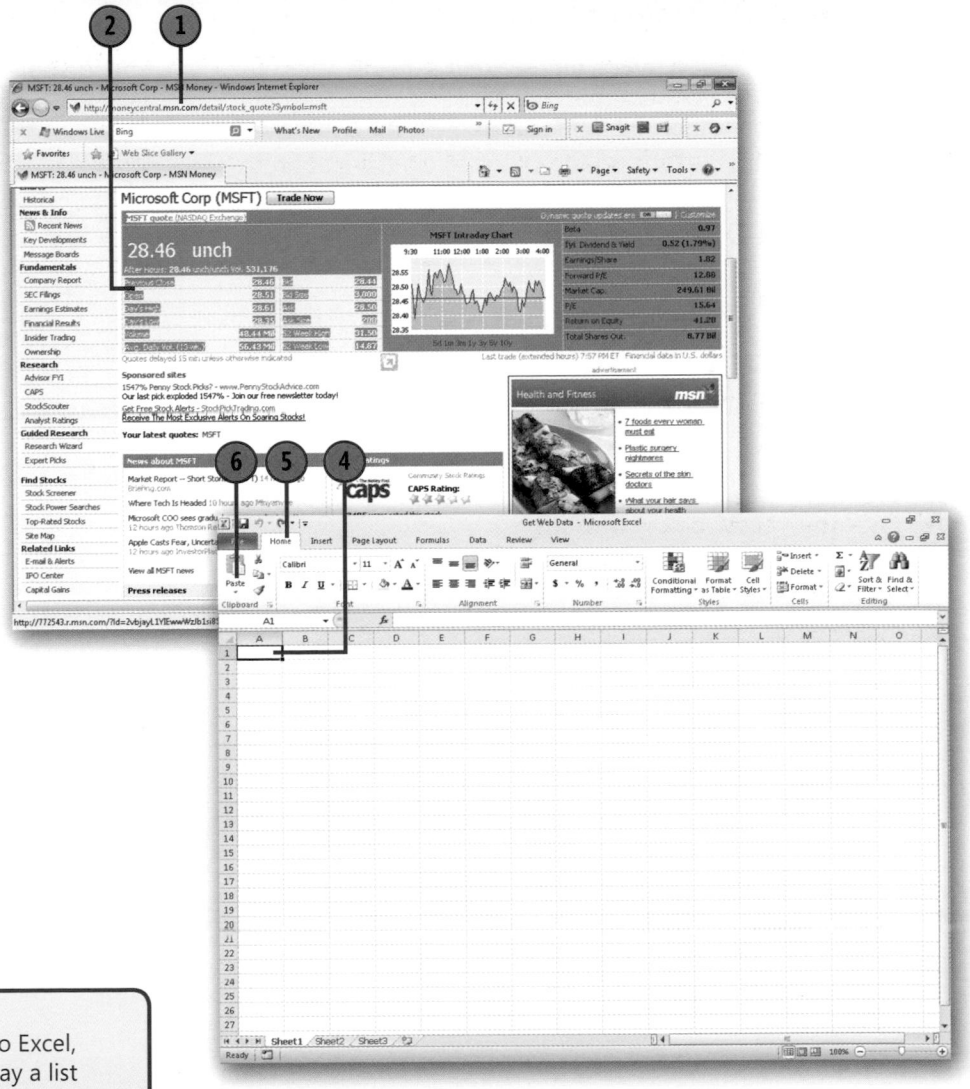

Tip

When you are ready to paste data from the Web into Excel, you can click the Paste button's down arrow to display a list of options. The last option is Create Refreshable Web Query, which displays the New Web Query dialog box.

Modifying Web Queries

When you create a Web query, you make it possible to use data from tables on your company's intranet or the Internet in your worksheets. Financial data can change, though, so you should use the buttons on the Data tab on the ribbon to change how Excel deals with data drawn from other sources. One way you can ensure that the external data is current is to have Excel refresh the data regularly.

Schedule Web Query Data Refreshes

1. Click the Data tab.
2. Click any cell that contains query data.
3. Click Properties in the Connections group.
4. Select the Refresh Every check box.
5. Type the number of minutes between refreshes in the Minutes box.
6. Click OK.

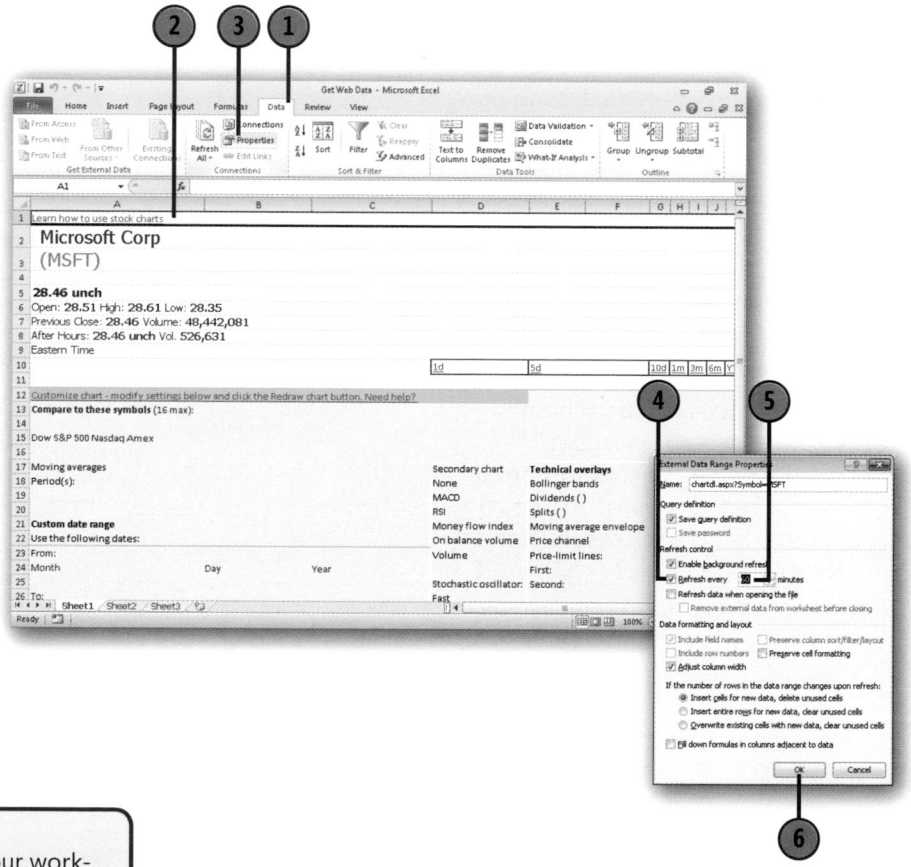

Tip

To have Excel refresh the data every time you open your workbook, select the Refresh Data When Opening The File check box.

Introducing XML

Although the Hypertext Markup Language (HTML) is great for describing how a Web page should be displayed in a browser, the language isn't designed to communicate anything about the contents of a document. For example, telling Internet Explorer to display a worksheet as an HTML table tells you nothing about the data shown on that Web page. When you save your worksheet data to an XML document, however, Excel annotates the data with tags describing which program generated the data, the name of the worksheet, and the data that belongs in each cell. With that information, Excel or another spreadsheet program that understands XML can read your worksheet data and retain your original meaning.

Although a full discussion of XML is beyond the scope of this book, the following bit of XML code shows how to identify an Excel workbook in XML:

```
<?xml version="1.0"?>
<Workbook xmlns="urn:schemas-microsoft-com:office:spreadsheet"
xmlns:o="urn:schemas-microsoft-com:office:office"
xmlns:x="urn:schemas-microsoft-com:office:excel"
xmlns:ss="urn:schemas-microsoft-com:office:spreadsheet"
xmlns:html="http://www.w3.org/TR/REC-html40">
```

Also, XML can identify rows and cells within the spreadsheet, as in the following example:

```
<Row>
 <Cell><Data ss:Type="String">Atlantic</Data></Cell>
 <Cell><Data ss:Type="Date">1/1/2010</Data></Cell>
 <Cell><Data ss:Type="Number">2010</Data></Cell>
 <Cell><Data ss:Type="String">January</Data></Cell>
 <Cell><Data ss:Type="Number">1</Data></Cell>
 <Cell><Data ss:Type="Number">1</Data></Cell>
 <Cell><Data ss:Type="String">Monday</Data></Cell>
 <Cell><Data ss:Type="Number">120933</Data></Cell>
</Row>
```

This XML code fragment represents the highlighted row in the following worksheet.

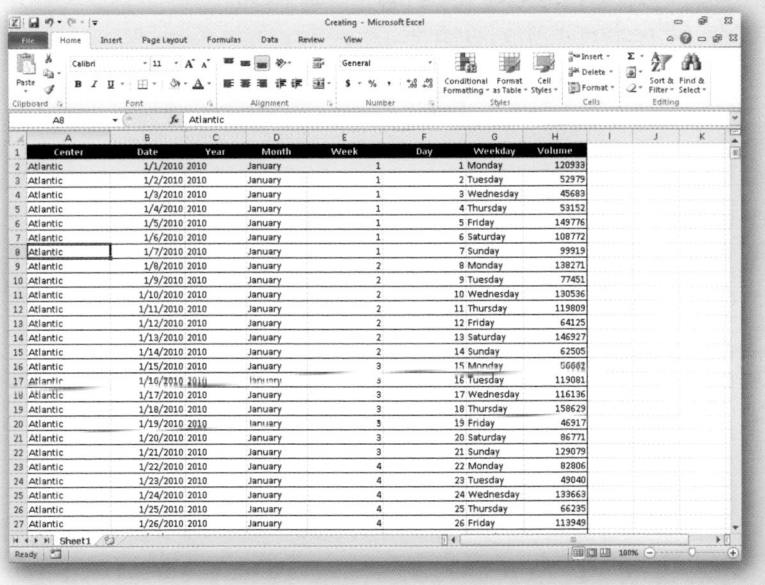

	Center	Date	Year	Month	Week	Day	Weekday	Volume
2	Atlantic	1/1/2010	2010	January	1	1	Monday	120933
3	Atlantic	1/2/2010	2010	January	1	2	Tuesday	52979
4	Atlantic	1/3/2010	2010	January	1	3	Wednesday	45683
5	Atlantic	1/4/2010	2010	January	1	4	Thursday	53152
6	Atlantic	1/5/2010	2010	January	1	5	Friday	149776
7	Atlantic	1/6/2010	2010	January	1	6	Saturday	108772
8	Atlantic	1/7/2010	2010	January	1	7	Sunday	99919
9	Atlantic	1/8/2010	2010	January	2	8	Monday	138271
10	Atlantic	1/9/2010	2010	January	2	9	Tuesday	77451
11	Atlantic	1/10/2010	2010	January	2	10	Wednesday	130536
12	Atlantic	1/11/2010	2010	January	2	11	Thursday	119809
13	Atlantic	1/12/2010	2010	January	2	12	Friday	64125
14	Atlantic	1/13/2010	2010	January	2	13	Saturday	146927
15	Atlantic	1/14/2010	2010	January	2	14	Sunday	62505
16	Atlantic	1/15/2010	2010	January	3	15	Monday	56682
17	Atlantic	1/16/2010	2010	January	3	16	Tuesday	119081
18	Atlantic	1/17/2010	2010	January	3	17	Wednesday	116136
19	Atlantic	1/18/2010	2010	January	3	18	Thursday	158629
20	Atlantic	1/19/2010	2010	January	3	19	Friday	46917
21	Atlantic	1/20/2010	2010	January	3	20	Saturday	86771
22	Atlantic	1/21/2010	2010	January	3	21	Sunday	129079
23	Atlantic	1/22/2010	2010	January	4	22	Monday	82806
24	Atlantic	1/23/2010	2010	January	4	23	Tuesday	49040
25	Atlantic	1/24/2010	2010	January	4	24	Wednesday	133663
26	Atlantic	1/25/2010	2010	January	4	25	Thursday	66235
27	Atlantic	1/26/2010	2010	January	4	26	Friday	113949

Interacting over the Web Using XML

The goal of XML is to be a universal language, allowing data to move freely from one application to another. That means that saving an Excel worksheet as an XML document allows any other spreadsheet program to read the XML file, separate out the cell names and data, and use the annotations to re-create the worksheet. By the same token, you can take a worksheet saved as an XML file and, regardless of the program in which the file was created, import it into Excel.

Save a Workbook As an XML Spreadsheet

1. Click the File tab.
2. Click Save As.
3. Click the Save As Type down arrow.
4. Click XML Spreadsheet 2003.
5. Type the file name you want.
6. Click Save.

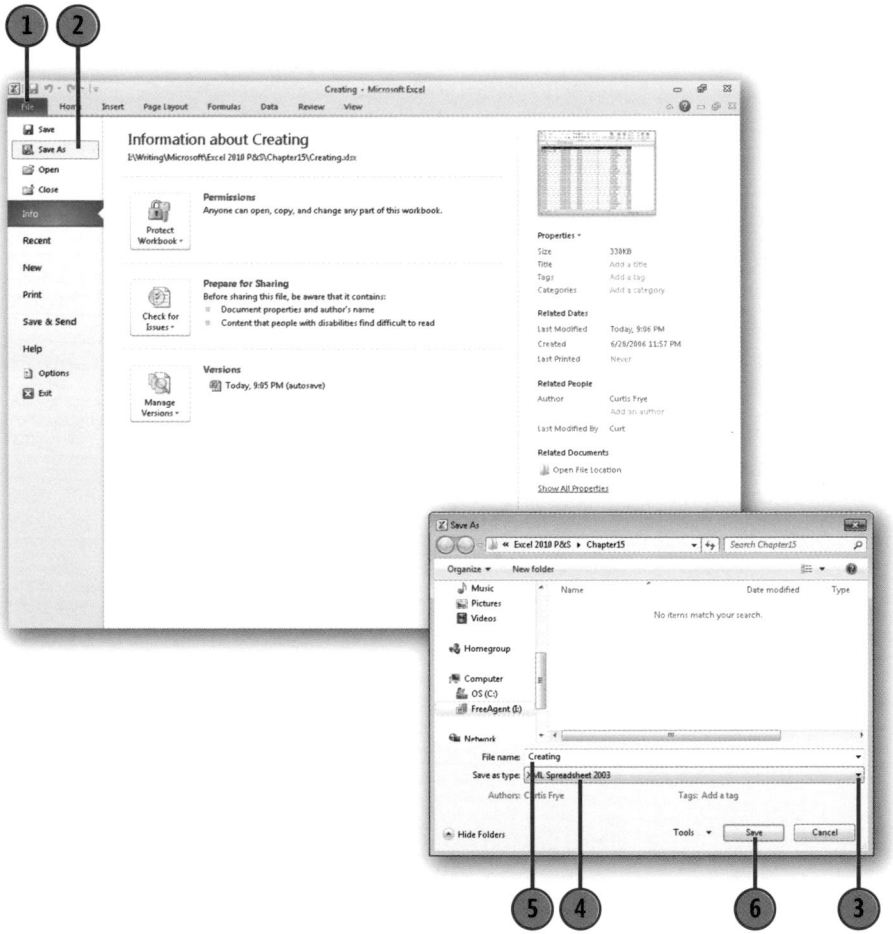

Import Spreadsheet XML

1. Click the File tab.
2. Click Open.
3. Navigate to the folder containing the XML document you want.
4. Double-click the XML document.

Tip

If you don't see any XML documents in the Open dialog box, click the file type button and click All Excel Files.

Index

Numbers

3D charts, 226
3D references, 84
3D rotating objects, 242

A

accepting
  Track Changes, 278–279
Access 2010
  sharing data between Access tables and worksheets, 269
Add Assistant, 255
advanced filters
  creating, 205–206
  removing, 206
advanced paste options, 51
aligning
  drawing objects, 246–248
Align Left button, 119
alignment
  cell text, 119
Align Right button, 119
apostrophes
  typing numbers as text values, 36
appearance
  charts, 215–216
area charts, 212
ascending order
  sorting worksheet data, 198
AutoComplete
  data entry, 40
AutoCorrect
  creating entries, 192–193
  deleting entries, 194
AutoFill
  inserting data into cells, 39
AutoFilters
  creating, 202–204
AutoFormat
  controlling rules, 195
AutoSum formula
  creating, 94

B

backgrounds
  cells, 111, 112
  removing from pictures, 245
Backstage view, 2, 6, 156–157
  exiting, 19
  setting print margins, 164–165
backups
  workbooks, 279
bar charts, 212
blank workbooks
  creating, 19
  starting Excel 2010, 12
blank worksheets
  inserting, 67
bodies (chart)
  changing, 219–221
borders
  cells, 113–114
    drawing, 113
Bottom Align button, 119
breaking links, 91
bubble charts, 212

C

calculations, 3, 30, 83, 84
  creating SUM formula, 94
  formulas
    debugging, 102–103
  functions, 97–98
    IF, 99
  grand totals, 95–96
  relative references, 84
  subtotals, 95–96
  summing cells, 93
cascading workbooks, 20
categories
  pie charts, 225
cell dependents, 100–101
cell precedents, 100–101
cell references, 10
cells, 10
  3D references, 84
  active, 10
  backgrounds, 111, 112
  borders, 113–114
    drawing, 113
  clearing, 53
  comments, 275
    deleting, 276
    editing, 276
    names, 276
    viewing, 275
  copying
    from worksheets to groups of worksheets, 77
  copying values, 50–51
  cutting values, 50–51
  deleting, 70
    formulas, 147
  dragging, 71

cells (*continued*)
editing, 44
formatting, 105
conditional formatting, 121–125, 126, 127
copying formats with Format Painter, 131
dates, 110
deleting conditional formats, 130
fonts, 106
formatting parts of, 107
numbers, 108–109
ranges, 107
text, 107
formulas, 83, 84
creating, 85, 89
creating with cell references, 90–92
editing, 85
names, 88
spaces, 85
inserting data into
multiple worksheets, 76–77
inserting dates into, 37, 38
inserting into worksheets, 70
inserting symbols into, 45
inserting times into, 37, 38
locking, 153
merging, 132–133
moving, 70
numbers
inserting, 36
orienting contents, 119
pasting values, 50–52
ranges
deleting, 87
names, 86–87
validation rules, 209
relative references, 84
selecting, 32–33
shading, 111, 112
splitting, 132–133
styles, 115–118
applying, 115
creating, 116
deleting, 118
modifying, 117
summing, 93
AutoSum formula, 94
grand totals, 95–96
subtotals, 95–96
text
alignment, 119
inserting, 34–35
orienting, 120
wrapping, 120
Track Changes, 277
accepting/rejecting tracked changes, 278–279
XML, 285
Cell Styles gallery, 116
cells (worksheets)
series, 223
deleting, 224
Center button, 119
Change History
creating, 279
character delimiters, 272
Chart (Linked To Excel Data) option, 268
charts, 211, 212
appearance, 215–216
area, 212
bar, 212
bodies of charts, changing, 219–221
bubble, 212
column, 212
cone, 212
copying data into PowerPoint, 267–268
creating, 213–214
customizing data, 222
cylinder, 212
doughnut, 212
formatting, 216
legends, 217–218
titles, 217–218
gridlines
displaying, 219
hiding, 219
layout, 214
line, 212
organization, 233
creating, 254–257
design, 257
layouts, 256
pie, 212, 225
exploded, 226
pyramid, 212
radar, 212
scale, changing
value axis, 220
X-axis, 221
scatter plot, 212
sparklines, 2, 3
column, 230
line, 229
Win/Loss, 231
stock, 212, 227
styles, 214
surface, 212
trendlines
adding to data series, 228
clearing
cells, 53
filters from lists, 204
Office Clipboard items, 55
clip art
inserting into worksheets, 251
Close Full Screen command, 23
closing
workbooks, 24–25, 25
code (XML), 285

colors
displaying error messages, 191
gridlines, 140
sheet tabs, 139
themes, 136
WordArt, 250
worksheet tabs, 69
color scales
displaying, 129
Colors dialog box
displaying, 69
column charts, 212
Column heading, 10
columns, 10
deleting, 72–74, 147
displayed grouped columns, 149
grouping, 148–149
headings
printing, 159
hiding, 35, 75, 150–151
hiding grouped columns, 148–149
inserting, 72–74
inserting into worksheets, 144–145
moving, 146
worksheets, 72–74
selecting, 33
sizing, 43, 142–143
tables
creating formulas that reference, 89
ungrouping, 148–149
unhiding, 75, 151
widths
changing in Page Layout View, 157
worksheets
sorting data, 198–199, 199
column sparklines
creating, 230
commands
adding to Quick Access Toolbar, 175, 179–180
adding to Ribbon, 181
Close Full Screen, 23
icons, 186
removing from Quick Access Toolbar, 180
reordering on Ribbon, 182
shortcut menus, 26–27
comments, 4
deleting, 276
editing, 276
in cells, 275
names, 276
viewing, 275
conditional formats
visualizing data, 7
conditional formatting, 121–125
based formulas, 123
based on values of cells, 121–122
changing order of conditions, 127
deleting conditional formats, 130
deleting rules, 125
editing rules, 124
stopping when conditions are met, 126
cone charts, 212
contiguous cells
selecting, 32–33
Copy As Picture option, 51
copying
cells
from worksheets to groups of worksheets, 77
cell values, 50–51
charts into PowerPoint, 267–268
data between Word tables and Excel tables, 265–266
styles with Format Painter, 131
Web data to Excel, 283
worksheets, 66
Create Refreshable Web Query option, 283
Create Table dialog box
displaying, 41
Ctrl key
dragging Fill handles, 39
currency
displaying numerical values as, 108
custom equations
adding to shapes, 259
custom groups
creating, 185
customizing
chart data, 222
objects, 243–245
pictures, 243–245
Quick Access Toolbar, 6
Ribbon, 6, 181–188
custom lists
defining, 200–201
custom properties, 18
custom styles
creating, 116
custom tabs
creating, 184
custom views, 81
custom zoom levels, 22
cutting
cell values, 50–51
cylinder charts, 212

D

data
merging, 132–133
pasting
Paste Preview, 6
sharing, 3
splitting, 132–133
summarizing
sparklines, 7
statistical functions, 6
visualizing, 7
conditional formats, 7

data (*continued*)
Web
copying to Excel, 283
retrieving using Excel, 282
data bars
displaying, 128
data entry, 3, 29, 30, 34–35
AutoComplete, 40
dates, 30, 37, 38
fractions, 30
lists, 40
multiple worksheets, 76–77
numbers, 36
saving workbooks as templates, 177
series, 39
shortcuts, 40
times, 30, 37, 38
validation, 207–209
data lists
creating tables, 41–43
data refreshes
Web queries, 284
Data Validation dialog box, 209
dates
formatting, 30, 110
inserting into cells, 37–38, 38
debugging
formulas, 102–103
decimal places
setting, 109
defaults
file folders
changing, 25
deleting
AutoCorrect entries, 194
cells, 70
formulas, 147
columns, 72–74, 147
comments, 276
conditional formats, 130
conditional formatting rules, 125
pictures, 235
ranges, 87
rows, 72–74, 147
series, 224
sparklines, 232
styles, 118
watches, 103
worksheets, 67
delimiters, 271, 272
descending order
sorting worksheet data, 198
design
organization charts, 257
diagrams, 233
inserting, 252–253
organization charts, 233
styles, 253
Venn, 233
dialog boxes
Colors, 69
Create Table, 41
Format Cells, 30, 106
Highlight Changes, 279
Insert Hyperlink, 48
directories
saving templates, 177
Display As Icon check box, 263
displaying. *See also* viewing
chart legends, 217–218
color scales, 129
Colors dialog box, 69
columns, 151
comments, 275
Create Table dialog box, 41
data bars, 128
error messages, 189–191
colors, 191
formula bar contents, 34–35
gridlines, 141, 219
grouped columns, 149
grouped rows, 149
icon sets, 129
math equations, 8
Office Clipboard contents, 54
Pick From Drop-Down List items, 40
Ribbon elements, 188
rows, 151
workbooks, 20
worksheets, 68, 156–157
doughnut charts, 212
dragging
cells, 71
Fill handles, 39
drawing
borders, 113
drawing objects, 234–235
adding to worksheets, 236–237
aligning, 246–248
effects, 241
fills, 238–240
grouping, 246–248
ordering, 248
ungrouping, 247
dynamically updating worksheets, 281

E

editing
cells, 44
conditional formatting rules, 124
formulas, 85
pictures, 8
shadows, 241
styles, 117
templates, 178
effects
drawing objects, 241
text effects
WordArt, 249

embedding, 262–264
enabling
  in-cell editing, 44
  Live Preview, 11
  Track Changes, 277
equations
  adding to shapes, 258–259
  math
    creating, 8
    displaying, 8
error messages, 189–191
  colors, 191
  resetting ignored messages, 190
Esc key
  undoing edits to cells, 44
Evaluate Formula dialog box, 102
Excel 2010
  exiting, 25
  Help system, 26–27
  new features, 5
  sharing data between Access tables and worksheets, 269
  sharing table data with Word tables, 265–266
  starting, 12
Excel Chart (Entire Workbook) option, 268
exiting
  Backstage view, 19
  Excel, 25
exploded pie charts, 226
exponents
  inserting numbers into cells, 36
Extensible Markup Language. *See* XML

F

fields
  Keywords, 17
file folders
  changing, 25
file properties
  custom properties, 18
  finding workbooks, 17–18
files
  adding hyperlinks to, 47
  embedding, 262–264
  linking, 262–264
  recently used
    viewing, 47
  text files
    importing, 271
File tab, 5, 6
  printing worksheets, 158
Fill handles
  dragging, 39
fills
  drawing objects, 238–240
  inserting data into cells, 39
  pictures, 240
filtering
  worksheet data
    advanced filters, 205–206
    AutoFilters, 202–204
    clearing filters, 204
    creating advanced filters, 205–206
    creating search filters, 204
    creating selection filters, 202
finding
  templates on Office.com Web site, 176
  text, 57–58
  workbooks, 14–16
    file properties, 17–18
Fluent interface, 11
folders
  changing, 25
  saving templates, 177
fonts
  cells, 106
footers
  adding graphics to, 171–172
  creating, 168–170
  formatting, 172
  height, 170
  previewing, 168
  text, 169
Format Cells dialog box, 30, 106
Format Painter, 131
formatting, 11, 107
  cell borders, 113–114
  cells, 105
    conditional formatting, 121–125, 126, 127
    copying formats with Format Painter, 131
    dates, 110
    deleting conditional formats, 130
    fonts, 106
    formatting parts of, 107
    numbers, 108–109
    ranges, 107
    text, 107
  charts, 216
    legends, 217–218
    titles, 217–218
  dates, 30
  fractions, 30
  headers and footers, 172
  numbers, 108–109
  sparklines, 232
  text
    footers, 169
    headers, 169
    in shapes, 237
  times, 30
  worksheets, 135
    coloring sheet tabs, 139
    gridlines, 140–141
    multiple worksheets, 76–77
    protecting worksheets, 152

formatting, worksheets (*continued*)
sizing columns/rows, 142–143
themes, 136–138
Formatting option, 51
formula bar
editing cells, 44
scrolling contents of, 34–35
formulas, 3, 83, 84
AutoSum
creating, 94
cell dependents, 100–101
cell precedents, 100–101
conditional formatting, 123
creating, 85
cell references, 90–92
table references, 89
debugging, 102–103
deleting cells, 147
deleting watches, 103
editing, 85
error messages, 189–191
mistakes, 175
names, 88
relative references, 84
removing tracer arrows, 101
saving workbooks as templates, 177
spaces, 85
SUM, 94
Formulas & Number Formatting option, 51
Formulas option, 51
fractions
formatting, 30
freezing panes, 79
Full Screen mode
viewing in Full Screen mode, 23
Function dialog box, 97
functions, 83, 97–98
IF, 99
ScreenTips, 97–98
statistical, 6

G

galleries, 3, 11
Cell Styles, 116
Shape Styles
displaying, 238
grand totals, 95
graphics. *See also* images; pictures
adding to footers, 171–172
adding to headers, 171–172
worksheets, 234–235, 235
graphs. *See* charts
gridlines
changing, 140–141
charts
displaying, 219
hiding, 219
colors, 140–141
displaying, 141, 219
hiding, 141
printing worksheets, 159
grouping
columns, 148–149
drawing objects, 246–248
rows, 148–149
groups
adding to Ribbon, 185
cells
deleting, 70
inserting, 70
moving, 70
names, 86–87
worksheets
copying cells to, 77
groups of cells
selecting, 32–33

H

hard shadows, 234
headers
adding graphics to, 171, 171–172
creating, 168–170
formatting, 172
height, 170
previewing, 168
text, 169
headings
printing worksheets, 159, 163
height
footers, 170
headers, 170
rows, 142–143
changing in Page Layout View, 157
Help, 26–27
Help button, 85
hiding
chart legends, 217–218
columns, 35, 75, 150–151
gridlines, 141, 219
grouped columns, 148–149
grouped rows, 148–149
Ribbon elements, 183, 187
rows, 75, 150–151
worksheets, 68
Highlight Changes dialog box, 279
Horizontal scroll bar, 10
hyperlinks, 46–49
adding to files, 46
adding to other files, 47
adding to Web pages, 48
mailto hyperlinks, 49

I

icons
  Ribbon commands, 186
icon sets
  displaying, 129
IF function, 99
ignored errors
  resetting, 190
images. *See also* graphics; pictures
  editing, 8
  reflection, 234
importing
  text files, 271, 272
  XML spreadsheets, 287
in-cell editing
  turning on, 44
Insert Hyperlink dialog box, 48
inserting
  cells into worksheets, 70
  clip art into worksheets, 251
  columns into worksheets, 72–74, 144–145
  comments into cells, 275–276
  data into tables, 42
  data into worksheets
    multiple worksheets, 76–77
  dates into cells, 37, 38
  diagrams, 252–253
  drawing objects into worksheets, 236–237
  hyperlinks, 46–49
    into Web pages, 48
    mailto hyperlinks, 49
    same files, 46
    to other files, 47
  numbers into cells, 36
  pictures into worksheets, 235
  rows into worksheets, 72–74, 144–145
  shapes
    into worksheets, 236
  shapes into organization charts, 255
  symbols into cells, 45
  text into cells, 34–35
  text into headers and footers, 169
  times into cells, 37, 38
  worksheets, 67
Insert Options button, 73
Insert Options indicator, 145
interface (Ribbon), 11

K

Keep Source Column Widths option, 51
Keep Source Formatting option, 51
keyboard shortcuts
  navigating worksheets, 31
Keywords field, 17

L

layouts
  charts, 214
  organization charts, 256
legends (charts), 217–218
  adding, 218
  removing, 218
libraries
  functions, 97–98
Linear Trendline option, 228
line breaks
  creating, 34–35, 35
line charts, 212
line sparklines
  creating, 229
Linked Picture option, 51
linking, 262–264
links (workbook)
  creating formulas, 90–92
list functions, 97–98
lists
  custom lists, 200–201
  data entry, 40
  validation rules, 209
Live Preview
  enabling, 11
locking
  cells, 153
Long Date format, 110

M

mailto hyperlinks
  adding, 49
manual page breaks
  setting, 173–174
  viewing, 173–174
margins
  setting, 164–165
math equations
  creating, 8
  displaying, 8
maximizing
  windows, 21
menus
  shortcut
    commands, 26–27
  Start
    opening recently opened workbooks, 13
merging
  cells, 132–133

Microsoft Excel Help, 26–27
Microsoft Office Access 2010
  sharing data between Access tables and worksheets, 269
Microsoft Office Button. *See* File tab
Microsoft Office Excel 2010
  exiting, 25
  sharing data between Access tables and worksheets, 269
  sharing table data with Word tables, 265–266
  starting, 12
Microsoft Office Excel 2010. *See* Excel 2010
Microsoft Office Fluent interface, 11
  See also Ribbon
Microsoft Office Online site, 27
Microsoft Office PowerPoint 2010
  copying Excel charts into, 267–268
Microsoft Office Word 2010
  sharing table data with Excel tables, 265–266
Middle Align button, 119
minimizing
  windows, 21
misspellings
  checking worksheets for, 59
  preventing Excel from turning off corrective behavior, 175
mistakes
  AutoCorrect
    creating entries, 192–193
    deleting entries, 194
  error messages, 189–191
    colors, 191
    resetting ignored messages, 190
  formulas, 175
model equations
  adding to shapes, 258–259
monitoring
  formulas, 102–103
mouse pointer
  cell styles, 115
Move Down button, 127
Move Up button, 127
moving
  cells, 70
  columns, 146
    worksheets, 72–74
  Quick Access Toolbar, 180
  rows, 146
    worksheets, 72–74
  worksheets, 64–65
multicolumn sorts, 199
multiple columns
  inserting into worksheets, 145
  moving, 74
  sizing, 143
multiple rows
  inserting into worksheets, 145
  moving, 74
  sizing, 143
multiple workbooks, 20
  viewing, 79
multiple worksheets
  formatting, 76–77
  inserting data into, 76–77
  printing, 158
  selecting, 62

N

names
  comments, 276
  formulas, 88
  ranges, 86–87
  Ribbon elements, 186
  searching for workbooks, 16
  tables, 42
  workbooks, 24–25
  worksheets, 63
  worksheet views, 80
navigating
  worksheets, 31
New Book option, 66
new features, 5
No Borders option, 51
noncontiguous cells
  selecting, 32–33
noncontiguous columns
  selecting, 33
noncontiguous rows
  selecting, 33
numbers, 211
  as text values, 36
  formatting, 108–109
  inserting into cells, 36

O

objects
  customizing, 243–245
  drawing, 234–235
    adding to worksheets, 236–237
    aligning, 246–248
    effects, 241
    fills, 238–240
    grouping, 246–248
    ordering, 248
    ungrouping, 247
  embedding, 262–264
  Excel Help system, 26
  filling with pictures, 240
  linking, 262–264
  rotating, 244
  rotating in 3-D, 242

sizing, 243
textures, 239
ungrouping, 247
Office Clipboard, 3
clearing items from, 55
displaying contents of, 54
pasting from, 54
Office.com Web site
finding templates on, 176
opening
workbooks, 13–15
existing workbooks, 14–16
ordering
buttons on Quick Access Toolbar, 180
commands on Ribbon, 182
drawing objects, 248
organization charts, 233
creating, 254–257
design, 257
layouts, 256
Orientation button, 120
orientation (page), 166
orienting
cell contents, 119

P

Page Break Preview mode, 173
page breaks
viewing, 173–174
Page Layout view, 156–157
changing column widths/row heights, 157
page orientation, 166
paper
selecting, 160–161
Paste As Hyperlink option, 51
Paste As Picture option, 268
Paste Link option, 51
Paste option, 51
Paste Preview, 6
Paste Special option, 51
pasting
advanced paste options, 51
cell values, 50–52
from Office Clipboard, 54
Paste Preview, 6
percentages
displaying numerical values as, 108
Pick From Drop-Down List items
displaying, 40
Picture option, 51
pictures. *See also* graphics; images
adding to worksheets, 235
customizing, 243–245
deleting, 235
editing, 8
filling objects with, 240
removing backgrounds from, 245
rotating, 244
sizing, 243
pie charts, 212, 225
exploded, 226
Portrait orientation
printing worksheets, 166
PowerPoint 2010
copying Excel charts into, 267–268
predefined custom properties, 18
previewing
footers, 168
headers, 168
worksheets, 156–157
print areas
printing parts of worksheets, 162
removing, 162
Print check box, 141
printers
selecting, 160–161
printing
worksheets, 155
creating headers and footers, 168–170
gridlines, 159
headings, 159, 163
margins, 164–165
multiple worksheets, 158
page orientation, 166
print areas, 162
scale, 166
selecting paper, 160–161
selecting printers, 160–161
proofreading
worksheets, 59
properties
custom properties, 18
finding workbooks, 17–18
protecting
worksheets, 152
publishing
worksheets to Web
dynamically updating, 281
pyramid charts, 212

Q

queries, Web
data refreshes, 284
Quick Access Toolbar, 3
adding commands to, 175, 179–180
adding Ribbon buttons to, 180
customizing, 6
moving, 180
ordering buttons on, 180
removing commands from, 180
Quick Print button, 158

R

radar charts, 212
ranges
  deleting, 87
  formatting, 107
  formulas
    names, 88
  names, 86–87
  validation rules, 209
recently used files
  viewing, 47
redoing
  actions, 56
references (formulas), 100–101
reflection
  images, 234
Refresh Data When Opening The File check box, 284
refreshing
  data, 284
  links, 92
rejecting
  Track Changes, 278–279
relative references, 84
removing. *See* deleting
  advanced filters, 206
  backgrounds from pictures, 245
  commands from Quick Access Toolbar, 180
  Office Clipboard items, 55
  print areas, 162
  Ribbon elements, 183
  splits, 78–79
  subtotals, 96
  tracer arrows, 101
repeating
  headings, 163
replacing
  text, 57–58
resizing. *See* sizing
restoring
  Ribbon, 181
  windows, 21
retrieving
  Web data using Excel, 282–283, 283
reviewing
  Track Changes, 278–279
Ribbon, 11
  adding buttons to Quick Access Toolbar, 180
  adding commands to, 181
  adding groups to, 185
  customizing, 6, 181–188
  displaying hidden elements, 188
  hiding elements, 183, 187
  naming elements on, 186
  removing elements from, 183
  reordering commands on, 182
  restoring, 181
  tabs
    creating, 184
rotating
  objects, 244
  objects in 3-D, 242
  pictures, 244
Row heading, 10
rows, 10
  deleting, 72–74, 147
  grouping, 148–149
  headings
    printing, 159
  height
    changing in Page Layout View, 157
  hiding, 75, 150–151
    grouped rows, 148–149
  inserting, 72–74, 144–145
  moving, 72–74, 146
    worksheets, 72–74
  selecting, 33
  sizing, 142
  ungrouping, 148–149
  unhiding, 75, 151
  worksheets
    sorting data, 198, 199
rules
  AutoFormat, 195
  conditional formatting
    changing order of conditions, 127
    deleting, 125
    editing, 124
    stopping when conditions are met, 126
  filtering rules
    creating, 203
  validation rules
    creating, 207–209

S

saving
  workbooks, 24–25
    as XML spreadsheets, 286
    to Web, 280
  workbooks as templates, 177
  worksheets
    to Web, 280
scale, 166
scale (charts)
  changing
    value axis, 220
    X-axis, 221
scatter plot charts, 212
scheduling
  data refreshes, 284
scientific notation
  inserting numbers into cells, 36

ScreenTips
functions, 97–98
scroll bars
Horizontal, 10
Vertical, 10
scrolling
formula bar contents, 34–35
search filters
creating, 204
searching
workbooks, 14–16
security
locking cells, 153
protecting worksheets, 152
selecting
cells, 32–33
columns, 33
printers, 160–161
rows, 33
worksheets, 62, 164
selection filters
creating, 202
series, 29, 39, 213–214
adding to charts, 223
adding trendlines to, 228
deleting, 224
shading
cells, 111, 112
shadows
adding, 241
editing, 241
hard shadows, 234
shapes
adding equations to, 258–259
adding to organization charts, 255
adding to worksheets, 236
styles, 238
text, 237
Shape Styles gallery
displaying, 238
sharing
data, 3
workbooks, 274
comments, 275–276
Track Changes, 277–279
sharing data
between Access tables and worksheets, 269–270
between Word tables and Excel tables, 265–266
copying Excel charts into PowerPoint, 267–268
embedding, 262–264
importing text files, 271, 272
linking, 262–264
Sheet tab, 10
sheet tabs
colors, 69, 139
themes, 139
shortcut keys
navigating worksheets, 31
shortcut menus
commands, 26–27
shortcuts
data entry, 40
Short Date format, 110
showing. *See* displaying; viewing
sizing
columns, 142–143
objects, 243
pictures, 243
rows, 142
tables, 43
windows, 21
sorting
worksheet data, 198, 199
custom lists, 200–201
Sort Largest To Smallest button, 198
Sort Newest to Oldest button, 198
Sort Oldest To Newest button, 198
Sort Smallest To Largest button, 198
source data (charts)
changing, 222
spaces
typing formulas, 85
sparklines, 2, 3
creating a column, 230
deleting, 232
formatting, 232
line, 229
summarizing data, 7
Win/Loss
creating, 231
spell checking
worksheets, 59
splits
worksheets, 78–79
splitting
cells, 132–133
SpreadsheetML, 273
starting
Excel 2010, 12
Start menu
opening recently opened workbooks, 13
statistical functions, 6
status bars, 10
stock charts, 212, 227
stopping
conditional formatting, 126
styles
cells, 115–118
applying, 115
creating, 116
deleting, 118
modifying, 117
charts, 214
copying with Format Painter, 131
diagrams, 253
shapes, 238

subtotals
creating, 95
removing, 96
SUM formula
creating, 94
summarizing
data
sparklines, 7
statistical functions, 6
summarizing data. *See* charts
summary worksheets
sparklines, 229–232
summing
cells, 93
AutoSum formula, 94
grand totals, 95
subtotals, 95
surface charts, 212
switching
between workbooks, 20
views, 81
Switch Windows button, 20
symbols
inserting into cells, 45

T

tables
adding data to, 42
columns
creating formulas that reference, 89
sizing, 43
creating, 41–43
creating formulas that reference, 89
names, 42
sharing data between Access tables and worksheets, 269
sharing data between Word tables and Excel tables, 265–266
sizing, 43
tabs
creating, 184
creating custom groups, 185
creating custom tabs, 184
File, 5, 6
printing worksheets, 158
Ribbon, 10
Sheet, 10
sheet tabs
colors, 139
themes, 139
View
Switch Windows button, 20
worksheets
colors, 69
templates, 3, 175
creating workbooks from, 176
editing, 178
finding on Office.com Web site, 176
saving workbooks as, 177
text
cells, 107
alignment, 119
orienting, 120
wrapping, 120
finding, 57–58
formatting
headers and footers, 169
in shapes, 237
headers and footers, 169
inserting into cells, 34–35
replacing, 57–58
shapes, 237
WordArt
colors, 250
text effects
WordArt, 249
text files
importing, 271, 272
textures, 239
themes
applying, 136–138
colors, changing, 136
creating, 138
sheet tabs, 139
three-dimensional
rotating objects, 242
three-dimensional charts, 226
times
formatting, 30
inserting into cells, 37, 38
titles
charts, 217–218
adding, 218
To Book list, 66
toolbars
Quick Access Toolbar, 3
adding commands to, 175, 179–180
adding Ribbon buttons to, 180
customizing, 6
moving, 180
ordering buttons on, 180
removing commands from, 180
Top Align button, 119
tracer arrows
removing, 101
Track Changes
accepting/rejecting changes, 278–279
Change History
creating, 279
enabling, 277
reviewing, 278–279
viewing, 278–279
Transpose option, 51
trendlines (charts)
adding to data series, 228
troubleshooting
formulas, 102–103

turning on
in-cell editing, 44
Live Preview, 11
Track Changes, 277
typing
AutoCorrect
creating entries, 192–193
numbers as text values, 36

U

undoing
actions, 56
edits to cells, 44
ungrouping
columns and rows, 148–149
objects, 247
unhiding
columns and rows, 75, 151
worksheets, 68
user interface (Ribbon), 11

V

validation
data entry, 207–209
workbooks, 209
value axis
changing chart scale, 220
Values & Number Formatting option, 51
Values option, 51
Values & Source Formatting option, 51
Venn diagrams, 233
Vertical scroll bar, 10
view
Backstage
exiting, 19
View check box, 141
viewing. *See also* displaying
3D charts, 226
comments, 275
page breaks, 173–174
recently used files, 47
Track Changes, 278–279
worksheets, 62, 78–79
in Full Screen mode, 23
views
Backstage, 2, 6, 156–157
setting print margins, 164–165
Page Layout, 156–157
changing column widths/row heights, 157
worksheets
custom views, 81
naming, 80
switching, 81
View tab
Switch Windows button, 20
visualizing
data, 7
conditional formats, 7

W

watches, 102
deleting, 103
Watch Window, 102
Web
copying data to Excel, 283
dynamically updating worksheets, 281
Excel Help system, 27
retrieving Web data using Excel, 282
saving workbooks to, 280
saving worksheets to, 280
Web pages
adding hyperlinks to, 48
Web queries
data refreshes, 284
Web sites
Office.com Web site, finding templates on, 176
width
columns, 142–143
changing in Page Layout View, 157
windows
maximizing, 21
minimizing, 21
restoring, 21
sizing, 21
Win/Loss sparklines
creating, 231
Word 2010
sharing table data with Excel tables, 265–266
WordArt
creating text effects, 249
text colors, 250
words. *See also* text
finding, 58
replacing, 58
workbooks, 4
backups, 279
blank
starting Excel 2010, 12
cascading, 20
closing, 24–25, 25
creating, 19
creating formulas
cell references, 90–92
table references, 89
displaying, 20
embedding, 262–264
finding, 14–16
file properties, 17–18
hyperlinks, 46–49
adding to other files, 47
adding to Web pages, 48
mailto hyperlinks, 49

workbooks (*continued*)
linking, 262–264
links
creating, 90–92
multiple workbooks, 20
opening, 13–15
existing workbooks, 14–16
saving, 24–25
as templates, 177
as XML spreadsheets, 286
to Web, 280
sharing, 274
comments, 275–276
Track Changes, 277–279
switching between, 20
templates, 175
creating workbooks from, 176
editing, 178
finding on Office.com Web site, 176
saving workbooks as, 177
themes
applying, 136–138
colors, 136
creating, 138
Track Changes
accepting/rejecting changes, 278–279
Change History, 279
enabling, 277
reviewing, 278–279
viewing, 278–279
validation, 209
worksheets
copying, 66
deleting, 67
displaying, 68
hiding, 68
inserting, 67
moving, 64–65
worksheets, 3, 10, 205
adding drawing objects to, 236–237
cells. *See* cells
accepting/rejecting tracked changes, 278–279
backgrounds, 111, 112
borders, 113–114
clearing, 53
comments, 275–276, 276
conditional formatting, 121–125
copying from worksheets to groups of worksheets, 77
copying values, 50–51
cutting values, 50–51
deleting, 70, 224
dragging, 71
editing, 44
fonts, 106
formatting, 105
formatting parts of, 107
inserting, 70
inserting dates into, 37, 38
inserting numbers into, 36
inserting symbols into, 45
inserting times into, 37, 38
locking, 153
merging, 132–133
moving, 70
numbers, 108–109
orienting contents, 119
pasting values, 50–52
selecting, 32–33
series, 223
shading, 111, 112
splitting, 132–133
styles, 115–118
text, 107
Track Changes, 277
clip art
inserting, 251
columns, 10
changing width in Page Layout View, 157
deleting, 72–74, 147
displayed grouped columns, 149
grouping, 148–149
headings, 159, 163
hiding, 35, 75, 150–151
hiding grouped columns, 148–149
inserting, 72–74, 144–145
moving, 72–74, 146
selecting, 33
sizing, 142–143
sorting data, 198, 199
ungrouping, 148–149
unhiding, 75, 151
comments, 4
copying, 66
deleting, 67
displaying, 68
dynamically updating, 281
embedding, 262–264
error messages, 189–191
colors, 191
resetting ignored messages, 190
filtering data
advanced filters, 205–206
AutoFilters, 202–204
footers
adding graphics to, 171–172
creating, 168–170
formatting, 172
formatting, 135
coloring sheet tabs, 139
gridlines, 140–141
multiple worksheets, 76–77
protecting worksheets, 152
sizing columns/rows, 142–143
themes, 136–138

formulas
  mistakes, 175
freezing panes, 79
graphics, 234–235, 235
gridlines
  colors, 140
  displaying, 141
  hiding, 141
headers
  adding graphics to, 171–172
  creating, 168–170
  formatting, 172
hiding, 68
inserting, 67
inserting data into
  multiple worksheets, 76–77
linking, 262–264
moving, 64–65
names, 63
navigating, 31
page breaks
  setting, 173–174
  viewing, 173–174
pasting data in
  Paste Preview, 6
previewing, 156–157
printing, 155
  creating headers and footers, 168–170
  gridlines, 159
  headings, 159, 163
  margins, 164–165
  multiple worksheets, 158
  page orientation, 166
  print areas, 162
  scale, 166
  selecting paper, 160–161
  selecting printers, 160–161
proofreading, 59
protecting, 152
rows, 10
  changing height in Page Layout View, 157
  deleting, 72–74, 147
  grouping, 148–149
  headings, 159, 163
  hiding, 75, 150–151
  hiding grouped rows, 148–149
  inserting, 72–74, 144–145
  moving, 72–74, 146
  selecting, 33
  sizing, 142
  sorting data, 198, 199
  ungrouping, 148–149
  unhiding, 75, 151
saving
  to Web, 280
selecting, 62, 164
shapes
  adding, 236
sharing data between Access tables and, 269
sorting data, 198, 199
  custom lists, 200–201
splits, 78–79
tables
  adding data to, 42
  columns, 43
  creating, 41–43
  names, 42
  sharing data with Word tables, 265 266
  sizing, 43
tabs
  colors, 69
text
  finding, 57–58
  replacing, 57–58
validation rules
  creating, 207–209
  viewing, 62, 78–79
    in Full Screen mode, 23
  views
    custom views, 81
    naming, 80
    switching, 81
  worksheet data
    creating advanced filters, 205–206
  XML, 285
  zooming in/out, 22
wrapping
  cell text, 120
Wrap Text button, 120

X

X-axis
  changing chart scale, 221
XML
  code, 285
  importing XML spreadsheets, 287
  saving workbooks as XML spreadsheets, 286
  SpreadsheetML, 273
XML (Extensible Markup Language), 4

Z

zooming in/out
  worksheets, 22

About the Author

Curtis Frye is the author of more than 20 books, including *Microsoft® Office Excel® 2007 Step by Step* and *Microsoft® Office Excel® 2007 Plain & Simple.*

What do you think of this book?

We want to hear from you!

To participate in a brief online survey, please visit:

microsoft.com/learning/booksurvey

Tell us how well this book meets your needs—what works effectively, and what we can do better. Your feedback will help us continually improve our books and learning resources for you.

Thank you in advance for your input!

Microsoft® Press

Stay in touch!

To subscribe to the *Microsoft Press® Book Connection Newsletter*—for news on upcoming books, events, and special offers—please visit:

microsoft.com/learning/books/newsletter